The International Criminal Court and Nigeria

If Nigeria fails to prosecute the crimes recognised under the Rome Statute, then the International Criminal Court (ICC) will intervene. The ICC is only expected to complement the criminal justice system in Nigeria and is not a court of first instance but one of last resort. This is what is known as the principle of complementarity. Before the ICC can step in, it must make a finding of 'unwillingness' or 'inability' on the part of Nigeria. It is only after this finding is made that the ICC can take over the prosecution of the crimes recognised under the statute from Nigeria. This book examines the criminal justice process in Nigeria and discovers that the justice system is latent with the requirements of 'unwillingness' and 'inability.' The requirements, which serve as tests for assessment, are as they are laid down by the Rome Statute and interpreted by the ICC. This book offers recommendations as to what Nigeria must do in order to avoid the ICC intervention by reversing those parameters that give rise to 'unwillingness' and 'inability.'

The International Criminal Court and Nigeria: Implementing the Complementarity Principle of the Rome Statute offers a contribution to the advancement of international law and will be of practical use to African countries. It aims to sensitise policy makers in different African countries with respect to policy options open to them to close impunity gap in their respective countries. This volume addresses the topics with regard to international criminal law and comparative public law and will be of interest to researchers, academics, organisations and students in the fields of international law, governance and comparative criminal justice.

Muyiwa Adigun is a lecturer in the Faculty of Law, University of Ibadan, Ibadan, Nigeria, West Africa.

Routledge Research in International Law

For a full list of titles in this series, visit www.routledge.com/Routledge-Research-in-International-Law/book-series/INTNLLAW

Available:

The Rule of Law in the United Nations Security Council Decision-Making Process
Turning the Focus Inwards
Sherif Elgebeily

Universal Jurisdiction in International Criminal Law
The Debate and the Battle for Hegemony
Aisling O'Sullivan

The Right to Democracy in International Law
Between Procedure, Substance and the Philosophy of John Rawls
Khalifa A Alfadhel

Latin America and the International Court of Justice
Contributions to International Law
Edited by Paula Wojcikiewicz Almeida and Jean-Marc Sorel

Fragmentation vs the Constitutionalisation of International Law
A Practical Inquiry
Edited by Andrzej Jakubowski and Karolina Wierczyńska

Legal Accountability and Britain's Wars 2000–2015
Peter Rowe

Means of Transportation and Registration of Nationality
Transportation Registered by International Organizations
Vincent P. Cogliati-Bantz

Regionalism in International Law
Ján Klučka

The International Criminal Court and Nigeria
Implementing the Complementarity Principle of the Rome Statute
Muyiwa Adigun

The International Criminal Court and Nigeria

Implementing the Complementarity Principle of the Rome Statute

Muyiwa Adigun

Routledge
Taylor & Francis Group
LONDON AND NEW YORK

First published 2018 by Routledge

2 Park Square, Milton Park, Abingdon, Oxfordshire OX14 4RN
52 Vanderbilt Avenue, New York, NY 10017

Routledge is an imprint of the Taylor & Francis Group, an informa business

First issued in paperback 2019

Library of Congress Cataloging-in-Publication Data
A catalog record has been requested for this book

ISBN: 978-1-138-29868-2 (hbk)
ISBN: 978-0-367-89080-3 (pbk)

Typeset in Galliard
by Apex CoVantage, LLC

Dedicated to my mother who loves me without reservation and my children whom I love without reservation.

Contents

Acknowledgements

I give thanks to Allah, the Most Beneficient, the Most Merciful for sustaining me. I am grateful to my parents, Alhaji Gbadegesin Adigun and Mrs Maryam Adigun. I am especially grateful to my mother for her exceptional sacrifice. I am also grateful to my wife, Mrs Folake Ajoke Adigun, and my children, Maryam Ifeoluwani Adigun, Muhammed Olumuyiwa Adigun and Aliyah Olusolape Adigun. I appreciate the following people for their support; their contributions are known to them, and I valued them much more than they would have ever thought: Justice M.O. Bolaji-Yusuf of the Court of Appeal, Nigeria; Professor Vincent O. Nmehielle and Professor Pamela Andanda, Oliver Schreiner School of Law, University of the Witwatersrand, Johannesburg; Aare Afe Babalola OFR, CON, SAN, FNIALS, FCIArb, LL.D, D. Litt (founder Afe Babalola & Co., Nigeria—one of the best law firms in Nigeria known for forensic advocacy); Mr Adebayo Adenipekun, SAN, FCIArb (Managing Partner, Afe Babalola & Co.,) and his wife, Mrs Yemisi Adenipekun; Professor Tam David-West, former petroleum minister, Nigeria; Chief G.M. Adedeji, former Attorney-General and Commissioner for Justice, Osun State of Nigeria; Dr J.O.A. Akintayo, Reader in Law, University of Ibadan, Ibadan, Nigeria; Mr Adekunle Olaosebikan (my uncle), Brianna Ascher, Mary Del Plato and Lucy Buchan (Taylor and Francis editors); Jennifer Bonnar (Project Manager, Apex CoVantage), Wendy Jo Dymond (Copyeditor, Apex CoVantage) and Julie Grady (Indexer, Apex CoVantage); Mrs Olukemi Adijah Amoo, Dr Ibraheem Olufemi Adigun, Dr Abiodun Adigun, Mrs Olubukola Abdul-Azeez and Mrs Omotayo Adeleke (my siblings); Dr Olusegun Adewuyi and his wife, Mrs Adebukola Adewuyi; Ms Adelaide Mongalo, University of the Witwatersrand, Johannesburg; Professor John-Mark Iyi, University of Venda, South Africa; Dr Abiodun Osuntoogun and Dr Peter Oniemola, University of Ibadan, Ibadan, Nigeria; Prince Akeem Adedayo Olaniyan, Olusola Olorunfemi, Alhaji Lukman Ogunrinde, Gbenga Oyewale, Linet Imbosa and the late Mr Matthew Olu Ayoola (my friends); and others too numerous to mention.

Preface

It is commonly asserted that the International Criminal Court (ICC) is unfairly administering international criminal justice as it prosecutes Africans alone. But, what most people do not understand is that the ICC is a court of last resort as distinct from a court of first instance. Thus, if African states have shown a 'willingness' and have exhibited an 'ability' to prosecute those alleged to have committed international crimes in their domain, there would have been no reason for the ICC to prosecute them, and the issue of unfairness would not have arisen. This is known as complementarity principle, where the ICC is only expected to intervene when national criminal justice fails. This principle is embodied in articles 1 and 17 of the Statute of the International Criminal Court, otherwise known as the Rome Statute.

Nigeria is a party to the Rome Statute like its other African counterparts, and it is expected to implement the principle of complementarity. This book therefore inquires into how Nigeria can effectively implement the complementarity principle of the Rome Statute. It examines the Nigerian criminal justice system relative to its ability to implement complementarity principle. It examines how Nigeria can effectively prosecute international crimes recognised under the Rome Statute. The book is a case study exploring the peculiarities of the Nigerian criminal justice system with the expected outcome of carrying forward Nigeria's obligations to under the Rome Statute. While the book is essentially on Nigeria, nonetheless it is a textual analysis of relevant literature, legislation, case law and regulations not only on Nigeria but also on other jurisdictions relating to the implementation of the complementarity principle. This comparative approach is adopted in interrogating the Nigerian legal system with a view to making recommendations which have been adopted elsewhere and are found workable. The central idea of the book is the interplay of the principle of complementarity, treaty implementation and the Nigerian criminal justice system.

In making the preceding inquiry, the book examines the concepts of legal pluralism, legal universalism and sovereignty. The concept of legal pluralism recognises the diversity of legal systems and contends that once a legal system has what is minimally required to effectively prosecute crimes recognised in the Rome Statute, nothing more extensive is required. This concept is found to be arguably subsumed within the provisions of the Rome Statute, hence its adoption. The concept of legal pluralism is also found to converge with the concept of sovereignty which articles 1 and 17 of the Rome Statute seek to protect by allowing states to exercise their criminal jurisdiction on crimes recognised under the statute and to allow the ICC to intervene only when they fail.

In contradistinction to the concept of legal pluralism is the concept of legal universalism. The concept sees the ICC as a civilising institution and envisages reforms of the widest possibility all in the name of implementing complementarity. Such wide-ranging reforms like the abolition of the death penalty, the adoption of universal jurisdiction and elaborate prison reforms are within the contemplation of this concept in implementing complementarity. The concept is flatly rejected in the book because it is found to be baseless within the meaning of the provisions of the Rome Statute. Unlike the concept of legal pluralism, the concept is found to have eroded the concept of sovereignty contrary to the essence of the principle of complementarity.

Further, in making the inquiry into whether Nigeria can effectively prosecute the crimes recognised under the Rome Statute, the book takes cognisance of the existence of the Nigerian legal system as a subsisting legal fact and assumes that Nigeria, despite being a party to the Rome Statute, will not be able to exercise criminal jurisdiction regarding international crimes within the meaning of articles 1 and 17 of the Rome Statute unless and until its legal system is revamped. Based on this underlying assumption, the book then raises two questions, namely (1) Can the Nigerian legal system as it is, successfully prosecute international crimes as envisaged in articles 1 and 17 of the Rome Statute? and (2) What are the measures to be put in place for the Nigerian legal system to effectively prosecute international crimes as envisaged in articles 1 and 17 of the Rome Statute?

In answering the preceding questions, the book has recourse to articles 1 and 17 of the Rome Statute, bearing in mind the minimalist prescriptions of legal pluralism. In defining what is required of states to implement the principle of complementarity, articles 1 and 17 of the Rome Statute develop the concepts of unwillingness and inability.

In subjecting the Nigerian legal system to the test of unwillingness and inability stipulated in articles 1 and 17 of the Rome Statute, the Nigerian legal system is found to have abysmally failed. The book discovers that the Nigerian legal system, as it is, cannot successfully prosecute international crimes as envisaged in articles 1 and 17 of the Rome Statute. The book finds that Nigeria does not have any law in place to prosecute international crimes recognised under the Rome Statute and that the existing legal regime *inter alia* recognises amnesties, immunities and pardon/prerogative of mercy. The book then argues that all these features are latent with the possibility of giving rise to the concept of unwillingness within the meaning of articles 1 and 17 of the Rome Statute. Similarly, the book finds that the prosecuting authority (the attorney-general) in Nigeria and the Nigerian judiciary lack the requisite independence and impartiality for the successful prosecution of the crimes recognised under the Rome Statute in Nigeria and argues that the situation reflects unwillingness.

With respect to the concept of inability, the book finds that there is no witness protection regime in Nigeria that would enhance the effective prosecution of the crimes recognised under the Rome Statute and that fugitives of these crimes could readily escape prosecution because of a lack of treaty arrangement between Nigeria and other state entities on extradition. The book therefore argues that the situation reflects inability within the meaning of articles 1 and 17 of the Rome Statute.

Based on the preceding findings, the book goes ahead to recommend measures that have to be put in place for the Nigerian legal system to effectively prosecute international crimes as envisaged in articles 1 and 17 of the Rome Statute by reversing the situation which reflects the concepts of unwillingness and inability. In order to reverse the situation which reflects the concept of unwillingness, the book makes it imperative for Nigeria to recognise by way of legislation crimes recognised under the Rome Statute and recommends that such clogs like amnesties, immunities and pardon/prerogative of mercy should be completely outlawed. The book also makes a case for an independent prosecuting authority and the right of private prosecution subject to judicial scrutiny and calls for the re-composition of the National Judicial Council, a body responsible for the regulation of the judiciary in Nigeria, with a viewing to guaranteeing its independence and impartiality. The book also recommends that the Nigerian judiciary should be extensively financed and sufficiently equipped in order to make the effective prosecution of the crimes recognised under the Rome Statute feasible.

In order to reverse the situation which reflects the concept of inability, the book calls for a strong witness protection regime so as to encourage witnesses to testify in the prosecution of crimes recognised under the Rome Statute. The book also recommends that Nigeria should negotiate treaties with other states so as to facilitate the return of fugitives from its shores, and where a state will not extradite unless the death penalty will not be imposed, Nigeria should delegate its criminal jurisdiction to such a state.

Muyiwa Adigun
Iwo, Osun State, Nigeria
August 2017

Acronyms and Abbreviations

AC	Appeal Cases
ACHPR	African Charter on Human and People's Rights
AG	Attorney-General
ALL NLR	All Nigerian Law Report
Art(s)	Article(s)
Cap	Chapter (under Laws of the Federation of Nigeria)
CAR	Criminal Appeal Report
Ch	Chancery
CLR	Commonwealth Law Report
ECHR	European Convention on Human Rights and Fundamental Freedoms
ECtHR	European Court of Human Rights
ETS	European Treaty Series
FIDH	*Federación Internacional de los Derechos Humanos*
FSC	Federal Supreme Court
FWLR	Federation Weekly Law Report
GA	General Assembly
HCA	High Court of Australia
HL	House of Lords
HRC	Human Rights Committee
ICC	International Criminal Court
ICCLR	International Centre for Criminal Law Reform
ICCPR	International Covenant on Civil and Political Rights
ICJ	International Court of Justice
ICTR	International Criminal Tribunal for Rwanda
ICTY	International Criminal Tribunal for Yugoslavia
ILC	International Law Commission
ILM	International Legal Materials
ILR	International Law Reports
IMT	International Military Tribunal
IMTFE	International Military Tribunal for the Far East
InterAmCtHR	Inter-American Court of Human Rights
JICJ	Journal of International Criminal Justice

JLOS	Ugandan Justice Law and Order Sector
LFN	Laws of the Federation of Nigeria
NCLR	Nigerian Constitutional Law Report
NMLR	Nigerian Monthly Law Report
NSCC	Nigerian Supreme Court Cases
NSW	New South Wales
NSWLR	New South Wales Law Report
NWLR	Nigerian Weekly Law Report
NZLR	New Zealand Law Report
OTP	Office of the Prosecutor
PCIJ	Permanent Court of International Justice
PTC	Pre-Trial Chamber
QB	Queen's Bench
RCMP	Royal Canadian Mounted Police
Res	Resolution
RPE	Rules of Procedure and Evidence
SC	Security Council
SCM	Supreme Court Monthly
SCNLR	Supreme Court of Nigeria Law Report
Ss	section(s)
TIAS	Treaties and other International Acts Series
TRC	Truth and Reconciliation Commission
UDHR	Universal Declaration of Human Rights
UKTS	United Kingdom Treaty Series
UN	United Nations
UNTS	United Nations Treaty Series
VWU	Victims and Witnesses Unit
WACA	West African Court of Appeal
WRN	Weekly Report of Nigeria
YILC	Yearbook of the International Law Commission

Table of Cases

Nigerian Cases

Foreign Cases

Table of Statutes

Nigerian Statutes

Foreign Statutes

Table of Treaties

1 Introduction

The Creation of the International Criminal Court and the Duty of States to Prosecute

On 1 July 2002, the Statute of the International Criminal Court (ICC) came into force. As of August 2017, 124 states had ratified the statute,[1] and 34 of them are in Africa.[2] Nigeria ratified the Statute of the ICC (Rome Statute) on 27 September 2001.[3] The Rome Statute recognises genocide, crimes against humanity, war crimes and the crime of aggression which are considered to be the most serious crimes that are of concern to the international community.[4] With the wide adoption of the Rome Statute, the international community has shown its commitment to the ideal of ending impunity so that the most serious crimes of concern to the international community will not go unpunished.[5] The Rome Statute creates the ICC and makes it a permanent institution.[6] The permanence of the ICC indicates that the ideal of ending impunity has assumed an institutional dimension.[7] While the crimes recognised under the Rome Statute are considered the most serious because of their 'shocking cruelties'[8] impunity 'adds insult to the injury already suffered by victims'[9]

1. International Criminal Court, 'The States Parties to the Rome Statute'. https://asp.icc-cpi.int/en_menus/asp/states%20parties/Pages/the%20states%20parties%20to%20the%20rome%20statute.aspx accessed 6 August 2017.
2. Ibid.
3. International Criminal Court, 'States Parties-Chronological List'. https://asp.icc-cpi.int/en_menus/asp/states%20parties/Pages/states%20parties%20_%20chronological%20list.aspx accessed 6 August 2017.
4. Rome Statute of the International Criminal Court (Rome Statute) (adopted 17 July 1998, entered into force 1 July 200) 2187 UNTS 3, art 5.
5. Max du Plessis and Jolyon Ford (eds), 'Unable or Unwilling? Case Studies on Domestic Implementation of the ICC Statute in Selected African Countries'. (March 2008) Institute of Security Studies (ISS) Monograph Series No 141, viii.
6. Rome Statute, preamble.
7. Plessis and Ford, 'Unable or Unwilling? Case Studies on Domestic Implementation of the ICC Statute in Selected African Countries' (n 5), viii.
8. Ibid., 1.
9. Ibid.

when the victims realise that the perpetrators will go unpunished. Therefore, the creation of the ICC not only reflects the maintenance of high ideals; it also reflects 'a belief in the practical deterrent'[10] that the creation of the court can achieve.[11]

The ICC is at the heart of the international criminal justice system because it is the only 'independent permanent International Criminal Court in relationship with the United Nations system'[12] in contradistinction to the preceding ad hoc tribunals like the International Military Tribunal (IMT), International Criminal Tribunal for Yugoslavia (ICTY) and the International Criminal Tribunal for Rwanda (ICTR). However, despite this position, the Rome Statute recognises the role of the domestic criminal justice system. In the preamble to the statute, state parties recall that 'it is the duty of every state to exercise its criminal jurisdiction over those responsible for international crimes' and that effective prosecution of these crimes 'must be ensured by taking measures at the national level.' The preamble appears to acknowledge the customary law duty to prosecute or extradite.[13]

The Rome Statute, however, goes beyond acknowledging the customary duty of states to prosecute crimes of the most serious concern to the international community. It emphasises 'policy prescriptions in favour of national action'[14] by state parties. Article 1 of the Rome Statute provides that the ICC 'shall be complementary to national criminal jurisdictions.' Article 17 requires state parties to the statute to investigate and prosecute international crimes over which they have jurisdiction and that it is when they are 'unwilling' or 'unable' that the ICC will intervene and take over from them. The principle embodied in articles 1 and 17 of the Rome Statute is known as the principle of complementarity. Therefore, a state that investigates and prosecutes international crimes under the Rome Statute can be said to be acting for the international community against enemies of humankind considering the customary duty to prosecute or extradite which the preamble to the Rome Statute appears to have acknowledged. It becomes imperative for such a state to comply with the requirements under article 17 so that 'international justice is not brought into disrepute.'[15] A state that is poised to investigate and prosecute international crimes on behalf of the international

10. Ibid., 3; Rome Statute, preamble.
11. Plessis and Ford, 'Unable or Unwilling? Case Studies on Domestic Implementation of the ICC Statute in Selected African Countries'. ibid.
12. Rome Statute, preamble.
13. Darryl Robinson, 'The Inaction Controversy: Neglected Words and New Opportunities' in Carsten Stahn and Mohamed El Zeidy (eds), *The International Criminal Court and Complementarity: From Theory to Practice* vol I (Cambridge University Press 2011), 460, 495–496.
14. Ibid., 496–498.
15. Plessis and Ford, 'Unable or Unwilling? Case Studies on Domestic Implementation of the ICC Statute in Selected African Countries' (n 5), viii.

community must take 'credible ownership'[16] of its justice system. The credibility requirement arguably emphasises the need to comply with the provisions of article 17.

There are three certain concepts which are central to what is to be examined in this book. They are the concept of sovereignty, legal universalism and legal pluralism and domestic implementation of treaties. The concept of sovereignty denotes that a state entity has control over its territory. The requirement that a state party must show unwillingness and inability before the ICC can intervene shows deference to the concept of sovereignty. Therefore, the need for the domestic justice system of any state party to avoid what may give rise to unwillingness and inability is imperative; otherwise, its sovereignty will be compromised. The sovereignty of any state party to the statute can be said to be compromised when the ICC investigates and prosecutes any person that the state party would have ordinarily investigated and prosecuted. This is because the exercise of criminal jurisdiction by a state is a manifestation of its sovereignty.[17]

The recognition of the role of the domestic criminal justice system by the ICC raises the question of legal universalism on the one hand and legal pluralism on the other hand. The universalists conceive the ICC as a civilising institution which domestic justice system must mirror and that domestic criminal justice must be 'on all fours,' with justice being dispensed by the ICC. Most non-governmental organisations appear to adopt a universalist stance by stating that 'the local regulatory framework should reflect as faithfully as possible the actual regime of the ICC itself, and every step taken from it takes states closer to a finding of inability or unwillingness.'[18] Similarly, Edoardo Greppi maintains that 'a State wishing to give solid foundations to its right to investigate and to prosecute crimes, and to avoid being considered in a potential situation of inability, should conform its legal system to the requirements of the Rome Statute.'[19] In other words, domestic legal systems must mimic the ICC and investigate and prosecute 'exactly as the ICC would.'[20]

The pluralists, on the other hand, emphasise the goal of closing impunity gap and de-emphasise the means. They tolerate 'diversity not only of legal

16. Vincent O. Nmehielle, 'Taking Credible Ownership of Justice for Atrocity Crimes in Africa' in Vincent O. Nmehielle (ed), *Africa and the Future of International Criminal Justice* (Eleven International Publishing 2012), 223–242.
17. *The Case of SS 'Lotus' (France v Turkey)*, ICJ, Judgment, 7 September 1927.
18. Frédéric Mégret, 'Too Much of a Good Thing? Implementation and the Uses of Complementarity' in Carsten Stahn and Mohamed El Zeidy (eds), *The International Criminal Court and Complementarity: From Theory to Practice* vol I (Cambridge University Press 2011), 372–373.
19. Edoardo Greppi, 'Inability to Investigate and Prosecute Under Article 17' in Mauro Politi and Federica Gioia (eds), *The International Criminal Court and National Jurisdictions* (Ashgate 2008), 69.
20. Mégret, 'Too Much of a Good Thing? Implementation and the Uses of Complementarity' (n 18), 378.

traditions but even approaches to the problematique of accountability.'[21] Otto Triffterer opines that 'it may not be necessary that States 'copy' the procedure applicable in cases before the Court.'[22] Similarly, it has been argued that 'complementarity does not require that domestic prosecutions are carried out in precise accord with the legal regime under the ICC Statute'[23] and that states are not required to 'change their domestic law to ensure parity with the Statute in all aspects of domestic criminal law and procedure in order to avail themselves of the principle of complementarity.'[24] Darryl Robinson also argues that 'there is no obligation to adopt the procedures appearing in the Rome Statute'[25] and that 'it is not the purpose of the ICC to impose universal criminal procedure.'[26] Therefore, 'states have considerable leeway in the implementation'[27] of the crimes recognised under the Rome Statute and that what is required of a state is 'at best 'equivalent' rather than 'identical' standard.'[28]

One point that is undisputable is that both the universalist and pluralist positions are ideals. There is no protagonist of legal universalism that will maintain that every aspect of a domestic criminal justice system must conform in all specific details with the Rome Statute.[29] Similarly, there is no protagonist of legal pluralism that will maintain that anything will do to satisfy the requirements of international criminal justice.[30] Nonetheless, the debate strikes at the core of the implementation of the principle of complementarity. In this book, the position of legal pluralism is adopted because the provisions of the Rome Statute on the principle of complementarity clearly justify it. The universalists tend to subsume a reformist agenda of the broadest possibility within the process of implementing the principle of complementarity which cannot be sustained within the provisions of the Rome Statute. Therefore, the principle of complementarity is considered in this book 'not

21. Ibid., 363.
22. Otto Triffterer, 'Legal and Political Implications of Domestic Ratification and Implementation Processes' in Claus Kress and Flavia Lattanzi (eds), *General Aspects and Constitutional Issues* (Baden–Baden/Fagnano Alto (L'Aquila) 2000), 1, 14.
23. Hellen Duffy, 'National Constitutional Compatibility and the International Criminal Court' (2001) 11 *Duke Journal of Comparative & International Law* 32.
24. Ibid.
25. Darryl Robinson, 'The Rome Statute and Its Impact on National Law' in Antonio Cassese, Paola Gaeta and John R.W.D. Jones (eds), *The Rome Statute of the International Criminal Court: A Commentary* (Oxford University Press 2002), 1849.
26. Ibid.
27. Mégret, 'Too Much of a Good Thing? Implementation and the Uses of Complementarity' (n 18), 388.
28. Matthias Goldmann, 'Implementing the Rome Statute in Europe: From Sovereign Distinction to Convergence in International Criminal Law?' (2005) 16 *Finnish Yearbook of International Law* 5, 11.
29. Mégret, 'Too Much of a Good Thing? Implementation and the Uses of Complementarity' (n 18), 363.
30. Ibid.

only as a concession to sovereignty but [also] as . . . a device to accommodate diversity.'[31]

Whenever a state ratifies a treaty, it must carry out its obligations. Although Article 17 is not couched in a positive obligatory term but only considers crimes recognised under the Rome Statute as being suitable for investigation and prosecution domestically,[32] nonetheless Nigeria, as a state party, is required to implement the policy prescriptions embedded in it. In *Alabama Claims Arbitration*,[33] Britain undertook to be neutral in the US civil war but allowed a ship which was used in the war to be constructed on its territory. Britain was found to be in breach of its obligation to be neutral.[34] Similarly, in *Exchange of Greek and Turkish Populations Case*[35] the parties to the Treaty of Lausanne 1923 inserted a clause in the treaty to the effect that the parties agreed to modify their respective domestic laws to implement the treaty. The Permanent Court of International Justice stated that the clause only attests to a settled rule of international law that a party to a treaty must modify its domestic law to fulfil its obligations under that treaty.[36]

Darryl Robinson observes that implementing the principle of complementarity forces 'policy-makers, officials, legislators, politicians, and members of the civil society . . . to confront the persistent problem of impunity.'[37] Similarly, Amnesty International observes that implementing complementarity demonstrates that 'the state is aware of its primary responsibility under international law to ensure accountability'[38] for crimes recognised under the Rome Statute. In implementing the principle of complementarity, it is imperative to find out if the Nigerian legal system, as it is, can successfully prosecute international crimes as envisaged in articles 1 and 17 of the Rome Statute, bearing in mind the minimalist prescriptions of legal pluralism. This implies that the test of 'unwillingness' and 'inability' will be used to examine the Nigerian legal system, and if any aspect of the Nigerian legal system fails this test, it follows that measures must be put in place for the Nigerian legal system to be able to successfully prosecute the crimes recognised under the statute.

31. Ibid., 390.
32. The only obligation imposed in the Rome Statute is that states should facilitate cooperation with the ICC: article 88. For the argument that article 17 of the Rome Statute does not really impose obligation to prosecute see Robinson, 'The Inaction Controversy: Neglected Words and New Opportunities' (n 13), 495–496 and Rod Radstan, 'Situation and Case: Defining the Parameters' in Carsten Stahn and Mohamed El Zeidy (eds), *The International Criminal Court and Complementarity: From Theory to Practice* vol I (Cambridge University Press 2011), 449–450.
33. *US v GB Moore* (1872) 1 Int Arb 495.
34. Ibid., 656.
35. Advisory Opinion PCIJ Reports Series B No 10 (1925).
36. Ibid., 20.
37. Robinson, 'The Rome Statute and Its Impact on National Law' (n 25), 1849.
38. Amnesty International, 'The International Criminal Court: Checklist for Effective Implementation' AI Index IOR 40/011/00 (2000), 33.

2 The Nigerian Legal System and the Implementation of the Rome Statute Complementarity Principle

The Federal Constitution and the Separation of Powers

Nigeria operates a federal constitution.[1] The operative constitution is the Constitution of the Federal Republic of Nigeria, 1999 as amended by various Alteration Acts (the 1999 Nigerian Constitution, the Constitution or the Constitution as amended). Nigeria has a central government known as the federal government and 36 states under the control of various state governments.[2] It also has its capital in Abuja, called the Federal Capital Territory.[3] The Constitution is supreme and its provisions are binding 'on all authorities and persons throughout the Federal Republic of Nigeria.'[4] The supremacy of the Constitution suggests that the implementation of the principle of complementarity must be in accordance with the Constitution.

The Constitution creates and regulates the organs of the government. In line with the principle of separation of powers, the Constitution recognises the executive,[5] the legislature[6] and the judiciary.[7] In *Abraham Adesanya v President, Federal Republic of Nigeria*,[8] the president of the Federal Republic of Nigeria, who was the respondent in the case, made an appointment to the chairmanship post of the then Federal Electoral Commission (FEDECO; a body responsible for the conduct of elections in Nigeria at the time) which was subject to the confirmation of the Senate. The appellant was a senator who argued on the floor of the house that the appointment made by the respondent was unconstitutional. However, the appellant's position was defeated by the majority vote. The appellant thereafter approached the court

1. Constitution of the Federal Republic of Nigeria 1999 as amended (Nigerian Constitution 1999), s 2(2).
2. Ibid ss 2(2) and 3(1).
3. Ibid.
4. Ibid s 1(1).
5. Ibid s 4.
6. Ibid s 5.
7. Ibid s 6.
8. (1981) 5 SC 69; (1981) All NLR 1.

seeking, *inter alia*, an order to the effect that the appointment made by the respondent was unconstitutional.

The Supreme Court of Nigeria held that the appellant action was to obtain through the court, that is, the judiciary, what the appellant could not obtain on the floor of the house as a member of the legislature. The appellant was therefore declared to have no standing to institute the action. The court held *obiter* that if the appellant had not been a member of the legislative organ, its position might have been different. By this decision, the Supreme Court gave effect to the principle of separation of powers as enshrined in the Constitution. In addition, sections 147(4) and 192(3) of the Nigerian Constitution as amended provide that whenever any member of the legislature is appointed as a member of the executive, such a member is deemed to have resigned his position as a member of the legislature.

Although the preceding analysis on the doctrine of separation of powers tends to indicate a somewhat rigid concept, it is not as rigid as it appears.[9] There are checks and balances among the three organs of government. The president is empowered to substitute a less severe punishment for any punishment imposed by the court.[10] The president's assent is also required before a bill can metamorphose into law.[11] The National Assembly is empowered to perform an oversight function over the actions of the executive by conducting an investigation with respect to their activities.[12] In performing its oversight function, the National Assembly can cause evidence to be led and issue warrant to compel attendance.[13] In addition, both the legislature and the judiciary have their respective roles to play in removing the president, who is a member of the executive.[14] The judiciary will set up a panel to investigate while the legislature will pass a resolution to remove.[15] In appointing certain judicial officers, the appointment is to be made by the president as a member of the executive while the confirmation of the said appointment is to be made by the Senate, the legislative organ.[16]

Because Nigeria is a federation, the executive, the legislature and the judiciary are recognised at both the federal and states levels.[17] The executive

9. On the doctrine of separation of powers in respect of the Nigerian Constitution 1999, see Onyekachi Duru, 'The Doctrine of Separation of Powers Under the Nigerian Constitution: A Critical Overview' 6 September 2009. http://papers.ssrn.com/sol3/papers.cfm?abstract_id=2142933 accessed 6 August 2017.
10. Nigerian Constitution 1999; s 175(1)(c). See also Nigerian Constitution 1999, s 212(1)(c) where the governor as a member of the executive arm is empowered to perform the same function at the state level.
11. Ibid s 58.
12. Ibid s 88.
13. Ibid s 89.
14. Ibid s 143. See also Nigerian Constitution 1999, s 188 which distributes roles in removing governors at the state level.
15. Ibid s 143.
16. Ibid ss 231 and 271.
17. Ibid ss 4, 5 and 6.

power at the federal level is vested in the president who may exercise the power directly or through 'the Vice-President and Ministers of the Government of the Federation or officers in the public service of the Federation.'[18] The legislative power at the federal level is vested in the National Assembly.[19] The National Assembly consists of 'a Senate and a House of Representatives.'[20] The National Assembly can legislate only on matters within the Exclusive Legislative List.[21] At the federal level, judicial power is vested in the federal courts.[22] The federal courts which are relevant here are the Supreme Court of Nigeria, the Court of Appeal, the Federal High Court and the High Court of the Federal Capital Territory, Abuja.[23]

With respect to the federating states, the executive power is vested in the governor who may choose to exercise the power directly or 'through the Deputy Governor and Commissioners of the Government of that State or officers in the public service of the State.'[24] The legislative power is vested in the 'House of Assembly of the State.'[25] The House of Assembly of a State can legislate only on matters within the Concurrent Legislative List[26] and on those matters that are residual.[27] Residual matters are matters which are not listed in both the Exclusive Legislative List and the Concurrent Legislative List.[28] This means that states share legislative powers with the federal government with respect to matters in the Concurrent Legislative List. At the state level, judicial power is vested in the courts 'for a State.'[29] The only court which is relevant here is 'a High Court of a State.'[30]

Whenever there is conflict between the law (an Act) enacted by the National Assembly and the law (Law) enacted by any House of Assembly of a State, the law enacted by the National Assembly prevails.[31] While federalism is reflected in both the executive and the legislature, this is not so with the judiciary. This is because appeals from the high court of any state go to the Court of Appeal and the Supreme Court which are meant for all the federating states. Thus, the judiciary is unitary in structure.

18. Ibid s 5(1)(a).
19. Ibid s 4(1) and part I second schedule.
20. Ibid.
21. Ibid s 4(2).
22. Ibid s 6(1).
23. Ibid s 6(5).
24. Ibid s 5(2).
25. Ibid s 4(6).
26. Ibid s 4(4) (a) and part II second schedule.
27. Ibid s 4(7).
28. Ibid.
29. Ibid s 6(2).
30. Ibid s 6(5).
31. Ibid s 4(5).

The Judiciary

The judiciary is the body of the court system in Nigeria. The courts which are relevant here are the Supreme Court, the Court of Appeal, the Federal High Court, the High Court of the Federal Capital Territory, Abuja, the High Court of a State and the Court Martial. The Supreme Court is at the apex of judicial hierarchy in Nigeria.[32] The court cannot have more than 22 justices at a time. These justices are the chief justice and other justices not exceeding 21.[33] In exercising its jurisdiction, the court must not be composed of fewer than five justices. But, where constitutional interpretation or fundamental rights issues are involved, the court must be made up of seven justices.[34] It has both an original and an appellate jurisdiction. Original jurisdiction can be exercised with respect to disputes between states or between a state and the federation.[35] The National Assembly may, however, add to its original jurisdiction.[36] In exercising this power, the Supreme Court (Additional Original Jurisdiction) Act, 2002 was enacted, and the Act confers the court with original jurisdiction in disputes between the president and the National Assembly.[37] The court cannot, however, be conferred with original jurisdiction with respect to any criminal matter.[38]

With respect to appellate jurisdiction, section 6 of the Constitution of the Federal Republic of Nigeria (Second Alteration) Act, 2010 which repealed section 233(1) of the Constitution provides that the 'Supreme Court shall have jurisdiction, to the exclusion of any other court of law in Nigeria, to hear and determine appeals from the Court of Appeal.' The purport of this provision is that only the Supreme Court can hear appeals from the Court of Appeal, it does not foreclose the possibility of hearing appeals from other courts as may be created by the National Assembly. Thus, appeals from the Legal Practitioners Disciplinary Committee go directly to the Supreme Court.[39] The Legal Practitioners Disciplinary Committee is a creation of the National Assembly to punish erring lawyers.

The Court of Appeal is next in judicial hierarchy to the Supreme Court. The court is made up of the president and such a number of justices not fewer than 49.[40] In exercising its jurisdiction, the court must be composed

32. Ibid s 235.
33. Ibid s 230(1).
34. Ibid s 234.
35. Ibid s 232(1).
36. Ibid s 232(2).
37. Supreme Court (Additional Original Jurisdiction) Act 2002 Cap S16 Revised Laws of the Federation of Nigeria (LFN) 2004, s 1.
38. Nigerian Constitution 1999, s 232(2).
39. Legal Practitioners Act Cap L11 Revised LFN 2004, s 12(7).
40. Nigerian Constitution 1999, s 237.

of not fewer than three justices.[41] The court has both original and appellate jurisdiction. Original jurisdiction is with respect to an election petition of the president and the vice-president.[42] The appellate jurisdiction of the court is with respect to both civil and criminal matters.[43] The court has

> jurisdiction to the exclusion of any other court of law in Nigeria, to hear and determine appeals from the Federal High Court, the High Court of the Federal Capital Territory, Abuja, High Court of a State . . . and from decisions of a court martial or other tribunals as may be prescribed by an Act of the National Assembly.[44]

The Federal High Court is created pursuant to section 249 of the 1999 Nigerian Constitution as amended. The Federal High Court is a court of coordinate jurisdiction to the High Court of the Federal Capital Territory, Abuja and the High Court of a State. However, its jurisdiction is limited. It is largely confined to matters within the Exclusive Legislative List. These matters include companies and allied matters, bankruptcy, customs and so on.[45] Criminal jurisdiction is confined to 'treason, treasonable felony and allied offences'[46] and 'criminal causes' arising out of those matters on which it ordinarily has jurisdiction.[47] The National Assembly may, however, expand the jurisdiction of the court with respect to matters it can competently legislate on.[48] This arguably includes federal offences.

The High Court of the Capital Territory, Abuja is created pursuant to section 255 of the Constitution as amended. The number of judges that make up the court is the chief judge and such a number of judges as prescribed by the National Assembly at a point in time.[49] In exercising the jurisdiction of the court, the court must be composed of at least one judge.[50] The High Court of the Federal Capital Territory exercises its jurisdiction solely in Abuja. It has unlimited jurisdiction on all civil and criminal matters, except to the extent limited by the jurisdiction of the Federal High Court as defined under section 251 of the Constitution as amended.[51]

The high court of a state exists pursuant to section 270(1) of the Constitution as amended.[52] The court can exercise its jurisdiction by at least one

41. Ibid s 247.
42. Constitution of the Federal Republic of Nigeria (Second Alteration) Act 2010, s 7.
43. Nigerian Constitution 1999, s 241(1)(a).
44. Ibid s 240.
45. Ibid s 251(1).
46. Ibid s 251(2).
47. Ibid s 251(3).
48. Ibid s 252(2).
49. Ibid s 255(2).
50. Ibid s 258.
51. Ibid s 257(1).
52. Ibid 270(2).

judge.[53] The jurisdiction of the court covers the whole state, and it is with respect to all civil and criminal proceedings except to the extent limited by section 251 where the jurisdiction of the federal High Court is defined.[54]

As the Court of Appeal can hear appeals 'from decisions of a court martial,'[55] it is also relevant to discuss this court. The Court Martial (CM) is often referred to as military court. It is a special court with criminal jurisdiction. The court was established by Armed Forces Act 1993. The CM is divided into two, namely the Special CM and the General CM.[56] The General CM is properly constituted by a president, no fewer than four members, a waiting member, a liaison officer and a judge-advocate.[57] The Special CM, on the other hand, is properly constituted by a president, no fewer than two members, a waiting member, a liaison officer and a judge-advocate.[58] The Special CM has the same competence as that of a General CM except that it cannot impose a death sentence or a sentence of imprisonment that is more than one year if the members are two.[59]

The president presides on the proceedings of the court. His rank must not be under the rank of a major or equivalent rank in other services. But, where a major or an officer of an equivalent rank is not available, a captain can be appointed.[60] An officer cannot be prosecuted by others of a lower rank.[61] A liaison officer is not a member of the court. His duty is to facilitate an exchange of papers and to maintain a cordial relationship between the court and the public. A waiting member comes in whenever there is a vacancy in the panel. A judge-advocate must be a member of the armed forces, and he must also qualify as a legal practitioner. The judge-advocate must have qualified as a legal practitioner for at least three years.[62] His duty is to advise the court on practice and procedure and evidence. He does not participate in decision making.

The CM prosecutes persons who are subject to service law.[63] Persons who are subject to service law include members of the Nigerian army, the Nigerian navy and the Nigerian air force.[64] Police officers are not subject to service law. The General CM can also prosecute 'a person subject to service law . . . who by law of war is subject to trial by a military tribunal and may adjudge a

53. Ibid s 273.
54. Ibid s 272(1).
55. Ibid s 240.
56. Armed Forces Act 1993 Cap A20 Revised LFN 2004, s 129.
57. Ibid s 129(a).
58. Ibid s 129(b).
59. Ibid s 130(3).
60. Ibid s 133(a).
61. *Okoro v Nigerian Army Council* [2000] 3 NWLR (Pt 647), 77.
62. Armed Forces Act 1993, s 133(6).
63. Ibid s 130(1).
64. Ibid s 291.

punishment authorised by law of war or armed conflict.'[65] Offences that can be prosecuted are military offences or civil offences. Military offences include mutiny, cowardly behaviour, insubordination and aiding the enemy.[66] Civil offences are offences in the Criminal Code or Penal Code. A person who has been tried before a CM can still be tried again before the regular court. If the person was convicted by the CM, the regular court must take cognisance of the punishment imposed.[67] However, if it is the regular court that has tried the person, the CM can no longer try the person again.

General CM may be convened by the president and commander-in-chief of the armed forces of Nigeria, the chief of defence staff, the service chiefs, the general commanding officer and a brigade commander.[68] Special CM can be convened by any person who is competent to convene a General CM and the commanding officer of a battalion.[69] An officer who convenes cannot be the president or member of the CM.[70] The power to convene can be delegated once the order in respect thereof is in writing and signed by the delegating person.[71] A CM may be dissolved before or after the commencement of trial if justice so warrants, but this does not bar convening another CM.[72] The CM sits in an open court except when the interest of defence and security demand otherwise.[73] The accused must be present during trial.[74] The Criminal Procedure Act applies to the CM.[75] This implies that adversarial mode of trial prevails. The decision of the CM is subject to the confirmation of the convening authority.[76] Before the CM can impose the death penalty, it must be composed of seven members.[77] The execution of the death sentence requires the approval of the president.[78] A Special CM cannot impose death sentence.[79] When it is made up of only two members, it cannot impose imprisonment more than one year.[80] Appeals from a CM do not end in the Court of Appeal since the Supreme Court also has jurisdiction to hear such appeals.[81]

65. Ibid s 130(2).
66. Ibid ss 45–114.
67. Ibid s 170.
68. Ibid s 131.
69. *Airforce v Obiosa* [2003] NWLR (Pt 810), 283.
70. Armed Forces Act 1993, s 134(1).
71. *Airforce v Obiosa* [2003] NWLR (Pt 810) 283, 346.
72. Armed Forces Act 1993, s 136(1) and (6).
73. Ibid s 139(1) and (2).
74. Ibid s 139(1).
75. Criminal Procedure Act Cap C41 LFN 2004, s 56; Administration of Criminal Justice Act 2015, ss 2(1), 2(2), 86 and 493.
76. Armed Forces Act 1993, ss 148(1) and 151.
77. Ibid s 130(1).
78. Ibid s 153.
79. Ibid s 130(3).
80. Ibid.
81. Ibid s 202.

Criminal Law and Practice in Nigeria

Criminal law falls within residual matters upon which only states within the federation can exercise their powers. The Criminal Code Law applies in each state within the southern part of the federation. The Penal Code Law applies in each state within the northern part of the federation and the Federal Capital Territory, Abuja. The Criminal Code has its origin in 1904 when it was introduced by Lugard administration to northern Nigeria by way of proclamation.[82] In 1916, it was extended to the whole of Nigeria after the amalgamation of Nigeria in 1914.[83] The code was prepared by Sir James Fitzstephen, an eminent English criminal lawyer, in 1878.[84] In 1959, the Criminal Code was restricted in its application to the southern part of Nigeria because of the conflict between the principles of the code and that of Islamic law of the Maliki School, which was then prevalent in the northern part of Nigeria,[85] while the Penal Code was promulgated and made to apply in the northern part of Nigeria.[86]

The Penal Code was fashioned after the code of the Sudan which was designed for a predominantly Muslim community.[87] The Sudanese Code was fashioned after the 1860 Indian Penal Code prepared by Lord Macaulay.[88] Neither of the two codes contains any provision for punishing crimes recognised under the Rome Statute. Thus, the crime recognised under the Rome Statute cannot yet be the basis of prosecution of any person in Nigeria. The reason for this situation is not far-fetched. The Criminal Code was written at a time when international crimes were yet to have any meaningful significance to the whole world. The first trial of international crimes was the trial of Peter von Hagenbach in 1474, which undoubtedly far preceded 1878 when Sir James Fitzstephen prepared the Criminal Code; however, the meaningful prosecution of international crimes after Hagenbach trial was not until 1945 by the International Military Tribunal (IMT). Therefore, Sir James Fitzstephen could not have contemplated the inclusion of international crimes in any form at the time. There was a gap of over 400 years between the trial of Hagenbach and the period in which Sir James Fitzstephen was preparing the Criminal Code.

With respect to the Penal Code, which came into operation in 1959-a period after 1945, one would have thought that the situation would have been different from that of the Criminal Code. However, this should not be a surprise if one considers that the Penal Code took after the Sudanese Code

82. Cyprian Okechukwu Okonkwo, *Criminal Law in Nigeria* (2nd edn, Spectrum Books Limited 1980), 4.
83. Ibid., 5.
84. Ibid.
85. Ibid., 5–9.
86. Ibid., 9.
87. Ibid.
88. Ibid.

which was fashioned after the Indian Penal Code of 1860. If in 1878 when Sir James Fitzstephens prepared the Criminal Code international crimes were insignificant to the whole world, then it is logical to conclude that when Lord Macaulay prepared the Penal Code in 1860, international crimes were insignificant as well. Therefore, Lord Macaulay could not have contemplated the inclusion of international crimes in any guise.

While the Criminal and the Penal Codes do not contain any provision on international crimes, there is the Geneva Conventions Act which punishes war crimes or grave breaches of the conventions.[89] However, the Additional Protocols to the Geneva Conventions are yet to be made punishable in Nigeria. The Geneva Conventions Act is the only law that comes close to the Rome Statute in Nigeria with respect to punishing international crimes, but it does not obviate the need for the investigation and prosecution of crimes recognised under the Rome Statute. The reason is that the Geneva Conventions only relate to war crimes or grave breaches of the conventions and do not cover genocide and crimes against humanity. In addition, the content of war crimes or grave breaches of the conventions is not identical with that of war crimes under the Rome Statute.[90]

As crimes are solely within the legislative competence of states, the Criminal Code which applies to the southern part of Nigeria becomes the Criminal Code Law of each state of the federation falling within the southern part of Nigeria. Similarly, the Penal Code becomes the Penal Code Law of each state of the federation falling within the northern part of Nigeria. Since the National Assembly legislates directly for the Federal Capital Territory and since it falls within the northern part of Nigeria, the Penal Code operating there is the Penal Code Act. But the fact that crimes are residual matters solely for the federating states does not, however, suggest that the federal government cannot legislate on what is called 'federal offence.' A federal offence is defined as 'an offence contrary to the provisions of an Act of the National Assembly or any law having effect as if so enacted.'[91]

89. Cap G3 Revised Laws of the Federation of Nigeria (LFN) 2004.
90. The Rome Statute constitutes progressive development of international criminal law in certain respects which cannot be found in the Geneva Conventions Act. For example, under the four Geneva Conventions 1949, an occupying power will commit war crime with the transfer of civilian population of the occupied territories: art 85(4) Additional Protocol I Geneva Convention 1977 (adopted 10 June 1977, entered into force 7 December 1978) 1125 UNTS 3. Under the Rome Statute of the International Criminal Court (Rome Statute) (adopted 17 July 1998, entered into force 1 July 2002) 2187 UNTS 3, in addition to the transfer of civilian population of the occupied territories, it is also criminal for the occupying power to transfer its own population to the occupied territories: art 8(2)(b)(viii) of the Rome Statute. Similarly, before war crimes are committed under the Geneva Conventions, death, serious injury to body or health must have resulted whereas under the Rome Statute, they are not required: Compare art 85(3) Protocol I to the Geneva Conventions with art 8(2)(b) of the Rome Statute.
91. Nigerian Constitution 1999, s 286(3).

The Criminal Code and the Penal Code are, however, not the only codes generally regulating crimes in Nigeria. There is also the Sharia Penal Code Law enacted by various states in the northern part of Nigeria in 2000.[92] This is an exercise of their legislative competence. The Sharia Penal Code Law is, however, a personal system of law because it applies to Muslims alone.[93]

The Office of the Attorney-General

Crimes are prosecuted in Nigeria by the attorney-general. There is the attorney-general of the federation and the attorney-general of each state of the federation.[94] The attorney-general of the federation is the 'Chief Law Officer of the Federation and a Minister of the Government of the Federation.'[95] The attorney-general of the federation is appointed by the president subject to the confirmation of the Senate,[96] and only a legal practitioner who has practised law for a period not less than 10 years can be appointed.[97] Similarly, the attorney-general of the state is the 'Chief Law Officer of the State and Commissioner for Justice of the Government of the State.'[98] The attorney-general of the state is appointed by the governor of that state subject to the confirmation of the House of Assembly of that state,[99] and only a legal practitioner who has also practised law for a period not less than ten years can be appointed.[100]

The attorney-general of the federation or the attorney-general of the state may institute criminal proceedings against any person in any court of law other than a court martial.[101] The attorney-general may also take over any criminal proceeding instituted by 'any other authority or person'[102] and may discontinue any such proceeding instituted by 'him or any other authority or person' before a judgement is delivered.[103] The attorney-general may exercise his or her power by himself or herself or any officers of his or her

92. For example, see Sharia'h Penal Code Law of Zamfara State 2000 which came into operation on the 27th day of January 2000.
93. For example, issue C of the general part of the Sharia'h Penal Code Law of Zamfara provides that the Code shall apply only to 'every person who professes the Islamic faith and/ or every other person who voluntarily consents to the exercise of the jurisdiction of any of Sharia'h courts established under the Sharia'h Courts (Administration of Justice and Certain Consequential Changes) Law. . . .'
94. Nigerian Constitution 1999, ss 174 and 211.
95. Ibid s 150(1).
96. Ibid s 147(2).
97. Ibid s 150(2).
98. Ibid s 195(1).
99. Ibid s 192(2).
100. Ibid s 195(2).
101. Ibid ss 174(1)(a) and 211(1)(a).
102. Ibid ss 174(1)(b) and 211(1)(b).
103. Ibid ss 174(1)(c) and 211(1)(c).

department.[104] Because the attorney-general may take over or discontinue any criminal proceeding instituted by any other authority or person, it follows that other authority than the attorney-general may also institute criminal proceedings subject to the power of the attorney-general to take over or discontinue such proceedings. Thus, the police and private persons can institute criminal proceedings.[105] However, private persons cannot prosecute federal offences punishable by death or life imprisonment.[106]

The attorney-general of the federation prosecutes offences created by Acts of the National Assembly while the attorney-general of a state prosecutes offences created by the law of the House of Assembly of a state. Therefore, only the attorney-general of a state can prosecute offences created by the Criminal Code Law and the Penal Code Law of that state. With respect to federal offences, only the attorney-general of the federation can prosecute. However, federal offences can be prosecuted in a state. The most important consideration is if the tenor of the Act is to the effect that the crime is to be prosecuted in any state. Therefore, 'the State High Court [can] be used as a venue for the prosecution of cases,'[107] and the attorney-general of the federation cannot be 'prevented from exercising his functions on the ground that his jurisdiction does not extend to any particular state in Nigeria.'[108] The attorney-general of the federation may, however, delegate his or her power to prosecute to the attorney-general of the state,[109] and the power so delegated may be exercised by that attorney-general of the state or any officer in his or her department or ministry.[110]

The General Part of Criminal Statutes

Chapter 5 of the Nigerian Criminal Code provides for the general principles of criminal responsibility as applicable to the Criminal Code. The core of chapter five is section 24 which provides that

> [s]ubject to the express provisions of this Code relating to negligent acts and omissions, a person is not criminally responsible for an act or omission, which occurs independently of the exercise of his will, or for an event which occurs by accident.

104. Ibid ss 174(2) and 211(2).
105. With respect to the police, see Police Act Cap P19 Revised LFN 2004, s 23 and Administration of Criminal Justice Act 2015, s 268(2). With respect to private persons see Criminal Procedure Act, s 59(1); Criminal Procedure Code, s 143(e) and Administration of Criminal Justice Act 2015, ss 267(1), 383 and 384.
106. Administration of Criminal Justice Act 2015, s 267(1).
107. *Attorney General Ondo v Attorney General Federation* [2002] FWLR (Pt. 111) 1972, 2210–2211, paras E-A.
108. Ibid., 2167 paras D-E.
109. Administration of Criminal Justice Act 2015, s 268(4).
110. Ibid s 268(5).

Section 2(4) of the Criminal Code makes chapter 5 applicable to all other subsequent criminal legislation in Nigeria when except those other legislations expressly provide otherwise. In the words of the code, 'the provisions of chapters 2, 4 and 5 of the Criminal Code shall apply in relation to any offence against any Order, Act, Law or Statute and to all persons charged with any such offence.' This implies that the general principles of criminal responsibility in the Nigerian Criminal Code shall apply to any law which seeks to make operative in Nigeria the crimes recognised under the Rome Statute except otherwise stated.

Basis for the Assumption of Criminal Jurisdiction

The principle for the assumption of criminal jurisdiction is essentially territorial in Nigeria. Section 12A of the Criminal Code and section 4 of the Penal Code deal with the issue. Each code is essentially territorial in its sphere of operation. When an element of a crime occurs in a territory where any of the codes operates, it will be taken as if all the elements of the crime had taken place in that territory.[111] But, when the only element of the crime that occurs is the death of a person, then the code that will apply will be the code that operates where the act causing the death had occurred.[112]

Where a crime has an international dimension, the strong territorial link is still maintained. Section 13(1) of the Criminal Code provides that when someone who is outside Nigeria procured another person to do something which would amount to a crime in Nigeria, and that person who procured another would have been ordinarily guilty if he himself had done the act in Nigeria, then that person would be considered guilty upon entering Nigeria. Similarly, section 13 provides that when someone who outside Nigeria procured another person to commit a crime in Nigeria and the crime was committed in Nigeria, the person would be considered guilty upon entering Nigeria. Section 13A of the Criminal Code provides that reference to Nigeria means a state in Nigeria or Nigeria if federal law is the law being breached. In addition, section 14 of the Criminal Code provides for the principle of double criminality. It provides that if someone in Nigeria procured another to do outside Nigeria what will ordinarily amount to a crime in Nigeria and that place outside Nigeria, then the person who procured another shall be guilty of appropriate crime in Nigeria. Section 14A applies the principle of double criminality among states within the federation.

Under the Administration of Criminal Justice Act 2015, the principle of territoriality also applies although less rigidly. A suspect can be prosecuted when the offence was wholly or in part committed, or some act forming part of the offence was committed,[113] or the consequence of the offence has

111. Okonkwo, *Criminal Law in Nigeria* (n 82), 10.
112. Ibid.
113. Administration of Criminal Justice Act 2015, s 93(1)(a).

ensued.[114] When an offence is committed at sea or outside Nigeria, the suspect may be prosecuted any place in Nigeria where the suspect is first brought or any place to which he or she may be taken thereafter.[115] When an offence is commenced in a state and completed in another state, or is completed in the Federal Capital Territory, Abuja after being commenced in another state, the suspect may be prosecuted in any of the states or the Federal Capital Territory, Abuja.[116] When a court has wrongly assumed jurisdiction on territorial ground, the proceedings of that court shall be deemed valid.[117] The principle of territoriality in the codes is confined to the crimes recognised in the codes while the principle of territoriality under the Administration of Criminal Justice Act 2015 applies to all federal offences.

In contradistinction to the codes and the Administration of Criminal Justice Act 2015, the Geneva Conventions Act provides for universal jurisdiction and any person may be proceeded against, tried and sentenced in Nigeria for the grave breaches of the conventions irrespective of where the breaches occurred.[118]

Criminal Procedure

While both the Criminal Code and the Penal Code are substantive laws defining elements of crimes, Criminal Procedure Code, Criminal Procedure Act, Administration of Criminal Justice Law and Administration of Criminal Justice Act regulate criminal prosecution in Nigeria.[119] The Criminal Procedure Code applies to the states within the northern part of Nigeria. It is adopted by each state as its Criminal Procedure Code Law. The Criminal Procedure Act applies to the states within the southern part of Nigeria. It is also adopted by each state as its Criminal Procedure Law. However, some states have repealed their Criminal Procedure Law and enacted Administration of Criminal Justice Law. The Administration of Criminal Justice Act applies in prosecuting federal offences, except for offences prosecutable by CM.[120]

Criminal prosecution is adversarial in Nigeria because Nigeria is a member of the common law family. There is no trial *in absentia*.[121] It is the prosecution that must discharge the burden of proof which must be established

114. Ibid s 93(1)(b).
115. Ibid s 94.
116. Ibid s 96.
117. Ibid ss 101 and 103.
118. Geneva Conventions Act, ss 3(2) and 4(2).
119. On the outline of criminal procedure in Nigeria see John O. Asein, *Introduction to Nigerian Legal System* (2nd edn, Ababa Press Limited 2005), 308–319.
120. Criminal Procedure Act, s 56; Administration of Criminal Justice Act 2015, ss 2(1), 2(2), 86 and 493.
121. Criminal Procedure Act s 210; Criminal Procedure Code, s 153; *Adeoye v State* [1999] 6 NWLR (Pt 605) 74; *Eyisi v The State* (2000) 12 SC (Pt 1) 24, 33.

beyond reasonable doubt.[122] However, this does not absolve the defendant of leading evidence in support of his or her defence. Defences which are open to the defendant include insanity,[123] intoxication,[124] self-defence,[125] provocation,[126] duress[127] or mistake of fact.[128] Sentences that may be passed include death sentence,[129] imprisonment,[130] caning,[131] fines,[132] forfeiture,[133] seizure,[134] restitution,[135] disposition[136] and compensation.[137]

Constitutional Safeguards for Fair Hearing

The Nigerian Constitution provides for fair hearing. Section 36 provides among others for the presumption of innocence,[138] public trial unless circumstances occasion otherwise,[139] the right to be informed of charges in the language understood by the defendant,[140] the right of the accused to cross-examine witnesses against him[141] and his right not to be compelled as a witness in his own case,[142] the right not to be punished for any conduct which at the time of commission or omission did not constitute an offence[143] and the right not to be tried again for an offence or another one of the same ingredient for which the defendant had been acquitted or convicted (*ne bis in idem* or *autre vois convict* or *autre vois acquit*)[144] and the right to appeal.[145]

122. Nigerian Constitution 1999, s 45.
123. Criminal Code Act Cap C39 Revised LFN 2004, s 28.
124. Ibid s 29.
125. Ibid s 26.
126. Ibid.
127. Ibid.
128. Ibid s 25.
129. Nigerian Constitution 1999, s 33(1); Criminal Code, s 37; Penal Code, s 221; Criminal Procedure Act, s 367; Administration of Criminal Justice Act 2015, s 402; *Kalu v State* [1998]13 NWLR (Pt. 583) 531, 537–561; *Ogugu v State* [1994] 9 NWLR (Pt. 366) 1 (SC).
130. Criminal Procedure Act, s 377; Administration of Criminal Justice Act 2015, s 416(1).
131. Criminal Code, s 17; Penal Code, ss 68(1), 387, 388, 392, 393, 402, 403 and 404; Criminal Procedure Act, ss 384–388; Criminal Procedure Code, s 309.
132. Criminal Procedure Act, ss 382(1) and 389–400; Criminal Procedure Code, s 23(1); Administration of Criminal Justice Act 2015, s 420(1).
133. Criminal Procedure Act, s 263.
134. Ibid.
135. Ibid.
136. Ibid.
137. Ibid s 256.
138. Nigerian Constitution 1999, s 36(5).
139. Ibid s 36(4)(a).
140. Ibid s 36(6)(a).
141. Ibid s 36(6)(d).
142. Ibid s 36(11).
143. Ibid s 36(8).
144. Ibid s 36(9).
145. Ibid ss 233 and 240.

The Police System in Nigeria

The Nigerian police is established pursuant to section 214 of the Nigerian Constitution 1999. While the structure of government in Nigeria is essentially federal, the police is a unitary institution in Nigeria. The Nigerian police are under the command of the inspector-general of police.[146] At state level, the police is placed under the command of the commissioner of police of that state. However, the authority of the commissioner of police is subject to the overriding authority of the inspector-general of police.[147]

There are two bodies that regulate the affairs of the police in Nigeria. They are the Nigeria Police Council and the Police Service Commission. The Nigeria Police Council is made up of the president, who shall be the chairman; the governor of each state of the federation; the chairman of the Police Service Commission; and the inspector-general of police.[148] The functions of the Nigeria Police Council includes the organisation and administration of the Nigeria Police Force and all other matters relating thereto (not being matters relating to the use and operational control of the force or the appointment, disciplinary control and dismissal of members of the force), the general supervision of the Nigeria police force and advising the president on the appointment of the inspector-general of police.[149]

With respect to the Police Service Commission, the Nigerian Constitution 1999 stipulates that the commission shall comprise of a chairman, and such a number of other persons, no fewer than seven but not more than nine, as may be prescribed by an Act of the National Assembly.[150] Pursuant to this provision, the Police Service Commission (Establishment) Act 2001 was enacted. The Act stipulates that members of the commission shall be a chairman who shall be the chief executive of the commission; a retired justice of the Supreme Court or Court of Appeal; a retired police officer not below the rank of commissioner of police; one representative each of women interest, the Nigerian press, non-governmental human rights organisations in Nigeria and organised private sector; and a secretary to the commission.[151] The secretary shall be an officer in the civil service of the federation not below the rank of a permanent secretary.[152]

The president of Nigeria appoints the members of the commission subject to the confirmation of the Senate.[153] Each member of the commission serves for a term of four years[154] but may be removed from office by the president if

146. Ibid s 215(2).
147. Ibid.
148. Ibid Third Schedule Part I.
149. Ibid.
150. Ibid.
151. Police Service Commission (Establishment) Act 2001, s 2(1).
152. Ibid s 10(1)(a).
153. Ibid s 2(2)(a).
154. Ibid s 3(1)(a).

'he is satisfied that it is not in the interest of the Commission or the interest of the public that the member should continue in office.'[155] When any member is unable to discharge the functions of his or her office (whether arising from infirmity of mind or body or any other cause or for misconduct), he or she may be removed by the president acting on an address supported by a two- thirds majority of the Senate praying that he or she be so removed.[156] Unlike the Nigeria Police Council, the commission has the power to appoint persons to offices (other than the office of the inspector-general of police) in the Nigeria police force and to dismiss and exercise disciplinary control over such persons.[157] The commission is also empowered to formulate and implement policies aimed at the efficiency of the Nigeria police force.[158]

The police in Nigeria play two vital roles, namely the investigation of crimes and the prosecution of offenders. In investigating crimes, the police are charged with the duties of detecting crimes and apprehending offenders.[159] They investigate crimes with a view to detecting those who are responsible. In investigating crimes, they will often have to collect information which will be used as evidence at trial. They often obtain information from witnesses, suspects or those who are responsible. To effectively carry out their duty of investigating crimes, the police are imbued with wide powers of search and arrest although their exercise is subject to constitutional limit. Therefore, the police are vital to a successful prosecution of crimes recognised under the Rome Statute as required by the principle of complementarity.

Apart from the investigation of crimes, the police can also conduct prosecution of crimes.[160] Any police officer may conduct in person all prosecutions before any court in Nigeria[161] subject to the power of the attorney-general of the federation or of the state to institute and undertake, take over and continue or discontinue criminal proceedings against any person in a court of law in Nigeria.[162] In *FRN v Osahon*,[163] the Supreme Court of Nigeria held that the police can prosecute in the Federal High Court in Nigeria. The court added that while it is desirable for such a police officer to be legally qualified as a legal practitioner, it is not compulsory that he or she be so qualified.

While the investigative role of the police in a successful prosecution of the crimes recognised under the Rome Statute is undeniable, their competence to successfully prosecute these crimes is seriously doubtful. This is because the prosecution of crimes recognised under the Rome Statute is very complex and highly technical, and most police officers are non-lawyers. Even if all

155. Ibid s 4(2).
156. Ibid s 5(1).
157. Nigerian Constitution 1999, Third Schedule Part I.
158. Police Service Commission (Establishment) Act 2001, s 6(1)(e).
159. Police Act, s 4.
160. Ibid s 23.
161. Ibid; *Olusemo v COP* [1998] 1 NWLR (Pt 575) 547.
162. Nigerian Constitution 1999, ss 174 and 211.
163. [2006] 5 NWLR (Pt 973) 361.

police officers are lawyers, the technical nature of prosecuting international crimes means that only the most competent hands should be made to prosecute. While the police can, in law, prosecute any crime before any court of law in Nigeria, in practice, they only prosecute minor offences.

The Nigerian Prisons Service

The Nigerian Prisons Service, like the Nigeria Police Force, is centrally administered. Thus, every prison in Nigeria is a federal institution. The Nigerian Prisons Service was established via the Prisons Act[164] pursuant to item 48 of the Exclusive Legislative List in which prison is established as a subject matter of federal legislative competence. The comptroller general of prisons is the head of the Nigerian Prisons Service.[165] The president of the Federal Republic of Nigeria is, however, empowered to make regulations 'with respect to the organisation and administration of the prisons; and on the recommendation of the Federal Civil Service Commission, with respect to appointments to offices in the Nigerian Prisons Service.'[166] In addition, the president is empowered to

> make standing orders for the good order, discipline and welfare of prisons . . . with respect to the organisation and administration of prisons; and after consultation with the Federal Civil Service Commission, with respect to any matter relating to appointments to offices in the Nigerian Prisons Service, promotion, transfer, dismissal and discipline of members of the prisons staff.[167]

While the president is empowered to administer prisons, it is the minister of internal affairs who often performs the function on his or her behalf.[168]

The Criminal Code, the Penal Code, the Criminal Procedure Act, the Criminal Procedure Code, the Administration of Criminal Justice Law and the Administration of Criminal Justice Act all recognise imprisonment as a form of punishment. Thus, they are the basis for the establishment of prisons in Nigeria. While prisons keep in custody convicts who are serving their sentences pursuant to the judgement of the court, they also keep in custody suspects who are awaiting trial or those whose trials are pending but are not entitled to bail. Therefore, the relevance of prisons service to the principle of complementarity is self-evident. Prisons keep in custody those who are suspected of having committed crimes recognised under the Rome Statute.

164. Cap P29 Revised LFN 2004.
165. Prisons Act, s 1.
166. Ibid s 15.
167. Ibid s 16.
168. Ibid ss 2 and 19 and Prisons Regulations of 1 November 1947 made pursuant to the Prisons Act, s 76.

Because of the very serious nature of these crimes, bails may not be granted as a general rule to any suspect of these crimes. Similarly, after trial and conviction, prisons are inevitable in housing convicts of crimes recognised under the statute, who may often have to serve long terms of imprisonment when the death penalty is not imposed.

3 Complementarity Under the Rome Statute of the International Criminal Court

Historical Evolution of the Principle of Complementarity

The idea of complementarity is that both international and domestic tribunals should compensate for any deficiency inherent in either of them. Most scholars are divided as to the exact time the principle of complementarity began in international criminal law. Some naturally linked it with the 1998 Rome Statute[1] while others traced it to the 1994 International Law Commission Draft Statute for an International Criminal Court (ICC).[2] Some others also claimed that the principle is traceable to the Working Group of 1992[3] or the discussion that took place within the precinct of the 1991 Commission.[4] The farthest in time is the claim that the principle of complementarity evolved, starting from 'World War I until 1998.'[5] However, it can be argued that the principle of complementarity began from the trial of Peter von Hagenbach in 1474 (Breisach Trial).

Archduke Sigismund of the Austrian Tyrol was heavily indebted. Thus, he faced harassment from Charles the Bold, duke of Burgundy, and mortgaged Alsace which was part of his territory to Charles via the treaty of St Omer in

1. John T. Holmes, 'The Principle of Complementarity' in Roy S. Lee (ed), *The International Criminal Court: The Making of the Rome Statutes, Issues, Negotiations, Results* (Kluwer Law International 1999), 41; Sharon A. Williams, 'Issues of Admissibility' in Otto Triffterer (ed), *Commentary on the Rome Statute: Observers' Notes, Article by Article* (Baden Baden 1999), 390.
2. Flavia Lattanzi, 'The Complementarity Character of the Jurisdiction of the Court with Respect to National Jurisdictions' in Flavia Lattanzi (ed), *The International Criminal Court: Comments on the Draft Statute* (Editoriale Scientifica 1998), 9; Kai Ambos, 'Establishing an International Criminal Court and an International Criminal Code: Observations From an International Criminal Law Viewpoint' (1996) 7 *European Journal of International Law* 519.
3. Immi Tallgren, 'Completing the "International Criminal Order": The Rhetoric of International Repression and the Notion of Complementarity in the Draft Statute for an International Criminal Court' (1998) 67 *Nordic Journal of International Law* 107, 120.
4. Oscar Solera 'Complementarity Jurisdiction and International Criminal Justice' (2002) 84 *International Review of the Red Cross* 145, 151.
5. Mohamed M. El Zeidy, *Complementarity in International Criminal Law: Origin, Development and Practice* (Martinus Nijhoff Publishers 2008), 6.

1469.[6] Charles then appointed Hagenbach as his governor for the territory. While administering the territory, Hagenbach unleashed terror described as 'unique in their ferocity even in those rough and dangerous times'[7] on the inhabitants of the territory which eventually elicited the response of France, Austria and knights of the neighbouring towns as their citizens who were resident in Alsace also fell victim of Hagenbach's rule.[8]

In an ensuing war between Charles and the neighbouring knights as Allies, Hagenbach was captured.[9] He was tried under the order of the archduke, who had resumed his sovereign rights over Alsace, before a tribunal composed of 28 judges from the Allies.[10] Hagenbach would have been tried by a 'local court, [however] the Allies agreed on an ad hoc tribunal'[11] because local courts were considered unsuitable to achieve 'effective justice.'[12] The international tribunal established by the Allies therefore compensated for the deficiency of the local courts. After the end of the First World War, a number of peace treaties were negotiated. These treaties were intended to bring to book those who violated the customs of war. One of these treaties is the Treaty of Versailles. Article 228 of the Treaty of Versailles provides that

> [t]he German Government recognises the right of the Allied and Associated Powers to bring before military Tribunals persons accused of having committed acts in violation of the laws and customs of war . . . notwithstanding any proceedings or prosecution before a tribunal in Germany or in the territory of her allies . . .

This provision tends to show that the trials conducted by the Allies took precedence over any prosecution conducted in Germany with respect to those who violated customs of war. However, Germany indicated that it was willing to prosecute those accused of war in its territory. The subsequent agreement that Germany should try those alleged of war crimes was declared by the Inter-Allied Commission to be 'compatible with the execution of article 228'[13] in compliance with the spirit of complementarity.[14]

6. Deji Adekunle, 'International Criminal Court: A Historical Account' in J.O. Fabunmi (ed), *Themes on Jurisprudence and International Law* (Total Communications Ventures 2009), 109, 111.
7. Robert K. Woetzel, *The Nuremberg Trials in International Law* (Stevens & Sons 1960), 19.
8. Adekunle, 'International Criminal Court: A Historical Account' (n 6), 111.
9. Ibid.
10. El Zeidy, *Complementarity in International Criminal Law* (n 5), 212.
11. Georg Schwarzenberger, *International Law as Applied by International Courts and Tribunals: The Law of Armed Conflict* vol II (Stevens & Sons Ltd 1968), 463.
12. El Zeidy, *Complementarity in International Criminal Law* (n 5), 212.
13. Ibid., 4.
14. Ibid., 16.

While the Treaty of Versailles was being negotiated, other peace treaties were also being negotiated as well. The Treaty of St. Germain[15] was concluded with Austria while the Treaty of Neuilly[16] was concluded with Bulgaria. Similarly, the Treaty of Trianon[17] was concluded with Hungary while the Treaty of Sèvres[18] was concluded with Turkey. Articles 173 of the Treaty of St. Germain, 157 of the Treaty of Trianon, 118 of the Treaty Neuilly and 226 of the Treaty of Sèvres were all identical with article 228 of the Treaty of Versailles. Despite the emphasis on the exclusive jurisdiction and superiority of international tribunals by the texts of these treaties, complementarity was also the outcome as the Allies deferred to the request of each of these states to prosecute within its own domestic realm. However, the Treaty of Sèvres was not ratified let alone implemented.[19]

After the conclusion of the peace treaties after World War I, efforts were geared towards the actualisation of the international criminal court, but they were at an unofficial level.[20] The situation continued until 1934 when France suffered from the waves of terrorist attacks in the Balkans and in Central and Southern Europe.[21] The French government thereafter called for the establishment of an International Criminal Court which would be competent to exercise criminal jurisdiction on terrorism. The 1937 League of Nations Convention which eventually emerged gave primacy to states. States could choose to prosecute in their territory or send the accused to the International Criminal Court. The state determined whether it was capable, and if it was not capable, it could still choose not to send the accused for prosecution.

Before the end of the Second World War, there were preparations to punish those who committed war crimes. The Moscow Declaration of 1943 stipulated that only 'the major criminals, whose offences have no particular geographical localisation'[22] would be tried 'by joint decision of the Governments

15. Treaty of Peace between the Allied and Associated Powers and Austria (signed at Saint Germain-En-Laye 10 September 1919) UKTS No 11 (1919).
16. Treaty of Peace between the Allied and Associated Powers and Bulgaria and Protocol signed at Neuilly-sur-Seine 27 November 1919, (January 1922) 12(3) *The Journal of International Relations* 436–445.
17. Treaty of Peace between the Allied and Associated Powers and Hungary and Protocol and Declarations signed at Trianon 4 June 1920, (January 1921) 15(1) Supplement Official Documents *The American Journal of International Law* 1–4.
18. Treaty of Peace between the Allied Powers and Turkey (signed at Sèvres 10 August 1920) UKTS No 11 (1920).
19. Mohamed M. El Zeidy, 'The Principle of Complementarity: A New Machinery to Implement International Criminal Law' (2001–2002) 23 *Michigan Journal of International Law* 869, 873.
20. El Zeidy, *Complementarity in International Criminal Law* (n 5), 43.
21. Martin David Dublin, *International Terrorism: Two League of Nations Conventions 1934–1937* (Kraus Microform 1991), 7–11.
22. The Tripartite Conference at Moscow Oct 19–30 1943 reprinted in International Conciliation No 395 (1943) 599–605 (Moscow Declaration).

of the Allies.'[23] This declaration formed the basis of the establishment of the International Military Tribunal (Nuremberg Tribunal) through the London Agreement of 8 August 1945.[24] Other criminals would 'be sent back to the Countries in which their abominable deeds were done in order that they may be judged and punished according to the laws of these liberated countries and of free governments.'[25] In line with this stipulation, the Allied Control Council which was acting as the legislative body for Germany enacted Law No. 10 in December 1945. The law was meant to punish international crimes committed in Germany, and it was meant to be implemented by each commander in his zone.[26] There was a division of labour between the International Military Tribunal and the tribunal established under the Control Council Law. Each was to complement the other.

Similarly, there was the International Military Tribunal for the Far East (IMTFE). The major Japanese war criminals were selected 'on the basis of their position rather than direct evidence of culpability.'[27] The tribunal set out to punish only those who took 'advantage of their power and their official positions and their own personal prestige and influence'[28] leaving those who did not have 'leadership background' to be tried separately by each of the 'occupied or colonised territories.'[29] The IMTFE was also to complement tribunals set up domestically in Japan. The only difference was that leadership was the criterion to determine the cases to be tried between the IMTFE and the 'occupied or colonised territories.'

After the Nuremberg trials, the General Assembly was keen about the formulation of its principles. The General Assembly then directed the International Law Commission (ILC) to prepare a 'Draft Code of Offences against the Peace and Security of Mankind.'[30] Meanwhile, the General Assembly on 9 December 1948 had adopted the Convention on the Prevention and Punishment of the Crime of Genocide (Genocide Convention).[31] The relationship

23. Ibid.
24. Agreement for the Prosecution and Punishment of the Major War Criminals of the European Axis, and Charter of the International Military Tribunal, London, 8 August 1945, UNTS No 251 (1951) 280.
25. Moscow Declaration (n 22).
26. Allied Control Council Law No 10, Punishment of Persons Guilty of War Crimes, Crimes against Peace and Crimes against Humanity, 20 December 1945, Official Gazette of the Control Council for Germany, No 3, Berlin, 31 January 1946.
27. Neil Boister and Robert Cryer, *The Tokyo International Military Tribunal: A Reappraisal* (Oxford University Press 2008), 50–69.
28. International Military Tribunal for the Far East (Indictment). www.trumanlibrary.org/whistlestop/study_collections/nuremberg/documents/index.php?documentdate=0000-00-00&documentid=18-2&pagenumber=1 accessed 7 August 2017.
29. Nadia Bernaz and Rémy Prouvèze, 'International and Domestic Prosecutions' in M. Cheriff Bassiouni (ed), *The Pursuit of International Criminal Justice: A World of Study on Conflicts, Victimization, and Post-Conflict Justice* vol I (Intersentia 2010), 280.
30. GA Res, 177 (II), 2nd Session, 123rd Plenary Meeting, 21 November 1947.
31. GA Res, 260 (III), 3rd Session, 179th Plenary Meeting, 9 December 1948, 174–177.

between international tribunal and domestic courts could not be resolved during the period the convention was being negotiated.[32] Therefore, the General Assembly also mandated the ILC to consider establishing an international tribunal that would be competent to enforce the Code.

In 1950, the ILC submitted its report to the General Assembly. But, until 1983, the ILC did not have the opportunity to consider the issue of the relationship between domestic courts and international tribunal again.[33] Between 1983 and 1989, the views of the members of the ILC were divergent and could not be reconciled. The variants of views remained until the General Assembly passed three resolutions requesting the ILC to come up with a more concrete proposal on the issue of international criminal jurisdiction.[34] Between 1990 and 1994, the ILC deliberated extensively on the request of the General Assembly and came up with a draft statute in 1994.[35]

Motivated by the idea that the court was intended to 'supplement, rather than replace, existing national criminal jurisdictions,'[36] the ILC through its 1994 Working Group employed the adjective 'complementary' when it was emphasised that the international criminal court 'is intended to be complementary to national criminal justice systems in cases where such trial procedures may not be available or may be ineffective.'[37] This indicated that the court could not act if 'States concerned were willing and able to exercise their own jurisdiction over the offence.'[38] The draft statute which eventually emerged provided that states would have the jurisdiction to prosecute first and that the tribunal would not have compulsory jurisdiction with respect to international crimes on which a state party could exercise jurisdiction until a particular case is referred to the court. This implies that being a party to the statute does not automatically confer jurisdiction on the court. Each case would still have to be referred to it.

Following the Balkan massacre of 1991, the United Nations Security Council (UNSC) established the International Criminal Tribunal for Yugoslavia (ICTY) as a means of restoring peace.[39] In the same vein, the UNSC

32. See Convention on the Prevention and Punishment of the Crime of Genocide (adopted 9 December 1948, entered into force 12 January 1951) 78 UNTS 277, art 6.
33. Summary Records of the Meetings of the Thirty-Fifth Session (3 May–22 July 1983), 1983 Yearbook of International Law Commission, vol 1.
34. GA Res 43/164 (1988), 76th Plenary Meeting; GA Res 44/32 (1989), 72nd Plenary Meeting; GA Res 44/39 (1989), 72nd Plenary Meeting.
35. Mohamed M. El Zeidy, 'The Genesis of Complementarity' in Carsten Stahn and Mohamed El Zeidy (eds), *The International Criminal Court and Complementarity: From Theory to Practice* vol I (Cambridge University Press 2011), 115–116.
36. 1994 Yearbook of International Law Commission, vol I, 9 and 191.
37. 1994 International Law Commission Draft Statute in 1994 International Law Commission Report 37, preamble, para 3.
38. 1994 Yearbook of International Law Commission, vol I, 23.
39. Statute of the International Tribunal for the Prosecution of Persons Responsible for Serious Violations of International Humanitarian Law Committed in the Territory of the Former

established the International Criminal Tribunal for Rwanda (ICTR) after the 1994 genocide in Rwanda.[40] Article 9 of the ICTY Statute provides that 'the International Tribunal and national courts shall have concurrent jurisdiction'[41] and that 'the International Tribunal shall have primacy over national courts'[42] which may 'at any stage of the procedure . . . formally request national courts to defer to . . . [its] competence . . .'[43] Article 10 adds that the ICTY may prosecute a person already tried by national courts if 'the act for which he or she was tried was characterised as an ordinary crime'[44] or 'the national court proceedings were not impartial or independent, were designed to shield the accused from international criminal responsibility, or the case was not diligently prosecuted.'[45] The statute of the ICTR was more strongly worded. Article 8 provides that 'the International Tribunal for Rwanda and national courts shall have concurrent jurisdiction'[46] and that 'the International Tribunal for Rwanda shall have primacy over the national courts of all States'[47] which may 'at any stage of the procedure . . . formally request national courts to defer to its competence.'[48] The statute of the ICTR also contains article 10 which is the same as that of the ICTY.

In order to wind up the ICTY and the ICTR, the UNSC adopted 'completion strategies.'[49] This process necessitated amending the Rules of Procedure and Evidence (RPE) of the two tribunals. Rule 11bis of the ICTY[50] empowers the tribunal to refer a case 'after an indictment has been confirmed and prior to the commencement of trial'[51] to the State where the crime was committed, or where the accused was arrested or 'having jurisdiction and being willing and adequately prepared to accept such a case.'[52] In referring a case, the tribunal shall 'consider the gravity of the crimes charged and the level of responsibility of the accused.'[53] But the tribunal may 'upon having given to the state authorities concerned the opportunity to be heard, revoke the order

---

Yugoslavia Since 1991, SC Res 827, UN SCOR, 48th Sess, Annex, 3417th mtg., UN Doc S/Res/827 (1993) (ICTY Statute).

40. Statute of the International Tribunal for the Prosecution of Persons Responsible for Serious Violations of International Humanitarian Law Committed in Rwanda, SC Res 955, UN SCOR, 49th Sess, Annex, 3453rd mtg., UN Doc S/Res/955 (1993) (ICTR Statute).
41. Article 9(1).
42. Article 9(2).
43. Ibid.
44. Article 10(2)(b).
45. Ibid.
46. Article 9(1).
47. Article 9(2).
48. Ibid.
49. See SC Res 1503 (2003) UN Doc S/Res/1503 and SC Res 1534 (2004) UN Doc S/Res/1534.
50. ICTY Rules of Evidence and Procedure (RPE) IT/32/Rev 47, 28 August 2012 as amended.
51. Ibid 11bis(A).
52. Ibid 11bis(A)(iii).
53. Ibid 11bis(C).

[of referral] and make a formal request for deferral'[54] 'before the accused is found guilty or acquitted by a national court.'[55] The ICTR[56] Rule 11bis is identical to that of the ICTY; the only difference is that there is no provision requiring the ICTR to consider the gravity of the crimes charged together with the responsibility of the accused. However, the practice of the court shows deference to this principle.[57] The primacy of the ICTY and the ICTR is also meant to complement the judicial process in Yugoslavia and Rwanda, but a subordinate role is assigned to these states. It is the international tribunals that determine at will cases to be tried by these states.

On 9 December 1994, the General Assembly established an Ad hoc committee[58] with the mandate to critically re-examine the 'major substantive and administrative issues' generated by the 1994 draft.[59] The Ad hoc Committee dedicated its effort to refining the criteria for the functioning of the principle of complementarity in the 1994 ILC Draft Statute.[60] The terms *available* and *ineffective* in the preamble to the 1994 ILC Draft Statute were severely criticised and were considered vague by several delegations.[61]

In 1995, the Preparatory Committee replaced the Ad hoc Committee. The issue of the vagueness of the terms adopted in the preamble of the 1994 ILC Draft Statute resurfaced.[62] While some delegations favoured a definition with more clarity, some wanted the terms deleted completely.[63] In August 1997, John Holmes, the head of the Canadian delegation, presented a draft provision (article 35) on complementarity during the session of the Preparatory Committee. The draft provision was approved at the end of the session.[64] In addition, the terms *unwilling* and *unable* which had earlier found expression in the report of the 1992 Working Group were adopted by the draft provision with more detailed and thorough criteria for assessment.[65] This

54. Ibid 11bis(F).
55. Ibid.
56. ICTR Rules of Evidence and Procedure 1 October 2009 as amended.
57. Erik Møse, 'Main Achievements of the ICTR' (2005) 3 *Journal of International Criminal Justice* 920, 932; Mohamed M. El Zeidy, 'From Primacy to Complementarity and Backwards: (Re)-Visiting Rule 11 *Bis* of the Ad hoc Tribunals' (2008) 57 *International & Comparative Law Quarterly* 403, 410.
58. GA Res 49/53, 9 December 1994.
59. Report of the Ad hoc Committee on the Establishment of an International Criminal Court UN GAOR, 50th Sess, Supp No 22, UN Doc A/50/22 (1995), para 154.
60. El Zeidy, 'The Genesis of Complementarity' (n 35), 130.
61. Report of the Ad hoc Committee 1995, para 41.
62. Report of the Preparatory Committee on the Establishment of an International Criminal Court UN GAOR, 51st Sess, vol 1, Supp No 22, UN Doc A/51/22 (1995), paras 154 and 161.
63. Ibid para 161.
64. Decisions Taken by the Preparatory Committee at its Session Held 4 to 15 August 1997, UN GAOR, 52 mtg, UN Doc A/AC.249/1997/L.8/Rev.1 (1997).
65. Ibid., 10–12.

eventually formed part of the draft final act.[66] Deliberations on complementarity continued in Rome, especially during the plenary meetings.[67] The final outcome of deliberations was embodied in article 17 of the Rome Statute.[68] The principle of complementarity in the Rome Statute confers both compulsory and optional jurisdiction on the International Criminal Court.[69] When a state ratifies the Rome Statute, the International Criminal Court automatically has compulsory jurisdiction which can be exercised on the fulfilment of certain conditions.[70] The optional jurisdiction is with respect to self-referral[71] reminiscent of the 1474 Hagenbach trial.

The historical background to the principle of complementarity shows that there are five formulations of the principle. The first one is the 1937 League of Nations complementarity. In this formulation states have primacy and solely determine if an international tribunal will have any case to adjudicate upon. The second one is the IMT complementarity. In this formulation, there is a division of labour between an international tribunal and a domestic court. The third one is the 1994 ILC complementarity. In this formulation, the international tribunal cannot assume compulsory jurisdiction because of the membership of a state to the draft statute. Each case will still be referred to the court before it can compulsorily assume jurisdiction. The fourth one is the primacy of the ad hoc tribunals. This is a complete opposite of the 1937 formulation. In this instance, it is the international tribunals that determine if the state will have any case to adjudicate upon. The fifth one is the Rome Statute complementarity. It has both compulsory and optional jurisdiction. Once a state ratifies the statute, the court can exercise compulsory jurisdiction if the state concerned is 'unwilling' and 'unable.' The optional jurisdiction is when a state party refers itself to the court. Because this book is about Rome Statute complementarity, it is this formulation that is discussed in this chapter.

66. Report of the Preparatory Committee on the Establishment of an International Criminal Court, Draft Statute and Draft Final Act, UN Doc A/Conf. 183/2/Add.1 (1998), art 15.
67. Report of the Preparatory Committee on the Establishment of an International Criminal Court, UN Doc A/Conf. 183/2 (14 April 1998), art 15; UN Doc A/Conf. 183/SR.2, para 70; UN Doc A/Conf. 183/SR.3, paras 48 and 88; UN Doc A/Conf. 183/SR.4, paras 27 and 42; UN Doc A/Conf. 183/SR.5, paras 21 and 39; UN Doc A/Conf. 183/SR.6, paras 31 and 100; UN Doc A/Conf. 183/SR.7, para 101; UN Doc A/Conf. 183/SR.8, paras 1 and 77.
68. Rome Statute of the International Criminal Court (Rome Statute) (adopted 17 July 1998, entered into force 1 July 2002) 2187 UNTS 3, art 17.
69. El Zeidy, 'The Genesis of Complementarity' (n 35), 134–137.
70. Rome Statute, art 17 provides that the 'Court shall determine that a case is inadmissible where. . . .'
71. *Prosecutor v Thomas Lubanga Dyilo, Decision on the Prosecutor's Application for a Warrant of Arrest* ICC-01/04-01/06-8-Corr, Pre-Trial Chamber 1, 10 February 2006, para 18.

Rome Statute Complementarity

As previously stated, the principle of complementarity under the Rome Statute is embodied in articles 1 and 17 of the Statute. Article 1 of the Rome Statute provides that

> [a]n International Criminal Court ('the Court') is hereby established. It shall be a permanent institution and shall have the power to exercise its jurisdiction over persons for the most serious crimes of international concern, as referred to in this Statute, and shall be complementary to national criminal jurisdictions. The jurisdiction and functioning of the Court shall be governed by the provisions of this Statute.

Article 17 of the Rome Statute reinforces the provisions of article 1 by providing that

1. Having regard to paragraph 10 of the Preamble and article 1, the Court shall determine that a case is inadmissible where:
    (a) The case is being investigated or prosecuted by a State which has jurisdiction over it, unless the State is unwilling or unable genuinely to carry out the investigation or prosecution;
    (b) The case has been investigated by a State which has jurisdiction over it and the State has decided not to prosecute the person concerned, unless the decision resulted from the unwillingness or inability of the State genuinely to prosecute;
    (c) The person concerned has already been tried for conduct which is the subject of the complaint, and a trial by the Court is not permitted under article 20, paragraph 3;
    (d) The case is not of sufficient gravity to justify further action by the Court.
2. In order to determine unwillingness in a particular case, the Court shall consider, having regard to the principles of due process recognised by international law, whether one or more of the following exist, as applicable:
    (a) The proceedings were or are being undertaken or the national decision was made for the purpose of shielding the person concerned from criminal responsibility for crimes within the jurisdiction of the Court referred to in article 5;
    (b) There has been an unjustified delay in the proceedings which in the circumstances is inconsistent with an intent to bring the person concerned to justice;
    (c) The proceedings were not or are not being conducted in a manner which, in the circumstances, is inconsistent with an intent to bring the person concerned to justice.

3. In order to determine inability in a particular case, the Court shall consider whether, due to a total or substantial collapse or unavailability of its national judicial system, the State is unable to obtain the accused or the necessary evidence and testimony or otherwise unable to carry out its proceedings.

Considering the preceding provision, article 17 does not expressly mention the word *complementarity*. However, article 1 uses the word *complementary*. Paragraph 10 of the Preamble referred to in article 17 reinforces the principle of complementarity by emphasising that 'the International Criminal Court established under this Statute shall be complementary to national criminal jurisdictions.' Article 20 paragraph 3 which is referred to in article 17 mentions *ne bis in idem* principle. This principle means that a person shall not be tried for the same crime twice. Within the context of articles 1 and 17 of the Rome Statute, it means that once a person has been genuinely tried by a domestic court, the ICC cannot try that same person for that same crime again. With respect to article 5 of the statute which is also referred to, this article only mentions crimes to which the principle of *ne bis in idem* applies, which, in this instance, are genocide, crime against humanity, war crimes and aggression.

Against the backdrop of the above provisions of the Rome Statute, the Federación Internacional de los Derechos Humanos (FIDH) considers complementarity 'not only a key element of the functioning of the Rome Statute system but . . . also the most essential aspect of the Court's legacy.'[72] Therefore,

> with the complementarity principle, much of the work done to achieve the goals of the Statute may take place in national judiciary around the world . . . [and that] the number of cases that reach the Court is not a positive measure of [its] effectiveness.[73]

Complementarity can be viewed from various perspectives. In *Prosecutor v Katanga and Ngudjolo*,[74] the ICC held that 'complementarity can be considered from various points of view such as those of the States-parties, the ICC or the accused.'[75] The perspective that is most relevant here is that of states. The concepts central to the understanding of the principle of complementarity

72. *Federación Internacional de los Derechos Humanos* (FIDH), 'Comments on the ICC's Prosecutorial Strategy' 1 December 2009 para 3. www.fidh.org/IMG//pdf/FIDHCommentsProsecStrategy2009-12_FINAL_REV.pdf accessed 7 August 2017.
73. Report on Prosecutorial Strategy (RPS) 2009–2012 of 1 February 2010, para 79; Report on Prosecutorial Strategy (RPS) of 14 September 2006, para 15.
74. ICC-01/04–01/07–891-Conf-Exp. The Challenge was made available to the other parties on 25 February 2009 and a public redacted version, ICC-01/04–01/07–949 was filed on 11 March 2009.
75. Ibid para 17.

are 'inaction,' 'unwillingness' and 'inability,' and they are considered in the following.

Inaction

Article 17 of the Rome Statute is couched in a negative sense. It provides that 'the Court shall determine that a case is inadmissible . . .' In *Prosecutor v Thomas Lubanga Dyilo*,[76] this provision came up for consideration. In this case the defendant was charged with enlisting and conscripting children younger than the age of 15 by the ICC following the armed conflict in the Ituri region of the Democratic Republic of the Congo (DRC). At the time of the charge by the ICC, the defendant was held in custody in the DRC having been charged with international crimes under the Rome Statute. However, the crimes with which the defendant was charged in the DRC did not include the crime of enlisting and conscripting children younger than the age of 15. Conscious of the implication of the negative manner in which art 17 is couched, the Pre-Trial Chamber (PTC) I held that it is not the finding of unwillingness or inability that must first be decided whenever a state challenges the competence of the ICC to intervene; rather, the appropriate finding is whether a state that has jurisdiction is investigating or prosecuting the same case before the court.[77] Thus, mere inaction on the part of the state which has jurisdiction automatically means the ICC can intervene. The court then held that whereas Lubanga was detained when his case came before the ICC, the fact that he was not charged by the DRC with the crime of enlisting and conscripting children younger than the age of 15 with which he was charged by the prosecutor was sufficient to justify the intervention of the ICC.[78] Similarly, in *Prosecutor v Francis Kirimi Muthaura*,[79] the Appeals Chamber held that the failure of the Kenyan government to prefer any charge against the suspects justified the intervention of the ICC. However, if the ICC finds that the state that has jurisdiction is investigating or prosecuting the same case and is thus 'active,' then the ICC will proceed to make a finding of 'unwillingness' or 'inability.'

Unwillingness

Where the court finds that the case is being investigated or prosecuted by the state which has jurisdiction to do so, the question of that state's unwillingness or inability becomes relevant. In determining unwillingness some technical difficulties may be involved as the exercise requires drawing inferences

76. *Prosecutor v Thomas Lubanga Dyilo, Decision on the Prosecutor's Application for a Warrant of Arrest* ICC-01/04–01/06–8-Corr, Pre-Trial Chamber 1, 10 February 2006.
77. Ibid para 30.
78. Ibid paras 39–40.
79. *Prosecutor v Francis Kirimi Muthaura* ICC-01/09–02/11–274 30 August 2011.

from circumstantial evidence.[80] In addition, the exercise may be politically sensitive as it may amount to accusing state authorities.[81] Article 17(2) states the requirements to be met for the court to determine unwillingness. These requirements are where the purpose of the prosecution is to shield the person concerned from criminal responsibility, unjustified delay inconsistent with the intent to bring the person to justice and lack of independence and impartiality inconsistent with the intent to bring the person concerned to justice. But what amounts to 'shielding,' 'unjustified delay' and 'independence and impartiality' are broad in their operative scope. Thus, the Office of the Prosecutor (OTP) has sought to determine the operative scope of each of these requirements through the Informal Expert Group by listing certain 'indicia' to determine unwillingness.

Criteria for Assessment: Shielding From Criminal Responsibility

Historically, it can be argued that the trial of German war criminals of World War I at Leipzig is the precursor to the idea of 'shielding' in the Rome Statute.[82] Only a few of these criminals were punished out of the initial list of 850.[83] Those who were punished received ridiculously low punishment.[84] For example, Karl Heynen charged with ill treatment of prisoners of war received 10 months' imprisonment[85] while Emil Muller[86] and Robert Neumann,[87] who were similarly charged, received six months' imprisonment. Cruscius, who was found guilty of killing several war prisoners, was punished with two years' imprisonment.[88] Dithmar and Boldt convicted of 'intermediate degree of killing' and 'second degree murder' were sentenced to four years in prison.[89] Apart from the fact that the sentences were ridiculously low, most of the convicts 'were not even made to serve the sentence[s]'[90] as they were 'treated

80. Office of the Prosecutor (OTP), Informal Expert Paper 2003, para 44.
81. Ibid.
82. El Zeidy, *The Principle of Complementarity in International Criminal Law* (n 5),172.
83. M. Cherif Bassiouni, 'International Criminal Investigations and Prosecutions: From Versailles to Rwanda' in M. Cherif Bassiouni (ed), *International Criminal Law: Enforcement* vol II (2nd edn, Transnational Publishers Inc 1999), 38.
84. Ibid.
85. Supreme Court at Leipzig Judgment in the Case of Karl Heynen 26 May 1921 (1922) 16 *American Journal of International Law* 674.
86. Supreme Court at Leipzig Judgment in the Case of Emil Müller 30 May 1921 (1922) 16 *American Journal of International Law* 684.
87. Supreme Court at Leipzig Judgment in the Case of Robert Neumann 6 February 1921 (1922) 16 *American Journal of International Law* 696.
88. The United Nations War Crimes Commission, *History of the United Nations War Crimes Commission and the Development of the Laws of War* (HMSO 1948) 47 (*History of the UNWCC*).
89. Supreme Court at Leipzig Judgment in the Case of Lieutenants Dithmar and Boldt Hospital Ship, 'Landovery Castle' 16 July 1921 (1922) 16 *American Journal of International Law* 708.
90. *History of the UNWCC* (n 88), 48.

as heroes'[91] and allowed to escape by the prison warders.[92] The prison warders were 'publicly congratulated'[93] for a job well done.

Long after the German shoddy trials, the notion of shielding appeared in article 10(2) of the statute of the ICTY and rule 9(ii) of the Rules of Procedure and Evidence (RPE) of the court.[94] Article 10(2) of the Statute of the ICTY stipulates that the ICTY can prosecute a person who had already been prosecuted before a national court 'if the national court proceedings were not impartial or independent, were designed to shield the accused from international criminal responsibility, or the case was not diligently prosecuted' while rule 9(ii) of the RPE stipulates that the ICTY can take over a case from a national court if 'there is a lack of impartiality or independence, or the investigations or proceedings are designed to shield the accused from international criminal responsibility, or the case is not diligently prosecuted.' In *Prosecutor v Duško Tadić*,[95] the Appeals Chamber held that 'there would be a perennial danger of . . . proceedings being "designed to shield the accused" . . . if not effectively countered by the principle of primacy . . .' Thus, shielding is a ground for the intervention of the tribunal.

It was during the time the ICTY took its decision on primacy by referring to the idea of shielding that the Rome Statute was in the process of being drafted.[96] Thus, article 17(2)(a) of the Rome Statute reflects shielding.[97] The OTP enumerated the indicia of 'shielding.'[98] These indicia to determine shielding are direct or indirect proof of political interference, general institutional deficiencies, procedural irregularities or a combination of these factors.[99] Various courts of human rights have also shed light on the idea of shielding. Although these courts gave their analysis in a different context, their jurisprudence can be a useful guide.

In *Makaratzis v Greece*,[100] the European Court of Human Rights (ECtHR) considered an effective prosecution which invariably is not calculated to shield to be one 'capable, firstly, of ascertaining the circumstances in which the incident took place and secondly, of leading to the identification and punishment of those responsible. This is not an obligation of results, but of means.'[101] Similarly, in *Nachova and Others v Bulgaria*,[102] the ECtHR

91. James F. Willis, *Prologue to Nuremberg: The Politics and Diplomacy of Punishing War Criminals of the First World War* (Greenwood Press 1982), 140.
92. El Zeidy, *Complementarity in International Criminal Law* (n 5), 173.
93. *History of the UNWCC* (n 88), 48.
94. El Zeidy, *Complementarity in International Criminal Law* (n 5), 170.
95. Case No IT-94–1-AR72, Decision on the Defence Motion for Interlocutory Appeal on Jurisdiction, 2 October 1995.
96. El Zeidy, *Complementarity in International Criminal Law* (n 5), 171.
97. Ibid.
98. OTP Informal Expert Paper (n 80) para 44.
99. Ibid para 47.
100. App no 50385/99 (ECtHR, 20 December 2004).
101. Ibid paras 73–74.
102. App nos 43577/98, 43579/98 (ECtHR, 6 July2005).

upheld shielding by declaring that 'authorities ignored those significant facts and, without seeking any proper explanation, merely . . . terminated the investigation. The investigator and the prosecutors then shielded Major G. from prosecution.'[103]

Where an investigation is 'perfunctory and superficial,'[104] it has been held to be ineffective and invariably considered amounting to shielding.[105] In *Velasquez Rodrigues v Honduras*,[106] the Inter-American Court of Human Rights (InterAmCtHR) held that investigations are 'effective search for the truth'[107] and must be conducted in a 'serious manner and not as mere formality pre-ordained to be ineffective.'[108] When an investigation lacks requisite seriousness, 'it must be presumed that the . . . authorities [so acted] in order to avoid punishment.'[109] In *Gangaram-Pandy v Suriname*,[110] the InterAmCtHR stated that the seriousness of a state to pursue justice can be gleaned by the court through 'circumstantial evidence and indications or presumptions.'[111] Because circumstantial evidence takes cognisance of the peculiarity of facts, it follows that the category of facts which can yield the notion of shielding is never closed.[112]

Unjustified Delay Inconsistent With Intent to Do Justice

Unjustified delay must be determined 'having regard with the principles of due process recognised by international law.'[113] The principle of due process recognised by international law which is most relevant here is the one that promotes expeditious trial. The International Covenant on Civil and Political Rights (ICCPR)[114] recognises the right 'to be tried without undue delay'[115] and trial within 'reasonable time.'[116] The African Charter on Human and Peoples' Rights (ACHPR)[117] provides for 'the right to be tried within a reasonable time.'[118] Similarly, the European Convention on Human Rights (ECHR) recognises 'right to a fair and public hearing within a reasonable time'[119] while the

103. Ibid para 116.
104. *Timurtas v Turkey* ECtHR Application No 23531/94, 13 June 2000, paras 88 and 110.
105. El Zeidy, *Complementarity in International Criminal Law* (n 5), 178.
106. Judgment (Series C) No 4 (InterAmCtHR, 29 July 1988).
107. Ibid para 177.
108. Ibid.
109. Ibid para 188.
110. Judgment Series C No 16 (InterAmCtHR, 21 January 1994).
111. Ibid para 49.
112. El Zeidy, *Complementarity in International Criminal Law* (n 5), 178.
113. Rome Statute, art 17(2).
114. (Adopted 16 December 1966, entered into force 23 March 1976) 999 UNTS 171.
115. Article 14(3).
116. Article 9(3).
117. (Adopted 27 June 1981, entered into force 21 October 1986) (1982) 21 ILM 58.
118. Article 7(1)(d).
119. Article 6(1).

American Convention on Human Rights (ACHR)[120] provides for the 'right to a hearing . . . within a reasonable time.'[121]

There are two problems with the right recognised by human rights instruments mentioned earlier in relation to the principle of complementarity. First, the right is within the context of an expeditious trial. This means that within the context of complementarity principle of the Rome Statute, investigations are left out. This point is further reinforced if one considers that unjustified delay is 'unjustified delay in the proceedings', and the proceedings here include investigation and prosecution.[122] In addition, the indicia of the OTP with respect to a delay include investigative and prosecutorial delay.[123] Second, the right is expected to guarantee fair trial for the accused, not to determine a state's unwillingness. The implication is that a defendant might have his right to an expeditious trial violated and yet be a beneficiary if the state violated his right to prevent his prosecution.[124] Despite these reservations, these human rights instruments can still serve as guidelines.[125]

'Unjustified delay in the proceedings' must take place 'in the circumstances . . . inconsistent with an intent to bring the person concerned to justice.' Reference to circumstances here means conditions peculiar to a legal system. The OTP has stated that delay in this context must be assessed in comparison with what normally obtains.[126] Rule 51 of the RPE also reinforces this position. It provides that 'in the context of the circumstances of the case, the Court may consider, *inter alia*, information that the State . . . may choose to bring to the attention of the Court.' The problem with this position is that prosecution of an ordinary crime in a domestic legal system is radically different from prosecution of international crimes. It may be somewhat difficult to see how the time it takes to prosecute ordinary crimes in a legal system can be used as a guide for the time it will take to prosecute an international crime in that same legal system.[127]

But it can be argued that reference to circumstances here means the time it takes a legal system to prosecute international crimes so that in prosecuting a specific case if the time taken is unusually lengthy, an unjustified delay can be inferred. If this is the case, the test breaks down completely for states that have never prosecuted international crimes before. This is because the idea of what normally obtains does not exist.[128] However, if the use of the word *inter alia* in the clause 'the Court may consider, *inter alia*, information that the State . . . may choose to bring to the attention of the Court' is anything to

120. (Signed 22 November 1969, entered into force 18 July 1978) 1144 UNTS 144.
121. Article 8(1).
122. El Zeidy, *Complementarity in International Criminal Law* (n 5), 183.
123. OTP Informal Expert Paper 2003 (n 80) Annexe 4, 29.
124. El Zeidy, *Complementarity in International Criminal Law* (n 5), 183.
125. Ibid., 183–184.
126. OTP Informal Expert Paper 2003 (n 80) Annexe 4, 29.
127. El Zeidy, *Complementarity in International Criminal Law* (n 5), 194–195.
128. Ibid.

go by, it follows that information available elsewhere may be considered. In this respect, international best practices may be considered together with the peculiar circumstances of a domestic legal system to determine unwillingness through undue delay.[129]

In *Prosecutor v Rwamakuba*,[130] the ICTR held that 'reasonableness of the period of the proceedings cannot be translated into a fixed number of days, months or years.'[131] Similarly, in *König v Germany*,[132] ECtHR held that 'the reasonableness of the duration of proceedings . . . must be assessed in each case according to its circumstances.'[133] In the same vein, the Human Rights Committee (HRC) stated in *Ratiani v Georgia*[134] that 'what constitutes "undue delay" depends on the circumstances of each case.'[135] While there may be variants of facts in considering the circumstances of each case, nonetheless some factors have been identified.

In *König* the court identified the complexity of the case, the applicant's conduct and the attitude of the judicial authorities as factors to be considered.[136] The InterAmCtHR also adopted these factors in *Genie-Lacayo v Nicaragua*.[137] A case will manifest complexity by the large amount of documentary evidence involved,[138] the number of suspects involved,[139] the size and complexity of the acts committed,[140] the nature of the charges,[141] the number of witnesses,[142] the possibility of reaching witnesses,[143] whether investigation is to be carried out abroad,[144] the need for expert evidence[145] and technical difficulties in general.[146]

129. Ibid.
130. Case No ICTR-98-44C-PT, Decision on Defence Motion for Stay of Proceedings Pursuant to Article 20 of the Statute, 3 June 2005.
131. Ibid para 26.
132. App no 6232/73, Judgment (Merits) (ECtHR, 28 June 1978).
133. Ibid para 99.
134. HRC, Communication No. 975/2001, UN Doc. CCPR/C/84/D/975/2001, 4 August 2005.
135. Ibid para 10.7.
136. App no 6232/73, Judgment (Merits) (ECtHR, 28 June 1978) para 99.
137. Judgment, Series C No 30 (InterAmCtHR, 29 January 1997) para 77.
138. *Hagert v Finland* App no 14724/02, Judgment (Merits and Just Satisfaction) (ECtHR, 17 January 2006) para 29.
139. *Neuimester v Austria* App no 1936/63, Judgment (Merits) (ECtHR, 27 June 1968) para 20.
140. Ibid.
141. *Calleja v Malta* App no 75274/01, Judgment (Merits and Just Satisfaction) (ECtHR, 7 April 2005) para 128.
142. *Wemhoff v Germany* Application No 2122/64, Judgment (Merits and Just Satisfaction) (ECtHR, 27 June 1968) para 20.
143. *Neuimester v Austria* App no 1936/63, Judgment (Merits) (ECtHR, 27 June 1968) para 20.
144. Ibid.
145. *Krasuki v Poland* App no 61444/00, Judgment (Merits) (ECtHR, 14 June 2005) para 56.
146. *Papachelas v Greece* App no 31423/96, Judgment (Merits and Just Satisfaction) (ECtHR, 25 March 1999) para 38.

The Principles and Guidelines on the Right to a Fair Trial and Legal Assistance in Africa appears to take cognisance of some of these factors by providing that

> factors relevant to what constitutes undue delay include the complexity of the case, the conduct of the parties, the conduct of other relevant authorities, whether an accused is detained pending proceedings, and the interest of the person at stake in the proceedings.[147]

The ICC appears to be conscious of the relevance of the complexity of the case. In *Prosecutor v Saif Al-Islam Gaddafi & Abdullah Al-Senussi*,[148] the Pre-Trial Chamber I of the ICC noted that a finding of unjustified delay cannot be made 'against an abstract ideal of "justice", but against the specific circumstances surrounding the investigation concerned'[149] and added that any finding of unjustified delay must take cognisance of the 'chronology of the domestic proceedings and the complexity of the domestic case.'[150]

With respect to the applicant's conduct, the court held in *Klamecki v Poland*[151] that where hearings had to be adjourned at the request of the applicant together with the fact that the applicant changed his counsel and the new counsel had to be given time to conduct the case, any allegation of delay could not be attributed to the state and that there was no violation of the requirement of reasonable time.[152] With respect to the conduct of judicial authorities or state officials, the court held in *Ekle v Germany*[153] that a delay of 15 months in opening a formal investigation after the date the complaint was lodged was not reasonable.[154] In *Genie-Lacayo v Nicaragua*,[155] the InterAmCtHR held that in spite of 'the excuses, impediments and substitution of judges of the Supreme Court of Justice, the two years that have elapsed since the application for judicial review was admitted is not reasonable.'[156]

Lack of Independence and Impartiality Inconsistent With Intent to Do Justice

The third requirement for determining unwillingness is where 'the proceedings were not or are not being conducted independently or impartially, and

147. Para N(5)(c).
148. *Prosecutor v Saif Al-Islam Gaddafi & Abdullah Al-Senussi* 'Decision on the admissibility of the case against Abdullah Al-Senussi' ICC-01/11-01/11, dated 11 October 2013.
149. Ibid para 223.
150. Ibid.
151. App no 25415/94, Judgment (Merits) (ECtHR, 28 March 2002).
152. Ibid paras 92–94.
153. App no 8130/78, Judgment (Merits) of (ECtHR, 15 July 1982).
154. Ibid paras 74 and 83–84.
155. Judgment, Series C No 30 (InterAmCtHR, 29 January 1997) para 77.
156. Ibid para 80.

they were or are being conducted in a manner which in the circumstances is inconsistent with an intent to bring the person concerned to justice.'[157] The requirement of independence and impartiality was initially planned to be placed under 'inability.' It was thought that a state that could not guarantee a fair proceeding could be considered unable.[158] However, it was countered that procedural failings should not be the basis for ICC intervention.[159]

The preceding provision reflects this debate. Failure to secure independence and impartiality is not sufficient; it must have benefited the accused by not being brought to justice.[160] When the trial process is at the detriment of the defendant, the ICC cannot intervene, although this is regrettable. A fair trial can only become relevant if the outcome reflects unwillingness or inability. In the *Prosecutor v Saif Al-Islam Gaddafi & Abdullah Al-Senussi*,[161] the Appeals Chamber of the ICC held that violations of the fair trial rights of the defendant may not necessarily justify ICC intervention as long as the proceeding in question does not lead to evasion of justice and that fair trial guarantees would only become relevant if their violations are so egregious that no genuine trial could be said to have taken place *ab initio*.[162] Therefore, where a defendant was wrongly prosecuted and made a culprit to divert attention from the actual culprit, then unwillingness can be said to have been made out, and ICC intervention justified.[163]

This position, however, contrasts with the position in the ICTR (and of course the ICTY)[164] where the fair trial guarantee is part of what is required to implement the principle of complementarity. In the *Prosecutor v Jean Nwinkindi*,[165] the ICTR applied fair trial guarantees as one of its criteria before it could allow Rwanda to prosecute Jean Nwinkindi.[166] As previously noted, article 17(2) enjoins the court to be guided by 'principles of due process recognised by international law' and these principles of due process apply to trial alone whereas proceedings include trial and investigation.[167] But rule 51 of the RPE seems to limit the applicable principles to prosecution

157. Rome Statute, art 17(2)(c).
158. Williams, 'Issues of Admissibility' (n 1), 394.
159. Holmes, 'The Principle of Complementarity' (n 1), 50.
160. Markus Benzing, 'The Complementarity Regime of the International Criminal Court: International Criminal Justice Between State Sovereignty and the Fight against Impunity' (2003) 7 *Max Planck Yearbook of United Nations Law* 591, 613.
161. *Prosecutor v Saif Al-Islam Gaddafi & Adbullahi Al-Senussi*, Judgment on the appeal of Mr Abdullah Al-Senussi against the decision of Pre-Trial Chamber I of 11 October 2013 entitled 'Decision on the admissibility of the case against Abdullah Al-Senussi' ICC-OI/II-OI/IIOA6 dated 24 July 2014.
162. Ibid paras 2–3.
163. Kevin John Heller, 'The Shadow Side of Complementarity: The Effect of Article 17 of the Rome Statute on National Due Process' (2006) 17 *Criminal Law Forum* 255.
164. ICTY Rule 11bis(B).
165. *Prosecutor v Nwinkindi* Case No ICTR -01–75-AR11bis.
166. Ibid para 22.
167. El Zeidy, *Complementarity in International Criminal Law* (n 5), 197.

alone and exclude investigation. It provides that states concerned have the right to inform the ICC 'that its Courts meet internationally recognised norms and standards for the independent and impartial prosecution of similar conduct.'[168] However, it is inconceivable that RPE can supersede the Rome Statute because it derives its validity from the statute. Thus, it can be argued that the RPE is null and void to the extent of its inconsistency with the Rome Statute.[169] Therefore, these principles can still be applied to investigation and prosecution in line with the purpose of complementarity irrespective of the ostensible limitation imposed by rule 51 of the RPE.

In *Prosecutor v Abdullah Al-Senussi*,[170] the Appeals Chamber of the ICC states that the notion of independence and impartiality as enshrined in human rights instruments and applied by various human rights courts are relevant in understanding the notion of independence and impartiality under article 17 of the Rome Statute.[171] These human rights instruments and the decisions of various human rights courts will now be considered in discussing the notion of independence and impartiality under article 17 of the Rome Statute. The Eight United Nations Congress on the Prevention of Crime and the Treatment of Offenders in its Guidelines on the Role of Prosecutors[172] provides for certain criteria to secure the independence and impartiality of prosecutors. These criteria are qualification, selection and training; status and conditions of service; objective regulation of discretionary power; and security of tenure. With respect to qualification, selection and training, it is stipulated that 'persons selected as prosecutors shall be individuals of integrity and ability with appropriate training and qualifications'[173] and that the criteria for selection shall 'embody safeguards against appointments based on partiality or prejudice.'[174]

With respect to status and conditions of service, it provides that states 'shall ensure that prosecutors are able to perform their professional functions without intimidation, hindrance, harassment, improper interference or unjustified exposure to civil, penal or other liability.'[175] In regulating the discretionary powers of prosecutors, states are obliged to subject the exercise of their discretions to such guidelines that make the exercise objective and

168. Jo Stigen, *The Relationship Between the International Criminal Court and National Jurisdictions: The Principle of Complementarity* (Martinus Nijhoff Publishers 2008), 300.
169. Rome Statute, arts 51(4) and (5).
170. *Prosecutor v Saif Al-Islam Gaddafi & Abdullah Al-Senussi* Judgment on the appeal of Mr Abdullah Al-Senussi against the decision of Pre-Trial Chamber I of 11 October 2013 entitled 'Decision on the admissibility of the case against Abdullah Al-Senussi' ICC-OI/II-OI/IIOA6, dated 24 July 2014.
171. Ibid para 250.
172. A/CONF. 144/28/Rev.1.
173. Ibid para 1.
174. Ibid para 2(a).
175. Ibid para 4.

predictable.[176] Tenure of service is to be secured by setting out clearly 'by law or published rules or regulations'[177] 'adequate remuneration and where applicable, tenure, pension and age of retirement.'[178] In addition, the disciplinary procedure must be clearly spelt out, must not be arbitrary, must guarantee the outcome of the objective decision and must be reviewable.[179]

The International Association of Prosecutors' Standards of Professional Responsibility and Statement of the Essential Duties and Rights of Prosecutors also contain identical provisions to secure the independence and impartiality of prosecutors. In securing the independence of prosecutors, it provides that the exercise of prosecutorial discretion should be independent and 'free from political interference.'[180] With respect to impartiality, 'prosecutors shall perform their duties without fear, favour and prejudice'[181] and ensure that 'all necessary and reasonable enquiries are made and the result disclosed.'[182] They are also to perform their duties 'fairly, consistently and expeditiously.'[183] Similarly, prosecutors are to be 'protected against arbitrary action by governments,'[184] and protection should be offered to their family whenever they are threatened.[185]

Similarly, the Principles and Guidelines on the Right to a Fair Trial and Legal Assistance in Africa developed by the African Union stipulates that prosecutors must be 'able to perform their professional functions without intimidation, hindrance, harassment, improper interference or unjustified exposure to civil, penal or other liability'[186] and that 'reasonable conditions of service of prosecutors, adequate remuneration and, where applicable, tenure, housing, transport, conditions of physical and social security, pension and age of retirement and other conditions of service shall be set out by law or published rules or regulations.'[187] It is also added that 'promotion of prosecutors, wherever such a system exists, shall be based on objective factors, in particular professional qualifications, ability, integrity and experience, and decided upon in accordance with fair and impartial procedures.'[188]

The preceding provisions are essentially institutional, although with a view to improving the behaviour of individual state actors in any instance.

176. Ibid para 17.
177. Ibid para 6.
178. Ibid.
179. Ibid para 22.
180. The International Association of Prosecutors' Standards of Professional Responsibility and Statement of the Essential Duties and Rights of Prosecutors, para 2.1.
181. Ibid para 3.
182. Ibid.
183. Ibid para 4.1.
184. Ibid para 6.
185. Ibid.
186. Para F(a)(2).
187. Para F(b).
188. Para F(c).

These provisions have found judicial adoption in one form or the other with a view to strengthening the office of the prosecutor. In *Güleç v Turkey*,[189] the ECtHR held that persons responsible for and carrying out the investigation must be independent of those implicated in the events. This means 'not only a lack of hierarchical or institutional connection but also a practical independence.'[190] Similarly, in *Koku v Turkey*,[191] Kahramanmara's governor investigated security forces who were themselves under his control and subject to his order. The ECtHR held that the requirements of independence and impartiality were not complied with. In *Kaya v Turkey*,[192] the prosecutor relied on the government's version of the story and failed to make his own independent inquiry; the court held that independence was lacking because 'as an independent investigating official he should have been alert to the need to collect evidence at the scene, to make his own independent reconstruction of the events.'[193]

In *McKerr v United Kingdom*,[194] the ECtHR held that 'there must be a sufficient element of public scrutiny of the investigation or its results to secure accountability in practice as well as in theory.'[195] In *Hugh Jordan v United Kingdom*,[196] it was held that 'it is of increased importance that the officer who decides whether or not to prosecute also gives an appearance of independence in his decision making'[197] and where no reasons are given . . . this may in itself not be conducive to public confidence.'[198]

The Universal Declaration of Human Rights (UDHR)[199] provides for the right to a fair and public hearing by a competent, independent and impartial tribunal established by law.[200] Article 14(1) of the ICCPR, article 6(1) of the ECHR, article 8(1) of the ACHR and article 7(1)(d) of the ACHPR also have identical provisions. Similarly, in 1985 the United Nations General Assembly adopted the Basic Principles on the Independence of the Judiciary (the Basic Principles).[201] Based on the recommendation of the Committee on Crime Prevention and Control, the Economic and Social Council of the

189. App no 21593/93, Judgment (ECtHR, 27 July 1998).
190. *McShane v United Kingdom* App no 43290/98, Judgment (ECtHR, 28 May 2002) para 95.
191. Judgment (ECtHR, 31 May 2005).
192. App no 22729/93, Judgment (ECtHR, 19 February 1998).
193. Ibid para 89.
194. App no 28883/95, Judgment (ECtHR, 4 May 2001).
195. Ibid para 115.
196. App no 24746/94, Judgment (ECtHR, 4 May 2001).
197. Ibid para 123.
198. Ibid.
199. (Adopted 10 December 1948 UNGA Res 217 A(III).
200. Article19.
201. Adopted by the Seventh United Nations Congress on the Prevention of Crime and Treatment of Offenders held at Milan from 26 August to 6 September 1985 and endorsed by General Assembly Resolutions 40/32 of 29 November 1985 and 40/146 of 13 December 1985.

United Nations adopted the Procedures for the Effective Implementation of the Basic Principles on the Independence of the Judiciary (the Procedures) in 1989.[202]

The Basic Principles provides for the independence of the judiciary in terms of separation of powers; qualifications, selection and training; conditions of service and tenure; and discipline, suspension and removal of judges.[203] In all these, certain core values run through them. They are independence, impartiality, integrity, propriety, equality, competence and diligence.[204] The OTP largely agrees with these principles in its list of the indicia of independence which include the degree of independence of the judiciary and prosecutors; the appointment and dismissal of judges; nature of governing body; patterns of political interference in investigation and prosecution and patterns of preordained outcomes.[205]

The Basic Principles provides that 'it is the duty of all governmental and other institutions to respect and observe the independence of the judiciary'[206] and that the judiciary 'shall have jurisdiction over all issues of a judicial nature.'[207] Arguably, the rationale behind judicial independence is to free the judiciary from any form of interference. The Basic Principles provides that 'there shall not be any inappropriate or unwarranted interference with the judicial process'[208] and that 'the judiciary shall decide matters before them impartially, on the basis of facts and in accordance with the law, without any restrictions, improper influences, inducements, pressures, threats or interferences, direct or indirect, from any quarter or for any reason.'[209] In *Campbell and Fell v The United Kingdom*,[210] the ECtHR held that there must be an 'existence of guarantees against outside pressures.'[211]

With respect to qualification, selection and training, the Basic Principles provides that 'persons selected for judicial office shall be individuals of integrity and ability with appropriate training or qualifications in law'[212] and that 'any method of judicial selection shall safeguard against judicial appointments for improper motives.'[213] In safeguarding against appointment for improper motives, the Universal Charter of the Judge 1999 stipulates that the 'selection

202. Economic and Social Council Resolution 1989/60, 15th Plenary Meeting, 24 May 1989.
203. See generally the Basic Principles (n 201).
204. The Judicial Integrity Group, 'Commentary on the Bangalore Principles of Judicial Conduct' March 2007. www.coe.int/t/dghl/cooperation/ccje/textes/BangalorePrinciples Comment.PDF accessed 7 August 2017.
205. OTP Informal Expert Paper 2003 (n 80) Annexe 4, 29.
206. Basic Principles, para 1.
207. Ibid para 3.
208. Ibid para 4.
209. Ibid para 2.
210. App nos 7819/77; 7878/77, Judgment (Merits and Satisfaction) (ECtHR, 28 June 1984).
211. Ibid para 78.
212. Basic Principles, para 10.
213. Ibid.

and each appointment of a judge must be carried out according to objective and transparent criteria based on proper professional qualification.'[214]

Similarly, in the Commonwealth (Latimer House) Principles on the Three Branches of Government 2003 it is stipulated that 'judicial appointments should be made on the basis of clearly defined criteria and by a publicly declared process.'[215] With respect to conditions of service and tenure, the Basic Principles provides that the tenure of judges should be adequately secured.[216] Judges do not have to be appointed for life; it is sufficient if their tenure is not subject to the whims and caprices of the executive.[217] Thus, in the Commonwealth (Latimer House) Principles on the Three Branches of Government 2003 it is stipulated that 'arrangements for appropriate security of tenure and protection of levels of remuneration must be in place.'[218] In addition, regarding discipline, suspension and removal of judges, the Basic Principles provides that a judge can only be relieved of his or her job based solely on incapacity and such conducts that render him or her unfit.[219] In the Commonwealth (Latimer House) Principles on the Three Branches of Government 2003, it is stated that 'judges should be subject to suspension or removal only for reasons of incapacity or misbehaviour that clearly renders them unfit to discharge their duties,'[220] thus reinforcing the position of the Basic Principles. In *Campbell and Fell* the ECtHR held that regard must be had 'to the manner of appointment . . . and [the] term of office.'[221]

The preceding provisions of the Basic Principles relate to external judicial independence. There is another dimension to judicial independence which is internal.[222] This internal aspect is the same as impartiality. This can be gleaned from the provision in the Basic Principles that 'the judiciary shall decide matters before them impartially, on the basis of facts and in accordance with the law . . .'[223] It means that justice must not only be done, it must be seen to have been done.[224] In article 5 of the Universal Charter of the Judge 1999, it is stated that 'in the performance of the judicial duties the judge must be impartial and must so be seen.' In *Prosecutor v Furundžija*,[225] the Appeals Chamber of the ICTY held that 'there is an unacceptable appearance of bias

214. Article 9.
215. Paragraph IV(a).
216. Basic Principles, paras 11 and 12.
217. *Engel v The Netherlands* App nos 5100/71; 5101/71; 5102/71; 5354/72; 5370/72, Judgment (Merits) (ECtHR, 8 June 1976) paras 30 and 68.
218. Paragraph IV(b).
219. Basic Principles, para 18.
220. Paragraph IV(d).
221. App no 7819/77; 7878/77, Judgment (Merits and Satisfaction) (ECtHR, 28 June 1984) para 78.
222. Basic Principles, para 2.
223. Ibid.
224. *R v Sussex Justices ex parte McCarthy* [1924] 1 KB 256, 259, per Lord Hewart CJ.
225. *Prosecutor v Furundžija* Case No (IT-95-17/1-A) Judgment 21 July 2000.

if . . . the circumstances would lead a reasonable observer, properly informed, to reasonably apprehend bias.'[226]

The ICC follows the decision of the ICTY by declaring through its Plenary in the *Prosecutor v Jean Pierre Bemba Gombo, Aimé Kilolo Musamba, Jean-Jacques Mangenda Kabongo, Fidèle Babala Wandu and Narcisse Arido*,[227] that the applicable standard within the meaning of article 41(2)(a) of the Rome Statute is 'whether the circumstances would lead a reasonable observer, properly informed, to reasonably apprehend bias in the judge. This standard is concerned not only with whether a reasonable observer could apprehend bias, but whether any such apprehension is objectively reasonable.'[228] In *Prosecutor v Saif Al-Islam Gaddafi & Abdullah Al-Senussi*,[229] the Appeals Chamber of the ICC also applied the standard of a 'reasonable observer, properly informed.'[230] However, this decision was taken within the meaning of article 42(7) of the Rome Statute which relates to the impartiality of the prosecutor. Similarly, the ECtHR in *Campbell and Fell* held that the court must present 'an appearance of independence.'[231]

In relation to impartiality, the OTP's list of indicia seems to agree with the ICTY, the ICC and the ECtHR. It includes collusion between the authorities and suspected perpetrators, links between judges and perpetrators and reprisals against investigating officers,[232] all of which can present the outlook of bias and lack of independence. Therefore, judicial independence is not only the summation of respect accorded to the judiciary by other arms of government to allow it to discharge its function, it also relates to how the judiciary internally regulates itself to gain public confidence.

The internal dimension to judicial independence which constitutes its impartiality also shows the relevance of the Bangalore Principles of Judicial Conduct 2002 (Bangalore Principles). The Bangalore Principles provides that a judge must not relate to any of the parties in dispute,[233] must not allow his or her personal prejudices to affect his or her judicial function,[234] must avoid a situation where he or she has to recuse himself or herself[235] and must 'accept personal restrictions which might be viewed as burdensome by the ordinary

226. Ibid para 189.
227. In *Prosecutor v Jean Pierre Bemba Gombo, Aimé Kilolo Musamba, Jean-Jacques Mangenda Kabongo, Fidèle Babala Wandu and Narcisse Arido*, 'Decision of the Plenary of Judges on the Defence Applications for the Disqualification of Judge Cuno Tarfusser From the Case' ICC-01/05–01/13–511-Anx, dated 20 June 2014.
228. Ibid para 17.
229. *Prosecutor v Saif Al-Islam Gaddafi & Abdullah Al-Senussi*, 'Decision on the Request for Disqualification of the Prosecutor' ICC-01/11–01/11–175(OA3), 12 June 2012.
230. Ibid para 20.
231. App no 7819/77; 7878/77, Judgment (Merits and Satisfaction) (ECtHR, 28 June 1984) para 78.
232. OTP Informal Expert Paper 2003 (n 80) 29–30.
233. Bangalore Principles, para 1.2.
234. Ibid para 2.1.
235. Ibid para 2.3.

citizen and should do so freely and willingly.'[236] All these requirements appear to have been subsumed in the decision of the Appeals Chambers of the ICTY when it was held that not only does a court have to 'be subjectively free from bias, but also that there should be nothing in the surrounding circumstances which objectively gives rise to an appearance of bias.'[237]

The issue of independence and impartiality is relevant in relation to the establishment of special or military courts. While the establishment of these courts does not in itself violates the tenets of independence and impartiality, nonetheless the Human Rights Committee (HRC) has noted that 'the existence in many countries of military or special courts which try civilians'[238] present 'serious problems as far as equitable, impartial and independent administration of justice is concerned'[239] because 'quite often the reason for the establishment of such courts is to enable exceptional procedures to be applied which do not comply with normal standards of justice.'[240] In *Findlay v The United Kingdom*,[241] the petitioner was tried by a court martial in which the presiding officers were subordinate to the 'convening officer' who was also the prosecutor and the 'confirming officer' and in whose capacity as the 'confirming officer' could vary the sentence imposed. The ECtHR held that the court martial was neither independent nor impartial.[242] The court added that legal decisions should not be changed by an authority other than the judiciary and that the legal validity of a judicial decision should not be made subject to other branches of government.[243] The court then concluded that the fact that judicial decision cannot be varied by the executive arm of government is inherent in the notion of a tribunal and its independence.[244]

The OTP identifies some 'contextual issues' which may not indicate unwillingness on their own but may, in conjunction with the criteria to determine unwillingness discussed earlier, indicate unwillingness. These include constitutional role, the separation of powers and powers attributed to institutions of the criminal justice system; the parameters of prosecuting powers and discretion; the privileges and immunities of state authorities, the granting of amnesties, pardons, enforcement of sentences and parole regimes; and the creation of extrajudicial commission of inquiry and truth commissions.[245] Other 'indicators' include legal regime of witness protection, refusal

236. Ibid para 4.2.
237. *Prosecutor v Furundžija* Case No (IT-95–17/1-A) Judgment 21 July 2000, para 189.
238. Human Rights Committee (HRC), General Comment No 13: Equality before the courts and the right to a fair and public hearing by an independent court established by law, 13 April 1984, para 4.
239. Ibid.
240. Ibid.
241. *Findlay v The United Kingdom*, Judgment (ECtHR, 25 February 1997) Series 1997–I.
242. Ibid paras 74–77.
243. Ibid para 77.
244. Ibid.
245. OTP Informal Expert Paper (n 80) 28.

to allow observers or trial monitors without justification and incompatibility of substantive law of crime with international standards.[246]

Since the principles of due process recognised by international law appear to be broad while the contextual issues identified by the OTP also appear to be wide, the question of whether the list of what constitutes unwillingness is exhaustive or not has been raised. Some scholars contend that the list is exhaustive.[247] They seem to place an emphasis on the drafting history of the Rome Statute in which there were indications of efforts to avoid a situation in which the ICC would intervene on the slightest infraction of due process by states.[248] On the other hand, some scholars contend that the list is not exhaustive.[249] These scholars rely on the text of the Rome Statute itself to argue that the list was not intended to be exhaustive. The difference between the two schools may not be much pronounced if it is realised that the list in terms of various categories of facts cannot be limited but that these facts revolve around the concepts of unwillingness and inability which are undoubtedly narrow.

Inability

Article 17(3) contemplates two sets of considerations. The first is the 'collapse' of the domestic judicial system or its 'unavailability.' The second consideration is whether the state is 'unable to obtain the accused' or the 'necessary evidence and testimony' or 'otherwise unable to carry out proceedings.' Inability may be less complex to determine as opposed to unwillingness since an examination of the motive of the authorities is not involved.[250]

Criteria for Assessment: Collapse of a Domestic Judicial System or Its 'Unavailability'

'Collapse' within the meaning of article 17(3) may be total or substantial. A total collapse is such that the judicial system has been rendered completely ineffective having been damaged because of war, armed conflict or natural disaster of a magnificent proportion like a tsunami. Rwanda offers a good example during the genocide period in 1994. With respect to substantial collapse, the administration of justice is not completely dysfunctional;

246. Ibid., 30.
247. Markus Benzing (n 157) 604.
248. Draft Proposal by Italy 44 UN Doc A/AC 249/1997/WG 3/IP 4 (5 August 1997) cited in John Heller, 'The Shadow Side of Complementarity: The Effect of Article 17 of the Rome Statute on National Due Process' 255, 272.
249. Darryl Robinson, 'Serving the Interests of Justice: Amnesties, Truth Commissions and the International Criminal Court' (2003) 14 *European Journal of International Law* 481, 500.
250. OTP Informal Expert Paper 2003 (n 80) para 48.

nonetheless it lacks the requisite capability to investigate the case.[251] Therefore, when a state has only lost control of some parts of its territory but still able to exercise control on other parts, substantial collapse cannot be said to have taken place.[252]

Inability to Obtain Evidence or the Accused or to Carry Out Proceedings

The criterion of 'inability to obtain evidence' implies that once domestic courts are unable to obtain evidence, the ICC will intervene. One of the most important means of obtaining evidence is through witnesses. Witnesses will not come forward to give evidence unless they are certain that their safety will be secure. The necessary implication of this criterion is that a strong witness protection regime must be in place. In *Prosecutor v Saif Al-Islam Gaddafi & Abdullah Al-Senussi*,[253] the Pre-Trial Chamber I of the ICC considered the issue of inability to obtain evidence. In the instant case, the defendant was being held by a militia group in Zintan within Libya, but it was not within the control of the Libyan government. The Pre-Trial Chamber I expressed its concern about Libya's 'lack of capacity to obtain the necessary testimony due to the inability of judicial and governmental authorities to ascertain control and provide adequate witness protection.'[254] The chamber noted that 'Libya has indicated that the measures for witness protection applicable at pre-trial can be continued at trial as it is within the discretionary powers of the trial judge to receive evidence in whatever form he or she deems appropriate. However, further to its submission that trial judges have discretionary powers to order protective measures, Libya has presented no evidence about specific protection programmes that may exist under domestic law.'[255] Thus, Libya was found lacking in capacity to ensure protective measures.

With respect to the criterion of 'inability to obtain the accused' the necessary implication is that once the accused cannot be apprehended by the state concerned, ICC will automatically intervene. Therefore, having an accused extradited by way of treaty arrangement may be imperative for states concerned if ICC intervention is to be forestalled. In *Prosecutor v Saif Al-Islam Gaddafi & Abdullah Al-Senussi*,[256] the Pre-Trial Chamber I considered the issue of inability to obtain the accused. The chamber noted that 'Libya has

251. Jakob Pichon, 'The Principle of Complementarity in the Cases of the Sudanese Nationals Ahmed Harun and Ali Kushayb before the International Criminal Court' (2008) 8 *International Criminal Law Review* 185,196.
252. Ibid.
253. *Prosecutor v Saif Al-Islam Gaddafi & Abdullah Al-Senussi*, 'Decision on the admissibility of the case against Saif Al-Islam Gaddafi' ICC-01/11–01/11, dated 31 May 2013.
254. Ibid para 209.
255. Ibid para 211.
256. *Prosecutor v Saif Al-Islam Gaddafi & Abdullah Al-Senussi*, 'Decision on the admissibility of the case against Saif Al-Islam Gaddafi' ICC-01/11–01/11, dated 31 May 2013.

not yet been able to secure the transfer of Mr Gaddafi from his place of detention under the custody of the Zintan militia into State authority.'[257] The chamber also noted 'the submissions of Libya that *in absentia* trials are not permitted under Libyan law when the accused is present on Libyan territory and his location is known to the authorities.'[258] The chamber then found Libya unable to obtain the accused.

It is, however, worthy to mention that the legal propriety of relying on the above findings may be somewhat questionable. This is because the Appeals Chamber of the ICC held in the preceding case that the findings of unwillingness and inability should not have been made. The Appeals Chamber based its decision on the fact that since the Pre-Trial Chamber I had held that the case being investigated by Libya was not the same as that of the ICC, the ICC automatically had the competence to assume jurisdiction to prosecute the defendant and that there was no need for the Pre-Trial Chamber to make a finding of unwillingness and inability on the part of Libya.[259] Nonetheless, the previous findings appear to offer some guidance with respect to what is required of states to avoid the notion of inability.

With respect to the criterion of 'inability to obtain the accused' it appears somewhat pertinent to consider this question: If the state which cannot prosecute the accused *in absentia* can also not obtain the accused, can the ICC obtain the accused? This question appears pertinent because if the ICC cannot obtain the accused when the state concerned cannot, the ICC cannot intervene, the prevention of which is the goal of complementarity. The ICC cannot intervene because trial *in absentia* is not permitted by the Rome Statute,[260] just as it is not permitted under the law of certain states.

It appears that the ICC can obtain the accused in certain instances where the state concerned cannot. One, when a fugitive from a state party finds his or her way into the territory of another state party and that other state party receives a request for arrest and surrender of that person from the ICC, that fugitive may be transmitted into the custody of the ICC.[261] Two, a third state[262] into which the fugitive has escaped from a state party may enter an admissibility challenge, and when the decision made favours the exercise of jurisdiction by the ICC, the third state may be impelled to surrender the fugitive to the ICC.[263]

257. Ibid para 206.
258. Ibid para 208.
259. *Prosecutor v Saif Al-Islam Gaddafi & Abdullah Al-Senussi*, Judgment on the appeal of Libya against the decision of Pre-Trial Chamber I of 31 May 2013 entitled 'Decision on the admissibility of the case against Saif Al-Islam Gaddafi' ICC-01/11–01/11 OA 4, dated 21 May 2014, paras 213–214.
260. Rome Statute, art 63(1).
261. Ibid arts 86, 87(1)(a) and 89(1).
262. Vienna Convention on the Law of Treaties (signed 23 May 1969, entered into force 27 January 1980) 1155 UNTS 332, art 2(1)(h) defines a third state as 'a State not a party to the treaty'.
263. Rome Statute, arts 18(1) and 19(2).

Three, a state into which the fugitive has escaped may have a law giving that state a leeway to hand over the fugitive to the ICC or to the state from which the fugitive has escaped. For example, under the Belgian Preliminary Title of the Code of Criminal Procedure, it is stipulated that the federal prosecutor may refuse to initiate proceedings if

> the specific circumstances of the case show that, in the interest of the proper administration of justice and in order to honour Belgium's international obligations, said case should be brought either before the international courts, or before the court of the place in which the acts were committed, or before the court of the State of which the perpetrator is a national, or the court of the place in which he can be found, and to the extent that said court is independent, impartial and fair as may be determined from the international commitments binding on Belgium and that state.[264]

Four, the ICC may enter into a treaty with another state to the effect that, that state should hand over any fugitive from international criminal justice found on its territory. Article 4 of the Rome Statute stipulates that 'the Court shall have international legal personality. It shall also have such legal capacity as may be necessary for the exercise of its functions and the fulfilment of its purposes' while article 87(5)(a) states that 'the Court may invite any State not party to this Statute to provide assistance . . . on the basis of an *ad hoc* arrangement, an agreement with such State or any other appropriate basis.'

While the ICC can obtain the accused in certain instances where the state that has jurisdiction to prosecute cannot, the inability of the ICC to obtain the accused appears irrelevant. This is because in *Prosecutor v Saif Al-Islam Gaddafi & Abdullah Al-Senussi*,[265] the ICC did not consider the fact that it could not obtain the defendant the same way Libya could not obtain him before finding the case admissible by the ICC. Nonetheless, in practical terms, the ability of the ICC to obtain the accused is a necessary consideration.

Having established that the ICC can obtain the accused if a state party cannot and that this consideration may somewhat not be necessary, the need for an extradition arrangement between a state party and other states is no longer questionable. It is, however, worthy to mention that the need for extradition arrangement is between a state party and states that are not parties to the Rome Statute. This is because state parties to the Rome Statute are

264. Preliminary Title of the Belgian Code of Criminal Procedure, arts 10, 1bis and 12bis. English translation available in (2003) 42 ILM 1258, 1267 cited in Cedric Ryngaert, 'Horizontal Complementarity' in Carsten Stahn and Mohamed El Zeidy (eds), *The International Criminal Court and Complementarity: From Theory to Practice* vol II (Cambridge University Press 2011), 855–887, 872–873.

265. *Prosecutor v Saif Al-Islam Gaddafi & Abdullah Al-Senussi*, 'Decision on the admissibility of the case against Saif Al-Islam Gaddafi' ICC-01/11-01/11, dated 31 May 2013.

under obligation to give priority to the ICC request for arrest and surrender over extradition request from other state parties.[266]

The criteria of 'unavailability' and 'otherwise unable to carry out proceedings' are blanket provisions within which a lot of factual situations can be subsumed, and the OTP has listed certain indicia as it did in determining unwillingness. These indicia are a lack of necessary personnel, judges, investigators and prosecutor; a lack of judicial infrastructure; a lack of substantive or procedural penal legislation rendering system 'unavailable'; a lack of access rendering system 'unavailable'; obstruction by uncontrolled elements rendering system 'unavailable'; and amnesties, immunities rendering system 'unavailable.'[267] Similarly, the 'contextual issues' identified by the OTP which apply to the determination of unwillingness also apply to inability.[268] In *Prosecutor v Jean-Pierre Bemba Gombo*[269] the Trial Chamber III considered the question of the inability of Central African Republic (CAR) and held that due to insufficient number of judges and human resources, inadequate budgetary allocation and the general instability of the region, the CAR lacked the requisite capability to try the alleged offences, and thus, its judicial system was unavailable.[270]

Since a lack of substantive penal legislation may render a system unavailable, this raises the question of whether the crimes recognised at the national level must be the same as those identified in the Rome Statute. In other words, must the nomenclature and the applicable principles be the same? In *Prosecutor v Francis Kirimi Muthaura*,[271] the Appeals Chamber applied the 'same person/substantially the same conduct test.'[272] Therefore, the nomenclature does not necessarily have to be the same as the applicable principles, but the egregious nature of international crimes must be reflected with its accompanying stigma and grave punishment. In addition, while the applicable domestic principles of preventing impunity may be higher than the international benchmark, it must not be lower; otherwise, it may indicate inability. In *Prosecutor v Saif Al-Islam Gaddafi & Abdullah Al-Senussi*,[273] the Pre-Trial Chamber I of the ICC held that 'the assessment of domestic proceedings should focus on the alleged conduct and not its legal characterisation'[274] and that 'there is no requirement under the Statute that the investigation at the national level be aimed at the prosecution of "international" crimes as long

266. Rome Statute, art 90.
267. OTP Informal Expert Paper 2009 (n 80) para 50.
268. Ibid Annex 4.
269. *Prosecutor v Jean-Pierre Bemba Gombo*, 'Decision on the Admissibility and Abuse of Process Challenges' ICC-01/05–01/08–802 Pre-Trial Chamber III, 24 June 2010.
270. Ibid para 245.
271. *Prosecutor v Francis Kirimi Muthaura* ICC-01/09–02/11–274 30 August 2011.
272. Ibid para 1.
273. *Prosecutor v Saif Al-Islam Gaddafi & Abdullah Al-Senussi*, 'Decision on the Admissibility of the Case Against Saif Al-Islam Gaddafi' ICC-01/11–01/11, dated 31 May 2013.
274. Ibid para 85.

as the investigation covers the same conduct.'[275] The court added that 'a domestic investigation or prosecution for "ordinary crimes", to the extent that the case covers the same conduct, shall be considered sufficient.'[276]

The principle of subsumption developed by Latin American jurists is relevant here. In subsumption, the court retains the name of the crime since it cannot change it. However, the elements of international crimes are applied.[277] For example, the elements of genocide that an ethnic group must be destroyed in whole or in part may be used to make a finding of guilt with respect to multiple murders. This approach is predicated on the principle that 'core crimes can be prosecuted as ordinary crimes, as international crimes defined in national law, and by direct application of international offences.'[278] This is in line with the position of the International Law Commission that 'the characterization or the absence of characterization of a particular type of behaviour as criminal under national law has no effect on the characterization of that type of behaviour as criminal under international law.'[279] However, the principle of subsumption may be of limited value when domestic law, which defines crimes and their ingredients, is exhaustive and foreclose having recourse to external sources. For example, the Supreme Court of Nigeria held in *Odu v The State*,[280] that the Nigerian Criminal Code is exhaustive in its operative scope and that recourse would only be had to the common law of England if its wordings are 'obscure or capable of bearing more than one meaning.'[281] In addition, while the court can use its power of interpretation to bring domestic crimes in tandem with international crimes, its power is considerably limited in dispensing punishment which, when it is considerably low by international standard may indicate inability. Therefore, prosecuting domestic crimes as international crimes has been considered a least desirable option.[282]

Because the ICC will not intervene unless a 'State is unwilling or unable genuinely to carry out the investigation or prosecution;'[283] the question is sometimes raised whether the adverb *genuinely* qualifies *unable* or both *unwilling* and *unable* or 'to carry out the investigation or prosecution.'[284] If the preceding discussion is considered, the adverb could not have modified

275. Ibid para 108.
276. Ibid para 88.
277. Due Process of Law Foundation, *Digest of Latin American Jurisprudence on International Crimes* (Due Process of Law Foundation 2010), 173.
278. Ward N. Ferdinandusse, *Direct Application of International Criminal Law in National Courts* (TMC Asser Press 2006), 89.
279. United Nations International Law Commission Draft Code of Crimes Against Peace and Security of Mankind with Commentaries, Yearbook of the International Law Commission, vol 2 Pt 2 (1996) 18.
280. [1965] NMLR 129.
281. Ibid 131.
282. Ferdinandusse, *Direct Application of International Criminal Law in National Courts* (n 275), 89.
283. Rome Statute, art 17(1)(a).
284. OTP Informal Expert Paper 2003 (n 80) para 21.

anything else but investigation or prosecution. This appears to be reinforced by article 17(1)(b) of the Rome Statute. It provides that the ICC will not intervene 'unless the decision resulted from the unwillingness or inability of the State genuinely to prosecute.'[285] The adverb arguably addresses the question of *bona fide*, and it could not have applied to unwillingness because the question of *bona fide* is already implicit in it. With respect to *unable*, the adverb could not have applied because the issue of motive is not necessarily at issue.

In the light of the preceding analysis, unwillingness and inability will only be considered with respect to a case and that the test will not be applied by the ICC unless there is a fact on ground. In other words, the tests will not be applied in the abstract. Nonetheless, the tests offer a guide to assess whether any legal system can effectively investigate and prosecute international crimes for which it has jurisdiction. These tests will be adopted in interrogating the Nigerian legal system to discover if as a matter of policy (because there is no case at issue) the Nigerian legal system is (un)willing and (un)able.

285. Ibid.

4 Inaction

Adoption of Implementing Legislation as an Aspect of Complementarity

In the preceding chapter, where the principle of complementarity was discussed, it was established that the assessment of unwillingness or inability will not be the first thing to be considered by the International Criminal Court (ICC), rather mere 'inaction' is sufficient to trigger the exercise of the compulsory jurisdiction of the ICC.[1] It is only when a finding of inaction is not made that the ICC will now proceed to consider unwillingness and inability. Inaction simply implies no domestic criminal proceeding, although the crimes recognised under the Rome Statute have been committed. There are several facts that can lead to a situation in which there will be no criminal proceeding although the crimes recognised under the Rome Statute have been committed. The categories of facts that can lead to a situation of 'inaction' are never closed, and it is not here being attempted to be exhausted. Nonetheless, one obvious instance in which there will be no proceeding, although the crimes recognised under the statute might have been committed, is when there is no legislation that can serve as the basis of prosecution. When there is no legislation, even if there is an effective investigation, the state concerned cannot proceed to prosecute.

As previously stated, there is no legislation in Nigeria which punishes the crimes recognised under the Rome Statute. This implies that Nigeria will perpetually be in a situation of inaction as no criminal proceeding can be initiated because of absence of implementing legislation. Therefore, the issue of how Nigeria can successfully implement the principle of complementarity by way of legislation to avoid being inactive is what will be considered in this chapter. In any criminal legislation, five issues must be addressed. They are the definition of the crime, the defences that are available to the defendants, the court that will assume jurisdiction, the principle for the assumption of jurisdiction and punishment to be meted out. But implementing legislation in this instance is not only a criminal legislation; it is also a legislation that seeks to put into effect Nigeria's obligation under a treaty. This largely determines the legislative options open to Nigeria.

1. *Prosecutor v Thomas Lubanga Dyilo, Decision on the Prosecutor's Application for a Warrant of Arrest* ICC-01/04–01/06–8-Corr, Pre-Trial Chamber 1, 10 February 2006, para 30.

Incorporation of the Crimes Recognised Under the Rome Statute by Attachment

The first legislative option which is open to Nigeria in implementing the complementarity principle of the Rome Statute is to attach articles 6, 7 and 8 of the statute where the crimes are defined by an enabling law. This is the approach adopted by Kenya and Uganda in their respective implementing legislation.[2] Where the Rome Statute is attached, the advantage is that the egregious nature of the crimes contained in the Rome Statute will be readily reflected. This is germane to implementing the principle of complementarity; otherwise, the context of the crimes would be lost. However, an amendment may be required in each case whenever the Rome Statute is amended to keep abreast with the definition in the statute. In order to obviate this clog, it is recommended in the Report of the Commonwealth Expert Group on the implementation of the Rome Statute that a state may

> include a provision that will allow for additional crimes to be included as domestic offences without the need for subsequent amendment to the law if a state accedes to a convention in future with new genocide, war crimes or crimes against humanity offences or if a new crime of the same nature is recognised under customary international law.[3]

In the Kenyan International Crimes Act, it is provided that crime against humanity 'includes an act defined as a crime against humanity in conventional international law or customary international law that is not otherwise dealt with in the Rome Statute or in this Act.'[4]

As the definition of war crimes in the Rome Statute is not identical in content with the definition of war crimes in the Geneva Conventions, incorporating it domestically presents a peculiar challenge because most Commonwealth states have laws implementing the Geneva Conventions already. Therefore, it is recommended in the Report of the Commonwealth Expert Group on the implementation of the Rome Statute that states must 'ensure that the provisions covering grave breaches and other serious violations covered by a Geneva Conventions Act are not adversely affected by the law incorporating the Rome Statute.'[5] Thus, Uganda provides in its implementing law that nothing affects or limits the application of the Geneva Conventions Act which makes grave breaches of the Act an offence under Ugandan law.[6]

2. International Crimes Act 2008 (Kenya), s 6 and First Schedule; International Criminal Court Act 2010 (Uganda), ss 7, 8, 9 and First Schedule.
3. Report of the Commonwealth Expert Group on Implementing Legislation for the Rome Statute of the International Criminal Court Revised April 2011 para 10 (Report of the Commonwealth Expert Group).
4. Section 6.
5. Report of the Commonwealth Expert Group (n 3) para 13.
6. International Criminal Court Act 2010, s 9(4).

With respect to ancillary offences like conspiracy, aiding and abetting, both Kenya and Uganda adopt the general part of the Rome Statute.[7] Under the Kenyan International Crimes Act 2008, it is provided that the general part as embodied in the Rome Statute together with the general principles of criminal law in Kenya shall apply and that whenever there is conflict the general principles as embodied in the Rome Statute shall prevail.[8] The same position is also adopted by Uganda in its International Criminal Court Act 2010.[9]

Perhaps, both Kenya and Uganda adopt the general part of the Rome Statute as contained in part III of the statute based on the suggestion that the 'principles of criminal responsibility in national legislation should be at least as strict as in Part 3 of the Rome Statute'[10] and that 'all crimes of accessory criminal responsibility, such as aiding, abetting and direct and public incitement as contained in Article 25 should be punishable under national law.'[11] It also appears that both Kenya and Uganda are influenced by such argument canvassed by Bruce Broomhall that 'the application of narrower general principles than contemplated by the Statute could make a case admissible before the Court if national law thereby allowed impunity where the Court would punish.'[12]

However, it is not required that the general part of the Rome Statute must be adopted before a state party to the Rome Statute can effectively implement complementarity. Frédéric Mégret contends that the general part was elaborated upon in the Rome Statute because of the concerns of state parties about the operation of the principle of *nullum crimen sine lege* at the international plane and not because of any strong conviction that the general part as embodied in the statute is the 'only good 'general part'' through which international crimes could be prosecuted.[13] According to him, 'this is an area of international criminal law that has been fraught with tensions, contradictions and evolutions so that the idea that it should now be transposed as such to domestic systems strikes one as odd.'[14]

In the light of Frédéric Mégret's argument, the general part of the Nigerian Criminal Code which applies to all criminal legislation apart from the

7. International Crimes Act 2008, s 7(1)(d); International Criminal Court Act 2010, s 19(1)(a)(iv).
8. Sections 7(1), 7(2)(a) and 7(2)(b)(i).
9. Sections 19(1)(a), 19(1)(b) and 19(3).
10. Amnesty International, 'The International Criminal Court: Checklist for Effective Implementation' AI Index IOR 40/011/00 (2000) 5.
11. Ibid 5–6.
12. Bruce Broomhall, *International Justice and the International Criminal Court: Between Sovereignty and the Rule of Law* (Oxford University Press 2003), 91.
13. Frédéric Mégret, 'Too Much of a Good Thing? Implementation and the Uses of Complementarity' in Carsten Stahn and Mohamed El Zeidy (eds), *The International Criminal Court and Complementarity: From Theory to Practice* vol I (Cambridge University Press 2011), 361, 374.
14. Ibid.

code is sufficient. Although the Report of the Commonwealth Expert Group on the implementation of the Rome Statute recognises the approach adopted by both Kenya and Uganda,[15] it also recognises that a state may choose not to adopt the general part under the Rome Statute, implying that failure to adopt the general principles as embodied under the Rome Statute is not contrary to implementing complementarity.[16]

Elements of crimes are necessary for interpreting the definitions of crime. As a matter of fact, elements of crimes are inherent in the definition of crimes. The ICC is not, however, confined to those elements.[17] This is to allow for greater flexibility to take care of wide arrays of factual situations. Uganda provides that courts 'may' have regard to those elements[18] while Kenya provides that courts 'shall' have regard to those elements.[19] The use of the word *may* permits much flexibility and appears preferable. In addition, apart from the specific mental element which is reflected in each element of a crime, the general mental element is also required in interpreting a criminal legislation. Uganda and Kenya adopt the general mental element in article 30 of the Rome Statute.[20] While the general part of the Rome Statute is not required to be adopted in implementing complementarity, any general part which is adopted would contain a provision on elements of crime both in specific and general content. Although international legal concepts are often adopted in interpreting a treaty where it is attached to an enabling law,[21] this will not necessarily apply here. In the Report of the Commonwealth Expert Group, it is acknowledged that the concept of *mens rea* under the common law is sufficiently broad to accommodate the mental elements of the crimes recognised under the Rome Statute.[22] In Nigeria, the courts in interpreting section 24 of the Criminal Code which applies to all criminal legislation in Nigeria have subsumed the concept of *mens rea* within it.[23]

With respect to defences, Kenya and Uganda adopt defences that are available under international law and domestic law and provide for the supremacy of international law in a situation of conflict.[24] This is in line with the Report of the Commonwealth Expert Group, where it is stated that states

15. Report of the Commonwealth Expert Group (n 3) para 51.
16. Ibid.
17. Rome Statute of the International Criminal Court (Rome Statute) (adopted 17 July 1998, entered into force 1 July 2002) 2187 UNTS 3, art 9(1).
18. International Criminal Court Act 2010, s 19(4)(a).
19. International Crimes Act 2008, s 7(5)(a).
20. International Crimes Act 2008, s 7(1)(h); International Criminal Court Act 2010, s 19(1)(a)(viii).
21. *Abacha v Fawehinmi* [2000] 6 NWLR (Pt 660) 228, 342–343.
22. Report of the Commonwealth Expert Group (n 3) para 69.
23. Cyprian Okechukwu Okonkwo, *Criminal Law in Nigeria* (2nd edn, Spectrum Books Limited 1980), 43.
24. International Crimes Act 2008, s 7(2)(b); International Criminal Court Act 2010, ss 19(1)(a)(ix), 19(1)(c) and 19(3).

may choose defences in their domestic law, international law or both and that where defences under the two are permitted, there must be a provision in the implementing legislation to resolve any possible conflict.[25] The position adopted by both Kenya and Uganda reflects the suggestion that 'defences in national law to crimes under international law should be consistent with customary international law.'[26] The position of both Kenya and Uganda is also synonymous with the suggestion made by the International Federation for Human Rights to Cambodia that the definition given to the concepts of constraint and state of necessity should be changed by Cambodia to be in tandem with the meaning assigned to these concepts in the Rome Statute.[27] In addition, Kenya and Uganda appear to be influenced by the argument canvassed by the International Centre for Criminal Law Reform (ICCLR) that 'all States wishing to rely upon the complementarity principle should review existing defences under their national criminal law in order to ensure that these defences do not potentially shield persons from criminal responsibility for acts amounting to ICC crimes.'[28]

However, states do not have to adopt the defences in the Rome Statute before the principle of complementarity can be fully implemented. As previously indicated, states are not obliged to adopt the Rome Statute general part to which defences constitute a part hook, line and sinker. In fact, defences largely depend on the circumstances of each case.[29] The International Criminal Tribunal for Yugoslavia (ICTY) and the ICTR did not have any provision for defences, yet the courts have had to consider defences when raised.[30] In *Public Prosecutor v Van Kouwenhoven*[31] before The Hague District Court, the defendant was charged with complicity in war crimes and acts contrary to the provisions of the Dutch Sanction Act. The purport of the Dutch Sanction Act is to prevent aggressive war. The defendant was alleged to have supplied weapons to Mr Charles Taylor when the latter was the president of Liberia. The defendant pleaded self-defence under article 51 of the United Nations Charter. The logic of this defence is that states can plead self-defence when engaged in war. Therefore, those who assisted the state in question to defend itself should be able to plead self-defence as well. The court considered the

25. Report of the Commonwealth Expert Group (n 3) para 73.
26. Amnesty International, 'The International Criminal Court: Summary Checklist for Effective Implementation' AI Index IOR 40/015/2000 (2000) 1.
27. International Federation for Human Rights (IFHR), International Criminal Court: Implementation of the Rome Statute in Cambodian Law no. 443/2 (2006) 64–65.
28. International Centre for Criminal Law Reform, *International Criminal Court: Manual for the Ratification and the Implementation of the Rome Statute* (3rd edn, International Centre for Criminal Law Reform 2008), 91.
29. Harmen van der Wilt, 'Equal Standards? On the Dialectics between National Jurisdictions and the International Criminal Court' (2008) 8 *International Criminal Law Review* 229–272, 250.
30. *Prosecutor v Erdemović* Judgment Case No. IT-96–22-A, 7 October 1997.
31. LJNAX7098 (District Court of The Hague, 7 June 2006).

defence, although it decided that the facts on ground did not meet with the required standard under article 51 of the United Nations Charter. The Dutch parliament appears to be conscious of the fact that defences under the Rome Statute are not required to be adopted when, in the Explanatory Memorandum to the Code on International Crimes, it is stated that 'it would be impractical and involve legal uncertainty if the Dutch courts were to apply provisions on participation, justification and excuses [derived from the Rome Statute] which only slightly deviate from the ones with which they are familiar.'[32] In the *Public Prosecutor v Van Anraat*,[33] the Dutch Court of Appeals adopted the stipulation of the Explanatory Memorandum. Therefore, the defences under the Criminal Code in Nigeria are sufficient, and adopting them complies with implementing complementarity even though the contours of the defences under the code are not completely identical with those in the Rome Statute.[34] In the Report of the Commonwealth Expert Group on the implementation of the Rome Statute, it is stated that 'it is for the State to determine what defences will apply.'[35]

With respect to vesting a court with jurisdiction in prosecuting the crimes recognised under the Rome Statute, the approach has been to vest any of the existing courts with jurisdiction or to create a special branch or division within an existing court or to create a special court and vest it with jurisdiction. Kenya vests its High Court with the jurisdiction to prosecute the crimes recognised under the Rome Statute[36] which is already in existence within its constitutional provision.[37] Uganda on its part created an International Crimes Division in its High Court.[38] Any of these three approaches are open to Nigeria in adopting and implementing legislation.

In terms of having a division in an existing court, the International Crimes Working Document geared towards implementing the principle of complementarity in Uganda was generated in 2009. The document states that War Crimes Division (WCD) of the Ugandan High Court shall adopt its own Rules of Procedure and Evidence which may deviate from the adversarial system that obtains in Uganda and that 'the judges may adopt modifications

32. See Explanatory Memorandum to the Code on International Crimes, Parliamentary Papers II, 2001/2002, 28 337. no. 3, 29 cited in Wilt, 'Equal Standards? On the Dialectics between National Jurisdictions and the International Criminal Court' (n 29), 245.
33. *Public Prosecutor v Van Anraat*, ILDC 753 (NL 9 May 2007) para 7, under B.
34. Compare Rome Statute, arts 31–33 and Criminal Code Act Cap C39 Revised LFN 2004, ss 2(4) and 25–29.
35. Report of the Commonwealth Expert Group (n 3) para 73.
36. International Crimes Act 2008, s 8(2).
37. Constitution of Kenya 2010, art 165.
38. Vincent O. Nmehielle, 'Taking Credible Ownership of Justice for Atrocity Crimes in Africa: The African Union and the Complementarity Principle of the Rome Statute' in Vincent O. Nmehielle (ed), *Africa and the Future of International Criminal Justice* (Eleven International Publishing 2012), 235.

modelled after the best practices of international tribunals.'[39] Similarly, the document provides that 'representatives of victim's [*sic*] groups may present perspectives on matters related to sentencing.'[40] However, the Ugandan International Criminal Court Act 2010 does not have any provision for victim participation and the right to reparation.[41]

With respect to creating a special court, Uganda initially contemplated a War Crimes Court modelled after the ICC which was to comprise 'a bench of at least three judges and a Registry to which will be attached an OTP, and an Office of the Defence Counsel.'[42] In spite of the apprehension that having judges, registry, the prosecutor and the defence together might compromise the principle of separation of powers under Ugandan domestic law; nonetheless, an official of the court stated that 'if you are driving, you need a driving mirror. The War Crimes Court mirrors the ICC-van.'[43] An official of the Ugandan Justice Law and Order Sector (JLOS) also added that judges, registry, the prosecutor and the defence have to be 'under one roof' to satisfy the requirements for implementing the principle of complementarity.[44] One senior official of the Ugandan JLOS explained the rationale behind mimicking the ICC by stating that

> complementarity means that there will be two units: one in The Hague and one municipal. These two must not divorce each other. It must be complementary, must look like the real thing in The Hague: the benchmarks, the procedure, substantive definitions . . . even with sentences . . .[45]

In addition, a senior Ugandan judge states that 'the ICC wants us to do everything the way they did it: we must use the same Statute and the same standards.'[46] Aiming at a complete symmetry with the ICC is a serious misunderstanding of what the implementation of the principle of complementarity requires.

With respect to the principle for the assumption of criminal jurisdiction, both Kenya and Uganda adopt the principle of territoriality,[47] nationality,[48]

39. International Crimes Working Document 2009, art 20(4).
40. Ibid art 20(6).
41. Marieke Wierda and Michael Otim, 'Courts, Conflict and Complementarity in Uganda' in Carsten Stahn and Mohamed El Zeidy (eds), *The International Criminal Court and Complementarity: From Theory to Practice* vol II (Cambridge University Press 2011), 1155, 1177.
42. Administrative Circular No 1 of 2008, High Court Divisions and Circuits and Staff Deployment, 22 May 2008.
43. Sarah Nouwen, 'Complementarity in Uganda: Domestic Diversity or International Imposition?' in Carsten Stahn and Mohamed El Zeidy (eds), *The International Criminal Court and Complementarity: From Theory to Practice* vol II (Cambridge University Press 2011), 1120, 1139.
44. Ibid.
45. Ibid 1147.
46. Ibid 1146.
47. International Crimes Act 2008, s 8(a); International Criminal Court Act 2010, s 18.
48. International Crimes Act 2008, s 8(b)(1); International Criminal Court Act 2010, s 18(a).

active personality,[49] passive personality[50] and universal jurisdiction based on the presence of the defendant in their respective territories. Under the Nigerian Geneva Conventions Act, it is stipulated that

> a person may be proceeded against, tried and sentenced in the Federal Capital Territory, Abuja for an offence under this section committed outside Nigeria as if the offence had been committed in the Federal Capital Territory, Abuja and the offence shall, for all purposes incidental to or consequential on the trial or punishment thereof, be deemed to have been committed in the Federal Capital Territory, Abuja.[51]

This provision appears to suggest the widest possible expression of the principle of universal jurisdiction which may accommodate trial *in absentia*, and it can be argued that Nigeria should adopt same with respect to crimes recognised under the Rome Statute, having adopted same with respect to the Geneva Conventions.

However, the principle of universal jurisdiction so adopted is subject to the presence of the defendant. This conclusion is predicated on the fact that domestic implementation of the Geneva Conventions is subject to the overriding supremacy of the Nigerian Constitution which in this instance arguably prohibits trial *in absentia* because of its fair hearing guarantees.[52] It would be recalled that trial *in absentia* does not obtain in Nigeria. Thus, universal jurisdiction based on the presence of the defendant adopted by Kenya and Uganda is the same as that adopted by Nigeria under Geneva Conventions Act when read in conjunction with the fair hearing provision of the Nigerian Constitution.

At this point, it is pertinent to consider the issue of whether universal jurisdiction must necessarily be adopted by domestic courts to assume jurisdiction under the Rome Statute. The Rome Statute under the provision of article 70(4)(a) only requires state parties to assume jurisdiction based on the principles of territoriality and nationality only with respect to offences against the administration of justice. Article 17 leaves to each state to determine the basis for the assumption of criminal jurisdiction by providing that when states fail to prosecute and investigate crimes under the Rome Statute for which they have jurisdiction the ICC will intervene.

Therefore, recommending the principle of universality for the assumption of criminal jurisdiction as some non-governmental organisations (NGOs) have done with respect to crimes recognised under the Rome Statute is unwarranted. It is not part of what is required to implement the principle of complementarity. While one may be supportive of the principle of universal

49. International Crimes Act 2008, s 8(b)(1); International Criminal Court Act 2010, s 18(b).
50. International Crimes Act 2008, s 8(b)(iii); International Criminal Court Act 2010, s 18(c).
51. Section 3.
52. Nigerian Constitution 1999, ss 36(4)-36(6).

jurisdiction because its ideal is to close impunity gap, packaging it as part of what is required to implement complementarity by some of these NGOs is legally unsustainable. It is therefore understandable why the Netherlands 'called the bluff and opted to not implement universal jurisdiction, arguing that the 'trend in international practice' did not support an obligation to do so.'[53] In the same vein, Slovenia adopts the principle of territoriality for the assumption of jurisdiction with respect to crimes recognised under the Rome Statute.[54] In fact, it has been argued that the creation of the ICC has even done away with universal jurisdiction and that this constitutes one of its achievements.[55] Therefore, the push for the adoption of universal jurisdiction is part of the wide reformist agenda of the universalists contrary to legal pluralism permitted by the Rome Statute.

Regarding the punishment to be meted out which an implementing legislation must provide for, the maximum penalty is life imprisonment in Uganda.[56] This is identical with the maximum that the ICC can impose.[57] On the other hand, life imprisonment[58] or death penalty can be imposed in Kenya if murder forms the basis of the offence.[59] The position in Uganda is an outcome of the misconception surrounding the concept of complementarity within the provisions of the Rome Statute. Initially, the 2004 and 2006 bills for implementing complementarity in Uganda provided that existing penalties would apply which included the death penalty.[60] Later, the 2009 draft provided that 'the maximum penalty permissible under this law shall be imprisonment for the remainder of the convicted person's life.'[61]

The change in position in the 2009 draft which later culminated in the 2010 Uganda statute is completely baseless. It is therefore unwarranted that a senior JLOS official should state that '[i]f the ICC says 10 years, we cannot say 100 years or 10 days . . .,'[62] nor is there any basis for the suggestion of Amnesty International that 'it would be inappropriate for national courts to impose a more severe penalty for a crime under international law than the

53. Mégret, 'Too Much of a Good Thing? Implementation and the Uses of Complementarity' (n 13), 371. See also Alper Çinar and Sander van Nierkerk, 'Implementation of the Rome Statute in the Netherlands'. http://ssrn.com/abstract=996521 accessed 7 August 2017.
54. Cooperation between the Republic of Slovenia and the International Criminal Court of 14 November 2002, art 7. However, article 8 of the Act includes nationality whenever there is Security Council referral to the ICC.
55. Gabriel Bottini, 'Universal Jurisdiction After the Creation of the International Criminal Court' (2004) 36 *New York University International Law and Politics* 503.
56. International Criminal Court Act 2010, ss 7(3), 8(3) and 9(3).
57. Rome Statute, art 77.
58. International Crimes Act 2008, s 5(3)(b).
59. Ibid s 5(3)(a).
60. Nouwen, 'Complementarity in Uganda: Domestic Diversity or International Imposition?' (n 43), 1145.
61. International Crimes Working Document 2009, art 20(10).
62. Ibid.

one chosen by the international community itself.'[63] In the same vein, there is no basis for the position of the chairperson of the Legal and Parliamentary Affairs Committee that the imposition of death penalty is 'inconsistent with the Rome Statute.'[64]

The correct position is that the Rome Statute provides in article 80 that nothing 'affects the application by States of penalties prescribed by their national law,' implying that states can, indeed, impose the death penalty. While one may make a case for the abolition of the death penalty, packaging it as part of what complementarity requires is gross misconception. It may be submitted that the misconception with respect to the abolition of the death penalty is borne of unalloyed reliance on the jurisprudence of the International Criminal Tribunal for Rwanda (ICTR), which makes the abolition of the death penalty a condition precedent for a state before ceding case.[65] In the ICTR complementarity, the ICTR has a primacy status and it is at liberty to determine criteria at its whims and caprices which domestic criminal justice system must meet before cases can be assigned to it. In the Rome Statute complementarity, on the other hand, states have primary duty to investigate and prosecute, and it is when they are unwilling and unable that the ICC will intervene. The ICC, unlike the ICTR, cannot go beyond the narrow confines of the criteria already laid down in article 17. Therefore, the abolition of the death penalty imposed by the ICTR is not part of what article 17 requires.

In addition, the misconception of what complementarity requires is also fuelled by the ICC as well. In one of its outreach programmes, an ICC official stated that 'States Parties are obliged to implement all the provisions of the Rome Statute.'[66] Similarly, various NGOs have also advanced the arguments that international crimes must be prosecuted domestically 'in the same manner as in international proceedings.'[67] While the position of these NGOs is understandable because it reflects the universalist agenda of pushing for wide-ranging reforms all in the name of complementarity, the position of an official of the ICC is uncalled for. It is most difficult to see how the position of the official can be justified in the face of the policy paper issued by the Office of the Prosecutor (OTP) that in assessing the efforts of states in investigating and prosecuting crimes recognised under the Rome Statute 'the Office will take into consideration the need to respect the diversity of legal systems, traditions and cultures.'[68]

63. Amnesty International, 'The International Criminal Court: Checklist for Effective Implementation' 7.
64. Nouwen, 'Complementarity in Uganda: Domestic Diversity or International Imposition?' (n 43), 1145.
65. *Prosecutor v Nwinkindi* Case No ICTR -01–75-AR11bis.
66. Nouwen, 'Complementarity in Uganda: Domestic Diversity or International Imposition?' (n 43), 1147.
67. Ibid 1146.
68. Office of the Prosecutor (OTP), 'Paper on Some Policy Issues before the Office of the Prosecutor' September 2003 para 1.2, 5.

In Nigeria, since the crimes recognised in the Rome Statute are yet to be defined in any statute, there is no specific punishment ascribed for each crime at present. Although punishments recognised in the Criminal Code constitute an aspect of the general part applicable to other subsequent criminal legislation in Nigeria;[69] nonetheless, the tenor of the provision on punishments indicates that the punishments constitute a general guide as to what the court may do in addition to the specific punishments prescribed either in the Criminal Code or in any other criminal statute. This is understandable since no one can be punished in Nigeria unless the crime is defined and the penalty with respect to it is defined.[70] It is worthy of note that any implementing legislation where the Rome Statute is attached as a schedule will maintain a superior status relative to any other criminal statutes in Nigeria which does not implement a treaty.[71]

As earlier stated, articles 6, 7 and 8 of the Rome Statute will be attached to the enabling law where incorporation by attachment is adopted. What this implies is that the enabling law must always pass through the furnace of section 12 since section 12 of the Nigerian Constitution 1999 ordinarily governs treaty implementation in Nigeria. Section 12 provides that

> (2) The National Assembly may make laws for the Federation or any part thereof with respect to matters not included in the Exclusive Legislative List for the purpose of implementing a treaty.
> (3) A bill for an Act of the National Assembly passed pursuant to the provisions of subsection (2) of this section shall not be presented to the President for assent, and shall not be enacted unless it is ratified by a majority of all the Houses of Assembly in the Federation.

The provision of section 12 has various implications. While treaty negotiation is solely within the competence of the executive arm of government at the federal level, its implementation may, however, involve the National Assembly alone as the sole legislative organ for the federation or both the National Assembly and each of the House of Assembly of the 36 states.[72] Where the subject matter of the treaty is within the Exclusive Legislative List, the implementation of the treaty is the exclusive preserve of the National Assembly.[73] Where the subject matter of the treaty is within the Concurrent Legislative List or where it falls within residual matters, the implementation of the treaty will involve both the National Assembly and each House of Assembly of the

69. Criminal Code, s 2(4) and ch 4.
70. Nigerian Constitution 1999, s 36(12); *Aoko v Fagbemi* (1961) All NLR 40.
71. *Abacha v Fawehinmi* [2000] 6 NWLR (Pt 660) 228.
72. Nigerian Constitution 1999, s 12; *Attorney General Canada v Attorney General Ontario* [1937] AC 326, paras 8 and 12–13.
73. Nigerian Constitution 1999, item 31 Exclusive Legislative List.

federating states.[74] Because the Rome Statute is a treaty whose subject matter is crime and as crime is a residual matter in the Nigerian Constitution 1999, it implies that both the National Assembly and each House of Assembly of the 36 states in Nigeria will participate in its implementation.

If the subject matter of the Rome Statute is crime and crime not being under the Exclusive Legislative List of the Nigerian Constitution 1999 the participation of the state House of Assembly would be required to enact the Rome Statute into law, then it can be questioned why the National Assembly would have legislated into law Prevention of Terrorism Act 2011 and Terrorism (Prevention) (Amendment) Act 2013. In other words, how could the Prevention of Terrorism Act 2011 and the Terrorism (Prevention) (Amendment) Act 2013 which seek to punish the egregious crime of terrorism be validly legislated into law by the National Assembly in Nigeria without the participation of federating states whereas the National Assembly cannot likewise do with respect to egregious crimes recognised under the Rome Statute?

In answering the above question, two issues are relevant to be considered. The first one is to consider matters in the Exclusive Legislative List. The second one is to consider treaty (or treaties) which the Prevention of Terrorism Act 2011 and the Terrorism (Prevention) (Amendment) Act 2013 seek to implement. If the subject matter of the treaty (or treaties) which the two enactments seek to put into effect falls within the Exclusive Legislative List, then the competence of the National Assembly to so act as it had done would have been constitutionally valid.

Under the Exclusive Legislative List, the National Assembly can validly legislate on arms, ammunition and explosives (item 2); aviation, including airports, safety of aircraft and carriage of passengers and goods by air (item 3); banks, banking, bills of exchange and promissory notes (item 6); diplomatic, consular and trade representation (item 20); immigration into and emigration from Nigeria (item 30); implementation of treaties relating to matters on the Exclusive Legislative List (item 31); maritime shipping and navigation (item 36); nuclear energy (item 41) and any matter incidental or supplementary to any matter mentioned elsewhere in the Exclusive Legislative List (item 68). Under Part III of the Second Schedule headed 'Supplemental and Interpretation,' it is stated that incidental matters include offences.

Section 1(2) of the Prevention of Terrorism Act 2011 stipulates that act of terrorism include any act calculated to force a government to act in a particular way and adds that an attack on people may be involved which may occasion serious bodily injury or death. Section 19(g) of the Terrorism (Prevention) (Amendment) Act 2013 stipulates that terrorism means any definition given to it under the Prevention of Terrorism Act 2011 and the following treaties: (1) Convention for the Suppression of Unlawful Seizure of Aircraft, 1970; (2) Convention for the Suppression of Unlawful Acts against the Safety

74. Ibid s 12.

of Civil Aviation, 1971; (3) Convention on the Prevention and Punishment of Crimes against Internationally Protected Persons, including Diplomatic Agents, 1973; (4) International Convention against the Taking of Hostages, 1979; (5) Convention on the Physical Protection of Nuclear Material, 1980; (6) Protocol for the Suppression of Unlawful Acts of Violence at Airports Serving International Civil Aviation, supplementary to the Convention for the Suppression of Unlawful Acts against the Safety of Civil Aviation, 1988; (7) Convention for the Suppression of Unlawful Acts against the Safety of Maritime Navigation, 1988; (8) Protocol for the Suppression of Unlawful Acts against the Safety of Fixed Platforms located on the Continental Shelf, 1988; (9) The International Convention for the Suppression of Terrorist Bombing, 1997; (10) The Convention against Terrorist Financing; (11) Convention on Offences and certain other Acts committed on Board Aircraft; and (12) Convention on the Making of Plastic Explosives for the Purpose of Detection.

Considering the matters in the Exclusive Legislative List and the aforementioned treaties, only the National Assembly could have solely validly legislated the Prevention of Terrorism Act 2011 and the Terrorism (Prevention) (Amendment) Act 2013. This is because the subject matter of each of the treaties falls within the Exclusive Legislative List. Thus, the subject matter of the Convention for the Suppression of Unlawful Seizure of Aircraft, 1970 can be subsumed within items 3, 30, 31 and 68 of the Exclusive Legislative List; that of the Convention for the Suppression of Unlawful Acts against the Safety of Civil Aviation, 1971 can be subsumed within items 3, 30, 31 and 68; that of the Convention on the Prevention and Punishment of Crimes against Internationally Protected Persons; including Diplomatic Agents, 1973 can be subsumed within items 20, 31 and 68; that of the International Convention against the Taking of Hostages, 1979 can be subsumed within items 3 and 68; that of the Convention on the Physical Protection of Nuclear Material, 1980 can be subsumed within items 31, 41 and 68; while that of the Protocol for the Suppression of Unlawful Acts of Violence at Airports Serving International Civil Aviation, supplementary to the Convention for the Suppression of Unlawful Acts against the Safety of Civil Aviation, 1988 can be subsumed within items 3, 30, 31 and 68.

In the same vein, the subject matter of the Convention for the Suppression of Unlawful Acts against the Safety of Maritime Navigation, 1988 can be subsumed within items 30, 31, 36 and 68 of the Exclusive Legislative List; that of the Protocol for the Suppression of Unlawful Acts against the Safety of Fixed Platforms located on the Continental Shelf, 1988 can be subsumed within items 31, 36 and 68; that of the International Convention for the Suppression of Terrorist Bombing, 1997 can be subsumed within items 2, 39 and 68; that of the Convention against Terrorist Financing can be subsumed within items 2, 6, 31 and 68; that of the Convention on Offences and certain other Acts committed on Board Aircraft can be subsumed within items 3, 30, 31 and 68 while that of the Convention on the Making of Plastic Explosives for the purpose of Detection can be subsumed within items 2, 31 and 68.

Just as the competence of the National Assembly to solely validly legislate the Prevention of Terrorism Act 2011 and the Terrorism (Prevention) (Amendment) Act 2013 into law may be questioned in view of section 12 of the Nigerian Constitution 1999, its competence to solely validly legislate the Geneva Conventions Act may also be questioned as well. With respect to the Geneva Conventions Act, it can be argued that since the federal government can validly declare war by the president of the federation subject to the resolution of the National Assembly by virtue of section 5(4)(a) of the Nigerian Constitution 1999, the National Assembly is therefore competent to regulate the prosecution of war which is the purport of the Geneva Conventions 1949. If the competence of the National Assembly to enact the Geneva Conventions into law is legally sustainable, it can be argued that to the extent that the provisions of the Rome Statute incorporate the Geneva Conventions in its definition of war crimes, then the National Assembly can legislate with respect to the war crimes provisions of the Rome Statute.

The phrase 'a majority of all the Houses of Assembly in the Federation' in section 12 of the Nigerian Constitution 1999 may mean two things. First, it may mean the majority of the members in each House of Assembly. Because the majority is simple,[75] this means a simple majority of the members of the House of Assembly in each of the 36 states in Nigeria. The implication is that if a simple majority in each of 35 states ratify a bill which purports to implement a treaty and the simple majority cannot be secured with respect to the 36th state, then the bill cannot be passed into law. Second, it may mean a simple majority of all the Houses of Assembly in the federation. Simple majority appears to be involved twice: a simple majority of members in each House of Assembly and a simple majority of 36 states which is any number greater than 18.

In addition to the two possible meanings stated earlier, section 12(3) which provides that a bill implementing a treaty 'shall not be presented to the President for assent, and shall not be enacted unless it is ratified by a majority of all the Houses of Assembly in the Federation' also presents its own problem with respect to presidential assent. Two meanings are also probable. The first is that the president shall not assent until there is ratification by a majority of all the Houses of Assembly. In other words, ratification must precede presidential assent. If presidential assent is required, the way section 12(3) is couched suggests that presidential assent is required in all instances and that it cannot be overridden as it can be done with respect to other bills under section 58 of the Constitution which ordinarily applies in making law in Nigeria.[76] This suggestion will imply that section 12 governs treaty implementation alone and in a matter of procedure the court often enforces strict compliance.[77]

75. Nigerian Constitution 1999, s 98(1) and (2).
76. On how bills become law in Nigeria, see John O.A. Akintayo, 'Legislation in Democratic Governance in Nigeria' (1999) 11 *African Humanities Monograph* 14–26.
77. *Inakoju v Adeleke* (2007) 4 NWLR (Pt 1025) 427, 597.

But, it can also be contended that section 12 is to be read in conjunction with section 58 of the Constitution.[78] This way, it means that presidential assent can be overridden. The second probable meaning is that presidential assent is not required. The use of the conjunctive ***and*** between 'shall not be presented to the President for assent' and 'shall not be enacted unless it is ratified by a majority of all the Houses of Assembly' suggests two different actions where one is not contingent on the other. This means that the president shall not assent at all, but the ratification by the House of Assembly must be done. Once an implementing legislation is successfully passed, it becomes an Act of the National Assembly and crimes recognised in the Act constitute federal offences.

While the preceding analysis rests on the application of section 12, it has however been argued that section 12 of the Nigerian Constitution 1999 only applies to bilateral treaties and that multilateral treaties are not covered.[79] By necessary implication, a multilateral treaty like the Rome Statute is not covered. Thus, section 12 does not apply in implementing the Rome Statute. This argument tends to place an emphasis on section 12(1) of the Nigerian Constitution 1999 which stipulates that 'no treaty between the Federation and any other country' shall have the force of law except to the extent to which any such treaty has been enacted into law by the National Assembly. This argument will appear legally unsustainable if a multilateral treaty involving Nigeria is considered as an agreement between Nigeria and each of the state parties to the agreement. Articles 19, 20, 23, 30(3) and (4), 40, 41, 58, 60(2)(a) and (b), 69(2)(a) and 70(2) of the Vienna Convention on the Law of Treaties 1969 appear to lend credence to the argument that a multilateral treaty is considered an agreement between parties *inter se*. Thus, section 12 is very much applicable.

However, assuming without conceding that section 12 applies to bilateral treaties alone; nonetheless, the English common law is clear on the principle that treaties must be enacted into law before they can become effective in Nigeria.[80] In this wise, the Rome Statute would still need to be enacted into law before it can become operative in Nigeria. Meanwhile, common law is subject to the overriding provision of a statute or the Constitution.[81] The implication is that it is still subject to the Nigerian Constitution with respect to legislative competence of lawmaking organs in Nigeria in terms of subject matter. Because crime is within the legislative competence of states within the Nigerian Federation, the implication is that the National Assembly is completely precluded from participating in enacting the Rome Statute into law. In fact, it is each state of the federation that would be competent to validly

78. *Olisa Agbakoba v The National Assembly* Suit No: FHC/L/CS/941/2010.
79. Yemi Akinseye-George, *Improving Judicial Protection of Human Rights in Nigeria* (Centre for Socio-Legal Studies Abuja Undated), 367.
80. *Salomon v Commissioners of Customs and Excise* [1967] 2 QB 116.
81. Ibid.

legislate in implementing the Rome Statute. This would place the National Assembly, nay the federal government, in a more precarious position.

Enacting the Crimes Recognised in the Rome Statute as Ordinary Crimes

The second legislative option open to Nigeria is to enact the crimes recognised in the Rome Statute as ordinary crimes without any reference to the Rome Statute. In this instance, the enabling law adopts its own language, and there is that possibility that the words chosen may not reflect the egregious nature of crimes contained in the Rome Statute. This impediment can be avoided by copying verbatim the relevant provisions of the Rome Statute. In this implementing legislation like the first option, defences available to a defendant, the court that will be seized of jurisdiction, the principle for the assumption of jurisdiction and punishment to be imposed must also be reflected together with the definition of the crimes. For all intents and purposes, they will be substantially identical with those under the first option.

However, there is a difference at least in relation to other statutes. When implementing law copies verbatim the crimes recognised in the Rome Statute without directly stating that it is implementing the Rome Statute or adopts its own language, the implementing law does not enjoy a superior status unlike if the Rome Statute is attached. This deficiency can be obviated if the implementing law provides expressly that it enjoys a superior status. This can be done using such expression as 'notwithstanding anything to the contrary in any other law.'

In enacting the Rome Statute like an ordinary statute without an explicit reference that the Rome Statute is being implemented, the National Assembly must have competence to legislate on crime. This can only be done by National Assembly if it can assume criminal jurisdiction on some other grounds since crimes are residual matters within the legislative competence of the constituent states in Nigeria. In *Attorney General Ondo State v Attorney General Federation*,[82] the Supreme Court of Nigeria held that any law validly passed in Nigeria does not have to indicate under what provision of the Constitution it is passed and that it is sufficient once its validity can be justified under any provision of the Constitution.[83] It appears that the decision of the Supreme Court in *Attorney General Ondo State* may make it feasible for the National Assembly to assume criminal jurisdiction with respect to crimes embodied in the Rome Statute.

In this case, the National Assembly enacted the Corrupt Practices and Other Related Offences Act No. 5 of 2000. The Ondo State government contended that the Act was not validly enacted because crime was not within

82. [2002] FWLR (Pt 111) 1972.
83. Ibid 2150 para A.

the legislative competence of the National Assembly and that crime was a residual matter which fell squarely within the competence of Houses of Assembly of states. In deciding the matter, the Supreme Court considered sections 4(2) and 15(5) of the Nigerian Constitution 1999 together with item 60(a) of the Exclusive Legislative List of the same Constitution. Section 4(2) empowers the National Assembly to 'make laws for the peace, order and good government of the Federation or any part thereof with respect to any matter included in the Exclusive Legislative List.' Section 15(5) which is under the Fundamental Objectives and Directive Principles of State Policy (Fundamental Objectives) provides that 'the State shall abolish all corrupt practices and abuse of power.' The Fundamental Objectives contain the list of rights often regarded as economic, social and cultural rights. Under item 60(a) of the Exclusive Legislative List, the National Assembly can legislate on 'the establishment and regulation of authorities for the Federation or any part thereof . . . to promote and enforce the observance of the Fundamental Objectives and Directive Principles of State Policy . . .'

The Supreme Court held that the Act was validly passed because it was an attempt to 'abolish all corrupt practices' as enjoined under the Fundamental Objectives and Directive Principles of State Policy. The Supreme Court also held that the Act was meant to enforce and promote the observance of the Fundamental Objectives and Directive Principles of State Policy as provided under item 60(a) of the Exclusive Legislative List. Since corruption was a matter of serious concern in Nigeria, the Supreme Court held that legislating it amounted to making 'laws for the peace, order and good government of the Federation.'

The preceding holding of the Supreme Court can arguably be applied to confer legislative competence on the National Assembly with respect to crimes embodied in the Rome Statute. Section 17(2)(b) under the Fundamental Objectives provides that 'the sanctity of human person shall be recognised and human dignity shall be maintained and enhanced.' Therefore, any Act which is passed to punish international crimes can be said to be an attempt to recognise and enhance the sanctity of human person as enjoined under the Fundamental Objectives. Such an Act can be considered as meant to enforce and promote the observance of the Fundamental Objectives as provided under item 60(a) of the Exclusive Legislative List. Since the commission of international crimes has been a matter of serious concern in Nigeria, legislating on it can be said to amount to making 'laws for the peace, order and good government of the Federation.'

However, unlike section 15(5) which specifically refers to 'corrupt practices,' section 17(2)(b) does not specifically refer to international crimes or crimes *simpliciter*. This appears to constitute no problem. The combined reading of item 68 of the Exclusive Legislative List and Part III of the Second Schedule seems to put any reservation at rest. As previously noted, item 68 provides that the power of the National Assembly to legislate on matters in the Exclusive Legislative List shall include 'any matter incidental or supplementary' to those already contained in the List while Part III of the Second Schedule provides that 'references to incidental and supplementary matters include . . . offences.' It can therefore be argued that international crimes are offences which are incidental and supplementary to section 17(2)(b) under the Fundamental Objectives and Directive Principles of State Policy. In *Attorney General of Ondo State* the Supreme Court held that

> it is manifest from the provisions of section 2(a) Part III of the Second Schedule to the Constitution that it was enacted in order to expand the effect and the extent of the provisions of item 68. It is by virtue of this provision that offences may be enacted by the National Assembly if it is shown that such offences as may be created are incidental and supplementary to matters in which the National Assembly is vested to enact laws.[84]

The need to justify the implementation of a treaty under a different provision of the Constitution as distinct from the constitutional provision which ordinarily applies is often felt to avoid any clog that may be occasioned by federalism.[85]

If the law implementing the complementarity principle of the Rome Statute is enacted like any other law by the National Assembly having acquired its competence from other provisions of the Constitution, nothing precludes House of Assembly of any state from legislating on crimes that are of identical egregiousness with the Rome Statute since crimes are residual matters on which states can exercise their legislative competence. Of course, both the National Assembly and the House of Assembly of each state will not be relying on section 12 of the Constitution which ordinarily governs treaty implementation.

Enacting the Crimes Recognised Under the Rome Statute Into Law by Criminalising Gross Violations of Fundamental Rights

The third option open to Nigeria is to enact the crimes recognised under the Rome Statute by criminalising gross violations of fundamental rights. As previously established, the Nigerian Constitution 1999 provides for fundamental rights. Among the rights recognised are the right to life,[86] the right not to be subjected to torture, or to inhuman or degrading treatment[87] and the right to private and family life.[88] These fundamental rights are not contained

84. Ibid 2209 paras C-E.
85. Duncan B. Hollis, Merritt R. Blakeslee and L. Benjamin Ederington (eds), *National Treaty Law and Practice* (Martinus Nijhoff Publishers 2005), 96.
86. Section 33.
87. Section 34(1)(a).
88. Section 37.

in both the Exclusive Legislative List and the Concurrent Legislative List. Although residual matters are issues not listed in both the Exclusive and Concurrent Legislative Lists as they fall into the categories of 'any other matter with respect to which it [House of Assembly of a State] is empowered to make laws in accordance with the provisions of this Constitution';[89] nonetheless, fundamental rights cannot be regarded as residual matters reserved for component states within the Nigerian Federation alone. This is because the National Assembly is also empowered to legislate on 'any other matter with respect to which it is empowered to make laws in accordance with the provisions of this Constitution.'[90] The fundamental importance of these rights arguably makes them matters on which both the National Assembly and the House of Assembly of each state of the federation can legislate upon.

As a general principle of law, if an entity can legislate on a matter, it can also create offences in respect thereof.[91] Therefore, the National Assembly can validly create offences with respect to the violation of any of the fundamental rights recognised in the Nigerian Constitution. There is no doubt that the egregious crimes recognised under the Rome Statute are also gross violations of fundamental rights recognised in the Nigerian Constitution and both the National Assembly and House of Assembly of states could have validly made their gross violations criminal. Thus, the criminalisation of their gross violations could be made to be on par with crimes recognised under the Rome Statute. Similarly, the African Charter on Human and Peoples' Rights is operative in Nigeria by virtue of African Charter on Human and Peoples' Rights (Ratification and Enforcement) Act.[92] The provisions of the charter are substantially identical in content with the fundamental rights provisions of the Nigerian Constitution. Thus, the charter can also be the basis for criminalisation which could be made to be on par with the Rome Statute.

In *Branko Tomašić and Others v Croatia*,[93] the European Court of Human Rights held that the enforcement of human rights includes putting into effect criminal law to deter the commission of offences against these protected rights. This decision reinforces the earlier principle that the competence to legislate a matter includes competence to create offences in respect thereof. It is worthy to note that fundamental rights provisions interpreted by the European Court can serve as a persuasive authority in understanding the fundamental rights provisions under the Nigerian Constitution. This is because the Nigerian constitutional provisions are derived from the European Convention for the Protection of Human Rights and Fundamental Freedoms which is the subject matter of European Court interpretation.

89. Nigerian Constitution 1999, s 4(7)(c).
90. Ibid s 4(4)(b).
91. *R v Kidman* (1915) 20 CLR 425 (HCA).
92. Cap A9 Revised Laws of the Federation of Nigeria (LFN) 2004.
93. App no 46598/06 (ECtHR, 15 January 2009).

In fact, it can be asserted that Nigeria is a party to the European Convention for the Protection of Human Rights and Fundamental Freedoms at least as it was in 1950. When Britain ratified the convention, it extended it to Nigeria as part of its colonies.[94] In 1960 when Nigeria gained independence from Britain, Nigeria signed Devolution Agreement with Britain in which Nigeria agreed to be bound by all treaties (including the European Convention) entered on its behalf during colonial tutelage.[95] This assertion is further strengthened by the decision of the Supreme Court of Nigeria in *JSF Inv Ltd v Brawal Line Ltd*.[96] The Supreme Court of Nigeria held that pre-1960 treaties are existing laws[97] in Nigeria and that they are deemed to be Acts of the National Assembly. The court added that such treaties do not require domestication as envisaged under section 12 of the Nigerian Constitution 1999.[98] Therefore, because Nigeria has undertaken to continue with the obligations incurred under treaties entered on its behalf before its independence in 1960, including the European Convention, and because such treaties form part of Nigerian laws as existing laws, then the European Convention is directly applicable in Nigeria. Thus, Nigeria is not only a party; it has also put its provisions into effect. Hence, the interpretation of the European Court is all the more persuasive.

It may, however, be argued that reliance on fundamental rights provisions of the Nigerian Constitution 1999 may not be the basis for legislating on war crimes. With respect to the National Assembly, this may not be a problem as section 5(4)(a) of the Nigerian Constitution 1999 empowers the president to declare war subject to the resolution of the National Assembly. Thus, because the National Assembly can regulate war, it can validly legislate on war crimes. With the combined reading of the fundamental rights provisions and section 5(4)(a) of the Nigerian Constitution 1999, the National Assembly should be able to legislate on all facets of the Rome Statute, including war crimes. With respect to states within the federation, it can be argued that if states within the federation are capable of legislating gross violations of

94. Nihal Jayawickrama, *The Judicial Application of Human Rights Law: National, Regional and International Jurisprudence* (Cambridge University Press 2002), 107–108.
95. Devolution Agreement provides as follows: '1. All obligations and responsibilities of the Government of the United Kingdom which arose from any valid international instrument shall henceforth, in so far as such instrument may be held to have application to Nigeria, be assumed by the Government of Nigeria. 2. The rights and benefits enjoyed by the Government of the United Kingdom in virtue of the application of any such international agreement to Nigeria shall henceforth be enjoyed by the Government of Nigeria.' See the United States Consul General at Lagos (Emmerson) to the Secretary of State (Herter), Despatch No 137, 8 September 1960. M. S. Dept of State, file 641.4 5h 9/9–860 cited by Tiyanjana Maluwa in *International Law in Post-Colonial Africa* (Kluwer Law International 1999), 71 and 81 (footnote 31 at page 81) who relied on M Whiteman ADIC, vol II, p 1000.
96. [2010] 18 NWLR (Pt 1225) 495.
97. Nigerian Constitution 1999, s 315(4)(b) defines an existing law as any law which is in existence before the coming into force of the Nigerian Constitution 1999.
98. *JSF Inv Ltd v Brawal Line Ltd* [2010] 18 NWLR (Pt 1225) 495, 506–507.

fundamental rights in peacetime, they should be capable of legislating on this same subject matter in war time. Whether in peacetime or wartime, gross violations of human rights remain gross violations. Alternatively, it can be argued that because states have their residual competence on crimes generally, war crimes are included. However, it may be countered that the subject matter of war crimes is not completely identical with human rights. This argument may, however, be difficult to sustain in the light of the growing blurring of boundaries between international humanitarian law and human rights.

The advantage of enacting the crimes recognised under the Rome Statute into law by criminalising gross violations of fundamental rights is that the onerous section 12 of the Nigerian Constitution 1999 can be bypassed. Once the National Assembly has criminalised the gross violations of these rights, the question of whether states within the federation can legislate through their respective Houses of Assembly may depend on the tenor of the federal enactment. If the provisions of the enactment cover the whole field,[99] then states can be said to be precluded from enacting any law with respect to the gross violations of these rights again. This is because a 'concurrent' relationship of a kind can be said to exist between the National Assembly and the Houses of Assembly of the states because both could validly legislate on fundamental rights as any other matter with respect to which both are empowered to make laws in accordance with the provisions of the Constitution.

However, it can be argued that since fundamental rights are not specifically placed within the Concurrent Legislative List the doctrine of covering the field may not apply. In addition, the fundamental nature of these rights may trump the application of the doctrine of covering the field. Thus, states may legislate along with the federal government on the same subject matter even if the tenor of the federal enactment appears to have covered the whole field. Tolerating multiplicity of enactment in this regard may be welcomed.[100] This is because, if the federal government fails to investigate and prosecute the crimes recognised under the Rome Statute, other states can investigate and prosecute.

Making the Crimes Recognised in the Rome Statute Part of the Nigerian Constitution

The fourth legislative option that is open to Nigeria is to make the crimes recognised in the Rome Statute part of the Nigerian Constitution 1999. But any treaty implemented in Nigeria pursuant to section 12 is still subject to the overriding supremacy of the Nigerian Constitution.[101] In the preceding

99. On the Doctrine of Covering the Field see T Naidike Blog, 'Doctrine of Covering-The-Field in Federal Constitutional Theory'. http://tnaidike.wordpress.com/doctrine-of-covering-the-field-in-federal-constitutional-theory/ accessed 7 August 2017.
100. *Multiple Access Ltd v McCutcheon* [1982] 2 SCR 161.
101. *Abacha v Fawehinmi* [2000] 6 NWLR (Pt 660) 228, 315–316.

legislative options, any implementing legislation is still amenable to the overriding supremacy of the Nigerian Constitution. Therefore, to avoid the possibility of any conflict between the Nigerian Constitution and any provision of the Rome Statute as embodied in an enabling law which may prevent the implementation of the principle of complementarity, an ingenious means of making the Rome Statute part of the Constitution has been designed by some states.

Within the context of adopting an implementing legislation, the crimes recognised by the Rome Statute will become part of the Constitution of the Federal Republic of Nigeria 1999 through this approach. This is brought about through the process of adoption. The Constitution 'adopts' the Rome Statute, and the Rome Statute with the crimes defined thereunder (with defences and other general part and punishment) form part of the Constitution. With respect to jurisdiction, the principle of territoriality and nationality in the Rome Statute may form the basis for the assumption of jurisdiction while the high court for each state may be considered to have been seized of jurisdiction because the high court of a state has unlimited jurisdiction.[102] Although the adoption of the totality of the Rome Statute without any enabling legislation to define the scope of its domestic operation may suggest that all the provisions of the statute, including its institutions and procedures, are adopted, this is not necessarily so as the judiciary is expected to fine-tune its operation domestically.

The most popular form of adoption is the French approach to implementing the Rome Statute. Article 53–2 of the French Constitution 1958 provides that 'the Republic may recognise the jurisdiction of the International Criminal Court as provided for by the Treaty signed on 18 July 1998.' This approach has been described as an 'elegant solution'[103] which avoids having had to open 'the extensive and divisive debates that would probably have been sparked by more detailed reforms.'[104] While the advantage of making the Rome Statute part of the Nigerian Constitution is that extensive debate in implementing the principle of complementarity can be avoided, the disadvantages are however equally weighty. The first disadvantage is that the approach places much premium on the power of judicial review since the judiciary is expected to fine-tune the operation of the statute domestically. One way or the other, the debates that were avoided would still come to the fore by way of litigation, and the judiciary will be left to decide issues that would ordinarily have been addressed by the legislative organ.

The power of judicial review appears to have been very highly rated when it is stated that 'the advantage of this type of constitutional reform is that it implicitly amended the constitutional provisions in question, without opening an

102. Nigerian Constitution 1999, s 272(1).

103. International Centre for Criminal Law Reform, *International Criminal Court: Manual for the Ratification and the Implementation of the Rome Statute* (n 28), 20.

104. Ibid.

extensive public debate on the merits of the provisions themselves'[105] and that 'Nigeria may wish to follow the example of France, by making a general amendment to the constitution that allows the country to cooperate with the ICC in all situations.'[106] The only means of making this implicit amendment explicit is through the process of judicial review. The necessity for making them explicit is that there is no amendment until there is a pronouncement to that effect. This is because there is a presumption of regularity of any statute until the contrary is declared by the court.[107] This does not make for elegant jurisprudence. It could be avoided if the legislature has taken the gauntlet. Judicial review should be interventional instead of being a rule-making or a norm-creating mechanism.

In addition, the power of judicial review as it is envisaged to be exercised here is a very delicate one. It is expected to be exercised in such a way that one provision of the Constitution is to be declared invalid with respect to another provision unlike the traditional mode of its exercise where only the provision of a statute will be declared invalid in the light of a superior constitutional provision. In *INEC v Musa*,[108] the Supreme Court of Nigeria held that 'provisions in a constitution are of equal strength and constitutionality [and that] no provision is inferior to the other and a fortiori no provision is superior to the other.'[109] However, it can be argued that the judiciary should not find it difficult to carry out this task since it has done so in some other context. Where there is a conflict between a general provision and a specific one, the specific provision prevails. If the judiciary has applied this principle with respect to any two conflicting provisions of any statute, it should not find it difficult to apply the same principle with respect to the Constitution. In this instance, the Rome Statute can be regarded as specific with respect to the other provisions of the Constitution.

What is, however, missing in this argument is that declaring a provision as nullifying another in this instance involves serious policy consideration which the legislative organ is much more competent to address. Thus, 'deferring to the future the resolution of potential constitutional conflicts—rather than facing them head-on through amendment or interpretation—is the least desirable option.'[110] Although

> a small number of States decided that this was their only option in the face of an extraordinarily lengthy, complex and uncertain process of constitutional amendment . . . this . . . does not excuse or justify this

105. Muhammed Tawfiq Ladan, *Materials and Cases on Public International Law* (Ahmadu Bello University Press 2007), 246.
106. Ibid.
107. Evidence Act 2011, s 168(1).
108. [2003] NWLR (Pt 806) 72.
109. Ibid 102 para E.
110. International Centre for Criminal Law Reform, *International Criminal Court: Manual for the Ratification and the Implementation of the Rome Statute* (n 28), 21.

approach . . . as it leaves the State open to later violations of the Rome Statute and sets a bad example for others, whatever difficulty constitutional change might entail in some instances.[111]

Another disadvantage with respect to the French approach is that while the power of judicial review can declare a statutory provision invalid, it cannot create another one. That is, it can only delete; it cannot add. Therefore, it cannot on its own create institutions that will make prosecution of international crimes feasible which is the goal of complementarity. However, the example of Luxembourg appears to foreclose any form of judicial review where there may be conflict (as distinct from the judicial task of working out *simpliciter* the operation of the statute) by stating that the provision of the statute prevails over any other provision of the Constitution. Luxembourg amends its Constitution to read that 'the provisions of the Constitution do not hinder the approval of the Statute and the performance of the obligations arising from the Statute according to the conditions provided therein.'[112]

So far, the preceding analysis tends to suggest that the adoption of the Rome Statute automatically translates to having jurisdiction over ICC crimes whereas the purpose of adoption is just to avoid divisive debates over the details of the workings of complementarity and in avoiding divisive debates on such issues like immunity. In order words, despite adoption, is a domestic statute criminalising the egregious crimes recognised under the Rome Statute still not required? If one considers the adoption itself as legislation that is sufficient to confer criminal jurisdiction, it means that no further statute is required. On the other hand, if one considers the adoption as merely meant to avoid divisive debates, then a further legislation may be required as the basis for the exercise of criminal jurisdiction with respect to the crimes recognised under the Rome Statute.

The position that a further legislation to ground jurisdiction on the Rome Statute crimes may on the face of it appear somewhat stronger since states in both dualist and monist traditions have recognised in one form or the other the need for an implementing legislation. However, there are instances in which effect has been given to the crimes recognised under the Rome Statute without any implementing legislation most especially in a monist state to which France belongs. Therefore, if effect can be given to the Rome Statute directly without any implementing legislation, the adoption can indeed be considered sufficient legislation to ground jurisdiction with respect to the crimes recognised under the Rome Statute. The Military Tribunal of Mbandaka (DRC) gave effect to crimes against humanity as embodied in the Rome Statute without any implementing legislation.[113] Similarly, the Military

111. Ibid.
112. Ibid 20.
113. RP No 086/05, RMP No 279/GMZ/WAB/2005, 12 January 2006 cited in Cedric Ryngaert, 'Horizontal Complementarity' in Carsten Stahn and Mohamed El Zeidy (eds),

Tribunal also in DRC in *Military Prosecutor v Bongi Massaba*,[114] followed the practice of the Mbandaka tribunal by directly giving effect to the Rome Statute. It should be noted that DRC is a monist state like Belgium, its former colonial power, and it is a party to the Rome Statute.

Ordinarily section 12 of the Nigerian Constitution governs treaty implementation in Nigeria. By adopting the French approach, implementing the complementarity principle of the Rome Statute is taken away from the provision of section 12 and placed within the provision of section 9 which governs constitutional amendments. Section 9 of the Constitution provides that

> 9.-(1) The National Assembly may, subject to the provisions of this section, alter any of the provisions of this Constitution.
>
> (2) An Act of the National Assembly for the alteration of this Constitution . . . shall not be passed in either House of the National Assembly unless the proposal is supported by the votes of not less than two-thirds majority of all the members of that House and approved by resolution of the Houses of Assembly of not less than two-thirds of all the States.

With the preceding provision, a two-thirds majority of the National Assembly and a two-thirds of all the states must be involved in amending the Constitution. After the amendment, the normal legislative procedure under section 58 of the Constitution will now apply.[115] As the implementation of the complementarity principle by way of legislation is taken away from the provision of section 12 and placed within the provision of section 9, any ambiguity that section 12 may generate will be avoided. Where the French approach is adopted and constitutional amendment succeeds, the need for a future amendment to keep abreast with development on the international plane is obviated. Since the Constitution just refers to the Rome Statute and reference to the Rome Statute means Rome Statute at a point in time, any amendment done by state parties to the Rome Statute automatically takes effect in the Constitution.

Once the Rome Statute forms part of the Constitution, the legislative competence of both the National Assembly and House of Assembly of each state with respect to the crimes recognised under the Rome Statute is limited. This is because when a law is passed which reproduces the content of the Constitution, it is ineffective even though it is not necessarily void.[116] Therefore,

The International Criminal Court and Complementarity: From Theory to Practice vol II (Cambridge University Press 2011), 855–887, 868.

114. Criminal trial judgment and accompanying civil action for damages, RP No 018/2006, RMP No 242/PEN/06, ILDC 387 (CD 2006) cited in Cedric Ryngaert ibid.
115. *Olisa Agbakoba* (n 78) 119.
116. *AG Abia v AG Federation* (2002) 6 NWLR (Pt 763) 264.

the competence of states to legislate on crimes with identical egregiousness is not legally feasible unlike if the crimes are enacted into law as ordinary crimes by the National Assembly. In addition, once the crimes recognised under the Rome Statute form part of the Constitution, they are federal offences. This is because the Constitution itself is an Act of the National Assembly.[117]

117. Constitution of the Federal Republic of Nigeria (Promulgation) Act 1999 Cap C23 Revised LFN 2004.

5 Unwillingness

Shielding From Criminal Responsibility I

In discussing the notion of shielding from criminal responsibility, it would be recalled that the Office of the Prosecutor (OTP) of the International Criminal Court (ICC) listed certain criteria for assessing shielding from criminal responsibility. These criteria include direct or indirect proof of political interference; general institutional deficiencies; procedural irregularities or a combination of these factors.[1] In addition, The OTP stated that these criteria operate within the gamut of what the OTP called 'contextual issues' which include constitutional role, separation of powers and powers attributed to institutions of the criminal justice system; parameters of prosecuting powers and discretion; privileges and immunities of state authorities, granting of amnesties, pardons, enforcement of sentences, parole regimes; and creation of extrajudicial commission of inquiry and truth commissions.[2]

Scholars, in analysing the dynamics of political interference, institutional deficiencies and procedural irregularities within the gamut of 'contextual issues,' identified by the OTP have emphasised immunities manifesting in the form of executive immunity,[3] parliamentary immunity[4] and sovereign immunity;[5] amnesties;[6] pardon/prerogative of mercy;[7] plea bargain;[8] the

1. See Chapter 3.
2. Ibid.
3. Due Process of Law Foundation, *Digest of Latin American Jurisprudence on International Crimes* (Due Process of Law Foundation 2010), 141–146.
4. Alper Çinar and Sander van Nierkerk, 'Implementation of the Rome Statute in the Netherlands'. http://ssrn.com/abstract=996521 accessed 7 August 2017.
5. Dapo Akande and Sangeeta Shah, 'Immunities of State Officials, International Crimes, and Foreign Domestic Courts' (2011) 21 *European Journal of International Law* 815, 818.
6. Andrea O'Shea, *Amnesty for Crime in International Law and Practice* (Kluwer Law International 2002); Faustin Z. Ntoubandi, *Amnesty for Crimes against Humanity under International Law* (Martinus Nijhoff 2007).
7. Due Process of Law Foundation, *Digest of Latin American Jurisprudence on International Crimes* (n 3), 288–292.
8. Jimmy Gurule, 'United States Opposition to the 1998 Rome Statute Establishing an International Criminal Court: Is the Court's Jurisdiction Truly Complementary to National Criminal Jurisdictions?' (November 2001–February 2002) 35 *Cornell International Law Journal* 1, 23; Nancy Amoury Combs, 'Procuring Guilty Pleas for International Crimes: The Limited

ne bis in idem principle;[9] the principle of legality;[10] and statute of limitation.[11] The emphasis placed by these scholars on some of these contextual issues can be understood bearing in mind that immunities preclude subjecting someone to a legal process which, of course, may amount to shielding someone from criminal responsibility. This is also true of amnesties and pardons in certain instances. A plea bargain may also lead to shielding where a person pleads to a less serious offence so that the person may not be charged with a more serious one. To the extent that that person is not charged, the person is technically shielded from his or her criminal responsibility. The principle of *ne bis in idem* which prohibits trying a person twice for the same offence may give rise to the notion of shielding in which the first trial is a sham. Similarly, the principle of legality, which prohibits retroactive penal legislation, may give rise to shielding where international crimes committed before legislation is implemented cannot be prosecuted and punished. A statute of limitation ordinarily prohibits subjecting any person to a judicial process after an expiration of a period certain. This necessarily suggests that once that period has expired, the person can no longer be tried and thus shielded from criminal responsibility.

All these issues are considered in the following in detail with a view to discovering if they exist within the Nigerian legal system and if their existence within the Nigerian legal system has the potential of giving rise to the notion of shielding from criminal responsibility. In this chapter, immunity: executive, parliamentary and sovereign; amnesties and pardon/prerogative of mercy will be considered while plea bargaining, the *ne bis in idem* principle, the principle of legality and statute of limitation are considered in the next chapter. In addition to those that have caught the attention of scholars, the power of the attorney-general to amend the law of evidence in Nigeria[12] (which is probably peculiar to Nigeria) is also considered in the next chapter. As previously stated, some of the contextual issues identified by the OTP are powers attributed to institutions of the criminal justice system and

---

Influence of Sentence Discounts' (2006) 59 *Vanderbilt Law Review* 69, 84; Nancy Armoury Combs, *Guilty Pleas in International Criminal Law: Constructing a Restorative Justice Approach* (Stanford University Press 2007).

9. Christine Van den Wyngaert and Guy Stessens, 'The International Non Bis In Idem Principle: Resolving Some of the Unanswered Questions' (1999) 48 *International and Comparative Law Quarterly* 779; Christine Van den Wyngaert and Tom Ongena, 'Ne Bis in Idem Principle, Including the Issue of Amnesty' in Antonio Cassese, Paola Gaeta and John RWD Jones (eds), *The Rome Statute of the International Criminal Court: A Commentary* (Oxford University Press 2002), 705–729.
10. Pal Wrange, 'The ICC Bill, Complementarity and "Retroactivity"' 30 September 2008 cited in Sarah Nouwen, 'The ICC's Intervention in Uganda: Which Rule of Law Does It Promote?' University of Cambridge Faculty of Law Legal Studies Research Paper Series, Paper No 22/2012, August 2012, 16.
11. Ruth A. Kok, 'Statutory Limitations in International Criminal Law' (PhD thesis, University of Amsterdam 2007).
12. Evidence Act 2011, s 255.

parameters of prosecuting powers and discretion. The attorney-general as the prosecutor is an institution of the criminal justice system in Nigeria and the power to amend the law of evidence confers much latitude of choice in the Nigerian criminal justice process. With respect to this power of the attorney-general to amend the law of evidence, the question is, Is it not latent in the attorney-general's exercise of this power to deliberately raise the bar of admissible evidence to make prosecution difficult and consequently shield those responsible for commission of international crimes from responsibility?

It is worthy to mention that parole regime will not be considered separately, even though it is one of the contextual issues identified by the OTP. This is because Nigeria does not have a well-developed parole regime. Parole was recognised for the first time in Nigeria under the Administration of Criminal Justice Act 2015.[13] It is stipulated that a prisoner may be released by the court before completion of sentence based on the report of the comptroller-general of prisons attesting to the prisoner's 'good behaviour' and that the prisoner has served at least one-third of his or her prison term where the sentence is not less than 15 years or life imprisonment.[14] Once the prisoner is released, the prisoner 'shall' undergo rehabilitation programme in a government facility or any other appropriate facility to enable him or her to be properly reintegrated into the society.[15] The comptroller-general of prisons 'shall' make an adequate arrangement, including budgetary provision, for the facility.[16] Based on these stipulations, the parole process is incomplete in Nigeria without admission to a rehabilitation facility. There is no rehabilitation facility within the meaning of the Act on ground, and the comptroller-general of prisons has not made any budgetary provision for it. Because the parole process is incomplete without rehabilitation facility which is not on ground, it follows that parole regime has not taken effect in Nigeria. Similarly, the creation of extrajudicial commission of inquiry and truth commissions is not considered distinctly as it is discussed within the context of amnesties.

Immunities

Immunity has been defined as 'freedom or exemption from legal proceedings.'[17] It has also been defined as 'any exemption from a duty, liability or service of process.'[18] Immunity has been contrasted with impunity. Impunity has been defined as 'exemption from punishment; immunity from the detrimental

13. Section 468.
14. Section 468(1).
15. Section 468(2).
16. Section 468(3).
17. Elizabeth A. Martins (ed), *Oxford Dictionary of Law* (5th edn, Oxford University Press 2004), 242.
18. Bryan A. Garner and others, *Black's Law Dictionary* (9th edn, Thomson Reuters, 2009), 817.

effects of one's actions.'[19] Within the context of complementarity, immunity implies that a state party to the Rome Statute like Nigeria will not be able to prosecute and/or punish the perpetrators of egregious crimes recognised under the statute. The consequential effect of immunity is impunity, the negation of which is the goal of complementarity. As previously noted immunities may manifest in the form of executive immunity, parliamentary/legislative immunity and sovereign immunity. Each of these categories is considered relative to Nigeria in implementing the principle of complementarity.

Executive Immunity

Executive immunity is freedom from prosecution granted to certain classes of elected executive office holders in Nigeria.[20] The Constitution of the Federal Republic of Nigeria 1999 (Nigerian Constitution 1999) confers immunity on the president, the vice-president, governors and deputy-governors.[21] Because Nigeria has 36 states, it follows that immunity applies to 72 executive office holders at state level together with two office holders at the federal level, making a total of 74. The Nigerian Constitution 1999 provides that 'no civil or criminal proceedings shall be instituted or continued against a person to whom this section applies during his period of office'[22] and that 'a person to whom this section applies shall not be arrested or imprisoned during that period either in pursuance of the process of any court or otherwise.'[23] In addition, the Constitution provides that 'no process of any court requiring or compelling the appearance of a person to whom this section applies, shall be applied for or issued.'[24]

The provision of the Nigerian Constitution 1999 on immunity has a lot of implications. Since immunity enjoyed by the executive is only for a period when the person who enjoys it is in office, it means that it is temporary. The period of office is the period during which 'the person holding such office is required to perform the functions of the office.'[25] The temporary nature of the immunity explains the rationale behind it. It is meant to shield the office holder against any inhibition that may be occasioned by litigation while the office holder is in office.[26] Therefore, a claim of immunity is no defence; it is just an objection that forecloses or bars examination of the case on merit and prevents the court from exercising jurisdiction.[27] Because

19. Ibid., 826.
20. Constitution of the Federal Republic of Nigeria (Nigerian Constitution) 1999, s 308.
21. Ibid.
22. Ibid s 308 (1)(a).
23. Ibid s 308 (1)(b).
24. Ibid s 308 (1)(c).
25. Ibid s 308(3).
26. *Obih v Mbakwe* (1984) 1 SCNLR 192, 211.
27. *Tinubu v IMB Securities PLC* (2001) 16 NWLR (Pt 740) 670.

criminal prosecution is not statute barred in Nigeria, the prosecution can be brought after the beneficiary has left office.

The immunity conferred is personal and not official. Although the immunity is personal, the beneficiary cannot waive it.[28] Thus, a criminal indictment cannot lie against the beneficiary of immunity.[29] Also, the beneficiary does not necessarily have to be a party to the case before the grant of immunity can be violated.[30] It is sufficient if the implication of the proceeding is to subject the beneficiary to the process of the court.[31] This can happen where an order of mandamus is sought compelling the police to prosecute a serving governor. However, criminal proceedings may lie against the beneficiary when he or she is a nominal party.[32] It is the substance of the action and not the mere use of a name that determines whether the beneficiary is sued in his or her official or private capacity.[33] The beneficiary cannot be compelled to testify in court in his or her private capacity.[34] Although the beneficiary cannot be indicted or compelled to testify, he or she can be investigated and the outcome of the investigation published.[35]

While the 1999 Nigerian Constitution grants immunity, the Rome Statute appears to negate it. Article 27 of the Rome Statute provides that

> 1. This Statute shall apply equally to all persons without any distinction based on official capacity. In particular, official capacity as a Head of State or Government, a member of a Government or parliament, an elected representative or a government official shall in no case exempt a person from criminal responsibility under this Statute, nor shall it, in and of itself, constitute a ground for reduction of sentence.
> 2. Immunities or special procedural rules which may attach to the official capacity of a person, whether under national or international law, shall not bar the Court from exercising its jurisdiction over such a person.

To the extent that immunity in Nigeria constitutes a privilege for a class of people, it can be argued that it runs contrary to article 27 of the Rome Statute which prescribes equal application of the Statute without distinction. Although immunity in Nigeria is temporary as it lapses when the beneficiary ceases to be in office, the period of its temporary application is sufficient to reflect unequal application of the Rome Statute because others do not enjoy such temporary privilege. Similarly, to the extent that immunity in Nigeria

28. Ibid.
29. *Alamieyeseigha v Yeiwa* [2002] 7 NWLR (Pt 767) 581.
30. Ibid.
31. Ibid.
32. Nigerian Constitution 1999, s 308(2).
33. *Samuel Igbe v Ambrose Alli* (1981) 1 NCLR 129.
34. Nigerian Constitution 1999, s 308(1)(c).
35. *Fawehinmi v Inspector General of Police* (2002) 7 NWLR (Pt 767) 606.

operates as a bar to the courts' exercise of jurisdiction, it can be argued that it is contrary to article 27 of the Rome Statute. However, reference to the court in article 27 is reference to the ICC which means that article 27 applies to the ICC and not to domestic courts, including courts in Nigeria. This argument tends to reinforce the position that article 27 forms part of the general part of the Rome Statute which a state, including Nigeria, is not obliged to adopt. Nonetheless, the effect of immunity on implementing complementarity is apparent: beneficiaries of immunity are shielded from prosecution and thus escape responsibility.

States with laws conferring immunity in one form or the other have had to contend with article 27 of the Rome Statute and have invariably adopted varying approaches. Some have chosen not to address it within the context of complementarity but within the context of acceding to ICC request to surrender suspects. This is the approach adopted by Uganda. Article 98(4) of the Ugandan Constitution 2005 provides immunity for the president while in office while article 25 of the Ugandan International Criminal Court Act 2010 provides that official capacity shall constitute no bar to surrendering a person in fulfilling ICC request. The implication is that Uganda is not prepared to prosecute its own president but is prepared to surrender him or her for ICC to prosecute.

It is likely that states like Uganda that adopt this approach rely on the procedure for removing the president.[36] Article 107 of the Ugandan Constitution 2005 provides for the removal of the president of Uganda. But whether this is a realistic option will remain a matter of serious concern lurking underneath the viability of this approach. It is also likely that states that adopt this approach also have a procedure for a waiver of immunity.[37] In this instance, Uganda does not have a provision with respect to a waiver, and the way article 98(4) is couched does not appear to contemplate a waiver. Article 98(4) provides that 'while holding office, the President shall not be liable to proceedings in any court.' The use of the word *shall* makes an arguable case for foreclosure of waiver.

Like Uganda, sections 143 and 188 of the Nigerian Constitution provide for the removal of the president and the vice-president and of the governors and the deputy-governors, respectively. Also, a waiver proceeding does not exist with respect to immunity in Nigeria, and the provisions on immunity foreclose waiver of any kind. But, the possibility of removing these beneficiaries will cast doubt on the viability of this option just as it is in the case of Uganda. While Uganda has only the president to contend with, Nigeria has 74 beneficiaries to contend with. Political situation may largely determine the

36. See Argentina and Sweden in The International Centre for Criminal Law Reform and Criminal Justice Policy, *International Criminal Court: Manual for the Ratification and Implementation of the Rome Statute* (3rd edn, The International Centre for Criminal Law Reform and Criminal Justice Policy 2008), 22.
37. Ibid. See Brazil, France, Ireland, Latvia, Luxembourg, and Portugal.

success or otherwise of the removal of each of these beneficiaries, even when complicity could be established among some of them in each situation.

On the other hand, some states have chosen to amend their respective constitutions.[38] This is the approach adopted by Kenya. While article 27 of the Kenyan International Crimes Act 2008 provides that official capacity shall constitute no bar to surrendering a suspect in fulfilling ICC request, article 143(4) of the Kenyan Constitution 2010 provides that 'the immunity of the President under this Article shall not extend to a crime for which the President may be prosecuted under any treaty to which Kenya is party and which prohibits such immunity.' It is worthy to mention that Kenya generally maintains immunity for its president while in office.[39] The Kenyan approach appreciates the effect that immunity has on implementing the principle of complementarity.

Another approach is for the state to construe constitutional provision on immunity in compliance with article 27 of the Rome Statute. This is known as the interpretative approach.[40] It is the approach adopted by Norway. In the Norwegian constitution, it is stated that 'the King's person is sacred; he cannot be censured or accused.' This provision has been interpreted as inapplicable to crimes recognised under the Rome Statute. It is considered that a constitution exists to uphold the rule of law and not to subvert it.[41] There is also the 'probability ratio' approach adopted by Liechtenstein.[42] It is considered that it is unlikely for the head of state to commit crimes recognised under the Rome Statute. This approach is applicable when the head of state is a ceremonial figurehead.

Parliamentary/Legislative Immunity

Parliamentary immunity is a privilege enjoyed by members of the legislative organ. The Nigerian Constitution 1999 does not specifically provide for legislative immunity. However, the Constitution empowers the National Assembly to make laws with respect to the immunity and privileges of its members. The Legislative Houses (Powers and Privileges) Act[43] regulates the immunity of members of the National Assembly. With respect to states, the issue of immunity of the members of parliament is arguably a residual matter within the legislative competence of each state House of Assembly.[44] It may also be regarded as part of common law applicable in Nigeria. There is Legislative Houses (Powers and Privileges) Law of each state.[45] Each of these laws is *in*

38. Ibid.
39. The Constitution of Kenya (Kenyan Constitution) 2010, art 143(1).
40. Report of the Commonwealth Expert Group on Implementing Legislation for the Rome Statute of the International Criminal Court Revised April 2011 para 168 (Report of the Commonwealth Expert Group).
41. Ibid.
42. Ibid para 169.
43. Cap L12 Revised Laws of the Federation of Nigeria (LFN) 2004.
44. Nigerian Constitution 1999, s 4(7)(c).
45. For example, see Legislative Houses (Powers and Privileges) Law Cap 62 Laws of Oyo State.

pari materia with the Legislative Houses (Powers and Privileges) Act. Therefore, any finding with respect to Legislative Houses (Powers and Privileges) Act is applicable to each of the Legislative Houses (Powers and Privileges) Laws. One hundred and nine senators[46] and 360 members of the House of Representatives[47] make up the National Assembly while each state also has its own members different in number from others. But there is no state with fewer than 34 members, and none has more than 40 members.[48] There is no doubt that the number of beneficiaries of parliamentary immunity is enormous when multiplied by 36 because Nigeria has 36 federating states.

Section 3 of the Legislative Houses (Powers and Privileges) Act provides that no civil or criminal proceedings may be instituted against any member of a legislative house 'in respect of words spoken before that House or a committee thereof' or 'in respect of words written in a report to that House or to any committee thereof or in any petition, bill, resolution, motion or question brought or introduced by him therein.' But what if the words spoken constitute a crime? This brings to the fore article 25(3)(e) of the Rome Statute which provides that directly and publicly inciting others to commit genocide constitute genocide. Therefore, if a parliamentarian on the floor of the House directly and publicly incites genocide, he or she cannot be prosecuted. It is worthy to note that article 25 of the Rome Statute like article 27 is a general part of the statute and may not be applicable to states that intend to implement complementarity. Nonetheless, the impact of this provision on complementarity cannot be seriously contested: a parliamentarian like its executive counterpart escapes prosecution.

In Kenya, any treaty ratified by Kenya is part of Kenyan law 'under' the Kenyan constitution.[49] This tends to imply that inciting genocide is criminal in Kenya because Kenya is a party to the Rome Statute in which inciting genocide is outlawed. However, because article 25 applies to the ICC, it can be argued that inciting genocide cannot be said to constitute a crime in Kenya. On the other hand, articles 4(2)(b), 7(1)(d) and 7(2) of the Kenyan International Crimes Act 2008 make article 25 applicable in Kenya,[50] which suggests much more strongly that inciting genocide may constitute a crime in Kenya. But parliamentary immunity with respect to words spoken subsists in Kenya which contravenes the provisions of the International Crimes Act.[51] Kenya, like Nigeria, does not provide for parliamentary immunity in its constitution but empowers the parliament to make law with respect to the immunity and privileges of its members.[52] With the position generally against implied repeal, immunity against prosecution with respect to inciting genocide may subsist in Kenya.

46. Nigerian Constitution 1999, s 48.
47. Ibid s 49.
48. Ibid s 91.
49. Kenyan Constitution 2010, art 2(6).
50. International Crimes Act 2008, arts 4(2)(b), 7(1)(d) and 7(2).
51. National Assembly (Powers and privileges) Act, s 4 (Kenya).
52. Kenyan Constitution 2010, art 117.

Uganda, like Nigeria and Kenya, does not specifically provide for immunity but empowers the legislature to enact law with respect to the privileges of its members.[53] Meanwhile, the Ugandan International Criminal Court Act 2010 makes article 25 applicable in Uganda,[54] which means that its provision contravenes the provision on parliamentary immunity in Uganda.[55] Just as immunity with respect to inciting genocide arguably subsists in Kenya, it also arguably subsists in Uganda.

Unlike Nigeria, Kenya and Uganda, South Africa appears to outlaw parliamentary immunity with respect to inciting genocide. Section 16 of the South African Constitution 1996 provides as follows:

(16) Freedom of expression. -(1) Everyone has the right to freedom of expression, which includes-

- (a) freedom of the press and other media;
- (b) freedom to receive or impart information or ideas;
- (c) freedom of artistic creativity; and
- (d) academic freedom and freedom of scientific research.

(2) The right in subsection (1) does not extend to-

- (a) propaganda for war;
- (b) incitement of imminent violence; or
- (c) advocacy of hatred that is based on race, ethnicity, gender or religion, and that constitutes incitement to cause harm.

Meanwhile, section 44(4) of the South African Constitution 1996 stipulates that 'when exercising its legislative authority, Parliament is bound only by the Constitution, and must act in accordance with, and within the limits of, the Constitution.' When section 16 is read in conjunction with section 44, the argument that inciting genocide appears to be outlawed is further reinforced. This is because inciting genocide can be subsumed within 'advocacy of hatred that is based on race [and] ethnicity . . . and that constitutes incitement to cause harm.' Since Parliament is bound by the Constitution, it follows that on no account should parliamentary debate degenerates to incitement to cause harm based on ethnicity or race.

Sovereign Immunity

Sovereignty is one of the attributes of statehood. It is the freedom of a state from external control. The concept of sovereign immunity brings into association certain notions which must be addressed before the impact of the concept

53. Constitution of the Republic of Uganda (Ugandan Constitution) 2005, art 97(1).
54. International Criminal Court Act 2010, art 19(1)(a)(iv).
55. Parliament (Powers and Privileges) Act 1955, s 2 (Uganda).

of sovereign immunity on the implementation of the principle of complementarity by Nigeria can be thoroughly addressed. The concept of sovereign immunity has brought into association the notions of immunity *ratione personae* which attaches to an office and immunity *ratione materiae* which attaches to official acts. Similarly, by virtue of the concept of sovereign immunity, the relationship between immunity and domestic jurisdiction of another state becomes relevant. In addition, since the law of state immunity is essentially customary, the domestic effect of customary international law becomes relevant.

Immunity Ratione Personae

Immunity *ratione personae* is also referred to as personal immunity. It is conferred on a person by virtue of his or her office and the person ceased to be immune once he or she no longer occupies that office.[56] Under customary international law, the head of state and diplomats are not amenable to the judicial process of other states.[57] Similarly, other treaties confer identical immunity on these officials and those on special missions.[58] This implies that they are shielded from responsibility with respect to crimes recognised under the Rome Statute. Therefore, Nigeria may not be able to implement the principle of complementarity relative to these officials.

However, the number of officials entitled to immunity is far from clear. In the *Arrest Warrant* case, the International Court of Justice (ICJ) stated that 'in international law it is firmly established that, as also diplomatic and consular agents, certain holders of high-ranking office in a state, such as the head of state, the head of government and the minister for foreign affairs, enjoy immunities from jurisdiction in other states, both civil and criminal.'[59] This tends to suggest that the number of officials entitled to immunity is not closed.[60] In this case, the ICJ stated that foreign ministers are entitled to immunity because the nature of their duties entails having had to travel to different parts of the world on behalf of their states to conduct governmental business.[61] This implies that any other official who may have to travel as well

56. Akande and Shah, 'Immunities of State Officials, International Crimes, and Foreign Domestic Courts' (n 5), 818.
57. Arthur Watts, 'The Legal Position in International Law of Heads of State, Heads of Government and Foreign Ministers' (1994-III) 247 *Recueil des Cours* 13.
58. Vienna Convention on Diplomatic Relations (adopted 18 April 1961, entered into force 24 April 1964) 500 UNTS 95, arts 29 and 31; Vienna Convention on Consular Relations (adopted 24 April 1963, entered into force 19 March 1967) 596 UNTS 261; UN Convention on Special Missions 1969, (adopted 8 December 1969, entered into force 21 June 1985)1400 UNTS 231, arts 21, 31 and 39.
59. *Case Concerning the Arrest Warrant of 11 April 2000 (Democratic Republic of the Congo v Belgium)* Judgment of 14 February 2002, ICJ Reports 2002 (*Arrest Warrant Case)*, para 51.
60. Akande and Shah, 'Immunities of State Officials, International Crimes, and Foreign Domestic Courts' (n 5), 821.
61. *Arrest Warrant Case* (n 59) para 53.

may be entitled to immunity.[62] But there seems to be no official of any state whose duties will not entail having had to travel in one form or another. Does this mean that any official of the state will be entitled to immunity?

With respect to special missions, it is not certain if state officials are entitled to immunity as a matter of treaty or under customary international law. By virtue of article 1 of the Convention on Special Missions,[63] a special mission is 'a temporary mission, representing the State, which is sent by one State to another State with the consent of the latter for the purpose of dealing with it on specific questions or of performing in relation to it a specific task.' If special missions are entitled to immunity from customary international law,[64] the implication is that the number of officials entitled to immunity would have been broader than those acknowledged by the ICJ in the *Arrest Warrant* case. This is because a special mission does not have to be a high-ranking member of government as indicated in the *Arrest Warrants* case.[65]

The nature of personal immunity is absolute once the beneficiary is in office. The beneficiary cannot be prosecuted for any acts whether sovereign or not. The nature of the act is not significant.[66] In the same vein, the time the alleged act took place is irrelevant. Whether the act was performed before or after the beneficiary assumed office is inconsequential.[67] It has been suggested that what distinguishes the personal immunity of the head of state from that of a special mission is that a head of state enjoys immunity on a private visit to any state whereas a special mission does not.[68] While this is correct, what appears to be the underlying factor behind this difference is that a head of state does not cease being a head of state even on a private visit whereas a special mission ceases being one once the person is on a private visit. Therefore, with the head of state, the question of immunity will always arise even on a private visit whereas with a special mission on a private visit immunity does not even arise at all. While it appears possible to separate a head of state from the official duty he or she performs, the duty performed by a special mission and his personality appear to conflate. A special mission on a private visit appears contradictory.

62. Akande and Shah, 'Immunities of State Officials, International Crimes, and Foreign Domestic Courts' (n 5), 821; Colin Warbrick, 'Immunity and International Crimes in English Law' (2004) 53 *International & Comparative Law Quarterly* 769, 773.
63. (Adopted 8 December 1969, entered into force 21 June 1985) 1400 UNTS 231.
64. See Yearbook of the International Law Commission, Volume II (1967) 358; *Re Bo Xilai* 128 ILR 713 (2005); *Tabatabai* case 80 ILR 388 (1989) (Criminal Chamber of the German Supreme Court). However, the Court in *USA v Sissoko* 121 ILR 599 (SD Fla, 1997) did not consider immunity of special missions a rule of customary international law.
65. Akande and Shah, 'Immunities of State Officials, International Crimes, and Foreign Domestic Courts' (n 5), 822.
66. *Arrest Warrant Case* (n 59) para 55.
67. Ibid.
68. Akande and Shah, 'Immunities of State Officials, International Crimes, and Foreign Domestic Courts' (n 5), 823.

The rationale behind conferring personal immunity is to allow free flow of intercourse among states in their quest for peaceful cooperation and coexistence.[69] The rationale is more justified considering the volume and the complexity of modern governmental business as opposed to the formerly rudimentary business of governance. With respect to the head of state, the personal immunity is conferred because he or she is a symbolic personification of his or her state together with the indispensable function he or she performs for the state. With respect to special missions and other officials of a state, it can be argued that immunity is conferred because of the functions performed by these officials. This implies that if Nigeria chooses to prosecute any of these officials, the proper functioning of their respective states will be impaired.

Immunity Ratione Materiae

Immunity *ratione materiae* is also known as functional immunity. It attaches to state conduct and serving officials and those who are no longer serving can rely on it. Whoever acts on behalf of the state can rely on this immunity whether he or she is a high-ranking official or not.[70] Where immunity *ratione materiae* is pleaded, the defendant to a criminal charge contends that his actions should be imputed to the state on behalf of which it is acting.[71] Therefore, immunity *ratione materiae* is immunity available to a state as an abstract entity. This immunity is invariably conferred on the agent of the state since a state cannot act on its own except through its agent.[72] Immunity *ratione materiae* hardly applies in criminal cases since the circumstances that may bring about an official facing a criminal prosecution with respect to his or her official conduct in another state is rare.[73] One possible instance is with respect to humanitarian law of war, where the conduct of a state official in prosecuting war may be prosecuted in another state.[74] Nonetheless, this immunity covers both civil and criminal cases.[75]

69. *Arrest Warrant Case* (n 59) para 53.
70. *Prosecutor v Blaškić* (Objection to the Issue of Subpoena duces Tecum) IT-95–14-AR 108 (1997) 110 ILR (1997) 607, 707, para 38; Ntombizozuko Dyani, 'Is the International Criminal Court Targeting Africa? Reflections on the Enforcement of International Criminal Law in Africa' in Vincent O. Nmehielle (ed), *Africa and the Future of International Criminal Justice* (Eleven International Publishing 2012), 205–206.
71. This dovetails into the Act of State doctrine. See *Attorney-General of Israel v Eichmann* 36 ILR (1962) 5, 308–309.
72. *Zoernsch v Waldock* [1964] 1 WLR 675, 692; Third Restatement of the Foreign Relations Law of the United States 1986, para 66.
73. Mizushima Tomonori, 'The Individual as Beneficiary of State Immunity: Problems of the Attribution of Ultra Vires Conduct' (2001) 29 *Denver Journal of International Law and Policy* 261, 262.
74. Akande and Shah, 'Immunities of State Officials, International Crimes, and Foreign Domestic Courts' (n 5), 826.
75. R.Y. Jennings, 'The Caroline and McLeod Cases' (1938) 32 *American Journal of International Law* 82, 92.

With respect to international crimes, it has been contended that immunity *ratione materiae* only applies to sovereign acts and that commission of international crimes do not constitute sovereign acts having been in contravention of the norm of *jus cogens*.[76] In the light of complementarity, it implies that immunity *ratione materiae* cannot be invoked before a Nigerian court because crimes recognised under the Rome Statute constitute norms of *jus cogens*. But whether an act is of sovereign nature has nothing to do with its legality. The test for determining a sovereign act is whether it is essentially governmental or not and not whether it is legal or illegal. International crimes including crimes recognised under the Rome Statute are often committed by those invested with state authority and they are often carried out as a state policy using state apparatuses. Therefore, they are sovereign acts irrespective of their illegality.[77] However, immunity *ratione materiae* does not apply to international crimes, including those recognised in the Rome Statute not because they are norms of *jus cogens* but because the principle of individual criminal responsibility has supplanted state immunity in customary international law.[78]

Therefore, immunity *ratione materiae* cannot be invoked before any Nigerian court with respect to crimes recognised under the Rome Statute because the principle of individual criminal responsibility supplants state immunity. It appears that the Rome Statute takes cognisance of this principle of individual criminal responsibility in customary international law. In the preamble to the Rome Statute state parties recall that 'it is the duty of every State to exercise its criminal jurisdiction over those responsible for international crimes.' By recalling the existence of this duty under customary international law, state parties appear to acknowledge individual criminal responsibility at the expense of state immunity.

In the *Arrest Warrant case*,[79] the ICJ held that while

> various international conventions on the prevention and punishment of certain serious crimes impose on States obligations of prosecution or extradition, thereby requiring them to extend their criminal jurisdiction,

76. Adam C. Belsky, Mark Merva and Naomi Roht-Arriaza, 'Implied Waiver Under the FSIA: A Proposed Exception to Immunity for Violations of Peremptory Norms of International Law' (1989) 77 *California Law Review* 365, 394; Andrea Bianchi, 'Denying State Immunity to Violators of Human Rights' (1994) 46 *Austrian Journal of Public & International Law* 195, 219; *Siderman de Blake v Republic of Argentina* 965 F 2d 699 (9th Cir 1992); *Prefecture of Voiotia v Federal Republic of Germany* (1998) 92 *American Journal of International Law* 765; *Prefecture of Voiotia v Federal Republic of Germany* (2001) 95 *American Journal of International Law* 198; *Princz v Federal Republic of Germany* 26 F 3d 1166 (DC Cir 1994) (Dissenting judgment of Wald J).
77. Akande and Shah, 'Immunities of State Officials, International Crimes, and Foreign Domestic Courts' (n 5), 830–832.
78. Ibid., 839–840.
79. *Arrest Warrant Case* (n 59) para 104.

> such extension of jurisdiction in no way affects immunities under customary international law, including those of Ministers of Foreign Affairs[80]

and that 'these remain opposable before the courts of a foreign State, even when those courts exercise such a jurisdiction under these conventions.'[81] This holding may appear to suggest that Nigeria cannot prosecute officials of other states before its courts. However, if it is realised that this pronouncement of the ICJ is with respect to immunity *ratione personae* and not immunity *ratione materiae*, it will be appreciated that Nigeria can prosecute officials of other states who are not entitled to immunity *ratione personae* but may want to invoke immunity *ratione materiae.* An arguable example is the defence minister of another state. If the minister does not fall within those entitled to personal immunity, the other immunity that may be invoked is state immunity which has been supplanted with the principle of individual criminal responsibility.

While immunity *ratione materiae* does not apply to state officials with respect to international crimes under customary international law, the position of diplomats appears to be different. This is because immunity *ratione materiae* for these officials is treaty based and not governed by customary international law. Article 39 of the Vienna Convention on Diplomatic Relations (VCDR) 1961[82] provides with respect to diplomats who are no longer serving that 'with respect to acts performed by such a person in the exercise of his functions as a member of the mission, immunity shall continue to subsist. . . .' Thus, these diplomats are immune *ratione materiae.* It is worthy of mention that the Diplomatic Immunities and Privileges Act No 42 of 1962 makes applicable in Nigeria the provisions of the VCDR 1961 because treaties do not operate in Nigeria unless implemented by way of statutory enactment.

Because the VCDR regulates diplomatic relations between the receiving state and the sending state, it follows that Nigeria cannot prosecute diplomats received in Nigeria for any of the crimes recognised under the Rome Statute once the acts which are the subject of prosecution were performed during the period the diplomat was in office acting on behalf of his or her state. These officials are thus shielded from prosecution in Nigeria. However, it can be argued that diplomats of another state which are not received in Nigeria can be prosecuted if their actions while in office disclosed the commission of any of the crimes recognised under the Rome Statute. This is because VCDR does not apply between Nigeria and any of these states.

Sovereign Equality and Territorial Jurisdiction

The concept of sovereign immunity exhibits two conflicting principles of international law, namely the principle of sovereign equality and territorial

80. Ibid para 59.
81. Ibid.
82. (Adopted 18 April 1961, entered into force 24 April 1964) 500 UNTS 95.

jurisdiction. This conflict has been appreciated as far back as 1812 when the US Supreme Court decided *The Schooner* Exchange *v McFaddon*.[83] In this case the *Exchange* was a vessel owned by two citizens of Maryland in the United States. The vessel was forcefully taken from them by the French navy sequel to the order of Emperor Napoleon Bonaparte and it was converted into a warship. Later, the *Exchange* was forced into the Philadelphia port by bad weather. The previous owner then filed an action to recover it. The French government invoked sovereign immunity and contended that France was not amenable to the judicial process of any kind in the United States. The French government argued that the warship was an extension of the French emperor and that because the emperor could not stand trial before the United States courts, the same privilege had to be extended to the warship. When the matter came on appeal before the US Supreme Court, the court noted that the 'jurisdiction of the nation within its own territory is necessarily exclusive and absolute'[84] but that because the world is made up of states with 'equal rights and equal independence'[85] one cannot sit in judgement over the action of another.

There are two competing rationales behind the doctrine of sovereign immunity.[86] The first is that immunity is fundamentally inherent in statehood by virtue of the principle of sovereign equality. The other one is that immunity is courtesy accorded to another state by the forum state in the exercise of the latter's territorial jurisdiction which is exclusive to it.[87] While the first one emphasises state equality, the second one emphasises territorial jurisdiction. And, as the concept of sovereign immunity exhibits the conflict between state equality and territorial jurisdiction, the two competing rationales are in conflict.

The implication for Nigeria in implementing the principle of complementarity is not difficult to fathom. If immunity is fundamentally inherent in statehood, the implication is that Nigeria will not be able to prosecute foreign officials for crimes recognised under the Rome Statute since the states which they represent are inherently entitled to immunity which extends to their officials as their agents. On the other hand, if the forum state has exclusive territorial jurisdiction and it only accords immunity as a matter of courtesy to another state, the implication is that Nigeria will be able to exercise its criminal jurisdiction with respect to crimes recognised under the Rome Statute against foreign officials except if Nigeria, on its own, chooses to accord immunity. In this way, Nigeria may choose not to grant immunity or introduce conditions in granting immunity since its competence so to do is exclusive to it.

83. 11 US (7 Cranch) 116 (1812).
84. Ibid., 136.
85. Ibid.
86. Lee M. Caplan, 'State Immunity, Human Rights and Jus Cogens: A Critique of the Normative Hierarchy Theory' (2003) 97 *American Journal of International Law* 741, 748.
87. Ibid., 748–751.

Because of the implications of the two competing rationales, it is pertinent to examine their respective viability. The principle that a state cannot sit in judgement over the action of another is often couched in the Latin maxim ***par in parem non habet imperium*** meaning 'an equal has no authority over an equal.'[88] The argument on the fundamental right of states assumes that the principle of state equality is the root of the principle that an equal has no authority over an equal. However, there is no basis for this assumption. What state equality means is that each state is absolute within its own territory to the exclusion of others. When a state enters the territory of another, it cannot claim any right in the territory of another because that other state enjoys its own absolute hegemony in its own territory.[89] This point is further buttressed by the doctrine of restrictive immunity.[90] If immunity is truly inherent in statehood, restricting immunity of a foreign state by the forum state should not have been possible. Similarly, the very fact that immunity is not an issue unless a forum state is competent to exercise jurisdiction suggests that immunity is an exception to the forum state's competence to exercise jurisdiction.[91] In the *Arrest Warrant* case, the ICJ stated that it 'is only where a State has jurisdiction under international law in relation to a particular matter that there can be any question of immunities with regard to the exercise of that jurisdiction.'[92]

With respect to the second argument which emphasises territorial jurisdiction, is it not arguable that courtesy often accorded foreign states has ossified to become a positive rule and makes foreign states untouchable in the territory of the forum state? The possibility of the emergence of a positive rule appears to gain credence considering the approach of immunity laws of some states like the United Kingdom and the United States, where immunity is often stated as a general rule while exceptions are listed out.[93] However, courtesy accorded to a foreign state is often accorded to foster mutually beneficial interstate relations.[94] With respect to state immunity laws, the fact

88. Caplan, 'State Immunity, Human Rights and Jus Cogens: A Critique of the Normative Hierarchy Theory' (n 86), 751.
89. Ibid., 751–753.
90. The doctrine of restrictive immunity differentiates between acts *jure imperii* (acts of a sovereign nature) which are not amenable to judicial process and acts *jure gestionis* (acts of a commercial nature) which are amenable to judicial process due to the growth and complexity of governmental business. See *Trendtex Trading Corp v Central Bank of Nigeria* [1977] QB 529, CA; [2004] All FWLR (Pt 238) 776. However, the difficulty in determining what constitutes acts of a sovereign nature as distinct from those of commercial nature led some states to enact immunity laws with the goal of stating clearly acts of a commercial nature in contradistinction to those of a sovereign nature. See Foreign Sovereign Immunities Act 1976 (US) and State Immunity Act 1978 (UK).
91. Caplan, 'State Immunity, Human Rights and Jus Cogens: A Critique of the Normative Hierarchy Theory' (n 86), 754–755.
92. *Arrest Warrant Case* (n 59) para 46.
93. Ibid., 755–756.
94. Ibid., 755.

that states that enact these laws often create exceptions at will reinforces the hegemony of states within their territories.[95] Therefore, the second rationale is the correct statement of the law. Nigeria can choose to prosecute officials of foreign states for crimes recognised under the Rome Statute and may accord courtesy to such officials to the extent that mutually beneficial interstate relations will be fostered.

Domestic Effect of Customary International Law

The domestic effect of customary international law in Nigeria follows the British practice. In giving effect to customary international law domestically, Britain adopts the doctrine of incorporation.[96] The doctrine of incorporation makes customary international law directly applicable domestically subject to the supremacy of a statute.[97] In *Ex Parte Pinochet (No 1)*, the court had recourse to the 'well-established principles of customary international law, which principles form part of the common law of England.'[98] While customary international law is directly applicable and subject to the overriding provision of a statute in Nigeria, like Britain, Nigeria operates a written constitution which makes the position in Nigeria slightly different from the British position. The supremacy clause in the Nigerian Constitution means that customary international law is inferior to both the statute and the Constitution.[99] It is not, however, clear whether customary international law is inferior to the Law of any of the federating states in Nigeria in addition to the Act of the National Assembly. It can, however, be argued that it is inferior to it if the matter is within the legislative competence of a state. When the subject matter is concurrent, the applicable rule of customary international law may be considered to have been 'adopted' by the National Assembly unless expressly declared otherwise by statutory enactment and considered superior to a state law. In the United States, customary international law is federal law[100] inferior to the US Constitution[101] and any statute enacted by the Congress[102] but superior to state law. The uncertainty with respect to whether customary international is inferior to state law does not, however, have any implication for diplomatic immunities since diplomatic matters are

95. Ibid., 761–762 and 764.
96. Malcolm N. Shaw, *International Law* (6th edn, Cambridge University Press 2008), 140.
97. *Trendtex Trading Corp* (n 90).
98. [2000] 1 AC 61, 90 and 98; 119 ILR 50, 87.
99. Nigerian Constitution 1999, s 1(1).
100. *Kadić v Karadžić* 70 F 3d 232, 246 (2d Cir 1995), 104 ILR 149, 159 and *In Re Estate of Ferdinand E. Marcos Human Rights Litigation* 978 F 2d 493, 502 (9th Cir 1992), 103 ILR 521, 529.
101. *Boos v Barry* 99 L Ed 2d 333, 345–347 (1988); 121 ILR 551.
102. *Committee of United States Citizens Living in Nicaragua v Reagan* 859 F.2d 929, 939 (1988) and *US v Yunis* (No 3) 724 F 2d 1086, 1091 (1991), 88 ILR 176, 181.

within the Exclusive Legislative List of the Nigerian Constitution 1999.[103] While customary international law directly applies, it is not subject to the doctrine of precedent. In *Ex Parte Pinochet (No 1)* it was held that the doctrine of precedent did not apply to customary international law.[104] Similarly, in *Trendtex Trading Corporation v Central Bank of Nigeria*, it was held that the doctrine of precedent did not apply to international law[105] and that any change in law could be effected by any court 'without waiting for the House of Lords to do it.'[106]

The doctrine of incorporation has an implication for the implementation of the principle of complementarity. Because customary international law on immunity is directly applicable in Nigeria, it follows that all those that are entitled to immunity under international law are also entitled to immunity under Nigerian law. This implies that they are shielded in Nigeria for the prosecution of crimes recognised under the Rome Statute. However, since customary international law is inferior to the Act of the National Assembly, it follows that Nigeria can choose to deny immunity to some officials who would have ordinarily enjoyed it under international law.

South Africa appears to be much conscious of the preceding implications. Section 232 of the South African Constitution 1996 provides that 'customary international law is law in the Republic unless it is inconsistent with the Constitution or an Act of Parliament.' This is a codification of the position in England and Nigeria. Meanwhile, section 4(2) of the South African Implementation of the Rome Statute of the International Criminal Court Act 2002 provides that

> [d]espite any other law to the contrary, including customary and conventional international law, the fact that a person-
>
> (a) Is or was a head of state or government, a member of a government or parliament, an elected representative or a government official; or
> (b) Being a member of a security service or armed force, was under a legal obligation to obey a manifestly unlawful order of a government or superior, is neither-
>
> (i) A defence to a crime; nor
> (ii) A ground for any possible reduction of sentence once a person has been convicted of a crime.

The obvious implication of the combined reading of section 232 of the South African Constitution and section 4(2) of the South African Implementation of the Rome Statute of the International Criminal Court Act 2002 is

103. Ibid item 20 Exclusive Legislative List.
104. [2000] 1 AC 61, 77; 119 ILR 50, 65.
105. [1977] 2 WLR 356, 365, 64 ILR 111, 128.
106. Ibid.

that immunities accorded certain officials under customary international law are completely outlawed and rendered inapplicable in South Africa.[107] In fact, some scholars have seen section 4(2) of the implementing Act as a departure from the 'unfortunate' *Arrest Warrant* case.[108]

It has, however, been contended that section 4(2) only affects immunity *ratione materiae* and not immunity *ratione personae*. The rationale behind this argument is that section 4(2) is modelled after article 27(1) of the Rome Statute which only affects immunity *ratione materiae*.[109] The implication of this argument is that section 4(2) is redundant. This cannot be the intendment of the drafters of the statute. As previously indicated, immunity *ratione materiae* does not only apply to international crimes before international tribunals like the International Criminal Court; it also does not apply to international crimes before domestic courts. Therefore, without section 4(2), immunity *ratione materiae* would still not have been able to be pleaded before any South African court seized with jurisdiction. This is because the principle of individual criminal responsibility has supplanted state immunity.

Despite the laudable provision of section 4(2) for its pro-complementarity stance, it is, however, worth mentioning that in *South African Litigation Centre v National Director of Public Prosecutions*,[110] the prosecuting authority in South Africa developed cold feet in investigating some Zimbabwean top police officers in South Africa alleged to have committed crime against humanity in Zimbabwe. One of the reasons given was that investigating such officers would hamper foreign relations between Zimbabwe and South Africa. If police officers who do not enjoy personal immunity will cause a diplomatic row, one wonders what the situation would have been for those who enjoy immunity. Perhaps, personal immunity accorded certain officials for the effective functioning of states they are representing at the international plane appears to be a necessary evil to contend with in implementing complementarity.

107. In addition, the provision also negates diplomatic immunities under Vienna Convention on Diplomatic Relations 1961. This convention was made applicable in South Africa through Diplomatic Immunities and Privileges Act 37 of 2001 as amended by Diplomatic Immunities and Privileges Act 35 of 2008. Since section 4(2) of the South African Implementation of the Rome Statute of the International Criminal Court Act 2002 provides that 'despite any other law to the contrary, including customary and conventional international law' those entitled to immunities are stripped of their immunities, it follows that the South African Implementation of the Rome Statute of the International Criminal Court Act 2002 prevails notwithstanding anything to the contrary in Diplomatic Immunities and Privileges Act 37 of 2001 as amended by Diplomatic Immunities and Privileges Act 35 of 2008.
108. Christopher Gevers, 'Immunity and the Implementation Legislation in South Africa, Kenya and Uganda' http://ssrn.com/abstract=1975788 accessed 7 August 2017.
109. Ibid.
110. High Court of South Africa (North Gauteng High Court) Case No: 77150/09. See the unsuccessful appeal of the decision by the South African Supreme Court of Appeal in *National Commissioner of the South African Police Service v South African Human Rights Litigation Centre Case* No: 485/2012.

Amnesties

Amnesty can be defined as 'an act of sovereign power designed to apply the principle of *tabula rasa* to past offences, usually committed against the State, to end proceedings already initiated or that are to be initiated, or verdicts that have already been pronounced.'[111] The grant of amnesty is an exercise of sovereign power. The exercise of this power often takes the form of statutory enactment. The statute may be general in scope covering all perpetrators of all crimes within a particular period or specific, in which case, it is limited to a class of people or crime or a combination of both.[112] While the idea of statutory enactment contemplates law made by a law-making organ, it can be argued that the idea is inclusive of executive orders that may qualify as 'law.'

In the *President of the Republic of South Africa and Another v John Phillip Peter Hugo*,[113] the president of South Africa under the interim constitution of South Africa signed a document styled Presidential Act No. 17. In the 'Act,' the president remitted the sentences of 'all mothers in prison on 10 May 1994, with minor children under the age of twelve (12) years.' The respondent contended that the so-called Presidential Act was discriminatory having excluded all fathers and was therefore unconstitutional. In the lead judgement delivered by Goldstone J, the Constitutional Court of South Africa noted that 'where the power of pardon or reprieve is used in general terms and there is an "amnesty" accorded to a category or categories of prisoners, discrimination is inherent'[114] but that unfair discrimination as a concept could not insist 'upon identical treatment in all circumstances.'[115] Goldstone J then concluded that

> the Presidential Act may have denied them an opportunity it afforded women, but it cannot be said that it fundamentally impaired their rights of dignity or sense of equal worth. The impact upon the relevant fathers was, therefore, in all the circumstances of the exercise of the Presidential power, not unfair.[116]

The relevant point here is that an executive order couched in general terms may grant amnesty. But, does it qualify as law? Mokgoro J answered in the affirmative.[117] In his concurring judgement, Mokgoro J relied on the judgement of the European Court of Human Rights in *The Sunday Times v The United Kingdom*.[118] The European Court in interpreting article 10 of the

111. Ntoubandi, *Amnesty for Crimes against Humanity under International Law* (n 6), 9.
112. Ibid., 12.
113. Case CCT 11/96 heard on 12 November 1996 and decided on 18 April 1997.
114. Ibid para 31.
115. Ibid para 41.
116. Ibid para 47.
117. Ibid paras 89–106.
118. (1979) 2 EHRR 245.

European Convention on freedom of speech which permits limitations on free speech only if they are 'prescribed by law' and 'are necessary in a democratic society' held that what qualifies as law must be accessible and sufficiently precise.[119] Thus, Mokgoro J held that the Presidential 'Act' qualified as law since it was accessible and sufficiently precise.[120]

But, it was a rule of common law as a limitation to free speech that was at issue in the European Court decision and not an executive order. Mokgoro J conscious of this important difference then considered the decision of the Supreme Court of Canada in *Committee for Commonwealth of Canada v Canada*.[121] In this case, the issue was whether government directives or guidelines which impinge on free speech could be regarded as 'law.' Lamer CJC did not consider them to be law since the requirement of accessibility was lacking as they are not generally published, only binding on the government and could be changed at will.[122] However, McLachlin J took a much broader view of law and considered executive directives and guidelines as law.[123] Mokgoro J adopted the position of McLachlin and concluded that the Presidential 'Act' could be accessed and was sufficiently precise which made it qualify as law.[124] Mokgoro J added that if delegated legislation as an executive rule making is law, there is no reason why an executive order should not be regarded as law. While a parent statute must exist for a delegated legislation, the constitution is also a parent statute for an executive order. Therefore, amnesty as a statutory enactment includes executive orders that qualify as law.[125]

The conflation of executive order and statutory enactment finds expression in *Ryan Albutt v Centre for the Study of Violence and Reconciliation*,[126] in which the president of South Africa issued an executive order to grant pardon to certain categories of people who did not participate in the Truth and Reconciliation process where amnesty was granted to those who were entitled based on certain strict criteria. The Truth and Reconciliation process was conducted by the Truth and Reconciliation Commission (TRC) pursuant to

119. Ibid para 49.
120. *President of the Republic of South Africa v John Phillip Peter Hugo* Case CCT 11/96 heard on 12 November 1996 and decided on 18 April 1997 para 102.
121. (1991) 77 DLR (4th) 385.
122. Ibid., 401.
123. Ibid., 461.
124. *John Phillip Peter Hugo* (n 120) para 102. The Supreme Court of Nigeria also takes a broader view of law in *Mbanefo v Molokwu* [2014] 6 NWLR (Pt 1403) 377, 396. In this case, the appellant had contested his ostracism by members of his community through the decision of the King-in-Council. The Supreme Court while interpreting section 45 of the Nigerian Constitution 1999 which permits the enactment of a law that limits the enjoyment of human rights if it can be justified in a democratic society held that 'the interpretation of "law" as prescribed under section 45 of the Constitution cannot be restricted only to statutes of Parliament. It would include the rules and regulations guiding communities which assist them in the maintenance of peace and tranquillity'.
125. *John Phillip Peter Hugo* (n 120) para 103.
126. Case CCT 54/09 [2010] ZACC 4.

the Promotion of National Unity and Reconciliation Act 1995. In the executive order, the president of South Africa adopted the criteria stipulated in the Promotion of National Unity and Reconciliation Act 1995 for granting amnesty. The president stated that the executive order was to conclude the 'unfinished business' of the Truth and Reconciliation Commission.

At the drafting stage of the Rome Statute, the issue of whether the ICC should take cognisance of amnesty granted by a state party before it could intervene was raised by the United States.[127] The United States in a 'non paper' suggested that the ICC 'should take account of domestic amnesties when deciding whether or not to exercise jurisdiction.'[128] South Africa welcomed the idea because of its concern that its TRC process might be considered by the ICC as an indication of unwillingness.[129] In the same vein, Colombia sought the right to be able to grant amnesty in appropriate circumstances. Colombia ratified the Rome Statute with a declaration that

> none of the provisions of the Rome Statute concerning the exercise of jurisdiction by the [ICC] prevent the Colombian State from granting amnesties, reprieves or judicial pardons for political crimes, provided that they are granted in conformity with the Constitution and with the principles and norms of international law accepted by Colombia.[130]

While no states objected to its declaration, nonetheless its relevance verges on whether the declaration is not a reservation inconsistent with the object of the Rome Statute since the statute permits no reservation.

However, the issue of amnesty could not be resolved. Those who supported the idea of ICC taking cognisance of amnesty contended that criminal prosecution could not alone restore peace and could in fact sometime exacerbate it. Opponents were not comfortable with the idea of perpetrators being indemnified against prosecution which was considered necessary to achieve justice.[131] Thus, the debate was torn between peace and justice. In the end, the drafters of the Rome Statute left the statute 'creatively ambiguous'[132] on the issue of amnesty.

127. H. Abigail Moy, 'The International Criminal Court's Arrest Warrants and Uganda's Lord's Resistance Army: Renewing the Debate Over Amnesty and Complementarity' 19 *Harvard Human Rights Journal* 267, 271–272.
128. Louise Mallinder, 'Amnesties and International Criminal Law'. http://ssrn.com/abstract=1531701 accessed 8 February 2014.
129. Ibid.
130. Kate Allan, 'Prosecution and Peace: A Role for Amnesty before the ICC?' (2011) 39 *Denver Journal of International Law & Policy* 239–301, 248.
131. Abigail Moy, 'The International Criminal Court's Arrest Warrants and Uganda's Lord's Resistance Army: Renewing the Debate Over Amnesty and Complementarity' (n 127), 190.
132. Dwight G. Newman, 'The Rome Statute, Some Reservations Concerning Amnesties, and a Distributive Problem' (2005) 20 *American University International Law Review* 293, 320–322.

Because the *travaux préparatoires* on the Rome Statute are blank on the resolution of the question of amnesty, one is only left with the consideration of the provisions of the Rome Statute. It appears that the issue of amnesty can be subsumed within the provision of article 53 of the statute. Article 53(1) stipulates that the ICC prosecutor shall initiate an investigation 'unless he or she determines that there is no reasonable basis to proceed.' Article 53(1)(c) adds that in deciding on whether to initiate an investigation or not, the prosecutor shall consider whether 'taking into account the gravity of the crime and the interests of victims, there are nonetheless substantial reasons to believe that an investigation would not serve the interests of justice.' While article 53(1) pertains to investigation, article 53(2) pertains to prosecution. Article 53(2)(c) empowers the prosecutor to decide if 'a prosecution is not in the interests of justice' after the prosecutor might have investigated. Article 53(2)(c) adds that in deciding if a prosecution is not in the interests of justice, the prosecutor has to take 'into account all the circumstances, including the gravity of the crime, the interests of victims and the age or infirmity of the alleged perpetrator, and his or her role in the alleged crime.'

To discover the position of the Rome Statute on amnesty therefore hinges on the meaning to be ascribed to the notion of 'interests of justice' within the provision of article 53. It should, however, be borne in mind that article 53 must be construed in conjunction with article 17 on which rests the principle of complementarity. Considering the provision of article 53(1)(c) which requires the prosecutor to consider the gravity of the crime and the interests of victims in determining if an investigation would serve the interests of justice, it can be argued that a broader conception of justice beyond retributive criminal justice can be subsumed within this provision. While it can be argued that there is no way an investigation would not serve 'the interests of victims,' the clause that 'nonetheless substantial reasons to believe that an investigation would not serve the interests of justice' acknowledges that investigation would always be in line with the interest of the victim but contemplates a broader conception of justice beyond justice done to the victim. The same can be said of article 53(2)(c) when after investigation, the prosecutor has to take 'into account all circumstances' to determine if prosecution will serve the 'interests of justice.' It follows therefore that if Nigeria enacts an amnesty law which accords with the notion of interests of justice under article 53 of the Rome Statute, the ICC cannot intervene.

If articles 53(1)(c) and 53(2)(c) permit a broader conception of justice, article 17 on complementarity arguably constitutes a limit. Therefore, amnesty granted by Nigeria must not reflect unwillingness or inability if the ICC is not to intervene. The Office of the Prosecutor (OTP) in 2007 issued its Policy Paper on the Interests of Justice which tends to subject article 53 to article 17. In the policy paper, the OTP leans towards prosecution. It is stated that 'there is a presumption in favour of investigation or prosecution'[133] and that a situation that will preclude ICC from intervening will be 'exceptional in its nature.'[134] It is also stated that the decision not to intervene must conform to the 'object and purpose of the Statute.'[135]

The OTP makes a distinction between 'the concepts of the interests of justice and the interests of peace'[136] and states that the concept of interests of peace 'falls within the mandate of institutions other than the Office of the Prosecutor.'[137] The OTP admits that the 'concept of interests of justice established in the Statute'[138] is 'broader than criminal justice in a narrow sense'[139] and that 'other forms of justice'[140] like 'truth seeking, reparations programs, institutional reform and traditional justice mechanisms'[141] can be subsumed within the concept of interests of justice to attain 'broader justice.'[142] The OTP, however, adds that the concept of interests of justice 'should not be conceived so broadly as to embrace all issues related to peace and security.'[143] Finally, the OTP 'fully endorses'[144] the 'complementary role'[145] that the pursuit of other forms of justice can play in 'dealing with large numbers of offenders and addressing the impunity gap.'[146]

Amnesty which is broad in its operative scope and which forecloses prosecution can be regarded as a 'national decision' with the consequence of 'shielding the person concerned from criminal responsibility' under article 17(2)(a) which is sufficient for ICC intervention contrary to the spirit of complementarity.[147] Similarly, under article 17(2)(a), amnesty after prosecution may be seen as a national decision to shield from criminal responsibility.[148] If the

133. OTP Policy Paper on the Interests of Justice (2007) 1.
134. Ibid.
135. Ibid.
136. Ibid.
137. Ibid.
138. Ibid 8.
139. Ibid.
140. Ibid.
141. Ibid.
142. Ibid.
143. Ibid.
144. Ibid.
145. Ibid.
146. Ibid.
147. Similarly, as previously established, ICC will not consider art 17 at all if a state has not acted as it will just proceed to intervene. Blanket amnesty can be said to yield positive inactivity to justify ICC intervention. Since amnesty is often granted due to practical necessity, it can also be argued that a state that grants blanket amnesty is 'unable to carry out its proceedings' under art 17(3).
148. With blanket amnesty after prosecution, a different picture can be seen. Unlike amnesty before prosecution, amnesty after prosecution cannot give rise to positive inactivity to justify ICC intervention since prosecution has demonstrated sufficient activity although willingness may be questioned.

historical background of shielding from prosecution is considered, amnesty after prosecution can be compared in a way with the ridiculously low punishment handed down to convicts in the German shoddy trials. If the ridiculously low punishment indicates shielding, then complete absence of punishment cannot be less indicative of shielding. While blanket amnesty can be said to amount to shielding from criminal responsibility, conditional amnesty presents a somewhat hazy outlook.

Darryl Robinson, relying on the example of the South African TRC,[149] has suggested that the ICC can take into account such amnesty where a state undertakes 'a diligent, methodical effort to gather the evidence and ascertain the facts relating to the conduct in question'[150] before deciding whether to grant amnesty in each individual case based on strict criteria and where prosecution is not completely ruled out for those who refuse to apply for amnesty or for those who though applied were refused amnesty. The position of Darryl Robinson appears to have been reinforced by the argument of the former UN secretary-general, Kofi Annan, that no

> one should imagine that [the ICC's power to intervene under Article 17] would apply to a case like South Africa's, where the regime and the conflict which caused the crimes have come to an end, and the victims have inherited power. It is inconceivable that, in such a case, the Court would seek to substitute its judgment for that of a whole nation which is seeking the best way to put a traumatic past behind it and build a better future.[151]

However, Kate Allan has argued that complementarity under article 17 envisages nothing but prosecution on the part of the state party. She hinges her argument on the preamble to the Rome Statute which affirms 'that the most serious crimes of concern to the international community as a whole must not go unpunished,' recalls that 'it is the duty of every State to exercise its criminal jurisdiction over those responsible for international crimes' and emphasises that 'the International Criminal Court established under this Statute shall be complementary to national criminal jurisdictions.' Furthermore, she hinges her argument on article 17 which uses such clauses as 'the case has been investigated,' the 'State has decided not to prosecute' and 'shielding the person concerned from criminal responsibility.'[152] She then concludes that 'amnesty does not just preclude admissibility because it shields a person

149. On the South African TRC see Antje du Bois-Pedain, *Transitional Amnesty in South Africa* (Cambridge University Press 2007).
150. Darryl Robinson, 'Serving the Interests of Justice: Amnesties, Truth Commissions and the International Criminal Court' (2003) 14 *European Journal of International Law* 481–505, 500.
151. Charles Villa-Vicencio, 'Why Perpetrators Should Not Always Be Prosecuted: Where the International Criminal Court and Truth Commissions Meet' (2000) 49 *Emory Law Journal* 205–222, 222.
152. Allan, 'Prosecution and Peace: A Role for Amnesty before the ICC?' (n 130), 250.

from prosecution in a trial, but because it shields them from the criminal consequences of guilt, namely, punishment.'[153]

What the preceding discussion has shown is that the issue of amnesty cannot completely be resolved on the reading of the provisions of the Rome Statute without some reservations. But, at least it gives a rough idea of what the ICC can do whenever a state party like Nigeria grants amnesty. It can safely be inferred that amnesty of the South African type which is granted in good faith and which does not completely foreclose any form of accountability may be taken cognisance of by the ICC. Arguably, such amnesty may tend to exhibit the following features, namely (1) the amnesty must be inevitable to peace and reconciliation,[154] (2) the amnesty must go *pari passu* with other accountability measures like truth commissions, (3) the amnesty must be a product of negotiated peace deal midwifed by international entities like the United Nations or it may be a product of peace negotiated between an outgoing government and an incoming one, (4) the amnesty will apply only to those that are least culpable[155] and (5) the amnesty would only cover the ring leaders in the most stringent circumstances.[156] Therefore, if Nigeria grants amnesty that exhibits the preceding features, the ICC may not intervene.

At this point article 10 of the Rome Statute becomes relevant. Article 10 stipulates that 'nothing in this Part shall be interpreted as limiting or prejudicing in any way existing or developing rules of international law for purposes other than this Statute.' Article 10 refers to part II of the Rome Statute in this provision. Article 17 which stipulates the grounds for ICC intervention is also under part II of the Rome Statute. By necessary implication, if the developing rules of international law for other purposes like the principle of 'prosecute or extradite' or the exercise of universal jurisdiction foreclose granting amnesty with respect to international crimes, nothing in part II, including article 17 shall be interpreted to prejudice these developing rules. Therefore, since article 53 can only be read in conjunction with article 17, it follows that article 17 cannot be read to prejudice developing rules of international law prohibiting granting amnesty to international crimes while it is being read in conjunction with article 53. The implication is that any broader concept of justice under article 53 is technically limited under article 17 to the extent determined by the developing rules of international law. Therefore, if the developing rules of international law crystalise into prohibiting

153. Ibid., 256.

154. *The Azanian Peoples Organization (AZAPO) v The President of the Republic of South Africa*, Case CCT 17/96, 1996 para 19. Judge Mahomed held that 'but for a mechanism for amnesty, the 'historic bridge' [transition from apartheid to a democratic rule] itself might never have been erected'.

155. Yasmin Naqvi, 'Amnesty for War Crimes: Defining the Limits of International Recognition' (2003) 85 *IRRC* 583, 617.

156. Robinson, 'Serving the Interests of Justice: Amnesties, Truth Commissions and the International Criminal Court' (n 150), 495–498.

international crimes, the implication is that any grant of amnesty by Nigeria will not be countenanced by the ICC.

Pardon/Prerogative of Mercy

The power of a constituted authority to pardon any person for any crime committed is as old as human civilisation. Nearly every state in the world empowers its organ(s) to grant a pardon.[157] The issue of pardon was raised in the deliberations of the Preparatory Committee in 1997, but it was not seriously considered.[158] Similarly, during the Rome Conference, any meaningful discussion of the issue was resisted because it was considered to interfere with the 'national decision making process.'[159] It has been argued that within the provision of article 20(3) 'the Court [ICC] would seem to be permanently barred from intervening.'[160] Article 20(3) stipulates that ICC will intervene if a domestic proceeding was to shield the person concerned from criminal responsibility or was calculated not to bring the person concerned to justice. However, it has been suggested that granting amnesty shortly after trial may make manifest an intention not to prosecute genuinely all along.[161] Amnesty in this context means pardon. But this argument will break down if a new administration granted the pardon.[162]

While the provision of article 20(3) may be debatable with respect to pardon, nonetheless pardon may be subsumed under article 17(2)(a) as it provides that the ICC may intervene when 'national decision was made for the purpose of shielding the person concerned from criminal responsibility.' A pardon arguably constitutes a national decision. Interestingly, delegations at the Rome Conference, too, recognised pardon as 'national decision making process.' This argument appears to accord with the position of the OTP that 'granting of amnesties, pardons, enforcement of sentences, parole regimes'[163] may be considered a relevant factor to determine unwillingness and inability.

157. Leslie Sebba, 'The Pardoning Power-a World Survey' (1977) 68 *Journal of Criminal Law & Criminology* 83.
158. Mohamed M. El Zeidy, *The Principle of Complementarity in International Criminal Law: Origin, Development and Practice* (Martinus Nijhoff Publishers 2008), 296.
159. Summary Record of the 11th Meeting, 22 June 1998, UN Doc A/CONF 183/C 1/SR 11, para 33.
160. William A. Schabas, *An Introduction to the International Criminal Court* (3rd edn, Cambridge University Press 2007), 192.
161. John T. Holmes, 'The Principle of Complementarity' in Roy S. Lee (ed), *The International Criminal Court: The Making of the Rome Statutes, Issues, Negotiations, Results* (Kluwer Law International 1999), 41, 77.
162. Paul Seils, *Handbook on Complementarity: An Introduction to the Role of National Courts and the ICC in Prosecuting International Crimes* (International Center for Transitional Justice 2016), 64–66.
163. Office of the Prosecutor (OTP), Informal Expert Paper: The Principle of Complementarity in Practice ICC-01/04–01/07–1008- Annexe 4, 28.

However, while pardon may be considered a national decision, it is questionable under what circumstances it would be considered to amount to shielding. Because a pardon is often granted after conviction, it can be argued that a pronouncement on guilt has already established criminal responsibility and that a pardon so granted may not be the basis for ICC intervention. In other words, a pardon after conviction may be considered consistent with complementarity. But this raises the question of whether there can be criminal responsibility without punishment. If the goal of criminal trial is to punish, the pronouncement of guilt is a sequel to that goal. By granting a pardon after conviction, that goal has been somewhat truncated. Therefore, it can be argued that there cannot be criminal responsibility without punishment once guilt has been established. As previously indicated, the idea of shielding is traceable to the trial of German criminals who were given ridiculously low punishment. This reinforces the argument that establishment of guilt without punishment amounts to shielding from criminal responsibility.

In *Motion submitted by the defense of Santiago Omar Riveros* the Argentine Supreme Court held that 'pardons granted to convicted individuals . . . constitute a breach of the State's duty to apply punishments in keeping with the nature of such crimes.'[164] While pardon is often granted after conviction, 'in exceptional cases, pardons have also been granted before the conclusion of a criminal proceeding, meaning before a final and non-appealable judgment has been issued.'[165] In this instance, a case of national decision calculated to shield is clearly made. In *Motion submitted by the defense of Santiago Omar Riveros* the Argentine Supreme Court also held that 'any pardon granted to defendants implicated in the commission of crimes against humanity would constitute a breach of the State's international obligation to investigate and determine responsibilities and punishment.'[166]

With respect to pardon in Nigeria, section 175 of the Nigerian Constitution 1999 provides as follows:

(1) The President may—

- (a) grant any person concerned with or convicted of any offence created by an Act of the National Assembly a pardon, either free or subject to lawful conditions;
- (b) grant to any person a respite, either for an indefinite or for a specified period, of the execution of any punishment imposed on that person for such an offence;

164. *Motion submitted by the defense of Santiago Omar Riveros*—Mazzeo, Julio Lilo y otros s/ rec. De casación e inconstitucionalidad, Expediente M. 2333. XLII, Corte Suprema de Justicia de la Nación, 13 de julio de 2007 cited in Due Process of Law Foundation, *Digest of Latin American Jurisprudence on International Crimes* (n 3), 292.

165. Due Process of Law Foundation, *Digest of Latin American Jurisprudence on International Crimes* (n 3), 289.

166. *Motion submitted by the defense of Santiago Omar Riveros* (n 164)

(c) substitute a less severe form of punishment for any punishment imposed on that person for such an offence; or
(d) remit the whole or any part of any punishment imposed on that person for such an offence or of any penalty or forfeiture otherwise due to the State on account of such an offence.

(2) The powers of the President under subsection (1) of this section shall be exercised by him after consultation with the Council of State.
(3) The President, acting in accordance with the advice of the Council of State, may exercise his powers under subsection (1) of this section in relation to persons concerned with offences against the army, naval or air-force law or convicted or sentenced by a court-martial.

The Council of State is made up of the president as the chairman, the vice-president as the deputy chairman, all former presidents of the federation and all former heads of the government of the federation, all former chief justices of Nigeria, the president of the Senate, the Speaker of the House of Representatives, all the governors of the states of the federation and the attorney-general of the federation.[167] While section 175 of the Nigerian Constitution 1999 regulates exercise of the power of pardon by the president,[168] section 212 regulates exercise of the power of pardon by state governors within the Nigerian Federation. Section 212 is in every way identical with section 175. The only difference is that state governors can only pardon any person who violates the law of a state the same way the president can only pardon with respect to the Act of the National Assembly. Also, state governors cannot issue pardon with respect to court martial. This is understandable since court martial is a federal court which belongs to the federal government. While the president can only exercise his or her power on the advice of the Council of State, the governor can only exercise his or her power 'after consultation with such advisory council of the State on prerogative of mercy as may be established by the Law of the State.'[169] Therefore, any analysis of the exercise of prerogative of mercy by the president automatically applies to the governors of the federating states.

By section 175 of the Nigerian Constitution 1999, the president may grant pardon to 'any person concerned with or convicted of' any of the offences recognised under the Rome Statute. The clause 'any person concerned with or convicted of' contemplates two classes of persons by the use of the disjunctive *or*. The first class is a 'person concerned with' an offence who has not been convicted while the second is a convicted person. While convicted persons are those who are often pardoned, the clause can accommodate such 'exceptional cases, [where] pardons have . . . been granted before the conclusion of

167. Nigerian Constitution 1999, Third Schedule Part 1 para B s 5.
168. See also Administration of Criminal Justice Act 2015, ss 409–411.
169. Nigerian Constitution 1999, s 212(2).

a criminal proceeding, meaning before a final and non-appealable judgment has been issued.' As previously stated, this is clearly a case of shielding from criminal responsibility since a person whose guilt cannot be established, cannot be said to be criminally responsible. Where pardon is granted after conviction, shielding will be inferred if the punishment received by the convict is proportionally low in relation to the crime committed.

Where pardon is 'subject to lawful conditions,' shielding from criminal responsibility can only be inferred depending on the circumstances of each case. Where the lawful condition is that the person concerned should freely confess his or her guilt and pay adequate compensation, this may somehow dovetail into amnesty of the South African type except that it is not with respect to a class of people but a single individual. Obviously, the tenor of the constitutional provision empowers the president to issue amnesty after all if the president can grant pardon with respect to an individual; nothing should preclude him or her from granting it with respect to several persons collectively either with laid-down criteria or not because the provision does not indicate the manner of exercising the power.

Where the president grants respite to a convict indefinitely when a sentence is to be executed with respect to the convict, it can also be argued that the convict has been shielded from criminal responsibility if it is accepted that there cannot be criminal responsibility without punishment. Where the respite granted is for a specified period, shielding from criminal responsibility may be inferred depending on the circumstances of each case. For example, if respite is granted for a specified period because of the ill health of the convict for making the convict recover, this may not amount to shielding from criminal responsibility.

Where the president substitutes a less severe punishment with the punishment imposed on the convict, it may indicate shielding depending on the circumstances of each case. For example when a death sentence is commuted to life imprisonment, this may not necessarily imply shielding. Life imprisonment is also a grave punishment. On the other hand, when a genocide convict sentenced to death has his or her sentence commuted to six months, this may amount to shielding reflective of the German shoddy trial and punishment after the Second World War. Similarly, when the whole of the sentence is remitted this may readily indicate shielding.

It can be questioned whether the president can pardon himself or herself. Since the president enjoys immunity he or she cannot be prosecuted while in office. But nothing precludes a president who is complicit in any of the crimes recognised under the Rome Statute from pardoning himself or herself once his or her tenure in office is about to expire.[170] Reference to 'any person' in section 175 arguably includes all natural and juristic persons. Because

170. On the possibility of self-pardon under the American Constitution, see Brian C. Kalt, 'Pardon Me? The Constitutional Case against Presidential Self-Pardons' 106 *The Yale Law Journal* 779.

the president is a natural person, he is included as well. While prerogative of mercy cannot be exercised with respect to impeachment proceedings in both England and the United States, it appears that it can be exercised with respect to impeachment proceedings in Nigeria. This is because the Nigerian Constitution is silent on it, unlike the United States, where it is clearly stated in the Constitution,[171] and England, where it is clearly stated in the Act of Settlement 1700.[172] Therefore, if pardon obliterates criminal blameworthiness as declared by the Supreme Court of Nigeria in *Falae v Obasanjo (No 2)*,[173] it follows that the president can pardon himself or herself before the commencement of removal proceedings and renders nugatory the basis on which removal could be justified. The situation makes it practically impossible to hold the president criminally responsible for any of the crimes recognised under the Rome Statute.

With respect to the Council of State, it can be argued that while the president is obliged to consult with them, he or she is not bound by their advice. However, where the president seeks to exercise the prerogative of mercy in 'relation to persons concerned with offences against the army, naval or airforce law or convicted or sentenced by a court martial,' he or she is bound by the advice of the Council of State since he or she can only exercise the power by 'acting in accordance with the advice of the Council of State.' All the preceding analysis applies to governors in their respective states except to the extent related to court martial and the people subject to service law.

So far, the preceding analysis considers section 175 of the Nigerian Constitution alone without more, and the tenor of the provision suggests an absolute power. But is the power truly absolute within the context of Nigeria's constitutional scheme? Is this approach not unduly simplistic by overlooking other provisions of the Nigerian Constitution? In *Gopalan v State of Madras*,[174] the Indian Supreme Court held that 'the Constitution is a logical whole, each provision of which is an integral part thereof, and it is, therefore, logically proper and, indeed, imperative to construe one part in the light of the provisions of the other parts.'[175] Therefore, if section 175 on the prerogative of mercy is considered in the light of other provisions of the Nigerian Constitution, a broader picture of the legal situation may be yielded.

Initially, the United States was concerned only with the clause granting the president the power of pardon. The provision was a codification of the royal prerogative in England. Thus, in *United States v Wilson*,[176] Marshall stated

171. Article 2, Section 2, Clause 1 of the United States Constitution provides that the President 'shall have power to grant Reprieves and Pardons for Offences against the United States, except in Cases of Impeachment'.
172. The Act stipulates that 'no pardon under the great seal of England [shall] be pleadable to an impeachment by the commons in parliament': 12 & 13 Will. 3, c. 2 (1700).
173. [1999] 4 NWLR (Pt 599) 476.
174. (1950) SCR 88.
175. Ibid para 109.
176. 32 US (7 Pet) 150 (1833).

that 'a pardon is an act of grace, proceeding from the power entrusted with the execution of the laws . . .'[177] However, the power of pardon was later placed within the ambit of the US Constitution. In *Biddle v Perovich*,[178] Oliver Wendell Holmes stated that

> we will not go into history, but we will say a word about the principles of pardons in the law of the United States. A pardon in our days is not a private act of grace from an individual happening to possess power. It is a part of the Constitutional scheme. When granted it is the determination of the ultimate authority that the public welfare will be better served . . .[179]

The idea of pardon as falling within the constitutional scheme was later reinforced by the US Supreme Court in *Schick v Reed*,[180] where the court held that the limit to the exercise of pardon 'must be found in the Constitution itself'[181] and not singly in the clause specifying the power.

In considering the power of pardon within Nigeria's constitutional scheme, the first provision to consider is section 6 of the Nigerian Constitution. Section 6(6)(a) of the Nigerian Constitution vests the power of judicial review on the judiciary in Nigeria. But, under section 6(6)(c) and (d), issues that are not amenable to judicial review are clearly stipulated. Since the issues that are excluded from judicial review do not include prerogative of mercy, it follows that the prerogative of mercy is subject to judicial review and that its exercise is not as absolute as it tends to appear when sections 175 and 212 are considered solely.

This argument is further reinforced by other provisions of the Constitution where the general power of the judiciary to assume jurisdiction is clearly ousted. Section 143 of the Nigerian Constitution empowers the National Assembly to remove the president. Pursuant to this power, the National Assembly may cause a panel to investigate any allegation made against the president. But section 143(10) specifically stipulates that 'no proceedings or determination of the Panel or of the National Assembly or any matter relating thereto shall be entertained or questioned in any court' and thus ousts the court's jurisdiction.

Similarly, section 215(3) empowers the president to give such lawful directions to the inspector-general of police with respect to securing public safety and public order. But section 215(5) clearly stipulates that the 'question whether any, and if so what, directions have been given under this section shall not be inquired into in any court.' Therefore, since the court has not

177. Ibid., 160.
178. 274 US 480 (1927).
179. Ibid., 486.
180. 419 US 256 (1974).
181. Ibid., 267.

been specifically precluded from reviewing the exercise of pardon, the court can review its exercise having been generally conferred with the power of review.

In *G Krishna Gouda v State of Andrah Pradesh*,[182] the Supreme Court of India held that the power of pardon can be reviewed and stated that 'all power, however majestic the dignitary wielding it, shall be exercised in good faith, with intelligent and informed care and honesty for the public weal.'[183] Similarly, in *Kehar Singh v Union of India*,[184] the Supreme Court of India held that 'it appears to us clear that the question as to the area of President's power under Article 72, falls squarely within the judicial domain and can be examined by the court by way of judicial review.'[185] In *Swaran Singh v State of Uttar Pradesh*,[186] the Supreme Court of India considered article 161 of the Indian constitution where governors are empowered to exercise the power of pardon. The court held that 'if such power was exercised arbitrarily, mala fide or in absolute disregard of the finer canons of the constitutionalism, the byproduct order cannot get the approval of law and in such cases, the judicial hand must be stretched to it.'[187] Having established that the exercise of the power of pardon can be reviewed when placed within constitutional scheme, it is only legally congruent that what will inform the court in reviewing the exercise of the power must be found in the constitution. This brings to the fore the fundamental rights provisions of the Nigerian Constitution. Thus, where any of the provisions on fundamental rights are violated in the exercise of prerogative of mercy, it can be argued that such exercise is unconstitutional.[188] Since commission of crimes recognised under the Rome Statute also amounts to gross violation of human rights under the fundamental rights provisions of the Nigerian Constitution, any actions by the president including the grant of pardon that tend to sustain such gross violation may be said to be unconstitutional. This argument appears to find support in section 1 of the Nigerian Constitution which provides that 'this Constitution is supreme and its provisions shall have binding force on all authorities and persons throughout the Federal Republic of Nigeria.' Therefore, the action of the president must conform to the fundamental rights provisions being part of the Constitution.

Fundamental rights which are more likely to be an issue are right to life, right not to be subjected to cruel, inhuman and degrading treatment and

182. *G Krishna Goud and J Bhoomaiah v State of Andhra Pradesh and Others*, Petition for Special Leave to Appeal (Crl) No 840 of 1975 decided by VR Krishna Iyer and AC Gupta JJ of the Supreme Court of India on 3 October 1975.
183. Ibid para 7.
184. 1989 AIR 653; 1989 (1) SCC 204.
185. Ibid.
186. (1998) 4 SCC 75.
187. Ibid.
188. Parul Kumar, 'The Executive Power to Pardon: Dilemmas of the Constitutional Discourse' (2009) 2 *NUJS Law Review* 9–30, 24.

right to privacy. When a victim of crimes recognised under the Rome Statute has lost his or her life, it is the relative of the victim who is in a position to obtain justice for the victim. Therefore, where pardon is granted before prosecution, Nigeria would have violated its obligation to investigate to secure accountability. In *Salman v Turkey*,[189] the ECtHR held that the duty to investigate the cause of death to secure accountability is incumbent on states. This is what has been characterised 'not an obligation of result, but of means,'[190] that is a procedural obligation as distinct from a substantive obligation. To the extent that a pardon tampers with the judicial process which is a procedural means of securing accountability, it can be regarded as failure of obligation of means.

When a pardon is issued after a conviction or a sentence, it can also be argued that the obligation of means has been violated. Although in some instances, the ECtHR has stated that when death occurred unintentionally, an effective remedy does not necessarily involve punishment and that compensation may be adequate.[191] But, the corollary of this dictum is that where death is intentional, then criminal remedy is the only adequate means. In fact, in *Budayeva and Others v Russia*,[192] the ECtHR held that when it comes to dangerous activities, failure to proceed criminally against those responsible for the deaths of others violates the obligation of means and that a compensatory procedure will not be adequate. Therefore, to the extent that the exercise of the prerogative of mercy forecloses adequate punishment, a breach of the obligation of means has occurred.

The logic applied with respect to the right to life can also be applied with respect to the right not to be subjected to cruel, inhuman and degrading treatment. Therefore, a pardon granted before prosecution makes accountability unachievable and constitutes a violation of obligation of means.[193] With respect to pardon after conviction, the ECtHR in *Aksoy v Turkey*[194] held that effective remedy is not only limited to compensation; it also includes investigation and prosecution of those responsible. Therefore, when a pardon leads to inadequate punishment or no punishment, it can be argued that there is no effective remedy.

189. App no 21986/93, (ECtHR, 27 June 2000).
190. *Makaratzis v Greece* App no 50385/99 (ECtHR, 20 December 2004) paras 73–74.
191. *Šilih v Slovenia* App no 71463/01, (ECtHR, 9 April 2009); *Branco Tomašić and Others v Croatia* App no 46598/06, (ECtHR, 15 January 2000).
192. App nos 15339/02; 21166/02; 20058/02; 11673/02; 15343/02 (ECtHR, 20 March 2008) paras 139–163.
193. See *Khashiyev and Akayeva v Russia* App nos 57942/00; 57945/00 (ECtHR, 24 February 2005); *Martinez Sala and Others v Spain* App no 58438/00, (ECtHR, 2 November 2004); *Kmetty v Hungary* App no 57967/00 (ECtHR, 16 December 2003); *Poltoratskiy v Ukraine* App no 38812/97, (ECtHR, 29 April 2003); *Veznedaroglu v Turkey* App no 32357/96, (ECtHR, 11 April 2000); *Assenov v Bulgaria* App no 24760/94 (ECtHR, 28 October 1998); *Aydin v Turkey* App no 23178/94 (ECtHR, 25 September 1997).
194. App no 21987/93 (ECtHR, 18 December 1996).

Another perspective to the issue of subjecting the exercise of prerogative to test is that where the exercise of the power will lead to a violation of Nigeria's obligation under a treaty, such exercise should be declared unconstitutional. In section 19 of the Nigerian Constitution 1999, it is stated that foreign policy objectives shall be 'respect for international law and treaty obligations.' Section 19 is under Fundamental Objectives and Directive Principles of State Policy and it is not on its own justiciable. But, in *INEC v Balarabe Musa*,[195] the Supreme Court of Nigeria gave effect to section 14 under Fundamental Objectives when read in conjunction with section 222 of the Constitution which is justiciable. This implies that any part of the Fundamental Objectives can be made effective when read in conjunction with other justiciable part of the Constitution. Therefore, reading section 19 which is non-justiciable with section 175 on pardon which is justiciable can make section 19 becomes justiciable. The implication is that exercise of prerogative of mercy can be subjected to the test of whether it will violate Nigeria's treaty obligation. In this respect, it can be tested against whether it will violate Nigeria's obligation under the Rome Statute.

Within the ambit of this logic, fundamental rights issues earlier discussed are still relevant to the extent that they constitute treaty obligations for Nigeria. Nigeria has ratified the International Covenant on Civil and Political Rights (ICCPR), International Covenant on Economic, Social and Cultural Rights (ICESCR), Convention against Torture and other Cruel, Inhuman and Degrading Treatment and African Charter on Human and Peoples' Rights. But it is arguable that ICCPR and ICESCR are yet to be domesticated in Nigeria and that the president's action should not be tested against non-domesticated treaties which do not have an effect in Nigeria in line with the doctrine of dualism. This argument will appear to be misplaced within the tenor of section 19 and the doctrine of dualism itself. Section 19 considers respect for treaty obligation as a foreign policy objective. It is therefore binding on the executive, headed by the president, which is saddled with the responsibility of formulating foreign policy. Also, while dualism does not make a non-domesticated treaty effective in Nigeria by way of legislation, it requires that steps towards its violation should not be taken unless expressly declared by the lawmaking organ.[196]

Even if the argument on dualism can be sustained with respect to ICCPR and ICESCR since they are yet to be domesticated, it cannot be sustained with respect to African Charter on Human and Peoples' Rights which has already been domesticated.[197] It can also not be sustained with respect to the European Convention for the Protection of Human Rights and Fundamental

195. [2003] NWLR (Pt 806) 72.
196. *Higgs v Ministry of National Security* The Times of 23 December 1999; *Salomon v Commissioners of Customs and Excise* [1967] 2 QB 116, 143.
197. African Charter on Human and Peoples' Rights (Ratification and Enforcement) Act Cap A9 Revised LFN 2004.

Freedoms. As previously stated, Nigeria is already a party to the convention to ensure continuity of obligations and rights at the international plane and that this convention is part of Nigerian law by virtue of the decision of the Supreme Court of Nigeria in *JSF Inv Ltd v Brawal Line Ltd.*[198] Therefore, it can be argued that the president is precluded to exercise a prerogative of mercy in violation of Nigeria's treaty obligation under the European Convention at least as it was in 1950.

While it can be argued that it was never within the contemplation of the drafters of the Nigerian Constitution that the exercise of the prerogative of mercy should be so subjected to judicial review, it is apposite to recall the dictum of Justice Stone of the US Supreme Court in *US v Classic*[199] where he held that

> in determining whether a provision of the Constitution applies to a new subject matter, it is of little significance that it is one with which the framers were not familiar. For in setting up an enduring framework of government, they undertook to carry out for the indefinite future and in all vicissitudes of the changing affairs of men, those fundamental purposes for which the instrument itself discloses. Hence, we read the words not as we read legislative codes-but as the revelation of the great purposes which were intended to be achieved by the Constitution as a continuing instrument of government.

It is most difficult to see the great purposes derivable from an unreviewable exercise of the prerogative of mercy in a democratic state like Nigeria. In fact, reviewing the prerogative of mercy is more in line with those great purposes.

The implication of the preceding analysis for the principle of complementarity is that if the provisions on pardon are considered solely, they are contrary to the spirit of prosecuting international crimes as required by the principle of complementarity. On the other hand, if the constitutional provisions on pardon are placed within the constitutional scheme, a pardon cannot be granted with respect to crimes recognised under the Rome Statute which is in tandem with the spirit of prosecuting crimes recognised under the Rome Statute as required by the principle of complementarity.

Having considered immunity in its executive, parliamentary and sovereign expressions; amnesties and pardon/prerogative of mercy; plea bargain; *ne bis in idem* principle; the principle of legality; the statute of limitation; and the power of the attorney-general to amend the law of evidence is considered in the next chapter as earlier intimated.

198. (2010) 18 NWLR (Pt 1225) 495.
199. (1941) 313 US 299.

6 Unwillingness

Shielding From Criminal Responsibility II

Plea Bargain

A plea bargain is 'a negotiated agreement between a prosecutor and a criminal defendant whereby the defendant pleads guilty to a lesser offense or to one of multiple charges in exchange for some concession by the prosecutor, usu. a more lenient sentence or a dismissal of the other charges.'[1] Plea bargains can be divided into two, namely charge bargaining and sentence bargaining.[2] In charge bargaining, 'a prosecutor agrees to drop some of the counts or reduce the charge to a less serious offense in exchange for a plea of either guilty or no contest from the defendant'[3] while in a sentence bargaining 'a prosecutor agrees to recommend a lighter sentence in exchange for a plea of either guilty or no contest from the defendant.'[4]

With respect to a guilty plea before the International Criminal Court (ICC), the consequence arising out of it was much debated. In states with the common law tradition, a confession of guilt puts an end to the trial whereas a guilty plea in states with the Civil Law tradition does not put an end to the trial. Thus, the two terms *confession* and *guilty plea* were altogether avoided in the Rome Statute.[5] Nonetheless, plea bargain can be subsumed within the provisions of article 65 of the Rome Statute which recognises 'admission of guilt.' Article 65 of the Rome Statute arguably takes after rules 62 bis and 62 ter of the International Criminal Tribunal for Yugoslavia (ICTY) Rules of Procedure and Evidence (RPE). Article 65(1) of the Rome Statute is in tandem with rule 62 bis of the ICTY RPE when it stipulates that an admission of guilt is valid only when 'the accused understands the nature and consequences of the admission of guilt; the admission is voluntarily made by the accused after sufficient consultation with defence counsel; and the admission

1. Bryan A. Garner and others, *Black's Law Dictionary* (9th edn, Thomson Reuters, 2009), 1269.
2. Ibid., 1270.
3. Ibid.
4. Ibid.
5. Regina E. Rauxloh, 'Plea Bargaining in International Criminal Justice: Can the International Criminal Court Afford to Avoid Trial?' (2011) 1(2) *The Journal of Criminal Justice Research* 1, 18–19.

of guilt is supported by the facts of the case' while article 65(5) of the Rome Statute accords with rule 62 ter of the ICTY RPE by stipulating that 'any discussions between the Prosecutor and the defence regarding modification of the charges, the admission of guilt or the penalty to be imposed shall not be binding on the Court.'

In Nigeria, plea bargain is of recent origin. The Administration of Criminal Justice Law of Lagos State 2011 first provides for its practice followed by the Administration of Criminal Justice Act 2015. Section 75 of the Administration of Criminal Justice Law 2011 stipulates that

> notwithstanding anything in this law or in any other law, the Attorney General of the State shall have power to consider and accept plea bargain from a person charged with any offence where the Attorney General is of the view that the acceptance of such plea bargain is in the public interest, the interest of justice and the need to prevent abuse of legal process.

Section 76(1) of the law adds that

> the prosecutor and a defendant or his legal practitioner may before the plea to the charge, enter into an agreement in respect of: (a) a plea of guilty by the defendant to the offence charged or a lesser offence of which he must be convicted on the charge and (b) an appropriate sentence to be imposed by the court if the defendant is convicted of the offence to which he intends to plead guilty.

This provision contemplates plea and charge bargaining.

Under the Administration of Criminal Justice Act 2015, the prosecutor may receive and consider a plea bargain from a defendant or on his behalf or may offer a plea bargain to a defendant.[6] A plea bargain may be undertaken by the prosecutor and the defendant before trial commences, and an agreement may be reached 'which may include the sentence recommended within the appropriate range of punishment stipulated for the offence or a plea of guilty by the defendant to the offence charged or a lesser offence of which he may be convicted on the charge' and 'an appropriate sentence to be imposed by the court where the defendant is convicted of the offence to which he intends to plead guilty.'[7] This provision also contemplates plea and charge bargaining. A plea bargain may also take place in the course of the trial. Thus, the prosecution 'may' enter into plea bargain with the defendant with the consent of the victim or his representative during or after the presentation of the evidence of prosecution but before the presentation of the evidence of the defence,[8] provided that the prosecution could not prove the offence

6. Section 270(1).
7. Section 270(4)
8. Section 270(2).

charged beyond reasonable doubt,[9] the defendant has agreed to return the proceeds of the crime or make restitution to the victim or his representative[10] or the defendant in a case of conspiracy has fully cooperated with the investigation and prosecution of the crime by providing relevant information for the successful prosecution of other offenders.[11] When the prosecutor is of the view that the offer or acceptance of a plea bargain is 'in the interest of justice, the public interest, public policy and the need to prevent abuse of legal process,' the prosecutor may offer or accept such plea bargain.[12] In offering or accepting such plea bargain, the prosecutor 'may' consult with the police officer who investigated the case and the victim or his representative[13] and pay due regard to the nature and the circumstances relating to the offence, the defendant and public interest.[14]

In determining what constitutes public interest, the prosecutor 'shall weigh all relevant factors, including' the defendant's willingness to cooperate in the investigation and prosecution of others, the defendant's history with respect to criminal activity, the defendant's remorse or contrition and his or her willingness to assume responsibility for his or her conduct, the desirability of prompt and certain disposition of the case, the likelihood of obtaining a conviction at trial and the probable effect on witnesses, the probable sentence or other consequences if the defendant is convicted, the need to avoid delay in the disposition of other pending cases, the expense of trial and appeal and the defendant's willingness to make restitution or pay compensation to the victim where appropriate.[15] The prosecution 'shall afford the victim or his representative the opportunity to make representations to the prosecutor' with respect to the content of the agreement and the inclusion in the agreement of a compensation and restitution order.[16] The presiding judge before whom the case is being prosecuted shall not participate in the plea bargain process.[17] When the presiding judge is satisfied that the sentence agreed on is appropriate, the judge 'shall' impose that sentence, but when the judge is of the view that a lesser sentence is appropriate, the judge 'shall' impose the lesser sentence. When the judge is, however, of the view that a heavier sentence should be imposed, the judge 'shall' inform the defendant accordingly.[18] Once the defendant is informed, the defendant may abide by his plea and agree to present an argument relevant to sentencing or withdraw from his or her plea agreement, in which case the trial begins afresh.[19]

9. Section 270(2)(a).
10. Section 270(2)(b).
11. Section 270(2)(c).
12. Section 270(3).
13. Section 270(5)(a).
14. Section 270(5)(b).
15. Section 270(5)(i)–(ix).
16. Section 270(6).
17. Section 270(8).
18. Section 270(11)(a)–(c).
19. Section 270(15).

Where the trial begins afresh, a new judge shall preside, no reference shall be made to the agreement and any admission contained therein is inadmissible and the prosecutor and defendant 'may' not enter into a 'similar plea and sentence agreement.'[20] Once a judgement is delivered based on a plea bargain, such a judgement is final and cannot be appealed except when fraud is alleged.[21]

The implication of a plea bargain for the implementation of the principle of complementarity is not difficult to decipher if one considers charge bargaining in the light of the decision of the Pre-Trial Chamber I (PTC I) in *Prosecutor v Thomas Lubanga Dyilo*[22] and sentence bargaining in the light of the historical evolution of the notion of shielding. With respect to charge bargaining in the light of the decision of the PTC I in *Prosecutor v Thomas Lubanga Dyilo*,[23] it would be recalled that the defendant was already in custody in the Democratic Republic of the Congo (DRC), having been charged with crimes recognised under the Rome Statute. However, the ICC took over the case from DRC because the DRC did not charge the defendant with the crime of enlisting and conscripting children younger than the age of 15 with which the defendant was charged by the ICC. The implication is that if the prosecutor agrees to drop some of the counts or reduce the charge to a less serious offence in exchange for a plea of guilt from the defendant, the ICC can still prosecute the defendant for those charges which were dropped or for those more serious offences for which the defendant could have been prosecuted.

It can, however, be argued that this may not necessarily be the case. This is because international crimes are broadly defined and are often overlap. For example persecution as a crime against humanity may also be committed in furtherance of genocide. It is because of this that the practice of charging suspects of international crimes with cumulative and alternative charges has been found acceptable. Thus, if genocide is dropped as a charge, persecution as a crime against humanity may still be sufficient and the ICC does not necessarily have to intervene when a plea agreement is that one of those crimes should be dropped in exchange for a guilty plea.

The problem with this argument is that if a given set of facts discloses a set of crimes, to charge one among all the crimes on the basis that the one with which the defendant is charged has the same factual basis with others with which the defendant is not charged does not remove the fact that the defendant committed multiple crimes and that he or she could still have been charged with these other crimes. In the example given earlier, to charge the defendant with crimes against humanity does not mean that the defendant could still not be charged with genocide, nor can it be seriously maintained

20. Section 270(16).
21. Section 270(18).
22. *Prosecutor v Thomas Lubanga Dyilo, Decision on the Prosecutor's Application for a Warrant of Arrest* ICC-01/04–01/06–8-Corr, Pre-Trial Chamber 1, 10 February 2006.
23. Ibid.

that crimes against humanity are the same as genocide. As a matter of fact, genocide is considered graver than crimes against humanity. Anna Petrig notes that

> even in cases where the factual basis underlying the conduct charged is not reduced by a plea agreement, the importance of the legal qualification of this conduct should not be underestimated. Not only might the stigma attached to genocide (the crime of crimes) be greater compared to a conviction for war crimes or crimes against humanity, but dropping the genocide charge might also erroneously be perceived as an admission by the Prosecutor that this crime did not take place and, hence, ultimately, facilitate denial.[24]

In a sentence bargaining, the prosecutor can agree to recommend a lighter sentence. This may not necessarily justify the intervention of the ICC until the sentence so recommended is passed by the court. It would be recalled that the genesis of shielding from criminal responsibility started with the ridiculously low sentences handed down to German convicts of war crimes during World War I at Leipzig, Germany. In addition, it can be argued that an extremely low sentence may somewhat justify the intervention of the ICC. Articles 81(2)(a) and 83(3) of the Rome Statute stipulate that disproportionate sentence may be a ground of appeal before the Appellate Chamber of the ICC. This indicates that the Rome Statute leans towards the idea that punishment must reflect the egregious nature of the crime recognised under the statute.

It can, however, be argued that if the Rome Statute permits plea bargain; any practice of plea bargain in Nigeria that satisfies a need for accountability at a minimum acceptable international standard would not have occasioned the ICC intervention. The problem with this argument is that what constitutes minimum acceptable standard which will satisfy the Rome Statute may be difficult to ascertain. Although articles 65(1) and 65(5) are identical in content with rules 62 bis and 62 ter of the ICTY RPE, nonetheless the context surrounding the provisions are different. The reason is that the practice of plea bargain by the ICTY and the ICTR is better understood within the context of completion strategy. As a matter of fact, while the ICTY formally accepted plea bargaining, it was not completely free of doubt whether plea bargaining was in line with its mandate by declaring that efficiency alone cannot be sufficient to justify plea bargain.[25]

24. Anna Petrig, 'Negotiated Justice and the Goals of International Criminal Tribunals With a Focus on the Plea-Bargaining Practice of the ICTY and the Legal Framework of the ICC' (2008) 8 *Chicago-Kent Journal of International & Comparative Law* 1, 15–16.
25. *Prosecutor v Momir Nikolić* Sentencing Judgement, Case No IT-02–60/1-S (December 2, 2003) para 67.

It is also pertinent to consider Article 78 of the Rome Statute and rule 145 ICC RPE. Both stipulate that an admission of guilt is not a mitigating factor to be considered in sentencing. The provisions discountenance the conduct of the defendant after the commission of the offence in sentencing. In addition, articles 15(3), 19(3), 53(1)(c), 54(1)(b), 65(4)(a) and 75(1) of the Rome Statute stipulate that victims are to be considered in all stages. When these articles are read in conjunction with articles 65(1) and 65(5), plea bargaining in the ICTY and the ICTR does not offer a strong precedent for the ICC, and what constitutes a minimum international standard permissible within the ambit of the Rome Statute remains cloudy. This point is further underscored by article 65(4), which is also a provision on 'admission of guilt' that the prosecutor may be required to present additional evidence including testimony of witnesses or the trial may be ordered to continue under ordinary procedure if the trial chamber 'is of the opinion that a more complete presentation of the facts of the case is required in the interests of justice, in particular the interests of the victims.'

Another dimension to this issue is to consider the constitutionality of plea bargain itself. The purport of this is that if plea bargaining is constitutional, it may negate the spirit of complementarity where the ICC finds it unacceptable. On the other hand, if plea bargaining is unconstitutional, complementarity is fostered since Nigeria, as a state party to the Rome Statute, must have to subject every commission of the crimes recognised under the Rome Statute to full trial in its domain. The relevant provisions to examine the constitutionality of plea bargain are section 33(1) which provides for right to life, section 34(1)(a) which provides for right to dignity of human person, section 37 which provides for right to privacy and section 36(5) which provides for right to presumption of innocence. All these rights are denied a victim when crimes within the Rome Statute are committed except the right to presumption of innocence which is only available to a defendant being charged with any of the crimes recognised under the Rome Statute.

With respect to charge bargaining, it can be argued that the rights of victims are violated where a defendant was not charged with the crimes he or she ought to be ordinarily charged. This is because a person cannot be punished for a crime for which he or she is not charged. Since the duty of the state to protect these rights also include the duty to punish their infractions, it follows that the duty has not been performed with respect to crimes for which the defendant was not charged. With respect to sentence bargaining, it can be argued that where it leads to a ridiculous sentence discounting, victims' rights are violated. This means that circumstances will determine whether sentence bargaining is constitutional or not. Thus, while charge bargaining is unconstitutional, the constitutionality of sentence bargaining will depend on if it leads to a ridiculous sentence discounting.

It is pertinent to point out that the preceding finding does not necessarily negate the competence of the prosecuting authority in Nigeria to exercise its prosecutorial discretion. What the earlier finding indicates is that any exercise of prosecutorial discretion 'would be based on a good faith assessment of the relevant law, facts, and evidence, and not made for the purpose of shielding the accused from criminal responsibility.'[26] But it is possible that the victims may agree to charge bargaining. Similarly, it is also possible that the victims may agree to a lighter sentence in place of a heavier one. The possibility of a victim to agree to charge or sentence bargaining is rife in the light of extreme poverty on the part of the victim coupled with the ability of the defendant to pay compensation. A ridiculous sentence discounting may be the result when an offer of compensation is part of the deal. This raises the question of whether a person (the victim in this instance) can waive the rights at issue. On the side of the defendant is also whether his or her right to full trial can be waived. The waiver of the defendant's right to presumption of innocence also has the consequence of absolving the state the duty to establish the guilt of the defendant. It is questionable whether the state can be absolved of this duty.

The jurisprudence on whether constitutional rights can be waived is replete with conflicts. In the South African case of *S v Shaba*[27] the court held that the doctrine of waiver as a private law concept cannot be applied to fundamental rights since a person has the option to exercise his or her constitutionally protected right without being punished. In *Basheshar Nath v The Commissioner of Income-Tax, Delhi & Rajasthan*,[28] the Indian Supreme Court held that rights to equality as enshrined in article 14 of the Indian constitution cannot be waived since it is enshrined as a matter of public policy. In *Olga Tellis v Bombay Municipal Corporation*,[29] the court held that litigants can never be estopped from claiming any fundamental right. In *R v Tran*,[30] the Canadian Supreme Court held that 'there will be situations where [a s 14 Charter] right simply cannot, in the greater public interest, be waived.'[31] In *R v Richard*[32] the court held that waiving constitutional rights will depend on 'the manner in which such a waiver may be made, the extent to which such rights can be waived and the effect of a waiver may vary with the nature and scope of the right in question.'[33] In the United States any right whether fundamental or not can be waived, and once it is waived, the person who waived is estopped from claiming it again. In *Peretz v US*[34] it was held that 'the most basic rights of criminal defendants are . . . subject to waiver.'[35]

26. Jimmy Gurule, 'United States Opposition to the 1998 Rome Statute Establishing an International Criminal Court: Is the Court's Jurisdiction Truly Complementary to National Criminal Jurisdictions?' (November 2001–February 2002) 35 *Cornell International Law Journal* 1, 23.
27. *1998* (2) BCLR 220 (T) 221HCI.
28. [1959] Supp 1 SCR 528, 550–553.
29. [1986] 73 AIR 180 (SC) paras 27–30.
30. [1995] 92 CCC (3d) 218.
31. Ibid., 254.
32. [1997] 110 CCC 3d 385.
33. Ibid., 396.
34. 501 US 923 (1991).
35. Ibid., 936.

Nancy Amoury Combs suggests that a plea bargain can be combined with the goal of prosecuting international crimes before international tribunals and that truth and reconciliation process can be combined with the practice of plea bargaining to achieve the goal of prosecuting international crimes before international tribunals.[36] Although this suggestion is within the context of prosecuting international crimes before international tribunals, it can be applied with the prosecution of international crimes domestically. This is because financial constraints and heavy workload in prosecuting international crimes is as much an issue domestically as it is an issue internationally. Thus, it can be argued that subsuming truth and reconciliation process of the South African type within the practice of plea bargain may justify waiver of right within Nigeria's constitutional scheme without necessarily compromising the victims' right to life, right not to be subjected to inhuman and degrading treatment and right to privacy of the relatives of the victim. Therefore, the practice of plea bargain to the extent that it is blended with truth and reconciliation process of the South African type in Nigeria is constitutional and at the same time accords with the principle of complementarity as embedded in the Rome Statute. It can be said to accord with the principle of complementarity as the factual basis of the crime committed will not be distorted with respect to charge bargaining while with respect to sentence bargaining, those who are not entitled to be considered for reprieve will still have to serve their sentences in full thus foreclosing ridiculous sentence discounting.

To the extent that the Administration of Criminal Justice Law 2011 and the Administration of Criminal Justice Act 2015 require the prosecution to consider the public interest (and public policy under the Administration of Criminal Justice Act 2015), the interest of justice and the need to prevent abuse of legal process, the prosecution can in practice subsume the truth and reconciliation process of the South African type within the practice of plea bargain. In a nutshell, a plea bargain will defeat the realisation of the principle of complementarity where its practice as charge bargaining leads to charging the accused with a much less serious crime with the attendant consequence of distorting the factual basis of the crime committed. Similarly, a plea bargain will defeat the realisation of the principle of complementarity when its practice as sentence bargaining leads to a ridiculous sentence discounting.

The *Ne Bis in Idem* Principle

Article 20 of the Rome Statute provides for the *ne bis in idem principle*. As previously stated, the principle means that a person shall not be prosecuted twice for the same offence. The principle is possibly one of universal expression. It has also been referred to as *non bis in idem*, double jeopardy[37]

36. Nancy Armoury Combs, *Guilty Pleas in International Criminal Law: Constructing a Restorative Justice Approach* (Stanford University Press 2007), 9–10 and 136–154.

37. Olaoluwa Olusanya, *Double Jeopardy Without Parameters: Re-Characterisation in Inter-National Criminal Law* (Instersentia 2004), 26.

or *autre fois aquit/convict.*[38] Almost all states with the common law tradition have embodied the principle either in their respective constitutions or in their statutes.[39] About 50 states have the principle in their respective constitutions.[40] The *ne bis in idem* principle is recognised by major international human rights instruments.[41] In the realm of international criminal jurisprudence, the principle first found expression in the Statute of the International Criminal Tribunal for Yugoslavia (ICTY)[42] followed by the Statute of the International Criminal Tribunal for Rwanda (ICTR).[43]

When the Statute of the ICC was being drafted, the International Law Commission provided for the principle in article 42. This article is the precursor to article 20 of the Rome Statute.[44] Article 20 of the Rome Statute states that a person shall not be prosecuted again after having been prosecuted domestically except if the domestic proceedings 'were for the purpose of shielding the person concerned from criminal responsibility for crimes within the jurisdiction of the Court [ICC]; or otherwise were not conducted independently or impartially in accordance with the norms of due process recognised by international law and were conducted in a manner which, in the circumstances, was inconsistent with an intent to bring the person concerned to justice.' This provision seeks to avoid prosecuting a person twice for the same offence, but it does so between domestic courts and the ICC.

As previously stated several states have embodied the principle, but the principle exists in various guises.[45] Thus, it is most difficult to generalise with respect to the scope of the principle,[46] even though the principle essentially seeks to avoid subjecting the same person to trial or punishment 'more than once for the same conduct or crime.'[47] This principle has been justified on at least two grounds. The first one is that the principle

38. Akhil Reed Amar, 'Double Jeopardy Law Made Simple' (1997) 106 *Yale Law Journal* 1807, 1810.
39. K. N. Chandrasekharan Pillai, *Double Jeopardy Protection: A Comparative Overview* (Mittal Publications 1988), 1.
40. M. Cheriff Bassiouni, 'Human Rights in Criminal Justice: Identifying International Protections in National Constitutions' (1993) 3 *Duke Journal of Comparative & International Law* 247, 289.
41. International Covenant on Civil and Political Rights (adopted 16 December 1966, entered into force 23 March 1976) 999 UNTS 171, art 14(7); American Convention on Human Rights (signed 22 November 1969, entered into force 18 July 1978) 1144 UNTS 144, art 8(4) and European Convention for the Protection of Human Rights and Fundamental Freedoms, art 6(1).
42. Article 10.
43. Article 9.
44. Mohamed M. El Zeidy, *The Principle of Complementarity in International Criminal Law: Origin, Development and Practice* (Martinus Nijhoff Publishers 2008), 285.
45. Christine Van den Wyngaert and Guy Stessens, 'The International Non Bis in Idem Principle: Resolving Some of the Unanswered Questions' (1999) 48 *International and Comparative Law Quarterly* 779.
46. Ibid.
47. Christine Van den Wyngaert and Tom Ongena, 'Ne Bis in Idem Principle, Including the Issue of Amnesty' in Antonio Cassese, Paola Gaeta and John R.W.D. Jones (eds), *The Rome*

protects people from the abusive use of state power. The second one is that where people are subjected to trial more than once, conflicting decisions can be arrived at and consequently brings judicial process to disrepute.[48]

The principle of *ne bis in idem* has three elements. The defendant must have been acquitted or convicted, the acquittal or conviction must be a final judgement, and the fresh trial must be founded on the same cause that led to the initiation of the former proceeding.[49] This principle has been offered as a defence by various defendants standing trial for international crimes at different times, relying on former proceedings which are shams or proceedings with respect to which pardon was granted.[50] As previously established, the defence proffered by defendants depends on the circumstances of each case. Generally, the principle can be a clog to the prosecution of international crimes where there had earlier been sham proceedings, when new evidence came to light after the former trial and when amnesty or a pardon had been granted with respect to the former proceeding.

In Nigeria, the *ne bis in idem* principle is embodied in sections 36(9) and (10) of the Nigerian Constitution 1999, sections 181 and 221 of the Criminal Procedure Act[51] and sections 238, 239, 240 and 277 of the Administration of Criminal Justice Act 2015. Section 36(9) provides that

> no person who shows that he has been tried by any court of competent jurisdiction or tribunal for a criminal offence and either convicted or acquitted shall again be tried for that offence or for a criminal offence having the same ingredients as that offence save upon the order of a superior court.

This provision will be a clog in prosecuting crimes recognised under the Rome Statute in Nigeria. For example, if in line with state policy, A, B and C were murdered, and D was charged with crimes against humanity by murdering A and B. The provision tends to suggest that D cannot be tried again for crimes against humanity with respect to the murder of C committed under the same state policy since it is 'a criminal offence having the same ingredients' as that of the first offence.

This argument appears to be reinforced by section 181 of the Criminal Procedure Act and section 238(1)(b) of the Administration of Criminal Justice Act 2015. Section 181(1)(b) of the Criminal Procedure Act and

---

Statute of the International Criminal Court: A Commentary (Oxford University Press 2002), 705–729.

48. Ibid., 705–706.
49. The Case of *Salazar Monroe, Julio Rolando* (Peru) of March 5, 2007 cited in Due Process of Law Foundation, *Digest of Latin American Jurisprudence on International Crimes* (Due Process of Law Foundation 2010), 317.
50. Ibid., 314.
51. Cap C41 Revised Laws of the Federation of Nigeria (LFN) 2004.

section 238(1)(b) of the Administration of Criminal Justice Act 2015 stipulate that a person charged with an offence shall not be tried again if 'he has previously been convicted or acquitted by a competent court on a charge on which he might have been convicted of the offence charged.' Since D might have been convicted for the murder of C when he was charged with the murders of A and B, this provision implies that D could not be charged again.

Similarly, section 181(1)(c) of the Criminal Procedure Act and section 238(1)(c) of the Administration of Criminal Justice Act 2015 stipulate that a person charged with an offence shall not be tried again if 'he has previously been convicted or acquitted by a competent court of an offence other than the offence charged, being an offence of which, apart from this section, he might be convicted by virtue of being charged with the offence charged.' This provision extends further the scope of the *ne bis in idem* principle in Nigeria. Suppose that the killing of A, B and C by D in pursuit of state policy which discloses crimes against humanity also discloses genocide and D was charged with crimes against humanity for the murder of A and B. D cannot be charged with genocide for the murder of C after the trial of D for crimes against humanity. This is because D has previously been convicted or acquitted by a competent court for crimes against humanity, which is an offence other than genocide for which D might be convicted by virtue of being charged with crimes against humanity.

Superior court within the provision of section 36(9) of the Nigerian Constitution 1999 refers to a court exercising an appellate jurisdiction over the decision of the court below. A superior court is the court superior to the one below it. This implies that a retrial can be ordered by an appellate court if the trial is a sham. This position is reinforced by section 181(2) of the Criminal Procedure Act and section 238(2) of the Administration of Criminal Justice Act 2015 which stipulate that nothing 'shall prejudice the operation of any law giving power to any court, on an appeal, to set aside a verdict or finding of any other court and order a re-trial.' A retrial which is being ordered here is not strictly speaking a second trial; it is as if the first trial did not take place at all. If all appellate jurisdictions have been exhausted or the case is not contested on appeal and the judgement of the trial court becomes final having passed a statutory period to lodge an appeal, it implies that the defendant cannot be tried again with respect to the same fact. Therefore, when the trial is a sham and the judgement is not contested on appeal, the defendant cannot be prosecuted again for that same crime. Also, when new pieces of evidence emerge, the defendant cannot be tried again.

Section 36(10) stipulates that 'no person who shows that he has been pardoned for a criminal offence shall again be tried for that offence.' In the same vein, section 221(1)(b) of the Criminal Procedure Act and section 277(1)(b) of the Administration of the Criminal Justice Act 2015 stipulate that a defendant may plead that 'he has obtained a pardon for his offence,' and the court is bound to verify the plea before the defendant can be made to plead to the charge or information filed against him.[52] This is a jurisdictional principle since it operates before a plea to the actual charge is taken. It can be argued that once the verification confirms the defendant's position, the court is precluded from examining the actual case on merit. The implication of the combined reading of section 36(10) of the Nigerian Constitution 1999, section 221(1)(b) of the Criminal Procedure Act and section 277(1)(b) of the Administration of the Criminal Justice Act 2015 is that pardon forecloses future prosecution with respect to the same crime.

But, if the exercise of pardon is unconstitutional for having violated other constitutional provisions, will it still foreclose prosecuting the person for the same offence? If a pardon was granted before the conclusion of a criminal proceeding (although in exceptional cases as previously shown) and it later turns out to be unconstitutional, it can be argued that section 36(10) of the Nigerian Constitution 1999 will not apply and the defendant can be prosecuted again. On the other hand, if a pardon was granted after prosecution but before sentencing and the pardon later turns out to be unconstitutional, the defendant can still not be prosecuted again. This is not because section 36(10) of the Nigerian Constitution will apply but because section 36(9) of the Nigerian Constitution will come to prevail. Since pardon was granted after prosecution, the fact of the defendant's prosecution remains intact and subjecting the defendant to another trial would have violated the *ne bis in idem* principle. Of course, it can be argued that a fresh sentence can be passed. This will not amount to double punishment since the defendant was never sentenced before. If the sentence was reduced and its reduction was unconstitutional, then the defendant would serve the remaining terms. This will also not violate the *ne bis in idem* principle since it is still the same case.

Section 270(17) of the Administration of Criminal Justice Act 2015 stipulate that where a person has been 'convicted and sentenced' based on plea bargain, such a person 'shall not be charged or tried again on the same facts for the greater offence earlier charged to which he had pleaded to a lesser offence.' Thus, in the example of the killing of A, B and C by D, once D has pleaded to the lesser crime of crimes against humanity with respect to the killing of A and B, D cannot be prosecuted for genocide which is a higher crime with respect to the killing of not only A and B but of C as well since both the crimes against humanity and genocide are predicated on the same fact. However, when plea bargaining as charge bargaining leads to charging the accused with a much less serious crime with the attendant consequence of distorting the factual basis of the crime committed and is unconstitutional, then the defendant can be charged again. Similarly, where plea bargain as sentence bargaining leads to a ridiculous sentence discounting and is unconstitutional, the defendant can be charged again.

52. Criminal Procedure Act Cap C41 LFN 2004, ss 221(2) and (3).

However, under section 211 of the Administration of Criminal Justice Act 2015 a defendant can be charged with more than one crime in a single trial if the defendant's acts or omissions are so connected to form the same transaction while under section 239 of the same Act, 'a defendant acquitted or convicted of an offence may afterwards be tried for a distinct offence for which a separate charge might have been made against him on the previous trial under the provisions of section 211. In the example of A, B and C murdered by D which discloses crimes against humanity, D under section 211 can be charged with the murder of A and B together in a single trial since they are so connected to form the same transaction of implementing state policy. After his trial, D can be charged again for the murder of C under section 239 since it constitutes a distinct offence with respect to C for which a separate charge might have been made against D on the previous trial. The provisions of section 211 and 239 appear to be in conflict with section 36(9) of the Nigerian Constitution 1999 and section 238(1)(c) of the Administration of Criminal Justice Act 2015. To the extent that they are in conflict with the Nigerian Constitution, they are void to the extent of their inconsistency.[53] With respect to section 238(1)(c) of the Administration of Justice Act 2015, it can be argued that immunity from prosecution as a right in favour of a defendant trumps the general right of prosecution in favour of the state.

Similarly, under section 240 of the Administration of Criminal Justice Act 2015 a defendant may be prosecuted again where the consequences of the defendant's action manifest as murder or manslaughter during the time the defendant was convicted but was unknown to the court or after the defendant's conviction. In the example of A, B and C, D may be prosecuted again for the murder of C as crime against humanity or genocide if C's death occurred during D's conviction for crimes against humanity with respect to the killing of A and B but was unknown to the court or after D was convicted of crimes against humanity with respect to the killing of A and B.

It is also relevant to consider the *ne bis in idem* principle from the perspective of prosecution by other states. As previously noted, section 36(9) of the Nigerian Constitution 1999 stipulates that

> no person who shows that he has been tried by any court of competent jurisdiction or tribunal for a criminal offence and either convicted or acquitted shall again be tried for that offence or for a criminal offence having the same ingredients as that offence . . .

It can be argued that the court of competent jurisdiction is not limited to Nigerian courts. However, if one considers the fact that section 36(9) ends with 'save upon the order of a superior court' and that only a court exercising an appellate jurisdiction can order a re-trial, then court of competent

53. Nigerian Constitution 1999, s 1(3).

jurisdiction is limited to Nigeria. Since a Nigerian court cannot sit in appellate jurisdiction over a foreign trial court, it can be argued that prosecution by other states is not contemplated. In *Macloed v Attorney General for New South Wales*,[54] it was held that 'all crimes are local. The jurisdiction over the crime belongs to the country where the crime is committed.'[55] Therefore, a person who had earlier been tried in another state may be prosecuted again in Nigeria. While this may be an injustice to the person, this favours the implementation of the principle of complementarity and reduces the chances of shielding the person from criminal responsibility by foreign sham proceedings.

Similarly, as earlier shown, section 36(10) stipulates that 'no person who shows that he has been pardoned for a criminal offence shall again be tried for that offence.' It can be argued that pardon in this provision is not limited to pardon granted in Nigeria. In this respect, a person who had been pardoned in another state to be shielded from criminal responsibility may also be shielded in Nigeria as well. However, a pardon is essentially a public act founded on public law of a state. In this wise, pardon granted by another state is an exercise of power under public law of that state which is essentially territorial and operative only in that state. In *The Antelope*,[56] Chief Justice Marshall of the United States stated that 'the courts of no country execute the penal laws of another.'[57] Penal law in this context means public law. Thus, in *Huntington v Attrill*,[58] the Privy Council held that '. . . crimes, including in that term all branches of public law . . . are local . . .'[59] The implication of this is that section 36(10) could not have contemplated pardon granted in another state. Therefore, excluding pardon granted by another state within the meaning of section 36(10) and making a person granted pardon in another state amenable to prosecution in Nigeria is more favourable to implementing complementarity.

Another dimension to this issue is: Can a state within the Nigerian Federation be bound by pardon granted by another state within the Nigerian Federation with respect to the same offence? Put in another way, what happens if a person granted pardon by one state for a crime recognised under the Rome Statute invoked the pardon when he or she is to be prosecuted for the same crime by another state within the Nigerian Federation? It would be recalled that states within the Nigerian Federation may legislate on crimes recognised under the Rome Statute in certain instances. The provision of section 36 is far from being explicit in this regard. Unlike pardon granted by another state outside Nigeria, this is pardon granted in Nigeria. Since section 36(10) does

54. (1891) AC 455.
55. Ibid., 458.
56. (1825) 10 Wheat 66, 123 (US 1825).
57. Ibid.
58. [1893] AC 150.
59. Ibid., 156.

not indicate whether pardon being pleaded by the defendant is state or federal, what a strict construction implies is that once a state has granted pardon with respect to the crimes recognised under the Rome Statute, no other state among the 36 states of the federation can subject the person to trial again thus shielding the person from criminal responsibility.

On the other hand, if the principle in *The Antelope* and *Huntington* is applied to the interstate relation as a conflict principle, then a state is not bound by pardon granted by another state with respect to the same crime recognised under the Rome Statute. It is worthy of note that each state within a federation in conflict of laws constitutes a state within the meaning of public international law.[60] This approach somehow coheres with the combined reading of section 36(10) and section 212 (on the exercise of prerogative of mercy by the governor) of the Nigerian Constitution 1999. Pardon in this way is considered a public act of one state limited to its territory. Of course, the public act is founded on the Constitution which jointly applies to all states within the federation; this does not make its exercise binding on other states that are also competent to act under the same constitution. Therefore, within the context of complementarity, the person who has benefitted from pardon granted by one state may not invoke the same pardon in another state. Thus, he or she is not shielded from criminal responsibility by another state which has failed to recognise it.

Can a state be bound by a pardon granted by the president with respect to the same crime recognised under the Rome Statute? It can be argued that since the president can only grant a pardon with respect to federal offences, states within the federation are not bound by it. With this argument, the potency of the prerogative of mercy in shielding from criminal responsibility may be whittled down. This is because, since the president cannot grant pardon with respect to state law, a beneficiary of pardon under the presidential prerogative may still have prosecution hanging around his or her neck under a state law. A combined reading of section 175 on presidential pardon, section 212 on governorship pardon and section 36(10) will tend to reinforce this argument.

On the other hand, it can be argued that a defendant is entitled to plead the pardon, and the court is precluded from further conducting the proceeding once it is found on its verification that a pardon has been granted with respect to the same offence. This argument will reinforce shielding from criminal responsibility since a grant of pardon by the president precludes states within the Nigerian Federation from further prosecution. This position will be on the strict construction of section 36(10). Similarly, a federal court may refuse a plea of pardon granted by a state on the ground that it was granted with respect to a state crime on the joint reading of sections 175, 212 and 36(10) or may uphold it on the strict construction of section 36(10).

Unlike Nigeria, the jurisprudence of the Latin American states in combating impunity by prosecuting and punishing international crimes has addressed

60. J.H.C. Morris and David McClean, *The Conflict of Laws* (5th edn, Sweet & Maxwell 2000), 2–3.

the issue of sham proceedings and the emergence of new evidence after final judgement. The Inter-American Court of Human Rights (InterAmCtHR) held in the *Case of the Rochela Massacre v Colombia*[61] that

> the principle of res judicata provides protection from another judgement only when this judgement is reached with due respect for the guarantees of due process, in conformity with the tribunal's jurisprudence on this subject. On the other hand, if new facts or evidence are discovered which make it possible to ascertain the identity of those responsible for grave human rights violations, investigations can be reopened, even if the case ended in an acquittal with the authority of a final judgment.[62]

Similarly, the court held in the *Case of Almonacid Arellano et al v Chile*[63] that where the first trial had no regard for due process or where new evidence came to light, a defendant can be tried again in the light of those developments.

In *Remedy of inconstitutionality (Article 220 of Law 200–2000, Code of Criminal Procedures)*[64] decided by the Constitutional Court of Colombia, the court acknowledged the conflict that may exist between the right of the defendant not to be subjected to trial twice on the same fact, on one hand, and the right of the victim to protection together with the duty of the state to prosecute and punish international crimes, on the other hand, and concluded that the defendant's right must yield because of the egregious nature of international crimes.[65] Apart from the egregious nature of international crimes, the court further noted that the principle of complementarity makes it incumbent on states to punish these crimes and that when the *ne bis in idem* principle will constitute a clog, it must inevitably give way.[66] Similarly, the Supreme Court of Argentina in *Motion submitted by the defense of Santiago Omar Riveros*[67] and *Motion submitted by Ragnar Erland Hagelin*[68] maintained the same position as that of the Colombian Constitutional Court.

With respect to the fact of A, B and C given earlier to illustrate the legal position in Nigeria, the Supreme Court of Argentina considered the similar

61. *Case of the Rochela Massacre v Colombia* Judgment (Merits, Reparations and Costs) Series C No 163 (InterAmCtHR, 11 May 2007).
62. Ibid para 197.
63. *Case of Almonacid Arellano et al v Chile* Judgment (Preliminary Objections, Merits, Reparations and Costs) Series C No 154 (InterAmCtHR, 26 September 2006) para 131.
64. *Remedy of inconstitutionality (Article 220 of Law 200–2000, Code of Criminal Procedures)*-Sentencia C-004/03, Expediente D-4041, MP Eduardo Montealegre Lynett, Corte Constitucional, 20 de enero de 2003 cited in Due Process of Law Foundation (n 49) xxx.
65. Ibid., 319–323.
66. Ibid.
67. *Motion submitted by the defense of Santiago Omar Riveros*-Mazzeo, Julio Lilo y otros s/ rec De casación e inconstitucionalidad, Expediente M. 2333. XLII, Corte Suprema de Justicia de la Nación, 13 de julio de 2007 cited in Due Process of Law Foundation (n 49) xxvi and 324.
68. *Motion submitted by Ragnar Erland Hagelin*-Hagelin, Ragnar Erland s/ rec art 445 bis CJM, Expediente H 381 XLII, Corte Suprema de Justicia de la Nación, 2 de diciembre de 2008 cited in Due Process of Law Foundation (n 49) xxvi and 324.

fact situation in *Motion submitted by the defense of Jorge Rafael Videla*[69] and held that an allegation is not 'whether the accused had committed crimes during a particular period in his life . . . or generally . . . but rather, whether the specific events could be imputed to him as crimes'[70] and that it must be 'a clear, precise, and detailed allegation of a specific and singular event in the life of a person, which is imputed to have actually occurred.'[71] Therefore, D could still be prosecuted for the crimes against humanity with respect to the killing of C even though his trial for crimes against humanity has been concluded with respect to the killing of A and B. Considering the issue of common plan the execution of which led to the killing of A, B and C, the court held that 'inasmuch as the examination of the conduct that gives rise to a potential situation of *ne bis in idem* looks not at the plan, but rather at the abduction of each and every one of the children'[72] the defendant can be subjected to the second trial.

With respect to the question of the finality of the first trial by virtue of amnesty law, the Peruvian Constitutional Tribunal in *Constitutional remedy (amparo) submitted by Santiago Enrique Martín Rivas*[73] held that the first trial could only be considered final if the amnesty law is constitutionally valid. This appears to converge with the argument earlier advanced with respect to the Nigerian situation.

The jurisprudence of Latin American states is essentially based on article 8.4 of the American Convention on Human Rights which stipulates that 'an accused person acquitted by a non-appealable judgment shall not be subjected to a new trial for the same cause.' The creative interpretation of the InterAmCtHR influenced the various highest courts in the region to adopt the position favourable to the principle of complementarity in interpreting the *ne bis in idem* principle. However, the position with respect to the European Convention for the Protection of Human Rights and Fundamental Freedoms is different. Articles 4(1) and (2) of Protocol No 7 to the Convention[74] specifically provide for sham proceedings and the emergence of new evidence. Article 4(1) stipulates that

> no one shall be liable to be tried or punished again in criminal proceedings under the jurisdiction of the same State for an offence for which he

69. *Motion submitted by the defense of Jorge Rafael Videla*-Videla, Jorge Rafael s/ incidente de excepción de cosa juzgada y falta de jurisdicción, Expediente V 34 XXXVI, Corte Suprema de Justicia de la Nación, 21 de agosto de 2003 cited in Due Process of Law Foundation (n 49) xxiv and 319.
70. Ibid.
71. Ibid.
72. *Motion submitted by the defense of Jorge Rafael Videla*-Videla, Jorge Rafael s/ incidente de excepción de cosa juzgada y falta de jurisdicción, Expediente V.34.XXXVI, Corte Suprema de Justicia de la Nación, 21 de agosto de 2003 cited in Due Process of Law Foundation (n 49) xxiv and 319.
73. *Constitutional remedy (amparo) submitted by Santiago Enrique Martín Rivas*-Expediente 679–2005-PA/TC, Tribunal Constitucional, 2 de marzo de 2007 cited in Due Process of Law Foundation (n 49) xxxvii and 325.
74. Article 4 of Protocol No 7 to the Convention for the Protection of Human Rights and Fundamental Freedoms (adopted 22 November 1980, entered into force 1 November 1998) ETS 117.

> has already been finally acquitted or convicted in accordance with the law and penal procedure of that State

while article 4(2) stipulates that

> the provisions of the preceding paragraph shall not prevent the reopening of the case in accordance with the law and penal procedure of the State concerned, if there is evidence of new or newly discovered facts, or if there has been a fundamental defect in the previous proceedings, which could affect the outcome of the case.

Thus, in *Nikitin v Russia*[75] the ECtHR held that

> the requirements of legal certainty are not absolute. In criminal cases, they must be assessed in the light of, for example, Article 4§2 of Protocol No. 7, which expressly permits a State to reopen a case due to the emergence of new facts, or where a fundamental defect is detected in the previous proceedings, which could affect the outcome of the case.[76]

But, in reopening a case, the power to reopen must be 'exercised by the authorities so as to strike, to the maximum extent possible, a fair balance between the interests of the individual and the need to ensure the effectiveness of the system of criminal justice.'[77] Similarly, in *Bratyakin v Russia*,[78] the court stated that 'the Convention requires that the authorities respect the binding nature of a final judicial decision, and allow the resumption of criminal proceedings only if serious legitimate considerations outweigh the principle of legal certainty.' In addition, the court also held in *Fadin v Russia*[79] that a case can be reopened 'owing to the fundamental defect in the previous proceedings, within the meaning of Article 4 § 2 of Protocol No. 7.' While it can be argued that the decisions of the ECtHR were taken not within the context of implementing complementarity, nonetheless, if Latin American jurisprudence is anything to go by, it can be argued that in all instances of the commission of any of the crimes recognised under the Rome Statute, the principles enunciated by the court will serve a useful purpose in implementing the complementarity principle vis-à-vis the *ne bis in idem* principle.

With respect to the issue of whether the *ne bis in idem* principle in Nigeria contemplates trial by another state, Canada and New Zealand specifically address the issue in their respective implementing legislations. Section 12(1) of Canada's Crimes against Humanity and War Crimes Act 2000 stipulates that

> if a person is alleged to have committed an act or omission that is an offence under this Act, and the person has been tried and dealt with

75. *Nikitin v Russia* 20 July 2004 Application No 50178/99.
76. Ibid para 56.
77. Ibid para 57.
78. *Bratyakin v Russia* App no 72776/01 (admissibility) (ECtHR, 9 March 2006).
79. *Fadin v Russia* App no 58079/00 (ECtHR, 27 July 2006).

> outside Canada in respect of the offence in such a manner that, had they been tried and dealt with in Canada, they would be able to plead autrefois acquit, autrefois convict or pardon, the person is deemed to have been so tried and dealt with in Canada.

However, section 12(2) denies a plea of *ne bis in idem* to a person

> if the person was tried in a court of a foreign state or territory and the proceedings in that court (a) were for the purpose of shielding the person from criminal responsibility; or (b) were not otherwise conducted independently or impartially in accordance with the norms of due process recognised by international law, and were conducted in a manner that, in the circumstances, was inconsistent with an intent to bring the person to justice.

Similarly, New Zealand in section 12(2) of its International Crimes and International Criminal Court Act 2000 also adopts an identical provision with that of Canada.

The Principle of Legality

The principle of legality is laden with a lot of meanings. It is generally understood that a criminal statute must not have a retroactive application. But it may also mean that reasoning by analogy to hold a person criminally culpable is forbidden. Similarly, it may also imply that a person cannot be made to suffer more than the stipulated punishment at the time of the commission or omission which constituted the crime even though heavier punishment was later prescribed.[80] The one that is relevant here is the principle that forbids retroactive penal legislation. In the Nigerian Constitution 1999, retroactive penal legislation is prohibited. Section 36(8) of the Nigerian Constitution provides that 'no person shall be held to be guilty of a criminal offence on account of any act or omission that did not, at the time it took place, constitute such an offence . . .'

This constitutional provision which prohibits retroactive penal legislation presents a great challenge to implementing the principle of complementarity. Thus, crimes recognised under the Rome Statute which can be prosecuted at the international sphere since 2002 when the statute came into force cannot be prosecuted in Nigeria if the period of commission of these crimes fall between 2002 and the date the statute is domesticated in Nigeria. An attempt to prosecute those crimes which precede the date of domestication of the Rome Statute will amount to retroactive penal legislation. In

80. Kenneth S. Gallant, *The Principle of Legality in International and Comparative Criminal Law* (Cambridge University Press 2009), 11–45.

the Report of the Commonwealth Expert Group on Implementing Legislation for the Rome Statute of the International Criminal Court,[81] it is noted that retroactive penal legislation can be made with respect to crimes recognised under the Rome Statute.[82] The Expert Group relies on article 15 of the International Covenant on Civil and Political Rights (ICCPR). Article 15(1) provides that 'no one shall be held guilty of any criminal offence on account of any act or omission which did not constitute a criminal offence, under national or international law, at the time when it was committed' while article 15(2) stipulates that 'nothing in this article shall prejudice the trial and punishment of any person for any act or omission which, at the time when it was committed, was criminal according to the general principles of law recognised by the community of nations.' In the report, it is contended that crimes recognised under the Rome Statute can be regarded as falling under article 15(2) of the ICCPR.

It is, however, conceded that it is debatable if all the crimes under the statute could be considered part of customary international law. Thus, to the extent that any of the crimes are part of customary international law, retroactive penal legislation is permitted.[83] Furthermore, it is noted in the report that

> retrospective application has advantages. First, if part of the purpose of incorporating the crimes is to be able to exercise jurisdiction under the complementarity regime, then retrospective application is necessary to provide a jurisdiction co-extensive with that of the ICC. Second, retrospective application helps reduce the prospect of impunity for crimes of the recent past.[84]

Since it is the Nigerian Constitution that prohibits retroactive penal legislation, article 15 could not be of help in Nigeria, and the laudable advantages recognised in the report could not be put into effect in Nigeria. Uganda has an identical constitutional provision with Nigeria, and an attempt has been made to wriggle out of this quagmire. Article 28(7) of the Constitution of the Republic of Uganda 1995 like the Nigerian Constitution 1999 provides that 'no person shall be charged with or convicted of a criminal offence which is founded on an act or omission that did not at the time it took place constitute a criminal offence.' Wrange has argued that the obstacle can be bypassed since

> [t]he Constitution does not say 'constitute a criminal offence under Ugandan law', but leaves it open whether it is restricted to domestic legislation or not. These acts did constitute criminal offences under

81. Report of the Commonwealth Expert Group on Implementing Legislation for the Rome Statute of the International Criminal Court Revised April 2011.
82. Ibid para 16.
83. Ibid para 17.
84. Ibid para 18.

> international law, which is a law binding also on Uganda. Hence, under this reading, there is no obstacle to introducing new legislation which criminalises acts under domestic law that have already been criminalised under international law.[85]

Sarah Nouwen has however contended that 'in a state with a dualist approach towards the international order,' the phrase 'constitute a criminal offence' could only mean constitute 'a criminal offence under Ugandan law' in contradistinction to a foreign law 'unless the Constitution would make an explicit exception for crimes pursuant to international law, in accordance with Article 15(2) of the International Covenant on Civil and Political Rights, which it does not.'[86] Sarah Nouwen's argument that domestic law is envisaged is more apposite to the Nigerian situation. Section 36(12) of the Nigerian Constitution 1999 provides that 'no person shall be convicted of a criminal offence unless that offence is defined and the penalty therefor is prescribed in a written law,' and a written law 'refers to an Act of the National Assembly or a Law of a State, any subsidiary legislation or instrument under the provisions of a law.'[87] Wrange in the light of Nouwen's argument appears to have offered a more plausible argument by distinguishing between 'act' and 'offence.' He states that

> the constitution provides that '[n]o person shall be charged with or convicted of a criminal offence which is founded on an act or omission that did not at the time it took place constitute a criminal offence.' Hence, it is not prohibited to introduce new crimes with retroactive application, as long as the acts or omissions in question were criminal at the time of commission. Otherwise the Constitution would have said '[n]o person shall be charged with or convicted of a criminal offence, which is founded on an act or omission that did not at the time it took place constitute that criminal offence.'[88]

While Wrange's latter argument appears to find an escape route for Uganda, it does not for Nigeria. The provision of the Nigerian Constitution 1999 in section 36(8) ends with 'such an offence' which is similar to 'that criminal offence' in Wrange's argument. Even if 'such an offence' is not similar to 'that criminal offence' in Wrange's argument, the Nigerian Constitution is emphatic by virtue of section 36(12) that only the law enacted in Nigeria

85. Pal Wrange, 'The ICC Bill, Complementarity and 'Retroactivity'' ' 30 September 2008 cited in Sarah Nouwen 'The ICC's Intervention in Uganda: Which Rule of Law Does It Promote?' University of Cambridge Faculty of Law Legal Studies Research Paper Series, Paper No 22/2012, August 2012, 16.
86. Nouwen, 'The ICC's Intervention in Uganda: Which Rule of Law Does It Promote?'.
87. See *Aoko v Fagbemi* (1961) 1 All NLR 40.
88. Wrange, 'The ICC Bill, Complementarity and 'Retroactivity'' ' (n 85).

can declare a conduct criminal. In contrast, the Constitution of Kenya 2010 (Kenyan Constitution) dispenses with the creative interpretation presented by Wrange. Article 50(2)(n) of the Kenyan Constitution provides that every accused person has the right to a fair trial which includes the right 'not to be convicted for an act or omission that at the time it was committed or omitted was not—(i) an offence in Kenya; or (ii) a crime under international law.'

Even if Wrange's argument offers an escape route for Nigeria, the decision of the ECOWAS Court in *Hissène Habré c/ Republique du Senegal*[89] is another obstacle to contend with. In the case, Senegal had sought to amend its Penal Code in 2007 to be able to prosecute former Chadian leader for torture and crimes against humanity alleged to have been committed by him between 1982 and 1990 almost 20 years before Senegal chose to amend its Penal Code to make the prosecution of the former Chadian leader legally feasible domestically. The argument of the former Chadian leader as the applicant was that the principle prohibiting retroactive penal legislation would be violated by Senegal by amending its Penal Code to prosecute the applicant. On the other hand, Senegal as the respondent argued that the crimes for which the applicant was to be prosecuted were already crimes at the international plane. The ECOWAS Court, surprisingly relying on article 15(2) of the ICCPR, held that domestic prosecution of the applicant would violate the principle prohibiting retroactive penal legislation and suggested an *ad hoc* international tribunal which in the view of the court could dispense with the principle prohibiting retroactive penal legislation.

This judgement fails to appreciate the difference between jurisdictional function and substantive function of a criminal legislation. What Senegal did in amending its law was just to be able to acquire jurisdiction for crimes already defined internationally at the time the Chadian leader was alleged to have committed the crimes. The legislative amendment did not create new crimes as a matter of substantive law.[90] With respect to implementing complementarity, it can be argued that the crimes recognised under the Rome Statute are already defined in the Rome Statute which, of course, had become operative for Nigeria in 2002 after Nigeria had ratified it and that implementing legislation in Nigeria would just be performing a jurisdictional function.

Despite this erroneous decision, the decision remains the position of the law in the West African subregion. While a judicial decision is only binding between the parties and constitutes just a subsidiary source of international law,[91] it is nonetheless a pronouncement on the position of the law in the

89. *Hissène Habré c/ Republique du Senegal* (ECW/CCJ/JUD/06/10) Judgment of 18 November 2010.
90. See Valentina Spiga, 'Non-Retroactivity of Criminal Law: A New Chapter in the Hissène Habré Saga' (2011) *Journal of International Criminal Justice* 1–19.
91. Statute of the International Court of Justice 3 Bevans 1179; 59 Stat 1031; TS 993; 39 *American Journal of International Law* Supp 215 (1945), arts 38(1)(d) and 59.

West African subregion.[92] Thus, while Nigeria initially has its constitutional order alone to contend with vis-à-vis the principle of legality, the decision has added an international dimension to it and compound an already difficult situation.

The position of the Expert Group regarding the Rome Statute as a codification of customary international law may offer another interesting insight. This is not from the perspective of justifying retroactive penal legislation but of dispensing with it altogether. Since customary international law are directly applicable in states with the common law tradition, including Nigeria,[93] it can be argued that the principle of legality will not apply since the crimes recognised under the Rome Statute would have formed part of Nigerian law at the time they become ossified as custom. Since the Rome Statute was adopted in 1998 (and could be considered reflective of customary international law at the time) which antedates 2002 when the implementation of the principle of complementarity within the Rome Statute provision devolves on Nigeria, the principle of legality would have technically become a non-issue.

The problem with this approach is that it assumes that all the crimes recognised under the Rome Statute have become customary international law. As recognised by the Expert Group, this is most difficult to sustain. While some of the crimes are arguably part of customary international law, not all of them can be so regarded as being part of customary international law.[94] But suppose crimes recognised under the Rome Statute are part of customary international law and that the Rome Statute just codifies them, they will still not operate in Nigeria. This is because customary international law relating to crime does not automatically operate in Nigeria. In *R v Jones*,[95] the House of Lords held that aggression as a crime in customary international law is of sufficient clarity to be regarded as a crime and that it would be absurd to contend otherwise because if it could be sufficiently clear in 1945 there is nothing to preclude it from being clear in the present age.[96] The court, however, held that in spite of its clarity it could not constitute a crime in England because only the legislature can declare a conduct criminal in line with the doctrine of separation of powers.[97] In Nigeria, this principle is reflected in the Nigerian Constitution which stipulates that a conduct can only be criminalised by an Act of the National Assembly or a Law of a state within the Nigerian Federation or any subsidiary legislation made pursuant to such Act

92. Sunday Babalola Ajulo, 'Sources of the Law of the Economic Community of West African States (ECOWAS)' (2001) 45 *Journal of African Law* 73–96, 89.
93. *Trendtex Trading Corp v Central Bank of Nigeria* [1977] QB 529.
94. The International Centre for Criminal Law Reform and Criminal Justice Policy, *International Criminal Court: Manual for the Ratification and Implementation of the Rome Statute* (3rd edn, The International Centre for Criminal Law Reform and Criminal Justice Policy 2008), 73–82.
95. [2006] UKHL 16.
96. Ibid para 19.
97. Ibid para 23.

or Law.[98] Thus, only a lawmaking organ can declare a conduct criminal in Nigeria which automatically forecloses placing reliance on customary international law with its period of formation antedating 2002.

Statute of Limitation

A statute of limitation can be defined as an enactment which stipulates the time within which criminal proceedings must be instituted or sentence enforced. The implication of a statute of limitation is that even if the defendant committed the alleged crimes, the defendant can still not be proceeded against once prosecution is outside the time frame legally stipulated nor can a convict be punished after a stipulated period. With respect to crimes recognised under the Rome Statute, the implication is that statute of limitation stipulates the time within which the crimes under the statute can be prosecuted, failing which any defendant to any of the crimes under the statute cannot be proceeded against nor can sentence be enforced against a convict after a stipulated period. As the definition of a statute of limitation indicates, a statute of limitation is of two kinds. The first one relates to the time within which criminal actions can be instituted. The second one relates to enforcement of sentences.[99] As a general rule, in states with the Civil Law tradition, crimes are subject to a statute of limitation unless expressly declared otherwise[100] while in states with the common law tradition, crimes are not subject to a statute of limitation unless expressly declared otherwise.[101]

In the realm of international criminal justice, the non-applicability of statute of limitation to international crimes was not addressed in the Charters establishing the International Military Tribunal (IMT)[102] and the International Military Tribunal for the Far East (IMTFE).[103] This is understandable since the crimes were intended to be prosecuted immediately after the war. However, the Control Council Law No 10[104] which was adopted in 1946 by the Allied Powers prohibited the applicability of the statute of limitation. Article II(5) of the Law stipulates that 'in any trial or prosecution for a crime herein referred to, the accused shall not be entitled to the benefits of any statute of limitation with respect to the period from 30 January 1933 to 1 July 1945, nor shall any immunity, pardon or amnesty granted under

98. Section 36(12).
99. See Ruth A. Kok, 'Statutory Limitations in International Criminal Law' (PhD thesis, University of Amsterdam 2007), para 29.
100. Ibid para 42.
101. Ibid para 44.
102. Charter of the International Military Tribunal UNTS No 251 (1951) 284.
103. Charter of the International Military Tribunal for the Far East, 19 January 1946, TIAS 1589.
104. Allied Control Council Law No 10, Punishment of Persons Guilty of War Crimes, Crimes against Peace and against Humanity, 20 December 1945, Official Gazette of the Control Council for Germany, No 3, Berlin, 31 January 1946.

the Nazi regime be admitted as a bar to trial or punishment.' In the Statutes of the International Criminal Tribunal for Yugoslavia (ICTY) and the International Criminal Tribunal for Rwanda (ICTR), the non-applicability of a statute of limitation was not addressed. Similarly, since the prosecution of the crimes committed were to take place almost immediately, it is understandable while the issue was not addressed.

With respect to the ICC, article 29 of the Rome Statute stipulates that 'the crimes within the jurisdiction of the Court shall not be subject to any statute of limitations.' Nigeria follows the tradition of states with the common law system. Thus, statute of limitation does not apply as a general rule to crimes in Nigeria. However, there are exceptions. The prosecution of treason and treasonable felonies must be commenced within two years of the commission of the offence.[105] Prosecution of sedition must be commenced within six months of the commission of the offence.[106] The prosecution of offences under the Customs and Excise Management Act must be commenced within seven years of the commission of the offence.[107] While limitation statute applies to these crimes, it does not apply with respect to conspiracy to commit any of these crimes even when the substantive crime has become statute barred.[108] It is worthy of note that protection enjoyed by public officers under section 2 of Public Officers Protection Act[109] does not apply to criminal proceedings.[110]

With respect to setting a time limit within which crimes under the Rome Statute can only be prosecuted, the implication is that a suspect of international crimes recognised under the Rome Statute cannot be prosecuted once the period of prescription has expired. Although article 29 is part of the general part of the Rome Statute and, as earlier indicated, it does not apply to domestic courts; nonetheless, it does not obviate the finding that statute of limitation shields a suspect of the crimes recognised under the Rome Statute from criminal responsibility. Similarly, while it appears to be a more persuasive argument that article 29 appears to be specific to the ICC by stating that the crimes within the jurisdiction of 'the Court' are not subject to statute of limitation; the potency of the preceding finding is not in any way whittled down. As a matter of fact, the French Constitutional Council decided in 1999 that once the period within which the prosecution of any of the crimes recognised under the Rome Statute could commence had expired, the ICC can validly intervene.[111] With respect to setting a time limit after

105. Criminal Code Cap C39 Revised LFN 2004, s 43.
106. Ibid s 52 (1).
107. Customs and Excise Management Act Cap C45 Revised LFN 2004, s 176(3).
108. *R v Simmonds* (1967) 51 CAR 316.
109. Cap P41 Revised LFN 2004.
110. *Yabugbe v COP* [1992] 4 NWLR (Pt 234) 152.
111. France, Constitutional Court, Decision 98–408 DC of 22 January 1999 (Treaty on the Statute of the International Criminal Court), Journal officiel, 24 January 1999, 1317.

which a convict of the crimes recognised under the Rome Statute can no longer be punished for the crimes committed, it can be asserted that so long as the punishment of the deserving remains the goal of the ICC, the spirit of complementarity is negated and that shielding from criminal responsibility will result. Considering the historical background of the notion of shielding as previously discussed, it can be argued that if a ridiculously low sentence will amount to shielding because the punishment does not reflect the gravity of the crime, then failure to punish at all cannot be less indicative of shielding. Similarly, the preamble to the Rome Statute stipulates that 'the most serious crimes of concern to the international community as a whole must not go unpunished.' By promulgating a statute of limitation prohibiting the imposition of punishment after some time, it can be argued that the purpose of the ICC as expressed in the preamble is defeated.

In addition, since articles 81(2)(a) and 83(3) of the Rome Statute stipulate that disproportionate sentence may be a ground of appeal before the Appellate Chamber of the ICC, thus indicating that sentence imposed must reflect the gravity of the crime committed, it is maintainable that a statute that forecloses serving the sentence imposed is contrary to the spirit of the Rome Statute. Furthermore, since the Rome Statute seeks 'to put an end to impunity' as reflected in its preamble, it is also maintainable that statute of limitation is in violation of this ideal of the Rome Statute to the extent that failure to punish may encourage impunity. The German Constitutional Court recognises the nexus between failure to impose punishment and impunity by stating that 'punishment after considerable time at any rate has a stronger general deterrent effect than impunity pursuant to expiration of prescription periods.'[112] It can therefore be asserted that since there is no statute of limitation generally in Nigeria, the prevailing legal regime fosters the implementation of the complementarity principle as envisaged in the Rome Statute by encouraging the prosecution of crimes recognised under the Rome Statute in Nigeria.

Meanwhile, in the Report of the Commonwealth Expert Group on Implementing Legislation for the Rome Statute of the International Criminal Court, the Expert Group appreciates the implication of a statute of limitation in the prosecution of crimes recognised under the Rome Statute but considers it a non-issue for states with the common law tradition.[113] However, the

112. BVerfG, 25, 269, 26 February 1969, at §IV, 2 cited in R A Kok (n 99) 143, para 345.

113. See the Commonwealth Expert Group on the Review of Implementing Legislation for the Rome Statute 23–25 February 2011, Annexe A para 10, where it is stated that 'it was recognised that international crimes of the nature dealt with in the Model Law are not subject to national Statutes of Limitation. As most Commonwealth jurisdictions do not have such statutes, it had not been felt necessary to include any provision on this in the original Model Law. However, for clarity, an optional provision (section 12 bis) has now been inserted.' See also the Report of the Commonwealth Expert Group on Implementing Legislation for the Rome Statute of the International Criminal Court Revised April 2011 at para 66 attached as Annexe B to the Commonwealth Expert Group on the Review of Implementing Legislation for the Rome Statute 23–25 February 2011.

fact that there are some exceptions in Nigeria by way of statutory enactment indicates that the National Assembly and the House of Assembly of each state within the Nigerian Federation can enact law subjecting the crimes recognised under the Rome Statute to a statute of limitation. It should be borne in mind that the rule in states with the common law tradition is that crimes of any kind including egregious crimes of the type recognised under the Rome Statute are not subject to a statute of limitation except otherwise declared. It is this potential to 'otherwise declare' that poses a serious threat to the implementation of the principle of complementarity in Nigeria.

Apart from the fact that the Commonwealth Expert Group relies on common law to consider the express prohibition of a statute of limitation with respect to crimes recognised under the Rome Statute a non-issue, the group also relies on the Convention on the Non-Applicability of Statutory Limitations to War Crimes and Crimes Against Humanity. By necessary implication, since Nigeria is also a party to this Convention,[114] express prohibition of statute of limitation with respect to crimes recognised under the Rome Statute is a non-issue. However, treaties do not automatically operate in states with the common law tradition due to the concept of dualism. Thus, even if these states with the common law tradition including Nigeria have ratified the Convention on the Non-Applicability of Statutory Limitations to War Crimes and Crimes Against Humanity, it does not make the convention operative domestically. Since Nigeria is to domestically prosecute crimes recognised under the Rome Statute in line with the principle of complementarity, the implication is that the Convention on the Non-Applicability of Statutory Limitations to War Crimes and Crimes Against Humanity would be required to be domesticated by way of a statutory enactment which has not been done in Nigeria.

But it can be suggested that the Convention on the Non-Applicability of Statutory Limitations to War Crimes and Crimes Against Humanity is a declaration of customary international law[115] which automatically operates in Nigeria without any need for an implementing legislation. While customary international law automatically operates in Nigeria without any need for statutory enactment, nonetheless it is subject to the supremacy of statutory enactment. Therefore, while customary international law prohibiting statute of limitation may be said to subsist in Nigeria; it can be overridden by statutory enactment. Thus, just as the potential to subject the crimes recognised under the Rome Statute to statute of limitation constitutes a threat to

114. Nigeria became a state party to the convention by accession on 1 December 1970. See parties to the Convention on the Non-Applicability of Statute of Limitations to International Crimes (adopted 26 November 1968, entered into force 11 November 1970) 754 UNTS 73. https://treaties.un.org/doc/Publication/MTDSG/Volume%20I/Chapter%20IV/IV-6.en.pdf accessed 7 August 2017.

115. Jean-Marie Henckaerts and Louise Doswald-Beck, *Customary International Humanitarian Law* vol I, Rules (Cambridge University Press 2005), 614–616.

complementarity despite the subsisting common law rule, so, too, does the threat remain under the applicable customary international law in Nigeria.

Having considered the common law position and that of customary international law, it is also apposite to consider the constitutionality or otherwise of a statute of limitation with respect to crimes recognised under the Rome Statute. This is because, if statute of limitation is unconstitutional, the potential to enact it to forestall the prosecution of crimes recognised under the Rome Statute contrary to the spirit of complementarity principle would have been rendered null. On the other hand, if its enactment is constitutional, the possibility to enact it to forestall the prosecution of these crimes or prevent having had to serve the sentence imposed after some time becomes imminent.

The constitutionality of a statute of limitation will be assessed in the light of the right of victims of crimes recognised under the Rome Statute to life, the right not to be subjected to inhuman or degrading treatment and the right to privacy as opposed to the defendant's right to speedy and expeditious trial. It is maintainable that, to the extent that a state should obtain redress for the victim by prosecuting the infractions of their rights and impose punishment accordingly, statute of limitation is unconstitutional. In *Chumbipuma Aguirre et al v Peru*,[116] the InterAmCtHR held that

> all amnesty provisions, provisions on prescription and the establishment of measures designed to eliminate responsibility are inadmissible, because they are intended to prevent the investigation and punishment of those responsible for serious human rights violations such as torture, extrajudicial, summary or arbitrary execution and forced disappearance, all of them prohibited because they violate non-derogable rights recognised by international human rights law.[117]

Therefore, since these human rights are also recognised under the Nigerian Constitution, it can be argued that statute of limitation is unconstitutional. Similarly, in *El Caracazo v Venezuela*,[118] the court held that 'provisions on prescription and the establishment of measures designed to eliminate responsibility are inadmissible.'[119]

In *R v Imre Finta*,[120] the Supreme Court of Canada was confronted with the question of whether prosecuting a defendant after 45 years would violate the defendant's right to the principles of fundamental justice under

116. *Chumbipuma Aguirre et al v Peru* (Merits) Series C No 75 (InterAmCtHR, 14 March 2001).
117. Ibid para 41.
118. *El Caracazo v Venezuela* (Reparations) Series C No 95 (InterAmCtHR, 29 August 2002).
119. Ibid para 119. See also *Trujillo Oroza v Bolivia*, (Reparations) Series C No 92 ((InterAmCtHR, 27 February 2002) para 106; *Myrna Mack Chang v Guatemala* Series C No 101 (InterAmCtHR, 25 November 2003), para 276.
120. [1994] 1 SCR 701.

section 7, the right to trial within a reasonable time under section 11(b) and the right to be presumed innocent under section 11(d) of the Canadian Charter of Rights and Freedoms. The Supreme Court held that the 'pre-trial delay of 45-odd years between the alleged commission of the offence and the laying of charges'[121] did not violate the provisions of the charter, since the 'Charter does not insulate accused persons from prosecution solely on the basis of the time that elapsed between the commission of the offence and the laying of the charge.'[122] The court added that 'indeed, it is far more likely that the delay was more prejudicial to the Crown's case than it was that of the defence'[123] and that the 'Defence counsel was entitled to argue that the witnesses' memories had become blurred with the passage of 45 years.'[124]

This necessarily implies that the rule prohibiting statute of limitation does not violate a defendant's right to expeditious trial and right to be presumed innocent and that procedural safeguards are sufficient to protect a defendant's right. Therefore, the combined dicta of the InterAmCtHR and the Supreme Court of Canada justify the inference that statute of limitation is unconstitutional in the light of the required balance of the victims' right and the defendant's right. This obviously fosters the complementarity principle under the Rome Statute of the ICC.

It is, however, worthy to note that despite the common law and customary international law prohibiting limitation period together with the possibility that statute of limitation may be unconstitutional, Australia finds it expedient to provide explicitly for prohibiting statute of limitation with respect to certain crimes. Article 75(6) of the Australian Penal Code 2003 stipulates that 'serious breaches of international humanitarian law during armed conflict or genocide are not subject to statutory limitations.' While the provision of the Australian statute is not explicit with respect to criminal proceedings and sentence imposed, the provision of the Genocide, War Crimes and Crimes against Humanity Act 1998 of the Democratic Republic of the Congo makes a clear-cut distinction between the two and categorically prohibits their applicability to international crimes. Article 14 stipulates that 'Statutes of limitation do not apply with regard to the prosecution and repression of war crimes or with regard to the pronounced penalty.' In the same vein, article 11 of the Argentine Act Implementing the ICC Statute 2006 stipulates that 'the right to prosecute and the execution of sentences of the crimes provided for in Article 8, 9 and 10 of the present Act . . . are imprescriptible.'

While Australia, Argentina and Democratic Republic of the Congo have statutory enactments with respect to statute of limitation, some states have preferred to subject the competence of their respective lawmaking organ to

121. Ibid., 717.
122. Ibid.
123. Ibid., 875.
124. Ibid.

constitutional supremacy by prohibiting statutes of limitation under their respective constitutions. Article 23(1) of the Ecuador Constitution 1988 stipulates that

> while taking into account the rights provided for in this Constitution and in international provisions that have entered into force, the State will recognise and guarantee the following to persons; 2. . . . the right to prosecute and the right to punish genocide, torture, forced disappearance of persons, kidnapping and murder for political or consciousness reasons are not subject to statutes of limitation.

Venezuela takes after Ecuador by providing in article 29 of its 1999 constitution that 'the state is obliged to investigate and punish legally crimes against humanity committed by its authorities. Criminal actions and enforcement of sentences to crimes against humanity, grave violations of human rights and war crimes are imprescriptible.' Egypt somewhat prefers to gravitate towards surplusage by stipulating in article 15(2) of its Code of Criminal Procedure that 'the statute of limitation does not apply to torture, as incorporated in Arts. 126, 127, 282 of the Penal Code' while concurrently stipulating in article 57 of its 1971 constitution that

> any assault on individual freedom or on the inviolability of the private life of citizens and any other public rights and liberties guaranteed by the Constitution and the law shall be considered a crime, whose criminal and civil lawsuit is not liable to prescription. The State shall grant a fair compensation to the victim of such an assault.

The Power of the Attorney-General to Amend the Law of Evidence

The attorney-general of the federation is empowered to amend the law of evidence. As previously raised, is it not possible for the attorney-general to raise the bar of admissibility and technically make prosecution difficult with the purpose of shielding a suspect from criminal responsibility? Section 255 of the Evidence Act 2011 provides that the 'Minister charged with responsibility for justice may from time to time make regulations generally prescribing further conditions with respect to admissibility of any class of evidence that may be relevant under this Act.' This provision may mean two things. First, it may mean that the attorney-general is empowered to lay down further conditions for admissibility of any evidence in addition to the conditions already laid down by the Evidence Act. Second, it may mean that as new pieces of evidence emerge with time (which, of course, would not have been provided for in the Act), the attorney-general may prescribe conditions for their admissibility.

The second condition appears to be the intendment of the National Assembly. It is most likely that the power to amend the law of evidence is given to the minister to avoid having had to bring the Evidence Act before the National Assembly for amendment any time there is need for amendment. However, the wordings of the Act tend to suggest the first situation. The implication of this power to the principle of complementarity is enormous. If the attorney-general removes certain classes of evidence from being tendered, it can be argued that this does not amount to prescribing further conditions. But, the attorney-general may raise the bar for admissibility higher by adding further conditions for admissibility. Therefore, previously admissible evidence under the Act may no longer be admissible until more onerous conditions are fulfilled. It is possible that the attorney-general may do this to shield from successful prosecution those who are politically powerful. Similarly, where the piece of evidence is not previously contemplated by the Act, the attorney-general may decide to prescribe conditions for admissibility and in the process laid down unduly onerous conditions to make prosecution difficult.

But, the decision of the Court of Appeal in *Abdullahi Haruna v Kogi State House of Assembly*[125] appears to put this fear at rest. In the instant case, the subject matter of litigation was the sale of some properties of the Kogi state government, a state within the Nigerian Federation. The governor of the state was among the defendants. While the case was pending, the governor purportedly revoked the Certificate of Occupancy with respect to those properties which consequently denied the owners, who were the plaintiffs, their alleged rights. The court held that the governor's act of revocation was null and void since it was exercised with respect to the subject matter of the case on which the parties have joined issues to defeat the outcome of the case. Therefore, if the attorney-general raises the bar of admissibility to make prosecution more difficult while prosecution is commencing, it can be argued that such exercise of power by the attorney-general will be null and void. Since the subject matter of the litigation will be the guilt or otherwise of the defendant, taking any step that will affect the outcome can be said to pre-empt the outcome of the litigation. However, it will be a different matter altogether if after investigation but before commencement, the attorney-general decides to raise the bar for admissible evidence. In this case the principle of *subjudice* in *Abdullahi Haruna* becomes inapplicable.

The power of the attorney-general to amend the law of evidence is a delegated legislation. It is therefore amenable to judicial review. The power can be reviewed if it is exercised before prosecution begins. When further conditions that are more onerous are prescribed with respect to evidence already provided for in the Evidence Act, it may be possible to impute *mala fide* on the part of the attorney-general, which is one of the grounds for judicial review. However, when conditions are prescribed with respect to evidence not contemplated by the Evidence Act, it may be much more difficult to

125. (2010) LPELR-CA/A/143/08.

succeed by imputing *mala fide* or by invoking other grounds for judicial review. The reason for the difficulty is that what the attorney-general honestly considers to be an appropriate law is what will be at issue.

What the attorney-general honestly considers to be an appropriate law presents a difficulty because issues of policy may be involved. But policy issues can also be subjected to the test of constitutionality. Any law enacted by the attorney-general may be asked to be reviewed if it is not a law 'reasonably justifiable in a democratic society'[126] for maintaining 'public order'[127] or 'protecting the rights and freedom of other persons.'[128] While it is possible to mitigate any abuse of the power of the attorney-general to amend the law of evidence, nonetheless, the implication of the power for the principle of complementarity is latent.

Since it is the minister responsible for justice who is empowered to amend the Evidence Act, it implies that the attorney-general of the state cannot exercise that power. When the attorney-general of the federation and the minister of justice intends to frustrate the prosecution of certain persons for the crimes recognised under the Rome Statute by the attorney-general of the state, the Evidence Act can be tampered with. However, the principle of *subjudice* earlier discussed may still apply since non-parties to a suit must not take any step to defeat the outcome of a pending suit like parties. The greatest difficulty will be with respect to judicial review. Since there will always be pending cases at any point in time when the attorney-general of the federation exercises the power to amend, it will be more onerous to impute *mala fide* with respect to the case being prosecuted by the attorney-general of the state. This is because other cases like the one being prosecuted by the attorney-general of the state will be affected. The need to prove that it was the case of the attorney-general of the state that was intended to be affected will be a difficult hurdle to cross. With respect to the test of constitutionality, it will not be in any way different from what it is when the attorney-general of the federation is the one who is prosecuting.

It may, however, be considered presumptive that the minister of justice is anti-criminal justice and may tamper with the Evidence Act by virtue of the fact that he or she is a politician. This reservation can be conveniently laid to rest in the light of the behavioural antecedents of attorneys-general in Nigeria. In *Attorney-General of Kaduna State v Mallam Umaru Hassan*,[129] the respondent's son was killed during communal violence and by virtue of which a charge of culpable homicide not punishable with death was preferred against some villagers. The prosecution of the case was discontinued through the issuance of *nolle prosequi* by the attorney-general without any lawful

126. Nigerian Constitution 1999, s 45.
127. Ibid.
128. Ibid.
129. [1985] 2 NWLR (Pt 8) 483.

justification. In *State v Ilori*,[130] the appellant who was a lawyer was charged with stealing and obtaining by false pretences by the director of public prosecution (DPP) of Lagos State, one of the federating states in Nigeria. After the charges were dismissed, the appellant requested the attorney-general to prosecute the DPP and two other police officers who investigated the case for conspiracy to bring false accusation against him and for conspiracy to injure him in his profession. The attorney-general refused the request. Following the attorney-general's refusal, the appellant then instituted a private prosecution. To prevent the prosecution of the DPP and the other police officers, the attorney-general entered a *nolle prosequi*. In *State v Adakole Akor*,[131] the attorney-general of Benue State entered *nolle prosequi* with respect to all the charges preferred against 27 accused persons for no reason. Similarly, six persons were charged to court for having committed assault and other crimes against members of a rival political party during electioneering campaign. The attorney-general who was a member of the same political party as that of the accused persons entered *nolle prosequi* to stall their prosecution.[132] In the same vein, several corruption cases initiated by the Economic and Financial Crimes Commission (EFCC) against politicians believed to have enriched themselves at the expense of Nigeria were discontinued in the exercise of the attorney-general's power to discontinue any case.[133] Therefore, it is not out of place to envisage the abuse of the power to amend the Evidence Act. In the words of an author,

> it must be remembered that the office of the Attorney-General is political and what assures one's membership of the cabinet is never one's personality and/or qualifications *per se* but one's access to the controlling machinery of the political echelons as well as one's relevance in balancing the prevailing power equations, among other factors. Experience shows that political office holders in Nigeria pay low regards, if any, to negative reactions by the electorate until they are embarking on fresh electoral campaigns.[134]

Having considered the first criterion of unwillingness which is shielding from criminal responsibility, the second criterion which is at issue is unjustified delay with intent not to do justice. However, this criterion will not be considered as a separate head. This is because the criterion of unjustified

130. (1983) 1 SCNLR 94.
131. (1981) 2 NCLR 410.
132. Dejo Olowu, 'Nolle Prosequi and the Law in Nigeria: Concept, Issues and Analysis' (2002) *Law Monograph Series 1 Demyaxs Law Publications* 33.
133. Ogidi Henry Tobechukwu and Stephen C. Chukwuma, 'Rethinking the Power of Nolle Prosequi in Nigeria: The Case of State v Ilori' (March 2014) 2(1) *Global Journal of Politics and Law Research* 1–11, 3.
134. Olowu, 'Nolle Prosequi and the Law in Nigeria: Concept, Issues and Analysis' (n 133), 32–33.

delay with intent not to do justice depends on the circumstances of each case. Since Nigeria has never prosecuted international crimes recognised under the statute, there are no materials on ground with which the Nigerian legal system could have been accessed. Although the Nigerian legal system can be said to be a bit slow in its general performance, nonetheless this is not sufficient to uphold unjustified delay with intent not to do justice. This is because what will amount to an unjustified delay with intent not to do justice is delay over and above what normally obtains in Nigeria.

7 Unwillingness

Independence and Impartiality of the Prosecuting Authority and the Judiciary

As indicated earlier, the principle of complementarity contemplates investigation and prosecution of crimes recognised under the Rome Statute. Two entities are relevant to a successful prosecution of these crimes. They are the attorney-general, who has the responsibility to prosecute, and the judiciary, which has the responsibility to establish guilt. Therefore, it is the independence and impartiality of these two entities that is considered in this chapter.

Independence and Impartiality of the Prosecuting Authority

The chief prosecutor who supervises the investigation and prosecution of crimes at both the federal and state levels is the attorney-general at the respective levels. The independence and impartiality of the attorney-general reflects how he or she is appointed and the mode of the exercise of his or her prosecutorial discretion. It would be recalled that the Eighth United Nations Congress on the Prevention of Crime and the Treatment of Offenders in its Guidelines on the Role of Prosecutors makes the provision for certain criteria to secure the independence and impartiality of prosecutors. These criteria include the requirement for qualification, selection and training of prosecutors which must embody safeguards against appointments based on partiality or prejudice. It is also stipulated that there should be security of tenure and objective regulation of discretionary power.[1] In the same vein, the International Association of Prosecutors in its Standards of Professional Responsibility and Statement of the Essential Duties and Rights of Prosecutors together with the Principles and Guidelines on the Right to a Fair Trial and Legal Assistance in Africa also contain identical provisions to secure the independence and impartiality of prosecutors. These provisions, as previously noted, have also found judicial adoption.[2] It is on the basis of these provisions

1. See Chapter 3.
2. Ibid.

that the independence and impartiality of the attorney-general is considered in this chapter.

With respect to qualification and training, the Constitution of the Federal Republic of Nigeria (Nigerian Constitution) 1999 provides that 10 years' post-call experience as a legal practitioner is required for any person to be appointed as an attorney-general. The attorney-general for the federation is a minister[3] while that of the state is a commissioner.[4] The attorney-general for the federation is to be appointed subject to the approval of the Senate[5] while the appointment of the attorney-general for a state is subject to the approval of the state House of Assembly.[6] The Constitution is silent on the factors to be considered, and in practice, political consideration has always been the most important issue. Thus, there is no safeguard against appointment based on prejudice and partiality. The implication is that the appointment of the attorney-general does not offer any guarantee against outside pressure nor does it project an appearance of the existence of such guarantee. Therefore, guarantee against outside pressure is lacking both in substance and in form.

In Kenya, the director of public prosecution (DPP) is identical to the attorney-general in Nigeria.[7] The DPP is to be appointed by the president subject to the approval of the National Assembly.[8] This is identical to the position in Nigeria. Ten years' experience as an academic or legal practitioner or both in the aggregate is required, but the Constitution is explicit in adding that the person to be appointed does not necessarily need to have acquired the experience in Kenya. It is sufficient if the person has acquired experience in other 'Commonwealth common-law jurisdictions.'[9] The possibility of appointing a foreigner may offer some protection against manipulation. Unlike Nigeria, it is also explicitly provided that the person to be appointed shall have high moral character, integrity and impartiality.[10]

In Uganda, the DPP is also identical with the attorney-general in Nigeria. The DPP is to be appointed by the president upon the recommendation of the Public Service Commission subject to the approval of the parliament.[11] The requirement for the recommendation of the Public Service Commission appears to offer some protection, but this is not necessarily so. This is because members of the commission are also appointed by the president subject to

3. Constitution of the Federal Republic of Nigeria (Nigerian Constitution) 1999, s 150(1).
4. Ibid s 195(1).
5. Ibid s 147(2).
6. Ibid s 192(2).
7. The Constitution of Kenya (Kenyan Constitution) 2010, art 157(1).
8. Ibid art 157(2).
9. Ibid arts 157(3), 166(2) and 166(5).
10. Ibid arts 166(2)(c).
11. Constitution of the Republic of Uganda 1995 as amended by the Constitution (Amendment) (No 2) Act, 2005, Act No 21 of 2005 (Ugandan Constitution 1995), art 120(1).

the approval of the parliament[12] and can be removed from the commission by the president.[13] Although the president can only remove any member of the commission on the grounds of 'inability to perform the functions of his or her office arising from infirmity of body or mind; misbehaviour or misconduct; or incompetence';[14] nonetheless, the grounds are sufficiently wide to permit the president much latitude, as the president is not required to consult any person or authority to determine that any of the grounds has been violated. Ten years' post-call experience as a legal practitioner is also required.[15] The requirement with respect to moral integrity is lacking, although they are required for the members of the commission who would recommend the DPP for appointment.[16]

With respect to security of tenure, the attorney-general in Nigeria does not enjoy the security of tenure. There is no specific number of years for the attorney-general to serve except that he or she may remain in office when his or her appointer is in power. In Kenya, the DPP can hold office for eight years but he or she is not eligible for reappointment.[17] The DPP can only be removed on the grounds of 'inability to perform the functions of office arising from mental or physical incapacity; non-compliance with Chapter Six; bankruptcy; incompetence; or gross misconduct or misbehaviour.'[18] Chapter six is on leadership and integrity. Where the DPP is to be removed, a petition shall be sent to the Public Service Commission, which, if satisfied that a case has been made, will forward it to the president.[19] The president shall then appoint a tribunal upon the advice of the Public Service Commission.[20] The tribunal shall be made up of judges or persons qualified to be appointed as such.[21] Since judges of other Commonwealth states can be appointed in Kenya,[22] it follows that they can also be appointed as a member of the tribunal. One person with 15 years' experience as an advocate is also to be appointed as a member of the tribunal by the statutory body for the regulation of advocates.[23] It appears that an advocate of other common law jurisdictions may be appointed since it is not stated that the statutory body shall be the body that regulates advocacy in Kenya. Two other persons learned in public affairs shall also be appointed as members of the tribunal.[24] The presi-

12. Ibid art 165(2).
13. Ibid art 165(8).
14. Ibid.
15. Ibid arts 120(2) and 143(1)(e).
16. Ibid art 165 (3).
17. Kenyan Constitution 2010, art 157(5).
18. Ibid art 158(1).
19. Ibid arts 158(2) and (3).
20. Ibid art 158(4).
21. Ibid art 158(4)(a).
22. Ibid art 166(2).
23. Ibid art 158(4)(b).
24. Ibid art 158(4)(c).

dent shall only remove the DPP on the recommendation of the tribunal.[25] The process is judicial and offers some protection, although it is questionable why the president should be the one to set up the tribunal.

In Uganda, the DPP can hold office until he or she attains the age of 65 years.[26] Like Kenya, the DPP can only be removed on the grounds 'of inability to perform the functions of his or her office arising from infirmity of body or mind; misbehaviour or misconduct; or incompetence.'[27] Similarly, judicial process is also required for the removal of the DPP. The Judicial Service Commission or the cabinet shall advice the president to set up a tribunal to determine whether the DPP should be removed.[28] The tribunal shall be made up of three judges or three persons who are qualified to be appointed as judges.[29] It should be noted that 10 years' post-call experience as a legal practitioner is required for any person to be appointed as a judge of a high court in Uganda.[30] The president shall remove the DPP if the tribunal so recommends.[31]

With respect to subjecting the exercise of prosecutorial discretion to objective criteria which will make its exercise predictable, this is also lacking in Nigeria. The prosecutorial discretion of the attorney-general consists in initiating prosecution, taking over prosecution already initiated by other entities or stopping prosecution already initiated by other entities. The power to stop prosecution already initiated is known as the power of *nolle prosequi*. While the power to enter a *nolle prosequi* is essentially conferred on the attorney-general, it can be delegated to any officer in his department.[32] The effect of the entry of *nolle prosequi* is that it puts an end to prosecution[33] but it does not operate as a bar to subsequent prosecution,[34] neither does it operate as an acquittal.[35]

In *State v Ilori*,[36] the Nigerian Supreme Court was confronted with the interpretation of the Nigerian Constitution 1979 on prosecutorial discretion with respect to *nolle prosequi*. Meanwhile, because of the abuse of the prosecutorial discretion under the Constitution of the Federal Republic of Nigeria 1963, the Constitution Drafting Committee on the 1979 Nigerian Constitution recommended that prosecutorial discretion 'shall only be exercised with

25. Ibid art 158(5).
26. Ugandan Constitution 1995, arts 120(2) and 144(1)(b).
27. Ibid art 144(2).
28. Ibid art 144(4).
29. Ibid art 144(4)(c).
30. Ibid art 143(1)(e).
31. Ibid art 144(3).
32. Nigerian Constitution 1999, ss 174(2) and 211(2).
33. Administration of Criminal Justice Act 2015, s 107(1); *Gilchrist v Gardener* (1891) 12 NSWLR 184.
34. Administration of Criminal Justice Act 2015, s 107(4); *Goddard v Smith* (1704) Salk 245.
35. *R v Ridpath* (1713) 10 Mod 152.
36. [1983] 1 SCNLR 94.

the permission of the court'[37] which 'in deciding whether or not to grant permission, shall have regard to the public interest, the interest of justice and the need to prevent an abuse of legal process.'[38] The government, however, rejected the recommendation. In its place, it was provided that in exercising his or her prosecutorial discretion, the 'Attorney-General . . . shall have regard to the public interest, the interest of justice and the need to prevent abuse of legal process.'[39] The Nigerian Supreme Court adopted the common law position on the prerogative power of the Crown and held that the prosecutorial power of the attorney-general, including the power of *nolle prosequi*, is unfettered and not amenable to judicial review. With respect to the provision that the attorney-general must have regarding the public interest, the interest of justice and the need to prevent the abuse of legal process, the court held that the provision is merely directory and not mandatory and that the attorney-general has always put public interest into consideration under the common law. The court appeared to be swayed by the rejection of the recommendation of the Constitution Drafting Committee since the recommendation would not have been rejected if the government had intended to curtail the power of the attorney-general.

Under the Nigerian Constitution 1999, sections 174 and 211 which recognise the office of the attorney-general of the federation and the attorney-general of each of the 36 states, respectively, are *in pari materia* with the provisions of the Nigerian Constitution 1979. Since the decision in *Ilori* is an interpretation of the 1979 constitutional provision which is identical with the Nigerian Constitution 1999, it implies that the decision is also an authoritative interpretation of the Nigerian Constitution 1999. The decision in *Ilori* is fraught with a lot of flaws. One, the emphasis placed on the common law prerogative as a source of the prosecutorial discretion of the attorney-general is misconceived. This is because common law prerogative was no longer applicable in Nigeria as far back as 1963 when the Republican Constitution took effect. While the Constitution of the Federation of Nigeria 1960 adopted royal prerogative but subjected it to constitutional limit, the Nigerian Constitution 1963 dispensed with it completely. Since then, no subsequent constitution in Nigeria adopted royal prerogative with respect to prosecutorial discretion.[40]

Two, common law prerogative is not the only source of prosecutorial discretion in England. Statute is also another source. Unlike common law, the prosecutorial discretion of the attorney-general under a statute has always

37. Draft Constitution of the Federal Republic of Nigeria 1979, s 159(2).
38. Ibid.
39. Nigerian Constitution 1979, ss 160(3) and 190(3).
40. Osita Mba, 'Judicial Review of the Prosecutorial Powers of the Attorney-General in England and Wales and Nigeria: An Imperative of the Rule of Law' (1 March 2010) *Oxford University Comparative Law Forum* 2 (2010) 23–27. http://ssrn.com/abstract=2056290 accessed 7 August 2017.

been amenable to judicial review.[41] The Nigerian Constitution 1979 came into operation through the Constitution of the Federal Republic of Nigeria (Enactment) Act 1978, implying that the prosecutorial discretion of the attorney-general was rooted in a statute and should have been subjected to judicial review. This argument also applies to the Nigerian Constitution 1999 which came into operation via the Constitution of the Federal Republic of Nigeria (Promulgation) Act 1999.

Three, the constitutional provision should have been given its ordinary meaning. Section 6(6) of the Nigerian Constitution 1979 subjected all matters to judicial review except those expressly excluded. Since the prosecutorial discretion of the attorney-general was not excluded, the court should have subjected it to judicial review. This will place Nigeria on par with other Commonwealth states such as Barbados,[42] Fiji,[43] Guyana,[44] Jamaica[45] and Samoa.[46] This argument also applies to the Nigerian Constitution 1999.

Four, while the provision requiring the attorney-general to have regard for the public interest, the interest of justice and the need to prevent the abuse of the legal process may appear to be directory if one considers the rejection of the recommendation of the Constitution Drafting Committee by the government, nonetheless, the provision should have been given its ordinary meaning since the words are clear and unambiguous. Putting into consideration the government's attitude is extraneous. This is more important since the word *shall* was used as distinct from the word *may*. In *Adegbenro v Akintola*,[47] the Privy Council held that it is the wording of the constitution that should be interpreted and that recourse should not be had on to extraneous matters. In *Matalulu v DPP*,[48] the Supreme Court of Fiji held that since the power of the DPP sprang from a written constitution, it cannot be considered to be a 'modern formulation of ancient prerogative power'[49] and that it must 'be exercised within constitutional limits.'[50] Similarly, in *Attorney-General of Fiji v Director of Public Prosecution*,[51] the Privy Council in interpreting the Constitution of Fiji 1970 with respect to the power of the DPP held that the

41. *R v Panel on Take-overs and Mergers Ex p Datafin Plc* [1987] QB 815, 847; *Mohit v DPP of Mauritius* [2006] UKPC 20 [14]; *R (Corner House Research and another) v Director of the Serious Fraud Office* [2008] EWHC 714 (Admin); [2008] UKHL 60.
42. *Re King's Application* (1988) 40 WIR 15.
43. *Matalulu v DPP* [2003] 4 LRC 712.
44. *Tappin v Lucas* (1973) 20 WIR 229.
45. *Tapper v Director of Public Prosecutions* (Supreme Court of Jamaica in the Constitutional Court, 8 February 1999 unreported) cited in *Mohit v DPP of Mauritius* [2006] UKPC 20 [11].
46. *Aii Taito Galu Teo v Attorney-General*, Court of Appeal of Samoa, judgement rendered 23 November 2001 cited in Mba, 'Judicial Review of the Prosecutorial Powers of the Attorney-General in England and Wales and Nigeria: an Imperative of the Rule of Law'.
47. [1963] AC 614.
48. [2003] 4 LRC 712.
49. Ibid., 735–736.
50. Ibid.
51. [1983] 2 AC 672.

provision 'amounted to a constitutional guarantee of independence from the direction or control of any person.'[52] In addition, the Privy Council in interpreting a similar provision held in *Mohit v DPP of Mauritius*[53] that the court can inquire into the exercise of any power.[54]

While in Ilori, it was *nolle prosequi* that was an issue, although the Supreme Court held that the prosecutorial discretion is unfettered generally, in *Abacha v State*[55] it was the prosecutorial discretion with respect to initiating prosecution that was at issue. The Nigerian Supreme Court held that when there is no *prima facie* evidence in support of prosecution, such prosecution initiated by the attorney-general is reviewable and liable to be quashed. The Supreme Court stated that the 'court must be vigilant . . . so that no accused person will be oppressed either directly or indirectly through act of prosecution; if not we shall have persecution in place of prosecution.'[56] The court added that

> [w]hile it is well said that section 211(1)(a) of the 1999 constitution empowers the Attorney-General of Lagos State to charge any person to court section 211(3) thereof empowers him to have regard to the public interest, the interest of justice and the need to prevent the abuse of legal process. Counts 3 and 4 are in clear breach of the foregoing provisions.[57]

It is worthy of note that the Supreme Court in *Abacha* did not mention *Ilori* and, thus, tends to create confusion. While the Supreme Court can overrule itself,[58] it is expected to clearly indicate which it failed to do in this instance. However, the combined *rationes* of the two cases tend to suggest that the power to initiate prosecution is amenable to judicial review while the power of *nolle prosequi* and the power to take over prosecution are not.

In Kenya, the power of the DPP to institute criminal proceedings or to take over proceedings already commenced appears not to be reviewable.[59] However, the power of *nolle prosequi* appears to be subject to judicial review. It is stated that the DPP 'may not discontinue a prosecution without the permission of the court.'[60] When the DPP exercises the power of *nolle prosequi* after the prosecution has closed its case but before the defence opens its case, the consequence is acquittal.[61] This appears to protect the defendant so that he or she would not be vexed twice. However, it could be a potent instrument to defeat the implementation of the principle of complementarity.

52. Ibid., 679.
53. [2006] UKPC 20.
54. Ibid para 13.
55. [2002] 11 NWLR (Pt 779) 437.
56. Ibid.
57. Ibid concurring judgement of SU Onu JSC.
58. *Johnson v Lawanson* [1971] 1 ALL NLR 56.
59. Kenyan Constitution 2010, art 157(6)(a) and (b).
60. Ibid arts 157(6)(c) and 157(8).
61. Ibid art 157(7).

This power can be compared with the power of the attorney-general of the federation to withdraw charges under the Administration of the Criminal Justice Act 2015.[62] When a withdrawal is made before the defendant enters his or her defence, the defendant shall be discharged.[63] However, if the court considers that an order of acquittal should be made, then such an order may be made.[64] When withdrawal is made after the defendant 'is called upon to make his defence, he shall be acquitted of the offence.'[65] The DPP in Kenya is not required to obtain the consent of any person in performing his or her duties,[66] and he or she 'shall not be under the direction or control of any person or authority.'[67] In performing his or her duties, the DPP 'shall have regard to the public interest, the interests of the administration of justice and the need to prevent and avoid abuse of the legal process.'[68]

In Uganda, the DPP in the exercise of the discretion to initiate or take over proceedings also appears unquestionable.[69] But, with respect to the power of *nolle prosequi*, the DPP 'shall not discontinue any proceedings commenced by another person or authority except with the consent of the court.'[70] The use of the word *shall* makes the position in Uganda stronger than that of Kenya. In addition, there is no provision that acquittal will be the consequence if the DPP exercises his or her discretion after the prosecution has closed its case but before the defence opens its case which also makes the position better in Uganda in implementing complementarity. Also, the power of *nolle prosequi* must 'be exercised by him or her exclusively.'[71] This makes the exercise of the power restricted. Like Kenya, however, the DPP is not subject to the control of any person or authority,[72] and he or she 'shall [also] have regard to the public interest, the interest of the administration of justice and the need to prevent abuse of legal process.'[73]

The need for judicial review of prosecutorial power, whether in initiating prosecution, taking over prosecution already initiated, stopping prosecution already initiated or withdrawing charges, is imperative because royal prerogatives can now be reviewed.[74] In *Council of Civil Service Unions v Minister*

62. Section 108.
63. Section 108(2)(a).
64. Section 108(3).
65. Section 108(2)(b).
66. Kenyan Constitution 2010, art 157(10).
67. Ibid.
68. Ibid art 157(11).
69. Ugandan Constitution 1995, art 120(3)(b) and (c).
70. Ibid art 120(3)(d).
71. Ibid art 120(4)(b).
72. Ibid art 120(6).
73. Ibid art 120(5).
74. *R v Criminal Injuries Compensation Board, ex p Lain* [1967] 2 QB 864, [1967] 2 All ER 182 (CA); Laker *Airways Ltd v Department of Trade and Industry* [1977] QB 643, [1977] 2 All ER 182 (CA).

for the Civil Service,[75] the House of Lords held that all prerogative powers are now subject to judicial review[76] and that the source of a power, whether statutory or prerogative, is irrelevant.[77] The court added that the privilege enjoyed by prerogatives is now 'overwhelmed by the developing modern law of judicial review.'[78] The relevant consideration for the exercise of the power of judicial review is whether the subject matter is justiciable or not.[79] While political decisions like foreign policy formulation are not justiciable, judicial decisions taken by the Crown are justiciable and can be reviewed.[80] The power of the attorney-general is a judicial decision because it involves evaluation of evidence.[81] Similarly, in the New Zealand case of *Burt v Governor-General*[82] it was held that

> the prerogative of mercy is a prerogative power in the strictest sense of that term, for it is peculiar to the Crown and its exercise directly affects the rights of persons. On the other hand it would be inconsistent with the contemporary approach to say that, merely because it is a pure and strict prerogative power, its exercise or non-exercise must be immune from curial challenge.[83]

Also, in the Australian case of *Minister for Arts Heritage and Environment v Peko-Wallsend Ltd*,[84] it was stated that

> the courts of this country should now accept responsibility for reviewing the decisions of Ministers or the Governor-General in Council notwithstanding the decision is carried out in pursuance of a power derived not from statute but from the common law or the prerogative.[85]

Apart from the attorney-general, there are other entities which prosecute in Nigeria. These entities which are relevant here are the police and legal practitioners who are prosecutors at the ministry of justice. These entities have a reasonable measure of independence when viewed in the light of appointment and tenure of service. With respect to the exercise of prosecutorial

75. [1985] AC 374 (HL).
76. Ibid.
77. Ibid 410.
78. Ibid 407.
79. Ibid.
80. Ibid 418.
81. *Mohit v DPP of Mauritius* [2006] UKPC 20 [14], [21]; *R (On The Application of) v Secretary of State For Foreign and Commonwealth Affairs* [2008] UKHL 61 (22 October 2008) para 35.
82. [1992] 3 NZLR 672 (CA).
83. Ibid 678 lines 31–39.
84. (1987) 75 ALR 218.
85. Ibid 224 lines 6–11.

discretion, it can be argued that these entities are amenable to judicial review. In *Westminster Corporation v L & NW Railway*,[86] the House of Lords stated that

> it is well settled that a public body invested with statutory power . . . must take care not to exceed or abuse its powers. It must act in good faith. And it must act reasonably. The last proposition is involved in the second, if not in the first.

Black's Law Dictionary defines *power* as 'the legal right or authorization to act or not act; a person's or organisation's ability to alter, by an act of will, the rights, duties, liabilities, or other legal relations either of that person or of another.'[87] Since other prosecutorial entities in Nigeria are public bodies that have power, this dictum can be said to apply to them. In *DPP v Humphreys*,[88] the House of Lords held that

> a judge has not and should not appear to have any responsibility for the institution of prosecutions, nor has he any power to refuse to allow a prosecution to proceed merely because he considers that, as a matter of policy, it ought not to have been brought. It is only if the prosecution amounts to an abuse of the process of the court and is oppressive and vexatious that the judge has the power to intervene . . . [T]he power of the court to prevent them is . . . of great constitutional importance and should be jealously preserved. For a man to be harassed and be put to the expense of perhaps a long trial and then given an absolute discharge is hardly from any point of view an effective substitute for the exercise by the court of the power to which I have referred.

While other entities can be said to enjoy some reasonable measure of independence in term of appointment and tenure, it should not be forgotten that they are subject to the control of the attorney-general with respect to the discharge of their prosecutorial duty. This is because the attorney-general possesses the power of *nolle prosequi* and any prosecution initiated by these other entities can be taken over or discontinued by the attorney-general. Since the attorney-general does not have independence the relative independence which these entities enjoy can hardly guarantee impartial prosecution.

The Right of Private Prosecution

As earlier stated the attorney-general prosecutes, but he or she prosecutes on behalf of the state or government. However, the right of private prosecution

86. (1905) AC 426.
87. Bryan A. Garner and others, *Black's Law Dictionary* (9th edn, Thomson Reuters, 2009).
88. (1977) AC 1.

also subsists in Nigeria.[89] Private prosecution in this context refers to a criminal proceeding initiated by any person other than a government official. The prosecution may be initiated by the complainant or by a private legal practitioner at his or her behest.[90] The right of private prosecution does not cover a situation in which the state briefs a private legal practitioner to prosecute on its behalf.[91] Since the state essentially prosecutes, private prosecution appears as a safety valve for any injustice that may be occasioned where the state fails to act. Within the context of complementarity, it may serve a useful purpose in prosecuting crimes recognised under the Rome Statute where the state fails to prosecute.

Section 342 of the Criminal Procedure Act provides that 'the registrar shall receive an information from a private person.' This provision does not limit the categories of persons who can initiate criminal proceedings. Therefore, anyone may be said to be competent to initiate criminal proceedings except when expressly limited by statute.[92] While the right to commence criminal proceedings may be vested in any person, there are, however, two conditions that must be met. The first condition is that a 'law officer' must endorse the information through which the private person seeks to commence the criminal proceeding.[93] The endorsement must indicate that the 'law officer' has seen the information but declined to prosecute at the public instance. 'Law Officer' means 'the Attorney-General and the Solicitor-General of the Federation, and includes the Director of Public Prosecutions and such other qualified officers, by whatever names designated, to whom any of the powers of a law officer are delegated by law or necessary intendment.'[94] The second condition is that the private person must enter into a recognisance in a specified sum together with a surety in the like sum to the effect that the private person will prosecute the case to conclusion. In lieu of entering into a recognisance, the private person may be asked to deposit a stated amount to court.[95]

While the right of private prosecution can foster prosecution of crimes recognised under the Rome Statute, there are a number of impediments which may limit its meaningful use. The first impediment is the requirement of endorsement. Endorsement here means that the law officer must give his or her consent before a private person can initiate criminal proceedings. In the Report of the Commonwealth Expert Group on Implementing Legislation for the Rome Statute of the International Criminal Court,[96] it is stated that

89. Criminal Procedure Act Cap C41 Revised Laws of the Federation of Nigeria (LFN) 2004, s 59(1); Criminal Procedure Code, s 143(e).
90. Isabella Okagbue, 'Private Prosecution in Nigeria: Recent Developments and Some Proposals' (Spring 1990) 34(1) *Journal of African Law* 53.
91. Ibid.
92. Criminal Procedure Act, s 59(1).
93. Ibid s 342(a).
94. Ibid s 2(1)(b); Criminal Code, s 1(1).
95. Criminal Procedure Act, s 342(b).
96. Report of the Commonwealth Expert Group on Implementing Legislation for the Rome Statute of the International Criminal Court Revised April 2011, para 32.

> a consent regime may also provide a protection against abuse and frivolous proceedings particularly in a system where private prosecutions are possible without the ability for intervention by state authorities to stop proceedings. At the same time, to guard against political interference with the prosecution of such cases, the consent responsibility should be vested in an authority that exercises independent judgement in the prosecution process.

While the position of the Commonwealth Expert Group would have made an arguable case for the requirement of endorsement in Nigeria, however, this is not to be, as the attorney-general is far from being independent in Nigeria as previously established. Since the attorney-general is the law officer or his or her delegate, he or she may refuse to endorse or may instruct his or her delegate not to endorse. This point is underscored in *Fawehinmi v Akilu*.[97]

In this case, a journalist who was a thorn in the flesh of government was killed by a parcel bomb. His attorney and friend sought to privately prosecute suspected government agents, but the DPP refused to endorse claiming that the evidence made available by the attorney was not sufficient for him to make up his mind as to whether prosecution should proceed and that he (the DPP) might have to further investigate. The attorney then sought an order of mandamus compelling the DPP to either endorse or prosecute. The High Court refused to grant the order sought on the ground that the DPP did not, in fact, refuse to endorse but could just not make up his mind pending further investigation. On appeal, the Nigerian Court of Appeal refused the order sought on the ground that the attorney had no *locus standi* since he did not have any particular vested interest. On appeal to the Supreme Court, the Nigerian Supreme Court held that the failure of the DPP to make up his mind amounted in substance to a refusal while the doctrine of *locus standi* relied on by the Court of Appeal was declared inapplicable to criminal as opposed to civil proceedings. The court stated that it was the duty of every Nigerian to maintain peace in the society and that regarding protection against crime, each person was his brother's keeper.[98] The order of Mandamus was then granted. In the meantime, the Criminal Procedure Law of Lagos State of Nigeria under which the attorney sought to privately prosecute the suspected government agents was amended to deny private prosecution except in case of perjury. Thus, the attorney was rendered incapacitated to privately prosecute suspected government agents.

The second impediment is that the amount required to enter into a recognisance may be raised to discourage private prosecution. When the court insists that the amount should be deposited, prosecution may be made much more difficult where the amount stipulated is prohibitive. Although 100

97. (1987) 4 NWLR 797.
98. Ibid., 832. See also *Fawehinmi v Akilu* 1987 11–12 SCNJ 151; *Akilu v Fawehinmi* 1989 1 NWLR (Pt 75).

naira is the amount statutorily required at present, which is nominal, nothing precludes the lawmaking organ from raising the amount to discourage private prosecution. Also, obtaining a surety may be difficult to achieve. The surety may fear reprisal or intimidation.

The third impediment is that the attorney-general may enter a *nolle prosequi*. Since the exercise of the power is still unfettered, this automatically forecloses private prosecution. In fact, it is possible for the attorney-general to endorse the information and later enter a *nolle prosequi* or when the attorney-general was compelled by way of mandamus, the attorney-general may later enter a *nolle prosequi* after the commencement of the trial by the private person. The emasculation of the right of private prosecution played out in Kenya and Uganda and, thus, reinforces the argument that the power of the Attorney-General to enter a *nolle prosequi* is a threat to any use to which the right of private prosecution could be put with respect to the prosecution of crimes recognised under the Rome Statute in Nigeria. In Uganda, private prosecution was initiated against Ivan Nkwasibwe, who was the divisional police commander in March 2007. The DPP took over the prosecution and suspended it indefinitely.[99] In fact, the DPP often takes over politically sensitive cases commenced by way of private prosecution, and such cases often ended up being quashed.[100] The Gambia appears to be much more conscious of the effect of the abusive use of *nolle prosequi* on private prosecution. Thus, it deprives the DPP of the power to take over and continue any private prosecution without the consent of private prosecutor and the court[101] or to discontinue any private prosecution without the consent of the private prosecutor.[102]

The fourth impediment is that public interest private prosecution by foreign counsel may be difficult. Although the Legal Practitioners Act does not allow any person to practice law in Nigeria unless the person has been called to the Nigerian Bar, nonetheless the Legal Practitioners Act[103] empowers the chief justice of Nigeria (CJN) to allow any person to practice law for a specific purpose in Nigeria if it appears to the CJN that the person is qualified to practice in a state with a similar legal tradition with Nigeria and that it is expedient in the opinion of the chief justice to permit the person to practice.[104] This provision appears favourable to a foreign counsel to some extent.

However, the decision of the Supreme Court of Nigeria in *Awolowo v Usman Sarki, Minister of Internal Affairs*[105] constitutes a serious impediment.

99. International Bar Association, 'Judicial Independence Undermined: A Report on Uganda' (September 2007), paras 4.49–4.50.
100. Ibid.
101. Constitution of the Republic of the Gambia 1997, s 85(1)(i).
102. Ibid s 85(1)(ii).
103. Cap L11 Revised LFN 2004.
104. Legal Practitioners Act, ss 2(1) and 2(2).
105. 1966 1 All NLR 178; 1966 NSCC 209.

In the case, the defendant who was standing trial for treasonable felony employed the services of a British barrister to defend him. The barrister had been permitted by the chief justice to practise in Nigeria for the specific purpose of the defendant's defence. The barrister, on his entry into Nigeria, was, however, declared *persona non-grata* and repatriated back to England by the then minister of internal affairs. The defendant invoked the constitutional provision that permitted him the right to counsel of his choice. However, the Supreme Court held that counsel of choice meant counsel that was available 'who could enter into the country as of right.' What this restrictive interpretation implies is that a foreign counsel interested in privately prosecuting any of the crimes recognised under the Rome Statute can be declared *persona non-grata* even if the CJN permits him or her to practise for the specific purpose of privately prosecuting a case.

Lord Denning has, however, suggested that whenever there is conflict between state right and an individual right, the individual right should be made to prevail.[106] If this suggestion is applied, then the impediment constituted by this decision can be mitigated. The last impediment is that the power of the attorney-general to amend the Evidence Act may be used to frustrate any private prosecution. It is possible for the attorney-general to raise the bar of admissible evidence to frustrate successful prosecution initiated by any private person.[107]

Under the Administration of Criminal Justice Act 2015, the right of private prosecution also subsists.[108] Endorsement by the attorney-general or any law officer acting on his behalf is also required.[109] When an application for endorsement is, however, refused, the attorney-general 'shall' give his reasons within 15 working days.[110] The private legal practitioner can then proceed to endorse and 'shall be entitled' to prosecute.[111] Recognisance is also required; however, no specific sum is stated in the Act which gives the court a wide discretion.[112] When the defendant is acquitted, the private prosecutor may be ordered to pay costs to the defendant.[113] While the impediment associated with endorsement can be said not to apply under the Administration of Criminal Justice Act 2015, all other impediments associated with the exercise of the right to private prosecution under the Criminal Procedure Act also apply under the Administration of Criminal Justice Act 2015. While the power to override the refusal of the attorney-general to endorse can be said to be favourable to implementing complementarity, however, section 267(1) has emasculated any

106. Alfred Thompson Denning, *The Family Story* (Butterworths 1981), 179.
107. Preceding analysis in respect of the power of the Attorney-General to amend the Evidence Act applies.
108. Sections 267(1), 322, 348(1)(d), 381(d), 383, 384 and 494(1).
109. Section 383(1)(a).
110. Section 383(2).
111. Section 384.
112. Section 383(1)(b).
113. Section 322(1).

advantage gained. Section 267(1) stipulates that 'the complainant and the defendant shall be entitled to conduct their cases by a legal practitioner or in person except in a trial for a capital offence or an offence punishable with life imprisonment.' This implies that international crimes under the Rome Statute which are likely to be punishable by death or life imprisonment because of their egregious nature cannot be prosecuted by private means.

Police Independence

While the attorney-general prosecutes, it is the duty of the police[114] to investigate. In fact, successful prosecution of international crimes rests on adequate investigation by the police. Therefore, if the investigation process is manipulated, successful prosecution has been jeopardised. Thus, the independence of the police as the investigator is as important as the independence of the attorney-general as the prosecutor.

The independence of the police under the English common law is best amplified in *R v Metropolitan Police Commissioner ex Parte Blackburn*.[115] In *Blackburn*, the Commissioner of London Police had instructed his officers not to enforce certain gambling laws because of the difficulty in enforcing those laws. The applicant brought an application with a view to compelling the police to enforce those laws. Lord Denning, however, in refusing the application held as follows:

> I have no hesitation in holding that, like every constable in the land, [the Commissioner of the London Police] should be, and is, independent of the executive. He is not subject to the orders of the Secretary of State, save that under the Police Act, 1964; the Secretary of State can call upon him to give a report, or to retire in the interests of efficiency. I hold it to be the duty of the Commissioner of Police, as it is of every chief constable, to enforce the law of the land. He must take steps so to post his men that crimes may be detected; and that honest citizens may go about their affairs in peace. He must decide whether or not suspected persons are to be prosecuted; and, if need be bring the prosecution or see that it is brought; but in all these things he is not the servant of anyone save of the law itself. No Minister of the Crown can tell him that he must, or must not, keep observation on this place or that; or that he must, or must

114. The word *police* is from French language which, in turn, derives from the medieval Latin word *politia*, meaning 'policy.' In this sense, the word is used as a noun. It may also be used as a verb or an adverb. In this sense, it may mean 'the arrangements made in all civilised countries to ensure that the inhabitants keep the peace and obey the law. The word also denotes the force of peace officers (or police) employed for this purpose.' Referring to the police as individuals reflects the use of the word as a noun while referring to police as a service reflects the use of the word as a verb or an adverb. See Andrew Halpenny, 'The Governance of Military Police in Canada' (2010) 48 *Osgoode Hall Law Journal* 1, 6–7.
115. [1968] 1 All ER 763.

> not, prosecute this man or that one. Nor can any police authority tell him so. The responsibility for law enforcement lies on him. He is answerable to the law and to the law alone . . . Although the chief officers of police are answerable to the law, there are many fields in which they have a discretion with which the law will not interfere. For instance, it is for the Commissioner of Police, or the chief constable, as the case may be, to decide in any particular case whether enquiries should be pursued, or whether an arrest should be made, or a prosecution brought. It must be for him to decide on the disposition of his force and the concentration of his resources on any particular crime or area. No court can or should give him direction on such a matter. He can also make policy decisions and give effect to them, as, for instance, was often done when prosecutions were not brought for attempted suicide . . .[116]

Lord Denning's exposition appears to be the most authoritative pronouncement of the common law on the independence of the police.[117] Phillip Stenning states that 'Lord Denning's exposition of the doctrine of police independence in the *Blackburn* case remains today the most oft-quoted statement of the doctrine . . . in Britain, Canada, Australia, and New Zealand'[118] and that the doctrine as enunciated by Lord Denning is the 'police chief's bible.'[119] Lord Denning's exposition that the commissioner of police may make policy decisions for the police and give effect to them together with wide discretion in investigation appears to imply for the police the widest form of independence. However, Lord Denning also appreciates the fact that his exposition of common law may also bend to the superiority of legislative enactment by stating that in line with the Police Act 1964 the commissioner of police may give a report to the Secretary of State. It can be argued that if the Police Act had required more than a report, police independence under the common law would have yielded to the extent it was encroached on by a statute.

In Nigeria, the extensive independence of police as enunciated by Lord Denning does not apply. Section 215(3) of the Nigerian Constitution 1999 provides that the

> President or such other Minister of the Government of the Federation as he may authorise in that behalf may give to the Inspector-General of

116. Ibid., 769.
117. See also the following cases in which the common law position on police independence was stated: *Buttrick v The City of Lowell* 83 Mass 172 (Sup Jud Ct, 1861) (USA); *Enever v The King* [1906] 3 CLR 969, 977 (Australia); *Attorney-General for New South Wales v Perpetual Trustee Co* [1955] AC 457 (Privy Council); *Nicholson v Haldimand-Norfolk Regional Board of Commissioners of Police* [1979] 1 SCR 311(Canada).
118. Philip Stenning, 'The Idea of the Political 'Independence' of the Police: International Interpretations and Experiences' in Margaret E. Beare and Tonita Murray (eds), *Police and Government Relations: Who's Calling the Shots?* (University of Toronto Press 2007), 198–199; Halpenny, 'The Governance of Military Police in Canada' (n 114), 19.
119. Ibid.

> Police such lawful directions with respect to the maintenance and securing of public safety and public order as he may consider necessary, and the Inspector-General of Police shall comply with those directions or cause them to be complied with.

In addition, section 215(5) of the Nigerian Constitution 1999 provides that the 'question whether any, and if so what, directions have been given under this section shall not be inquired into in any court.' It would be recalled that the inspector-general is the most senior police officer in Nigeria and that all police officers in Nigeria are under his or her command. Therefore, to the extent that the president may give a direction, police independence as enunciated by Lord Denning does not apply.

It can, however, be argued that at least with respect to the investigation of crimes (including international crimes recognised under the Rome Statute) and laying of charges, the directions of the president may not encroach. This appears to be justified by the decision of the Supreme Court of Canada in *R v Campbell.*[120] In *Campbell*, two people were charged with drug offences by the Royal Canadian Mounted Police (RCMP). The RCMP officers in a 'reverse sting operation' sold drugs to these people. The Crown sought to justify the action of the police in baiting the defendants and obtaining immunity for them, as well, by arguing that the officers concerned were agents of the Crown and that they were under the protection of the Crown public immunity. The Supreme Court of Canada rejected this argument and held that the

> Crown's attempt to identify the RCMP with the Crown for immunity purposes misconceives the relationship between the police and the executive government when the police are engaged in law enforcement. A police officer investigating a crime is not acting as a government functionary or as an agent of anybody. He or she occupies a public office initially defined by the common law and subsequently set out in various statutes.[121]

The court took cognisance of the fact that the police 'perform a myriad of functions apart from the investigation of crimes'[122] and that 'some of these functions bring the RCMP into a closer relationship to the Crown than others.'[123] Nonetheless, the court held that 'in this appeal, however, we are concerned only with the status of an RCMP officer in the course of a criminal investigation, and in that regard the police are independent of the

120. [1999] 1 SCR 565.
121. Ibid para 27.
122. Ibid para 28.
123. Ibid.

control of the executive government.'[124] The court invoked *Blackburn* to justify its position[125] and added that the principle of police independence from the executive 'underpins the rule of law'[126] and that it constitutes 'one of the fundamental and organizing principles of the Constitution.'[127] It is worthy to mention that just as the Nigerian Constitution 1999 empowers the president to issue lawful directives, section 5(1) of the Canadian RCMP Act places the commissioner of the RCMP 'under the direction of the Minister' who 'has the control and management of the Force and all matters connected therewith.'

While *Campbell* may serve as a persuasive authority in Nigeria in certain respects, the Supreme Court of Canada's reliance on the doctrine of rule of law to justify police independence is unacceptable in Nigeria even though the doctrine was invoked to justify equal subjection of every person to prosecution if occasioned. In *Attorney-General Ondo State v Attorney-General Federation*,[128] the Supreme Court of Nigeria held that doctrines cannot be relied upon to interpret the Constitution and that they are at best healthy political theory to analyse what the court has interpreted.[129] Nonetheless, *Campbell* can be subsumed within the provision of the Nigerian Constitution. Thus, an interpretation of the power vested in the president admits the proposition that the power is only limited to directions for securing public safety and public order and that investigative power of the police is excluded.

While police independence with respect to the investigation of crimes and laying of charges can be said to obtain in Nigeria, the appointment of the inspector-general of police, however, appears to undermine it. It would be recalled that the OTP in its list of the indicia of independence of prosecutors emphasises the nature of governing body. Although the police may not have to prosecute international crimes by the nature of their complexity as previously stated, nonetheless, the nature of governing body is also relevant for an impartial investigation. Thus, with the appointment of the inspector-general of police, what the constitution appears to give with the right hand, it takes with the left hand.

Sections 215(1)(a) and 216(2) of the Nigerian Constitution 1999 empower the president to appoint and remove the inspector-general of police on the advice of the Nigeria Police Council. The Nigeria Police Council is made up of the president as the chairman, the governor of each state of the federation, the chairman of the Police Service Commission and the inspector-general of police (this will be the outgoing officer when another is to be appointed). To the extent that the function of the Nigeria Police Council is limited to giving

124. Ibid para 29.
125. Ibid para 33.
126. Ibid para 18.
127. Ibid.
128. [2002] FWLR (Pt 111) 1972.
129. Ibid 2145–2146 paras F-D.

advice, the inspector-general of police holds his or her office at the mercy of the president. The provision is merely cosmetic as it is not compulsory for the president to accede to the advice given by the Nigeria Police Council. It is worthy to mention that other officers apart from the inspector-general of police are appointed, promoted and disciplined by the Police Service Commission.[130] Therefore, since all police officers are under the command of the inspector-general of police and since the inspector-general of police holds his or her appointment at the mercy of the president, police independence in Nigeria is arguably compromised. In addition, the police under the British control were pro-executive in their operation.[131] This orientation remains with the Nigerian police to date. Thus, with the subjection of the police to executive control coupled with their pro-executive orientation, the Nigerian police cannot effectively investigate crimes recognised under the Rome Statute when the interests of the executive will be affected.

Unlike Nigeria, the appointment of the inspector-general of police by the president in Kenya is subject to the approval of the parliament.[132] The inspector-general of police has the command of all police officers in Kenya as it obtains in Nigeria.[133] While the 'Cabinet secretary responsible for police services may lawfully give a direction to the Inspector-General with respect to any matter of policy for the National Police Service,' no person may give a direction to the inspector-general 'with respect to the investigation of any particular offence or offences.'[134] Any direction given by the cabinet secretary or the director of public prosecution must be in writing.[135] However, the president can unilaterally remove the inspector-general, which seriously undermines police independence.[136] Although the removal must be on the stipulated grounds of serious violation of the Constitution or any other law, including a contravention of chapter six,[137] gross misconduct whether in the performance of the office holder's functions or otherwise,[138] physical or mental incapacity to perform the functions of office,[139] incompetence[140] and bankruptcy,[141] the inclusion of 'any other just cause'[142] as a ground for removal appears to be too broad which further undermines police independence.

130. Nigerian Constitution 1999, Third Schedule Part I para M ss 30(a) and (b).
131. P.A.O. Oluyede, *Constitutional Law in Nigeria* (Evans Brothers (Nigeria Publishers) Limited 1992), 438.
132. Kenyan Constitution 2010, art 245(2)(a).
133. Ibid art 245(2)(b).
134. Ibid art 245(4)(a).
135. Ibid art 245(5).
136. Ibid art 245(7).
137. Ibid art 245(7)(a).
138. Ibid art 245(7)(b).
139. Ibid art 245(7)(c).
140. Ibid art 245(7)(d).
141. Ibid art 245(7)(e).
142. Ibid art 245(7)(f).

In Uganda, the command of the police is also placed under the inspector-general of police.[143] Like Kenya, the appointment of the attorney-general is also subject to the approval of the parliament.[144] However, the president can remove the inspector-general at will[145] as there is no stipulated ground. Unlike Kenya, where the cabinet secretary is empowered to give directions, it is the president that may give direction on policy matters in Uganda.[146]

Independence and Impartiality of the Judiciary in Nigeria

It would be recalled that the judiciary in Nigeria was discussed under the Nigerian legal system.[147] In this chapter, it is the independence and impartiality of this judiciary that is the focus. With respect to the independence and impartiality of the judiciary, it would be recalled that the Universal Declaration of Human Rights, the International Covenant on Civil and Political Rights, the European Convention on Human Rights, the American Convention on Human Rights, the African Charter on Human and Peoples' Rights, the Universal Charter of the Judge, the Commonwealth (Latimer House) Principles on the Three Branches of Government and the Basic Principles on the Independence of the Judiciary all provide for the independence of the judiciary in terms of separation of powers; qualifications, selection and training; conditions of service and tenure; and discipline, suspension and removal of judges.[148] Similarly, the OTP of the ICC in its list of the indicia of independence emphasises the degree of independence of the judiciary and prosecutors, the appointment and dismissal of judges, nature of governing body, patterns of political interference in investigation and prosecution and patterns of preordained outcomes.[149]

With respect to impartiality of the judiciary, the Universal Charter of the Judge and the Bangalore Principles of Judicial Conduct provide that justice must not only be done, it must be seen to have been done. The OTP, in its list of indicia, emphasises the avoidance of what can present the outlook of bias and lack of independence.[150] The ICC in *Prosecutor v Saif Al-Islam Gaddafi & Abdullah Al-Senussi*,[151] applied the standard of a 'reasonable observer, properly informed.'[152] Similarly, the Appeals Chamber of the ICC

143. Ugandan Constitution 2005, art 213(3).
144. Ibid art 213(2).
145. Ibid art 213(5).
146. Ibid art 213(4).
147. See chapter 2.
148. Ibid.
149. Ibid.
150. Ibid.
151. *Prosecutor v Saif Al-Islam Gaddafi & Abdullah Al-Senussi*, 'Decision on the Request for Disqualification of the Prosecutor' ICC-01/11-01/11-175(OA3), 12 June 2012.
152. Ibid para 20.

in *Prosecutor v Abdullah Al-Senussi*[153] adopted the notion of independence and impartiality as enshrined in human rights instruments and applied by various human rights courts.[154] It is the preceding criteria that are adopted in assessing the impartiality of the Nigerian judiciary in this chapter. Meanwhile, the Federal Republic of Nigeria Code of Conduct for Judicial Officers (Code of Conduct) largely guides how the judiciary should internally regulates itself so as not only to do justice but to be seen as doing justice and it accords with the stipulations of the Universal Charter of the Judge, the Bangalore Principles of Judicial Conduct and the OTP's position that justice must not only be done; it must also be seen to have been done.

As previously established, the Nigerian Constitution recognises the principle of separation of powers. With respect to the judiciary, this is arguably to prevent it from unlawful interference by the other arms of government. The Nigerian Constitution vests the judicial powers of the federation in the 'courts established for the Federation'[155] and in the courts established 'for a State.'[156] Judicial powers extend 'to all inherent powers and sanctions of a court of law'[157] and 'to all matters between persons, or between government or authority and to any person in Nigeria.'[158]

The Nigerian Constitution provides for the qualification, selection and training of judges in Nigeria. Only legal practitioners called to the Nigerian bar for a period not less than 15 years can be appointed as a justice of the Supreme Court[159] while only legal practitioners called to the Nigerian bar for a period not less than 12 years can be appointed as a justice of the Court of Appeal.[160] For any person to be qualified for appointment as a judge of the federal High Court, the High Court of the Capital Territory, Abuja and the state High Court he or she must have practised as a legal practitioner for a period not less than 10 years.[161] It appears that if a non-Nigerian has been called to the Nigerian bar for a period not less than those stipulated with respect to these courts, such a person is qualified to be appointed. But non-Nigerians cannot be called to the Nigerian bar unless they have a qualifying certificate and satisfy the Body of Benchers as to character.[162]

153. *Prosecutor v Saif Al-Islam Gaddafi & Abdullah Al-Senussi* Judgment on the appeal of Mr Abdullah Al-Senussi against the decision of Pre-Trial Chamber I of 11 October 2013 entitled, 'Decision on the admissibility of the case against Abdullah Al-Senussi' ICC-OI/II-OI/IIOA6, dated 24 July 2014.
154. Ibid para 250.
155. Nigerian Constitution 1999, s 6(1).
156. Ibid s 6(2).
157. Ibid s 6(6)(a).
158. Ibid s 6(6)(b).
159. Ibid s 231(3).
160. Ibid s 238(3).
161. Ibid ss 250(3), 256(3) and 271(3).
162. Legal Practitioners Act 2007, s 4(4).

With respect to selection, the Constitution empowers the president of the Federal Republic of Nigeria to appoint the chief justice of Nigeria and other justices of the Supreme Court,[163] the president of the Court of Appeal,[164] the chief judge of the federal High Court[165] and the chief judge of the High Court of the Federal Capital Territory, Abuja[166] on the recommendation of the National Judicial Council (NJC) subject to the confirmation of the Senate. Similarly, the president is empowered to appoint justices of the Court of Appeal,[167] judges of the federal High Court[168] and judges of the High Court of the Federal Capital Territory, Abuja[169] on the recommendation of the NJC but without Senate confirmation. With respect to the high court of a state, it is the governor that appoints the chief judge on the recommendation of the NJC subject to the confirmation of House of Assembly.[170] House of Assembly confirmation is not, however, required for other judges.[171]

The training of judges is subsumed within the precinct of the constitutional provision on freedom of association. Thus, the Federal Republic of Nigeria Code of Conduct for Judicial Officers (Code of Conduct or the Code)[172] provides that 'Judicial Officers shall be free to form and join associations of judges or other organisations to represent their interests, to promote their professional training and to protect their judicial independence.'[173] The National Judicial Institute is a professional body for judges that organises conferences and lectures for the training of judges.

The Nigerian Constitution also makes provision with respect to the conditions of service and tenure of judges in Nigeria. The age of retirement for the justices of the Supreme Court and the Court of Appeal is 70[174] while that of other judicial officers is 65.[175] Judges are also entitled to receive a pension for life on their retirement.[176] The salaries and allowances of the justices of the Supreme Court,[177] the justices of the Court of Appeal[178] and the judges of

163. Nigerian Constitution 1999, ss 231(1) and 231(2).
164. Ibid s 238(1).
165. Ibid s 250(1).
166. Ibid s 256(1).
167. Ibid s 238(2).
168. Ibid s 250(2).
169. Ibid s 256(2).
170. Ibid s 271(1).
171. Ibid s 271(2).
172. Federal Republic of Nigeria Code of Conduct for Judicial Officers, www.unodc.org/documents/nigeria//publications/Otherpublications/Nigeria_Code_of_Conduct_for_Judges_Poster1.pdf accessed 7 August 2017.
173. Ibid Rule 3B(ii) and (iii).
174. Nigerian Constitution 1999, s 291(1).
175. Ibid s 291(2).
176. Ibid s 291(3).
177. Supreme Court Act Cap S15 Revised LFN 2004, s 5.
178. Court of Appeal Act Cap C37 Revised LFN 2004, s 2(4).

the Federal High Court[179] are charged on and paid out of the Consolidated Revenue Fund.[180] In addition, the NJC 'control and disburse all moneys, capital and recurrent, for the judiciary'[181] and 'deal with all other matters relating to broad issues of policy and administration.'[182]

In *Judicial Staff Union of Nigeria v National Judicial Council*,[183] the constitutionality of the piecemeal release of the amount standing to the credit of the judiciary in the Federation Account/Consolidated Revenue Fund by the executive to the judiciary was challenged. The court held that the practice was unconstitutional. Similarly, in *Olisa Agbakoba v The Attorney General of the Federation*,[184] the constitutionality of the practice in which the judiciary submits its budgetary estimates to the executive for consideration and inclusion in the Appropriation Bill prepared by the executive was considered. The court held that the practice was unconstitutional. The court held that 'as the executive arm is required by the Constitution of the Federal Republic of Nigeria 1999 to submit its Budget Estimates to the National Assembly for deliberations, so is the judicial arm accorded the same right and independence to do so under sections 81 and 84 of the same Constitution.'[185] It is however worthy of note that the competence of the judiciary to prepare its own budget without having had to submit it to the executive for inclusion in the executive Appropriation Bill is only with respect to salaries, allowances, remuneration and recurrent expenditure while capital expenditure is excluded.[186]

In *Olisa Agbakoba* the court noted that the practice where the judiciary had to submit its estimates to the executive for the executive to include it in the Appropriation Bill

> undermines the financial independence of the judiciary in this country. For times without number, the estimates of salaries, allowances, remuneration and recurrent expenditure of the judiciary are being altered. This alteration has always been at the detriment of effective and efficient administration of justice in this country.[187]

Thus,

> each year, the judiciary Budget continues to decline. It has moved downwards from ₦90 Billion to ₦75 Billion. The Budget Office advises

179. Federal High Court Act Cap F12 Revised LFN 2004, s 5.
180. Supreme Court Act, s 5.
181. Nigerian Constitution 1999, Third Schedule s 21(e).
182. Ibid Third Schedule s 21(i).
183. Suit No FHC/ABJ/CS/667/13 delivered on 13 January 2014 by AFA Ademola J.
184. FHC/ABJ/CS/63/2013 delivered on Monday 26 May 2014 delivered by AR Mohammed J.
185. Ibid., 40.
186. See Nigerian Constitution 1999, ss 81(1), (2), (3) and 84(1), (2), (3), (4), (7).
187. FHC/ABJ/CS/63/2013 delivered on Monday 26 May 2014 delivered by AR Mohammed J, 38.

> the NJC not to go beyond a ceiling. In 2012, the ceiling was placed at ₦65 Billion . . . most judges do not have befitting office, furniture, court-room and personnel assistance to carry out judicial functions unhindered. Many judges write in torturing and judicial time-wasting long hand because the modern recording technology could not be acquired . . . court rooms are very dilapidated, stuffy and generally not conducive for serious judicial business. Courtrooms are not the "hallowed chambers" they should be . . . judiciary staff are always on one industrial action or the other across Nigeria as a result of the underfunding of the judiciary . . .[188]

Hence,

> the continued dependence of the judiciary on the executive arm for its budgeting and funds release is directly responsible for the present state of underfunding of the judiciary, poor and inadequate judicial infrastructure, low morale among judicial personnel, alleged corruption in the judiciary, delays in administration of justice and judicial services delivery and general low quality and poor out-put by the judiciary.[189]

With respect to discipline, suspension and removal, the Nigerian Constitution 1999 provides that a judge can only be removed before retirement based on infirmity of body or mind, misconduct or contravention of the Code of Conduct.[190] It appears that the Code of Conduct referred to is the Code of Conduct which generally applies to public officers and not the Code of Conduct for judicial officers. However, the inclusion of 'misconduct' should cover all prohibited conducts in the Code of Conduct for judicial officers. The chief justice of Nigeria, president of the Court of Appeal, the chief judge of the federal High Court and the chief judge of the High Court of the Federal Capital Territory, Abuja, can only be removed by the 'President acting on an address supported by two-thirds majority of the Senate'[191] while justices of the Supreme Court, justices of the Court of Appeal, judges of the federal High Court and judges of the High Court of the Federal Capital Territory, Abuja, can only be removed by the president 'acting on the recommendation of the National Judicial Council.'[192] It is the governor 'acting on an address supported by a two-thirds majority of the House of Assembly of the State' that can remove the chief judge of a state[193] while other judges

188. Ibid., 20–21.
189. Ibid 4 and 42.
190. Nigerian Constitution 1999, s 292(1).
191. Ibid s 292(1)(a)(i).
192. Ibid s 292(1)(b).
193. Ibid s 292(1)(a)(ii).

can only be removed by the governor 'acting on the recommendation of the National Judicial Council.'[194]

Apart from the preceding constitutional provisions, judicial immunity also obtains in Nigeria either as a statutory provision or English common law applicable in Nigeria. Section 88 of the High Court Law of Lagos State of Nigeria stipulates that

> no judge shall be liable for any act done by him or ordered by him to be done on the discharge of his judicial duty, whether or not within the limits of his jurisdiction provided that he at the time, in good faith, believed himself to have jurisdiction to do or order to be done the act in question.

On the other hand, statutes with respect to the Supreme Court, Court of Appeal and the federal High Court do not contain identical provisions. The implication is that judicial immunity with respect to judges of these courts is governed by English common law.

Against the backdrop of the preceding discussion, the judiciary in Nigeria appears to be independent, and it should be able to successfully adjudicate on international crimes. However, an examination of the composition of the National Judicial Council and its procedure may indicate that its independence is just a 'myth.'[195] The need to appraise this body is predicated on the emphasis placed by the OTP in its list of indicia of independence on the nature of governing body not only for the prosecutor but also for the judiciary. The NJC is made up of the chief justice of Nigeria (CJN) as the chairman; the justice of the Supreme Court, who is next in rank to the CJN as the deputy chairman; the president of the Court of Appeal; five retired justices to be appointed by the CJN from among the retired justices of the Court of Appeal or the Supreme Court, the chief judge of the federal High Court, five chief judges from state High Courts and the High Court of the Federal Capital Territory, Abuja, appointed by the CJN; one Grand Kadi appointed by the CJN from Grand Kadis of the Sharia Courts of Appeal; one president of the Customary Court of Appeal appointed by the CJN from presidents of the Customary Courts of Appeal, five members of the Nigerian Bar Association appointed by the CJN who must have practised for at least 15 years one of whom must be in the rank of a Senior Advocate of Nigeria; and two persons who are not legal practitioners 'who in the opinion of the chief justice of Nigeria, are of unquestionable integrity.'[196]

The NJC is therefore made up of the CJN and 22 members. Out of the 22 members, the CJN appoints 19. With respect to the procedure of the NJC, one-third of the 23 members (CJN and 22 members) are sufficient to form

194. Ibid s 292(1)(b).
195. Opeyemi Akanbi, 'The Myth of Judicial Independence in Nigeria'. 20 April 2012. http://ssrn.com/abstract=2175933 accessed 7 August 2017.
196. Nigerian Constitution 1999, para 20 Part 1 Third Schedule.

a quorum, which is eight.[197] And, the simple majority of eight, which is five, is sufficient to take decisions on behalf of the council[198] notwithstanding the absence of other members.[199] Therefore, the decision to recommend any person for appointment as a judge or to discipline any judge or recommend any judge for removal as the case may be can be taken by just four members and the CJN. The combined implication of the composition of the NJC and its procedure is that any person who does not enjoy the goodwill of the CJN can hardly be appointed. Since judges like other human beings also want to keep their job and be elevated, it means that those appointed as judges have to make sure they are in the good book of the CJN. Meanwhile, the CJN holds his office at the pleasure of the president since the president as a politician could cause his removal by instigating the members of the Senate, who are also politicians as well to authorise his removal. This is more feasible where the president belongs to the same political party as the majority of the members of the Senate. Therefore, all that is required to manipulate the judiciary is to take control of the CJN.[200]

While it can be argued that the Senate cannot authorise the removal of the CJN unless his actions amount to misconduct, the point is that categories of what constitutes a misconduct is never closed, nor can it be seriously suggested that the Senate cannot create new ones. Similarly, while it can also be argued that the CJN may challenge his removal by way of judicial review, the political question doctrine may be an obstacle[201] to a successful challenge although the CJN may presumably be expected to enjoy the support of his or her colleague and have the doctrine whittled down in his or her favour.[202] In addition, the cost in terms of time and money when it comes to obtaining justice may inform the CJN to make himself or herself malleable to both the executive and the legislature. The CJN might have realised quite well that the fear of politicians is the beginning of wisdom.

It is pertinent to mention that the NJC is to be advised by the Federal Judicial Service Commission (FJSC) in recommending any person for appointment to the office of the chief justice of Nigeria, a justice of the Supreme Court, the president of the Court of Appeal, a justice of the Court of Appeal, the chief judge of the federal High Court, a judge of the federal High Court, and the chairman and members of the Code of Conduct Tribunal.[203] But this does not offer any meaningful protection against manipulation. Apart from the fact that the NJC is not bound by the advice of the FJSC, it is just a mere

197. Ibid s 159(1).
198. Ibid 159(2).
199. Ibid s 159(4).
200. Akanbi, 'The Myth of Judicial Independence in Nigeria' (n 195), 60.
201. On the doctrine of political question in Nigeria, see Enyinna Nwauche, 'Is the End Near for the Political Question Doctrine in Nigeria?' in Charles Fombad and Christina Murray (eds), *Fostering Constitutionalism in Africa* (Pretoria University Law Press 2010), 31–60.
202. Ibid.
203. Nigerian Constitution 1999, Third Schedule Part I para E s 13.

subset of the NJC with respect to membership. The FJSC is made up of the chief justice of Nigeria, who shall be the chairman; the president of the Court of Appeal; the attorney-general of the federation; the chief judge of the federal High Court; two persons, each of whom has been qualified to practice as a legal practitioner in Nigeria for a period of not less than 15 years, from a list of not less than four persons so qualified recommended by the Nigerian Bar Association; and two other persons, not being legal practitioners, who in the opinion of the president are of unquestionable integrity.[204]

With respect to states within the Nigerian Federation, the State Judicial Service Commission (SJSC) advises the NJC with respect to the appointment and removal of the chief judge and other judges of the High Court of the state. The membership of SJSC includes the chief judge of the state, who shall be the chairman; the attorney-general of the state; the grand kadi of the Sharia Court of Appeal of the state, if any; the president of the Customary Court of Appeal of the state, if any; two members, who are legal practitioners and who have been qualified to practice as legal practitioners in Nigeria for no fewer than 10 years; and two other persons not being legal practitioners, who in the opinion of the governor are of unquestionable integrity. Just as the NJC is not bound by the advice of the FJSC, it is also not bound by the advice of the SJSC, and it is self-evident that the membership of the SJSC offers no protection of any kind against manipulation.

The court martial is even in a more precarious situation than the regular courts. It is nothing more pretentious than an extension of the will of the executive. The president of the Federal Republic of Nigeria can order one to be set up, and the judgement of the tribunal requires the endorsement of the convening authority. It would be recalled that independence is lacking where the validity of a judicial decision is subject to confirmation by the executive arm. As previously established, the fact that judicial decision cannot be varied by the executive arm of government is inherent in the notion of a tribunal and its independence. Since the tribunal is *ad hoc* it can readily give in to abuse and become a tool of truncating justice. For example, the tribunal can be set up to witch-hunt those opposed to government's genocidal policy and divert attention from actual culprits who align themselves with the policy of the government.

With respect to the issue of impartiality, the Code of Conduct states that it is 'desirable that standard of conduct which a Judicial Officer should observe be prescribed and published for the information of the Judicial Officer himself and the public in general . . .'[205] In the Code, judicial officers are the chief justice of Nigeria and other justices of the Supreme Court, the president and other justices of the Court of Appeal, the chief judges and other judges of

204. Ibid Third Schedule Part I para E s 12.

205. Code of Conduct for Judicial Officers Federal Republic of Nigeria, para 2 preamble.

the federal and state High Courts.[206] The Code further provides that it 'applies to all categories of judicial officers throughout the Federation.'[207] Arguably, this omnibus provision covers presiding officers in courts-martial and other courts that may be established in future.

The Code provides that a judicial officer must avoid relationship 'that cast doubt on the judicial officers ability to decide cases impartially.'[208] When the impartiality of a judicial officer might reasonably be questioned, he or she must recuse himself or herself.[209] Circumstances in which the impartiality of a judicial officer may be at issue include when the judicial officer has a personal bias or prejudice concerning a party or when the judicial officer has personal knowledge of the fact.[210] Another circumstance is when a judicial officer had previously acted as a legal practitioner in a matter or another person with whom he had earlier practised is a legal practitioner in the matter in which he is called to decide or that person with whom he had earlier practised is a witness in the matter he is called to decide.[211] Similarly, when a judicial officer or his spouse or child has an interest (whether financial or otherwise) which could be affected by the outcome of a proceeding, then his or her impartiality will be in issue.[212] In the same vein, impartiality will be an issue when a judicial officer or his or her spouse relates to one of the parties.[213] The bottom line of all these examples is that justice must not only be done; it must also be seen to have been done which is in line with the stipulations of the Universal Charter of the Judge, the Bangalore Principles of Judicial Conduct and the OTP's position.

In *Isiyaku Mohammed v Kano Native Authority*,[214] it was held that 'the true test of fair hearing is the impression of a reasonable person who was present at the trial whether from his observation; justice has been done in the case.'[215] The court added that 'such a bystander would be guided by two universally recognised principles. First, were the two sides to the case heard so as to fulfil the principle of *audi alteram partem*? Second, was the judge personally interested in the issue before him, thus violating the principle of *nemo judex in causa sua*?'[216] Similarly, in *Mika'ilu v State*,[217] it was held that 'where there is a breach of the principle of fair hearing, any decision arrived at would

206. Ibid Explanatory section, para i.
207. Ibid Explanatory section, para ii.
208. Ibid Rule 1(2)(a).
209. Ibid Rule C1.
210. Ibid Rule 2C(1)(a).
211. Ibid Rule 2C(1)(b).
212. Ibid Rule 2C(1)(c).
213. Ibid Rule 2C(1)(d).
214. [1968] 1 All NLR 33.
215. Ibid.
216. Ibid.
217. (2001) 5 WRN 74.

be cut down notwithstanding that the conclusion would not have been any different if the principle had been adhered to.'[218] While the impartiality of the judiciary appears to have to be established with respect to each specific case, there is no doubt that lack of independence of the judiciary has the propensity of producing a partial judiciary with intent not to do justice when the interests of the executive and the legislature are at stake.

218. Ibid., 80.

8 Inability

The Need for Witness Protection, Extradition Arrangement and Delegation of Criminal Jurisdiction to Other States

It would be recalled that the concept of inability within the meaning of article 17 of the Rome Statute envisages two distinct situations. The first one is the total collapse of a legal system.[1] This is not considered in this chapter. The reason is that this book assumes the existence of the Nigerian legal system. The second situation envisaged in article 17 of the Rome Statute is inability to obtain evidence or the accused or to carry out proceedings.[2] Obviously, inability to carry out proceedings appears to be a catch-all phrase, and it is not considered here. Therefore, what is left for consideration is the inability to obtain evidence and inability to obtain the accused.

With respect to inability to obtain evidence, it would be recalled that the Pre-Trial Chamber I of the International Criminal Court (ICC) in *Prosecutor v Saif Al-Islam Gaddafi & Abdullah Al-Senussi*,[3] held that Libya's lack of a strong witness protection regime culminated in its failure to obtain necessary evidence[4] and that this is sufficient for ICC intervention in spite of the fact that the trial judge in Libya has some measure of discretion in obtaining evidence in any manner the judge considers appropriate.[5] Thus, the case is made for a strong witness protection regime against which the Nigerian legal system is examined.

With respect to inability to obtain the accused, it would also be recalled that the Pre-Trial Chamber I found in favour of ICC intervention as Libya could not obtain the custody of the accused[6] coupled with the fact that *in absentia* trial is not permitted in Libya.[7] Thus, the case is made for extradition arrangements between Nigeria and other state entities which will also be the basis of assessment of the Nigerian legal system. Although the legal

1. See Chapter 3.
2. Ibid.
3. *Prosecutor v Saif Al-Islam Gaddafi & Abdullah Al-Senussi*, 'Decision on the admissibility of the case against Saif Al-Islam Gaddafi' ICC-01/11–01/11, dated 31 May 2013.
4. Ibid para 209.
5. Ibid para 211.
6. Ibid para 206.
7. Ibid para 208.

propriety of relying on the preceding findings has earlier been considered somewhat questionable since they ought not to have been made in the first place,[8] nonetheless, they have, at the same time, been considered to have offered some guidance.

Inability to Obtain Evidence

Modern prosecution of international crimes relies heavily on oral evidence unlike prosecution by the International Military Tribunal (IMT) which relied largely on documentary evidence.[9] Unlike the 'meticulous recordkeeping that made Nazi war crimes relatively easy to prove'[10] 'high ranking perpetrators today are not so careless as to leave a paper trail of their orders.'[11] This necessarily suggests the need for witness protection. In *Moore v Clarke of Assize Bristol*,[12] Lord Denning stated that 'the court will always preserve the freedom and integrity of witnesses and not allow them to be intimidated in any way, either before the trial, pending it or after it.'[13]

Witness protection first gained prominence in the United States in 1970. It was adopted as a strategy to destroy organisations run by mafias.[14] Thus, the Organised Crime Control Act was enacted in 1970. The Act empowered the US attorney-general to provide for the protection of witnesses that had chosen to testify in organised crime and other serious crimes. Thus, the Witness Security (WITSEC) programme of the United States was introduced. The programme ensured physical protection of witnesses who were at risk. Protection measures included resettlement to a new undisclosed place of residence with new identity details. Following some inadequacies in the programme after its operation for 10 years, the Witness Security Reform Act was enacted in 1984. The Act addressed fundamental issues which are central to any witness protection programme. The issues include well-articulated

8. *Prosecutor v Saif Al-Islam Gaddafi & Abdullah Al-Senussi*, Judgment on the appeal of Libya against the decision of Pre-Trial Chamber I of 31 May 2013 entitled 'Decision on the admissibility of the case against Saif Al-Islam Gaddafi' ICC-01/11-01/11 OA 4, dated 21 May 2014, paras 213–214.
9. Paulina Vega Gonzalez and Carla Ferstman, *Ending Threats and Reprisals Against Victims of Torture and Related International Crimes: A Call to Action* (Redress 2009), 51.
10. Terry Coonan, 'Prosecuting and Defending Violations of Genocide and Humanitarian Law: The International Tribunal for the Former Yugoslavia' 1994 American Society of International Law Proceedings 239, 248.
11. Regina E. Rauxloh, 'Plea Bargaining in International Criminal Justice: Can the International Criminal Court Afford to Avoid Trials?' (2011) 1(2) *The Journal of Criminal Justice Research (JCJR)* 1–25, 17–18.
12. [1972] 1 All ER 58 (CA).
13. Ibid. On witness protection in India, see also *Zahira Habibulla H Sheikh v State of Gujarat (Best Bakery Case)* (2004) 4 SCC 158 and contempt proceeding against *Zahira Habibulla H Sheikh* (2006) 3 SCC 374.
14. United Nations Office on Drugs and Crime, 'Good Practices for the Protection of Witnesses in Criminal Proceedings involving Organised Crime' (2008) 7.

admission criteria, including an appraisal of the danger posed by relocated former criminals to the public, the establishment of a fund to compensate victims of crimes committed by participants who have been admitted to the programme, signing of a memorandum of understanding in which the obligations of witnesses admitted to the programme are clearly outlined, setting forth in details the procedures to be followed should there be an infraction of the memorandum by the participant, instituting procedures for the disclosure of information with respect to programme participants and providing for punishment for any unauthorised disclosure of such information and safeguarding the rights of third parties, particularly honouring the debt of witnesses and the right of parents who are not relocated to the custody of their children or the rights of parents to visit their children.

Witness protection has assumed an international dimension. Article 24 of the United Nations Convention against Transnational Organised Crime[15] provides that state parties are to take appropriate measures towards ensuring the protection of witnesses from being intimidated. The measures contemplated include physical protection, relocation of witnesses, non-disclosure of the whereabouts of witnesses, limitation in disclosing the identity of any witness and amendment of the law of evidence to ensure the safety of witnesses while giving evidence. State parties are also to consider entering into agreements with other states in relocating witnesses.[16] Article 24 also applies to victims in so far as they are witnesses.[17] Similarly, article 26 of the convention provides that state parties are to take measures towards ensuring that participants in organised crimes cooperate with law enforcement authorities for investigative and evidentiary purposes. Such participants are also entitled to be protected under article 24.

Like the United States, other states have aligned themselves with the ideals stipulated in the United Nations Convention against Transnational Organised Crimes through various pieces of legislation.[18] For federal states like the United States and Australia, federating units have also enacted laws with respect to witness protection to complement federal enactment.[19] However,

15. General Assembly Resolution 55/25, Annex I.
16. Ibid art 24 para 3.
17. Ibid art 24 para 4.
18. Witness Protection Act 1994 (Australia); Witness Protection Programme Act 1996 (Canada); Law No 418 of 1997 (Colombia); Witness Protection Act 2001 (Germany); Witness Protection Ordinance 2000 (Hong Kong); Decree-Law No 82 of 15 March 1991 as amended in 2001 (Italy); Witness Protection Amendment Act 2010 (Kenya); Witness Protection, Security and Benefit Act No 6891 (1991) (Philippines); Witness Protection Act 112 of 1998 (South Africa); Witness Protection Act B E 2546/2003 (Thailand).
19. With respect to the United States, see the California Witness Protection Programme 1997 in California Penal Code, §§14020 through14033. As regards Australia, see Witness Protection Act 1996 (Australian Capital Territory); Witness Protection Act 1995 (New South Wales); Witness Protection (Northern Territory) Act 2002 (Northern Territory); Witness Protection Act 2000 (Queensland); Witness Protection Act 1996 (South Australia); Witness

there are states that have witness protection programme as a matter of policy as opposed to legislation. These include New Zealand, Austria, the Netherlands and Norway.[20] The list shows that adopting witness programme as a matter of policy cuts across legal traditions. Thus, states with common law legal tradition and those with Civil Law legal tradition have sometimes chosen policy as opposed to legislation. Nonetheless, the policy adopted must indicate protection measures that may be put in place, the criteria for admission of witnesses and conditions for their application, the procedure to be followed, the authority responsible for the implementation of the programme, the reason for the termination of the programme, the rights and obligations of the parties and the confidentiality of the operations of the programme. All these are at the heart of witness protection.

Apart from the importance that witness protection has assumed among states, it has also assumed an importance of high magnitude in international tribunals. This is understandable since these tribunals rely largely on oral evidence in contradistinction to their IMT counterpart which relied on documentary evidence. Article 22 of the Statute of the International Criminal Tribunal for Yugoslavia (ICTY) mandates the tribunal to provide for witness protection in its Rules of Procedure and Evidence (RPE). Pursuant to article 22 of the Statute, rule 34 of the RPE empowers the Registrar of the Court to set up a Victims and Witnesses section to recommend protective measures. The tribunal has a number of protective measures like expunging names and other identity information from the court record, testifying under a pseudonym, electronic facial distortion, voice distortion, closed session, testifying through video-link, and giving testimony from a remote witness room.[21] In some cases witnesses may be relocated to a state other than their home state. However, this is not part of witness protection measures that may be granted by the court. It is the registrar that concludes relocating arrangements with several states. Although relocation may address the concern of most witnesses, nonetheless, the registrar may request the relocating state to admit the witness to its own witness protection programme. While relocation may tend to induce testimony, the registrar must scrutinise thoroughly any situation that calls for relocation.

The legal regime of witness protection in the International Criminal Tribunal for Rwanda (ICTR) is identical with that of the ICTY. Articles 14 and 21 of the Statute of the ICTR mandate the RPE to provide for witness protection while rule 34 of the RPE provides for witness protection. However, while ICTR took effect in 1994, an efficient witness protection was not put in place

---

Protection Act 2000 (Tasmania); Witness Protection Act 1999 (Victoria); Witness Protection (Western Australia) Act 1996 (Western Australia).

20. United Nations Office on Drugs and Crime, 'Good Practices for the Protection of Witnesses in Criminal Proceedings involving Organised Crime' (n 14), 44.

21. RPE, r 75.

until 1996 when not less than 99 witnesses had been killed.[22] This further underscores the importance of witness protection. Unlike the ICTY and the ICTR which provide for witness protection in their respective RPEs, the Rome Statute of the ICC has its provision on witness protection in the statute itself.

Article 43(6) of the statute provides for the establishment of the Victims and Witnesses Unit (VWU) under the registrar. This tends to suggest that witness protection is accorded more priority than the earlier statutes. In addition, rule 17 of the ICC RPE empowers the VWU to provide witness protection services to witnesses who have appeared before the court and to those who are at risk on account of the testimony of those who have appeared. The ICC witness protection has proved to be the most successful of all international tribunals.[23] However, the prosecution of the Kenyan president, Uhuru Muigai Kenyatta, by the ICC has thrown up unprecedented challenges to the court's witness protection regime as witnesses were intimidated, and as 'time progressed, more and more witnesses disappeared, changed their accounts or simply refused to give their testimony.'[24] The special circumstance of a sitting president with enormous state machinery at his disposal overwhelms the ICC witness protection regime.[25]

Because of the preceding challenges, the Office of the Prosecutor (OTP) is contemplating the use of other forms of evidence such as forensic materials, electronic evidence including voice and cyber communications, remote sensing, satellite imaging and digital and video analysis.[26] This development

22. Chris Mahony, *The Justice Sector Afterthought: Witness Protection in Africa* (Institute for Security Studies 2010), 59.
23. Ibid., 16.
24. American Non-Governmental Organisations Coalition for the International Criminal Court (AMICC), 'Kenyatta Case at the ICC: Three Options Available for the ICC Judges, the Issue, the Importance of the Status Conferences for the International Community and for the African Countries'. http://amicc.blogspot.com/2014/10/kenyatta-case-at-icc-three-options.html accessed 7 August 2017. See also *Prosecutor v Uhuru Muigai Kenyatta* 'Public redacted version of the 16 July 2013 Prosecution notification of withdrawal of witnesses' ICC-01/09–02/11, dated 16 July 2013; *Prosecutor v Uhuru Muigai Kenyatta* 'Public redacted version of the Prosecution request for protective measures and protections against self-incrimination for its first ten witnesses' ICC-01/09–02/11, dated 11 October 2013 and *Prosecutor v Walter Osapiri Barasa* 'Warrant of arrest for Walter Osapiri Barasa' ICC-01/09–01/13, dated 2 August 2013.
25. The Office of the Prosecutor (OTP) once stated that 'the witness security issues are daunting, the incidents of witness tampering and interference unprecedented.': *Prosecutor v Francis Kirimi Muthaura and Uhuru Muigai Kenyatta*, ICC-01/09–02/11–437-Red2, Public Redacted Version of the Prosecution Response to 'Defence Application for (1) An Order prohibiting the Prosecution from contacting potential Defence witnesses without following the procedural safeguards stipulated in other cases before the ICC and (2) An Order to the Prosecution to disclose information on all contacts between the Prosecution and potential Defence witnesses,' dated 19 June 2012, para 45.
26. International Bar Association (IBA), 'Witnesses Before the International Criminal Court: An International Bar Association International Criminal Court Programme Report on the ICC's Efforts and Challenges to Protect, Support and Ensure the Rights of Witnesses' July 2013, 6.

may appear to undermine the need for witness protection at least in future. However, 'it is unlikely that the Court [or any other court] will ever fully be able to complete a case without the testimony of . . . witnesses'[27] since 'other forms of physical, documentary or electronic evidence require some human verification.'[28] Thus, the need for witness protection will always be relevant.

Witness protection is much more a relatively recent issue in Nigeria. Its rudimentary expression can be found in the Nigerian Terrorism Act 2011, Terrorism (Prevention) (Amendment) Act 2013 and the Administration of Criminal Justice Act 2015. In the Nigerian Terrorism Act 2011, it is stipulated that the identity and address of witness should be kept secret based on the court's own motion or a motion filed by a prosecuting authority[29] and that the place of trial may be determined by the court.[30] Under the Terrorism (Prevention) (Amendment) Act 2013, informants are to be protected by the relevant law enforcement or security agency while their information is to be treated as confidential.[31] The identity and address of witness can be kept secret by the court on its own motion or by a motion filed by the attorney-general or relevant law enforcement or security agency.[32] Steps which the court may take to protect the identity and address of witnesses include determining the venue of the trial,[33] avoiding mentioning the real name of witnesses in its orders and judgement and any documents that can be assessed by the public,[34] issuing orders to the effect that witnesses should be protected[35] and holding trial in camera.[36] In addition, the court may order that its proceedings which are pending shall not be published[37] and that such proceedings may be adjourned and the defendant detained until the safety of witnesses is guaranteed by the attorney-general.[38] The court may also exclude any person from its proceedings except the parties.[39] A violation of an order issued by the court to protect a witness is punishable by at least five years' imprisonment.[40]

Under the Administration of Criminal Justice Act 2015, when the court deems it necessary to protect the identity of the victim or witness, the court may receive evidence by video link,[41] permit the witness to be screened or

27. Ibid., 14.
28. Ibid., 18.
29. Section 29(1).
30. Section 29(2).
31. Section 33(1).
32. Section 34(1).
33. Section 34(2)(a).
34. Section 34(2)(b).
35. Section 34(2)(c).
36. Section 34(2)(d).
37. Section 34(3)(a).
38. Section 34(3)(b).
39. Section 34(4).
40. Section 34(5).
41. Section 232(3)(a).

masked,[42] receive written deposition of expert evidence[43] and take any other measure it considers appropriate in the circumstance.[44] The court may also decide not to conduct a trial in an open court;[45] the names, addresses, telephone numbers and identity of the victims of such offences or witnesses 'shall' not be disclosed in any record or report of the proceedings, and it 'shall' be sufficient to designate the names of the victims or witnesses with a combination of alphabets.[46]

Like the Nigerian Terrorism Act 2011, the Terrorism (Prevention) (Amendment) Act 2013 and the Administration of Criminal Justice Act 2015, the Nigerian Constitution 1999 also has some provisions which may accommodate the idea of witness protection. Section 33(1) of the Constitution of the Federal Republic of Nigeria (Nigerian Constitution) 1999 provides that 'every person has a right to life, and no one shall be deprived intentionally of his life, save in execution of the sentence of a court in respect of a criminal offence of which he has been found guilty in Nigeria.' This provision can be argued to permit witness protection whenever there is a risk of loss of life for the witness. The court may take such necessary steps to protect the life of the witness or the party for whom the witness is to testify may apply to the court to offer such protection as the circumstances of the situation may require. In addition, section 46(1) of the Nigerian Constitution 1999 provides that 'any person who alleges that any of the provisions of this Chapter has been, is being or likely to be contravened in any State in relation to him may apply to a High Court in that State for redress.' A combined reading of this provision with the right to life implies that whenever it is likely that a person may lose his or her life, such a person may seek refuge in court. Although section 46 is essentially jurisdictional, it nonetheless envisages a risk of loss of fundamental rights (including the right to life).

In *Killic v Turkey*,[47] a journalist who had received death threats and had complained to state authorities was not protected until he was eventually killed. The European Court of Human Rights (ECtHR) held that states are obliged to offer protection to those whose lives are at risk and that such risks are those which the state is aware of or ought to have been aware of. Similarly, in *Akkoc v Turkey*,[48] both husband and wife had received several death threats on the phone and had informed the state authorities. However, nothing was done until the husband was eventually killed on the way to his workplace. The failure of the state to act was held to be in violation of the right to life.

42. Section 232(3)(b).
43. Section 232(3)(c).
44. Section 232(3)(d).
45. Section 232(1).
46. Section 232(2).
47. App no 22492/93 (ECtHR, 28 March 2000).
48. App nos 22947/93; 22948/93 (ECtHR, 10 October 2000).

Section 34(1) of the Nigerian Constitution 1999 provides that 'every individual is entitled to respect for the dignity of his person and that 'no person shall be subjected to torture or to inhuman or degrading treatment.'[49] Witness protection may also be subsumed under this provision. The likelihood of the fact that a witness may be tortured is sufficient for the court to make such orders or take such steps as may be necessary to protect the witness. Similarly, section 29(2)(a) of the Evidence Act 2011 renders inadmissible any confessional statement made by a defendant if the confessional statement was obtained 'by oppression of the person who made it.' Meanwhile, section 29(5) of the Evidence Act 2011 provides that oppression 'includes torture, inhuman or degrading treatment and the use or threat of violence whether or not amounting to torture.' In the same vein, section 227 of the Evidence Act 2011 prohibits indecent and scandalous questions (which may be regarded as inhuman or degrading even if those questions do not amount to torture) while section 228 of the same Act forbids questions which are calculated to insult or annoy.

In *Ireland v United Kingdom*,[50] the ECtHR stated that a degrading treatment is 'such as to arouse in [its] victims feelings of fear, anguish and inferiority capable of debasing them and possibly breaking their physical or moral resistance'[51] and that it is only different from torture as a matter of intensity.[52] In *A v United Kingdom*,[53] the court was preoccupied with determining whether state could be held responsible for the beating of the applicant by his stepfather. The court held that states are obliged to adopt measures to prevent anyone from being subjected to cruel, inhuman and degrading treatment including such treatment administered by private individuals.[54] Similarly, in *Z v United Kingdom*,[55] the court stated that states are to provide effective protection against cruel, inhuman and degrading treatment and that reasonable steps must be taken to prevent ill treatment which the state is aware of or ought to have had knowledge of.[56]

Section 36(4) of the Nigerian Constitution 1999 provides that whenever any person is charged with a criminal offence, that person shall be entitled to a fair hearing in public within a reasonable time by a court or tribunal provided that

(a) a court or such a tribunal may exclude from its proceedings persons other than the parties thereto or their legal practitioners in the interest of defence, public safety, public order, public morality, the welfare of

49. Constitution of the Federal Republic of Nigeria (Nigerian Constitution) 1999, s 34(1)(a).
50. App no 5310/71 (ECtHR, 18 January 1978).
51. Ibid para 167.
52. Ibid.
53. App no 100/1977/884/1096 (ECtHR, 3 September 1998).
54. Ibid para 22.
55. App no 29392/95 (ECtHR, 10 May 2001).
56. Ibid para 73.

> persons who have not attained the age of eighteen years, the protection of the private lives of the parties or to such extent as it may consider necessary by reason of special circumstances in which publicity would be contrary to the interests of justice

The preceding provision tends to reinforce earlier provisions with respect to witness protection. Although section 36(4)(a) uses the word *exclude*, it can be argued that the provision contemplates total exclusion of the witness. However, the concluding part of the provision empowers the court to exclude 'to such extent as it may consider necessary by reason of special circumstances in which publicity would be contrary to the interests of justice.' This means that to exclude does not mean complete denial of participation. Rather, it means exclusion from participating to the extent that the interests of justice will be fostered. This provision will arguably permit anonymous testimony,[57] removal of the defendant from the courtroom once his or her legal practitioner is present and removal of the public from the courtroom, voice and face distortion, and testimony via closed-circuit television or videoconferencing, although the court may not close its eyes to what is realistic to be provided at a given moment.

Section 37 of the Nigerian Constitution 1999 provides that 'the privacy of citizens, their homes, correspondence, telephone conversations and telegraphic communications is hereby guaranteed and protected.' Protecting witnesses may be a measure to guarantee their right to privacy while protecting families of witnesses can be said to be a protection of their homes. In *X and Y v The Netherlands*,[58] someone had sexual intercourse with the daughter of the applicant without her consent, and the defendant's authorities failed to bring the culprit to book. The court held that the right to privacy of the daughter at whose instance the application was brought was violated. The court noted that the duty of a state to guarantee right to privacy and family life is not limited to restraining public authorities from arbitrarily interfering with the right but may involve 'positive obligations inherent in effective respect for

57. The use of anonymous witnesses may tend to violate the fair hearing provision of the Nigerian Constitution. However, the jurisprudence of the European Court of Human Rights on the implementation of article 6 (right to a fair trial) of the Convention for the Protection of Human Rights and Fundamental Freedoms may serve as a persuasive authority for Nigerian Courts. The European Court of Human Rights has created certain conditions which must be met before anonymous witnesses can be made to testify. These conditions are incorporated through legislation by state parties to the convention. They are also to guide the courts of state parties in their practices. However, the conditions limit the weight or probative value that may be placed on evidence obtained through anonymous witnesses. See *Kostovski v The Netherlands* App no 11451/85, Judgment Series A No 166 (ECtHR, 20 November 1989); *Windisch v Austria* App no 12489/86, Judgment Series A No 186 (ECtHR, 27 September 1990); *Lüdi v Switzerland* App no 12433/86, Judgment Series A No 238 (ECtHR, 15 June 1992); and *Doorson v The Netherlands* App no 20524/92, Judgment (Reports 1996-II) (ECtHR, 26 March 1996).
58. App no 8978/80, Judgment (ECtHR, 26 March 1985).

private or family life. These obligations may involve the adoption of measures designed to secure respect for private life even in the sphere of the relations of individuals between themselves.'[59]

However, the court did not address the issue of whether the applicant's right to family life was thus violated. The consequential violation of another person's right by virtue of a violation of someone's right was later considered in *Đorđević v Croatia*.[60] In this case, the first applicant, who was suffering from mental and physical disabilities, and the second applicant, who was the mother of the first applicant, brought an action before the ECtHR with respect to verbal and physical abuse of the first applicant because of his inabilities. The court held that the right to family life of the second applicant was violated for failure to prevent the abuse of the first applicant.[61]

While the preceding provisions in Nigerian law can offer some measure of protection, they are grossly inadequate for the prosecution of crimes recognised under the Rome Statute. This point is underscored by the decision of the ICC in *Prosecutor v Saif Al-Islam Gaddafi & Abdullah Al-Senussi*.[62] As previously stated, the ICC found Libya unable to ensure protective measures despite its submissions that trial judges have the discretion to provide some protections. As a matter of fact, lack of witness protection law informed the court to reach its conclusion. It can therefore be seen that the provisions on witness protection are not sufficiently comprehensive and cannot be relied on in case of the Nigerian Constitution or adopted as a model in case of the Prevention of Terrorism Act 2011, Terrorism (Prevention) (Amendment) Act 2013 and the Administration of Criminal Justice Act 2015 in prosecuting the crimes recognised under the Rome Statute.

All the core issues earlier identified like strict criteria for admitting any person to witness protection programme are conspicuously missing. In the first place, most of the provisions relate to protection during trial whereas witness protection involves pre-trial and post-trial protection. In addition, it is practically impossible for the judiciary to completely create an efficient witness protection programme in the absence of a comprehensive enactment or policy. The judiciary cannot practically order relocation to another state since it involves treaty negotiation, nor can it order evidence to be given in another state because it also requires treaty arrangement. There will always be the need for a policy framework or legislation irrespective of the creative enterprise of the judiciary.

Unlike Nigeria, Kenya and Uganda appear to have realised the importance of witness protection and the need for legislation in respect thereof in the successful prosecution of international crimes recognised under the Rome

59. Ibid para 23.
60. App no 41526/10 Judgment (ECtHR, 24 July 2012).
61. Ibid para 153.
62. *Prosecutor v Saif Al-Islam Gaddafi & Abdullah Al-Senussi*, 'Decision on the admissibility of the case against Saif Al-Islam Gaddafi' ICC-01/11-01/11, dated 31 May 2013.

Statute. In Kenya, witness protection is regulated by the Witness Protection Act 2006 and Witness Protection (Amendment) Act 2010 while Uganda's witness protection is regulated by the Whistleblowers Protection Act 2010. Under the Kenyan laws, the following are clearly indicated, namely the criteria for admission of witnesses[63] and conditions for their application,[64] the procedure to be followed,[65] the authority responsible for the implementation of the programme,[66] the reason for the termination of the programme,[67] the rights and obligations of the parties[68] and the confidentiality of the operations of the programme.[69]

However, the Ugandan Whistleblowers Act is not as impressive as the Kenyan laws. The Act conflates informants and witnesses.[70] While the Act punishes the disclosure of the informant in an attempt to maintain confidentiality,[71] it insists that the whistleblower must disclose his or her name, address and occupation as a procedural requirement[72] and that a person who makes an anonymous disclosure does not enjoy the protection of the Act.[73] The Act erroneously assumes that Ugandans have confidence in the institutions designated as competent to receive information.[74] These institutions include the directorate of public prosecutions and the Ugandan police force. The notion that the police often do the bidding of the executive and are often involved in the commission of egregious crimes is taken for granted.

Inability to Obtain the Accused

Another criterion to determine inability is the inability to obtain the accused. As previously established, failure to obtain the accused makes imperative extradition arrangement between Nigeria and states not parties to the Rome Statute.[75] Extradition is 'the formal legal process by which persons accused

63. Witness Protection Act 2006, s 6; Witness Protection (Amendment) Act 2010, s 8.
64. Witness Protection (Amendment) Act 2010, s 6.
65. Ibid s 7.
66. Ibid s 5.
67. Witness Protection Act 2006, s 10; Witness Protection (Amendment) Act 2010, s 12.
68. Witness Protection Act 2006, ss 7 and 8; Witness Protection (Amendment) Act 2010, ss 9 and 10.
69. Witness Protection Act 2006, ss 15, 22–24, 30, 33 and 34; Witness Protection (Amendment) Act 2010, ss 21–22, 29 and 32.
70. Whistleblowers Act 2010, s 11.
71. Ibid s 14.
72. Ibid s 6(3).
73. Ibid s 3(3).
74. Ibid s 4(3).
75. The Nigerian Extradition Act Cap E25 Revised Laws of the Federation of Nigeria (LFN) 2004, s 1(a) empowers Nigeria to enter into extradition agreement. The Act regulates extradition process in Nigeria. However, some continental European states may extradite without any existing extradition treaty between them and the requesting state. See Christopher L.

or convicted of crime are surrendered from one state to another for trial or punishment.'[76] At present some states would not extradite unless there is an assurance from the requesting state that the human rights of the fugitive would be observed. This is the practice of most European states.[77] The European Convention on Human Rights has been the standard of measure for these states. However, this is not to suggest that these European states expect the requesting state to observe these rights in the same manner as they would observe it. It suffices if there was no flagrant violation in case of a convict who escapes to avoid punishment,[78] while in the case of a fugitive who escapes to avoid prosecution, there must not be the risk of flagrant violation of the fugitive's human rights.[79]

Human rights which are more prominent in extradition practice are right to life, right not be subjected to torture, inhuman and degrading treatment, right to a fair trial and right to private and family life.[80] When European states (or states with identical practice) refuse to extradite, this will have an impact on Nigeria with respect to the implementation of the principle of complementarity. Among the prominent rights highlighted earlier, right to life and right not to be subjected to torture, inhuman and degrading treatment are the most relevant to Nigeria. The imposition of death penalty in Nigeria may become an issue for European states. It may be questionable if extraditing to Nigeria will not amount to a breach of their obligations under the European Convention with respect to the right to life and right not to be subjected to torture, inhuman and degrading treatment. Similarly, the prison conditions in Nigeria may become an issue to be considered by the European states vis-à-vis the right not to be subjected to torture, inhuman and degrading treatment. Each of these issues is considered in the following.

In *Kropiwnicki v Lord Advocate*,[81] the High Court of Justiciary considered the issue of whether surrendering the appellant would violate article 3 of the European Convention which prohibits inhuman or degrading treatment in the light of the overcrowding and poor conditions of prisons in Poland. In its decision, the court adopted the decision in *Orchowski v Poland*,[82] where the

Blakesley, 'The Practice of Extradition From Antiquity to Modern France and the United States: A Brief History (1981) 4 *Boston College International & Comparitive Law* 39, 53–59.

76. A Review of the United Kingdom's Extradition Arrangements (Following Written Ministerial Statement by the Secretary of State for the Home Department of 8 September 2010) Presented to the Home Secretary on 30 September 2011, 20.
77. *Soering v United Kingdom* (1989) 11 EHRR 439, para 86.
78. *Drozd & Janousek v France & Spain* (1992) 14 EHRR 645, para 110.
79. In *R (Ullah) v Special Adjudicator* [2004] 2 AC 323, para 24.
80. Ibid.
81. [2010] HCJAC 41.
82. Application No 17885/04, 22 October 2009. On EctHR declaring poor prison conditions as amounting to inhuman and degrading treatment see *Dougoz v Greece* App no 4907/98 (ECtHR, 6 March 2001); *Kalashnikov v Russia* App no 47095/99 (ECtHR, 15 July 2002); *Poltoratskiy v Ukraine* App no 38812/97 (ECtHR, 29 April 2003); *Khokhlich v Ukraine* App no 41707/98 (ECtHR, 29 April 2003); *Kuznetsov v Ukraine* App no 39042/97

European Court of Human Rights held that overcrowding and almost total confinement within a cell and transfers between prisons with similar conditions exceeded the threshold of unavoidable suffering inherent in detention. However, the court dismissed the appellant's case on the ground that Poland had started improving the conditions of its prisons.

The conditions of prisons in Nigeria are dismal.[83] Most prisons in Nigeria are intolerably overcrowded.[84] The Ikoyi prison had exceeded its capacity by over 250 per cent.[85] In addition, most of these prisons also lack basic needs like bed, food and medical services.[86] Supplies are often in accordance with the official capacity of the prisons. Since each of these prisons has exceeded its official capacity, the implication is that supplies fall short of what is needed by inmates.[87] A prison inmate once described his condition with that of other inmates in the following words: 'Our little cell rooms measured about seven feet by eight feet. We would bathe, sleep, eat, defecate, piss, play and pray in there. For us, it was our entire world.'[88]

The implication is that fugitives from Nigeria may not be extradited to Nigeria either for prosecution or for service of their terms of imprisonment. The options which are open for Nigeria are two. The first one is that Nigeria may choose to improve the conditions of its prisons. In this respect, complementarity has indirectly imposed the obligation to reform prisons in Nigeria. The case of the universalists would have been somewhat strengthened even if indirectly. In *Prosecutor v Nwinkindi*,[89] the Appellate Chamber of the International Criminal Tribunal for Rwanda (ICTR) considered conditions of detention in Rwanda[90] before remitting the trial of Nwinkindi to the Rwandan legal system. With respect to conditions of detention, the court held that Rwanda guaranteed the minimum standards adopted by the United Nations General Assembly Resolution 43/173.[91] In this respect, Rome Statute complementarity would have somewhat conflated with the complementarity principle under the ICTR as far as prison reforms are concerned. However, it is

(ECtHR, 29 April 2003); *Mayzit v Russia* App no 63378/00 (ECtHR, 20 January 2005); *Novoselov v Russia* App no 66460/01 (ECtHR, 2 June 2005); *Khudoyorov v Russia* App no 6847/02 (ECtHR, 8 November 2005); *Ostrovar v Moldova* App no 35207/03 (ECtHR, 13 September 2005); *Alver v Estonia* App no 64812/01 (ECtHR, 8 November 2005); *Karalevicius v Lithuania* App no 53254/99 (ECtHR, 7 April 2005); *Labzov v Russia* App no 62208/00 (ECtHR, 16 June 2005); *Romanov v Russia* App no 63993/00 (ECtHR, 20 October 2005); *Becciev v Moldova* App no 9190/03 (ECtHR, 4 October 2005).

83. Amnesty International, 'Nigeria: Prisoners' Rights Systematically Flouted' AI Index: AFR 44/001/2008 February 2008.
84. Ibid., 22–23.
85. Ibid., 22.
86. Ibid., 24–27.
87. Ibid., 24.
88. Ibid Glossary.
89. Case No ICTR -01–75-AR11bis.
90. Ibid paras 37.
91. Ibid.

worthy of note that even if Nigeria may have to reform its prisons, the standard required does not necessarily have to be on par with those of the most developed states. Thus, it is gross misconception on the part of the official in the Ugandan Department of Prisons to have stated that gym and DVD players in the Scheveningen detention centre in The Hague represent international standard.[92]

The second option is that Nigeria may delegate the state which has the fugitive to imprison the fugitive. Section 41(2)(b)(ii) of the Nigerian Constitution 1999 provides that any person may 'undergo imprisonment outside Nigeria in execution of the sentence of a court of law in respect of a criminal offence of which he has been found guilty' 'provided that there is reciprocal agreement between Nigeria and such other country in relation to such matter.'

With respect to the imposition of death penalty, some states will not extradite to other states that impose the death penalty for crimes with respect to which a fugitive is sought to be extradited. Most of these states are states that have abolished the death penalty. In the European Convention on Extradition 1960,[93] article 11 provides that when the offence with respect to which extradition is sought is punishable by death under the law of the requesting party but not that of the requested party, or the requested party does not normally carry out death penalty 'extradition may be refused unless the requesting Party gives such assurance as the requested Party considers sufficient that the death-penalty will not be carried out.' Also, the Inter-American Convention on Extradition 1981 similarly provides.[94] In the 'Model Treaty on Extradition' proposed by the Eighth United Nations Congress on the Prevention of Crime and Treatment of Offenders 1990,[95] it is stipulated in article 4 that

> [e]xtradition may be refused in any of the following circumstances . . . (c) If the offence for which extradition is requested carries the death penalty under the law of the requesting State, unless that State gives such assurance as the requested State considers sufficient that the death penalty will not be imposed or, if imposed, will not be carried out.[96]

After the Model Treaty on Extradition, the United Nations Commission on Human Rights passed a resolution in which states were requested to ask

92. Sarah Nouwen, 'Complementarity in Uganda: Domestic Diversity or International Imposition?' in Carsten Stahn and Mohamed El Zeidy (eds), *The International Criminal Court and Complementarity: From Theory to Practice* vol II (Cambridge University Press 2011), 1120, 1148.
93. (Signed 13 December 1957, entered into force 18 April 1960) 359 UNTS 273, ETS 24.
94. (Adopted 25 February 1981, entered into force 28 March 1992) (1981) 20 ILM 723, art 9.
95. UN Doc A/CONF 14/28/Rev 1.
96. Ibid., 68.

for assurances that death penalty would not be imposed when extraditing a fugitive.[97] States have found it expedient to adopt the provision similar to the Model Treaty and in line with the request of the United Nations Commission on Human Rights. Examples are the SADC Extradition Protocol[98] and the Extradition Treaty between Nigeria and South Africa 2002.[99]

The courts have had to consider the implications of not obtaining assurance that death penalty would not be imposed and if imposed would not be carried out. In *United States v Burns*,[100] the suspects were alleged to have murdered the father, mother and sister of one of them in a 'brutal and shocking cold blooded'[101] manner in the United States. In considering their extradition without obtaining assurance that death penalty would not be imposed and that, if imposed, it would not be carried out, the Supreme Court of Canada held that failure to obtain such assurance would violate section 7 of the Canadian Charter of Rights and Freedoms which guarantees to everyone 'the right to life, liberty and security of the person and the right not to be deprived thereof except in accordance with the provisions of fundamental justice.' The court noted that 'while the Canadian government would not itself inflict capital punishment, its decision to extradite without assurances would be a necessary link in the chain of causation to that potential result.'[102]

In *Khalfan Khamis Mohamed v President of the Republic of South Africa*,[103] the South African Constitutional Court considered the implication of failure to obtain assurances before extraditing. In this case, the applicant was alleged to have participated in the bombing of the US embassies in Nairobi and Dar es Salaam which led to the death of several people. He was then indicted by the federal grand jury in New York, where he faced the death penalty if convicted. He was arrested and detained in South Africa before being handed over to Federal Bureau of Investigation (FBI), who took him to the United States. The legality of his handing over was the issue before the court. The court held that by failing to obtain assurances that death penalty would not be imposed and, if imposed, would not be carried out, the handing over was unconstitutional. The court stated that the applicant's right to life and dignity and his right not to be subjected to cruel, inhuman and degrading punishment were violated. In *Minister of Justice and Constitutional Development v Emmanuel Tsebe*,[104] the applicants were each alleged to have murdered their wife in Botswana and Botswana refused to assure South Africa that death penalty would not be imposed. The South African Constitutional

97. The United Nations Commission on Human Rights Resolutions 1999/61 (adopted April 28 1999) and 2000/65 (adopted April 27 2000).
98. Article 5(c).
99. Article 3(1).
100. [2001] 1 SCR 283.
101. Ibid para 9.
102. Ibid para 54.
103. CCT 17/01 Judgment delivered by the South African Constitutional Court on 28 May 2001.
104. [2012] ZACC 16.

Court adopted *Mohamed* and declared that extraditing the applicants would be unconstitutional.

If Nigeria imposes the death penalty for crimes recognised under the Rome Statute, the implication is that these states will not extradite to Nigeria any fugitives of international crimes from its shore. The implication for Nigeria is that the principle of complementarity cannot be implemented with respect to such fugitives that succeed in escaping to such states that will not extradite them to Nigeria. Nigeria will invariably lack the requisite ability to prosecute.

In other to address this obstacle, there are a number of approaches that may be adopted by Nigeria. It is worthy of note that the Nigerian Constitution 1999 recognises death penalty. Section 33(1) of the Constitution provides that 'every person has a right to life, and no one shall be deprived intentionally of his life, save in execution of the sentence of a court in respect of a criminal offence of which he has been found guilty in Nigeria.' In *Kalu v State*,[105] the constitutionality of the death penalty was contested before the Nigerian Supreme Court. The court held that death penalty was constitutional and added that only the legislature could abolish the death penalty in Nigeria.

The first approach that may be adopted by Nigeria is to abolish the death penalty by way of constitutional amendment. It would be recalled that complementarity does not necessarily require the abolition of the death penalty. In this situation, the abolition of the death penalty is being indirectly induced by those states that will not extradite unless death penalty will not be imposed. This situation indirectly makes a case for the universalists with their toolkit of reform agenda. By abolishing the death penalty, the Rome Statute complementarity would have conflated with the complementarity principle under the ICTR as far as the abolition of the death penalty is concerned. In *Prosecutor v Nwinkindi*,[106] the abolition of the death penalty is one of the conditions laid down by the ICTR before ceding a case to the Rwandan judicial system.[107]

The death penalty is under Chapter IV of the Nigerian Constitution and Chapter IV is headed Fundamental Rights. Section 9(3) of the Constitution provides that in amending the Nigerian Constitution with respect to fundamental rights, any proposal for amendment is to be approved by 'the votes of not less than four-fifths majority of all the members of each House, and also approved by resolution of the House of Assembly of not less than two-third of all States.' This is especially onerous, and its successful passage may be doubtful apart from the heated debate it will generate.

The second approach that may be adopted by Nigeria is not to impose the death penalty for crimes recognised under the Rome Statute in implementing legislation so as to be able to obtain fugitives of international crimes from

105. (1998) 13 NWLR (Pt 583) 531 (SC).
106. Case No ICTR -01–75-AR11bis.
107. Ibid para 22.

Nigeria. The limitation of this approach is that while the federal government may choose not to impose the death penalty in its own implementing legislation, it cannot prevent states within the federation to impose the death penalty if it wishes so to do. As previously indicated, states can exercise competence with respect to crimes recognised under the Rome Statute. Therefore, if any one of them chooses to impose the death penalty, the federal government is completely helpless.

In *LaGrand*,[108] the US federal government could not prevent the execution of a German national by the state of Arizona while the suit between Germany and the United States with respect to the conviction of the German national was pending before the International Court of Justice. Similarly, in *Soering v United Kingdom*,[109] the European Court of Human Rights recognised the limitation of the US federal government in giving a convincing assurance that death penalty would not be imposed by the state of Virginia if the applicant was extradited to the United States. The court noted that

> the offence charged, being a State and not a Federal offence, comes within the jurisdiction of Virginia; it appears as a consequence that no direction could or can be given to the Commonwealth's Attorney by any State or Federal authority to promise more; the Virginia courts as judicial bodies cannot bind themselves in advance as to what decisions they may arrive at on the evidence; and the Governor of Virginia does not promise that he will later exercise his executive power to commute a death penalty.[110]

It is, however, worthy to mention that the United States successfully persuaded the state of Virginia not to impose the death penalty. Three days after the United Kingdom refused to extradite to the United States following the decision of the European Court that Soering should not be extradited in the absence of an assurance from the United States, the United States communicated to the United Kingdom that 'in the light of the applicable provisions of the 1972 extradition treaty, United States law would prohibit the applicant's prosecution in Virginia for the offence of capital murder.'[111] Soering was subsequently extradited, where he was sentenced on conviction to 90 years' imprisonment. Despite this encouraging development, federalism still poses a challenge to this approach.

108. *LaGrand (FRG v US)*, 2001 ICJ 104 (June 27), 40 ILM 1069. On the constraints that federalism may impose on treaty implementation, see Edward T Swaine, 'Does Federalism Constrain the Treaty Power?' (2003) 103 *Columbia Law Review* 403–533.
109. (1989) 11 EHRR 439.
110. Ibid para 97.
111. William A. Schabas, *The Abolition of the Death Penalty in International Law* (3rd edn, Cambridge University Press 2002), 275.

Apart from the helplessness of the federal government, the constitutionality of not imposing death penalty for crimes recognised under the Rome Statute while the same penalty is imposed for less egregious crimes like murder or armed robbery may become an issue. In *Jowad Kezaala v Attorney General*,[112] the constitutionality of not imposing death penalty with respect to Rome Statute crimes as recognised in the Ugandan International Criminal Act 2010 when death penalty was imposed on less egregious crimes was an issue. Under articles 7(3), 8(3) and 9(3) of the Act, the maximum penalty imposed for these crimes was life imprisonment while under section 189 of the Ugandan Penal Code Act, the maximum penalty was death. The petition therefore contended that articles 21(1), 21(2) and 21(3) of the Constitution of the Republic of Uganda (Ugandan Constitution) 2005 was violated as a convict under the ICC Act would suffer from discrimination.[113] This argument is predicated on the premise that death penalty is a higher punishment than life imprisonment. This premise appears to have been supported by the decision of the Human Rights Committee in *Errol Johnson v Jamaica*,[114] where it was held that '[l]ife on death row, harsh as it may be, is preferable to death.'[115]

Although the petition was later abandoned, nonetheless, the issue could be relevant if Nigeria chooses to abolish the death penalty for crimes recognised under the Rome Statute while retaining death penalty for less egregious crimes so as to obtain fugitives from states that will not extradite unless it is guaranteed that death penalty would not be imposed. It is worthy to mention that article 21 of the Ugandan Constitution 2005 is under chapter four of the Constitution and it is titled 'Protection and Promotion of Fundamental and Other Human Rights and Freedoms.' This is an equivalent of Chapter IV of the Nigerian Constitution which is also titled 'Fundamental Rights.' However, Nigeria does not appear to have an identical provision with article 21 of the Ugandan Constitution. Article 21 of the Ugandan Constitution provides that

> (1) [a]ll persons are equal before and under the law in all spheres of political, economic, social and cultural life and in every other respect and shall enjoy equal protection of the law.
> (2) Without prejudice to clause (l) of this article, a person shall not be discriminated against on the ground of sex, race, colour, ethnic origin, tribe, birth, creed or religion, social or economic standing, political opinion or disability.

112. Constitutional Petition 24 of 2010.
113. Christopher Mbazira, 'Prosecuting International Crimes Committed by the Lord's Resistance Army' in Uganda in Chacha Murungu and Japhet Biegon (eds), *Prosecuting International Crimes in Africa* (Pretoria University Law Press 2011), 217–218.
114. Communication No 588/1994 UN Doc CCPR/C/56/D/588/1994 (1996).
115. Ibid para 8.4.

(3) For the purposes of this article, "discriminate" means to give different treatment to different persons attributable only or mainly to their respective descriptions by sex, race, colour, ethnic origin, tribe, birth, creed or religion, social or economic standing, political opinion or disability.

On the other hand, section 42(1) of the Nigerian Constitution 1999 provides that

(1) [a] citizen of Nigeria of a particular community, ethnic group, place of origin, sex, religion or political opinion shall not, by reason only that he is such a person:—

(a) be subjected either expressly by, or in the practical application of, any law in force in Nigeria or any executive or administrative action of the government, to disabilities or restrictions to which citizens of Nigeria of other communities, ethnic groups, places of origin, sex, religions or political opinions are not made subject; or
(b) be accorded either expressly by, or in the practical application of, any law in force in Nigeria or any such executive or administrative action, any privilege or advantage that is not accorded to citizens of Nigeria of other communities, ethnic groups, places of origin, sex, religions or political opinions.

While discrimination in term of imposition of punishment can be said to have been outlawed by the Ugandan Constitution 2005 having provided that 'all persons are equal before and under the law in all spheres of political, economic, social and cultural life and in every other respect and shall enjoy equal protection of the law,' such may be difficult to sustain under section 42 of the Nigerian Constitution 1999. This is because section 42 outlaws only a situation in which the practical application of any law leads to a disability occasioned by the person's membership of a given community, ethnic group, place of origin, sex, religion or political opinion. However, sections 15 and 17 of the Nigerian Constitution appear to be capable of producing the same outcome as article 21 of the Ugandan Constitution. Section 15 of the Nigerian Constitution provides that

(1) [t]he motto of the Federal Republic of Nigeria shall be Unity and Faith, Peace and Progress.
(2) Accordingly, national integration shall be actively encouraged, whilst discrimination on the grounds of place of origin, sex, religion, status, ethnic or linguistic association or ties shall be prohibited.

The preceding provision tends to suggest that the pursuit of 'national integration' and the prohibition of 'discrimination on the grounds of place of origin, sex, religion, status, ethnic or linguistic association or ties' are two distinct but related goals. The use of the word *whilst* appears to justify this argument. Thus, while national integration is being actively encouraged, discrimination on the preceding grounds would be outlawed. Prohibition of discrimination on the ground of status may be employed to outlaw discriminatory punishment. A convict has a status, and his or her status is that of a person whose guilt has been determined and is subject to legal disabilities.

Black's Law Dictionary defines *status* as 'a person's legal condition insofar as it is imposed by the law without the person's consent, as opposed to a condition that the person has acquired by agreement.'[116] Similarly, *Merriam-Webster's Dictionary and Thesaurus* defines status as 'position or rank in relation to others, the condition of a person or thing in the eyes of the law, state or condition with respect to circumstances.' In the same vein, section 17 of the Nigerian Constitution 1999 tends to reinforce section 15. Section 17(1) stipulates that 'the State social order is founded on ideals of Freedom, Equality and Justice'[117] while section 17(2)(a) stipulates that in furtherance of the social order 'every citizen shall have equality of rights, obligations and opportunities before the law.' Therefore, if the right to equal punishment for equal offence does not exist, nonetheless, the right to equal treatment in like situation exists.

While sections 15 and 17 of the Nigerian Constitution can arguably produce the same outcome with article 21 of the Ugandan Constitution, there seems to be a limit with respect to the extent these provisions can extend. This is because these provisions are under the Fundamental Objectives and Directive Principles of State Policy, which are not justiciable. However, if one considers the decision of the Supreme Court of Nigeria in *INEC v Balarabe Musa*,[118] the clog of non-justiciability may be avoided. In this case, the Independent National Electoral Commission (INEC) laid down certain guidelines for registration of political parties. The guidelines were then challenged by some political parties on the ground that it was unconstitutional for imposing more conditions than what was stipulated under section 222 of the Nigerian Constitution 1999. In declaring the guidelines unconstitutional, the Supreme Court invoked section 14(1) of the Constitution which is under the Fundamental Objectives and Directive Principles of State Policy and is not justiciable. Section 14(1) stipulates that Nigeria shall be a state based on the principles of democracy and social justice; therefore, any other conditions over and above what was stipulated in the Constitution had the consequence of stifling the principles of democracy under section 14(1).

This judgement implies that any provision of the Fundamental Objectives and Directive Principles of State Policy can be made effective if read with other justiciable parts of the Constitution or statutes. Therefore, equal

116. Bryan A. Garner and others, *Black's Law Dictionary* (9th edn, Thomson Reuters, 2009), 1542.
117. In *Attorney-General Ondo State v Attorney-General Federation* [2002] FWLR (Pt 111) 1972, State was held to mean Federal, State and Local Governments at 2071 paras E-H.
118. [2003] NWLR (Pt 806) 72.

treatment envisaged in sections 15 and 17 of the Nigerian Constitution can be made effective when read in conjunction with the Criminal Code which imposes death penalty with respect to certain crimes, section 3(1) of the Nigerian Constitution which permits the imposition of death penalty and the implementation of legislation of the Rome Statute which may seek to avoid death penalty for the purpose of being able to obtain extradition of fugitives of crimes recognised under the Rome Statute.

While the earlier analysis under the Nigerian Constitution is circuitous, this is not so under the African Charter on Human and Peoples' Rights (Ratification and Enforcement) Act.[119] The African Charter on Human and Peoples' Rights (Ratification and Enforcement) Act implements the African Charter on Human and Peoples' Rights in Nigeria. Article 2 of the charter stipulates that every individual shall enjoy all the rights enumerated in the charter without distinction of any kind including 'status.' Article 3(1) stipulates that 'every individual shall be equal before the law' while art 3(2) stipulates that 'every individual shall be entitled to equal protection of the law.' Similarly, article 19 envisages equal treatment in like situation by stating that 'all peoples shall be equal; they shall enjoy the same respect and shall have the same rights.' Therefore, convicts of less egregious crimes facing the death penalty may challenge the propriety of not imposing the death penalty on the convicts of crimes recognised under the Rome Statute within the meaning of the above provisions of the African Charter on Human and Peoples' Rights (Ratification and Enforcement) Act.

The third approach which may be adopted is that the death penalty may be imposed with respect to crimes recognised under the Rome Statute the same way it applies to other crimes while moratorium may be granted as a matter of policy. In this respect, any alleged discrimination will be with respect to executive policy making as distinct from legislative enactment. But the policy itself is amenable to judicial review within the context of other policies or laws. Similarly, the policy itself like statutes may also be subjected to the test of constitutionality. Article 21 of the Ugandan Constitution 2005 which provides that 'all persons are equal before and under the law in all spheres of political, economic, social and cultural life and in every other respect and shall enjoy equal protection of the law' makes it possible to apply constitutionality test. The phrase 'in every other respect' can be said to accommodate executive policy making.

In the same vein, section 15 of the Nigerian Constitution which prohibits 'discrimination on the grounds of place of origin, sex, religion, status, ethnic or linguistic association or ties' makes it possible to subject such executive policy to constitutionality test within the context of other laws or policies. This is further reinforced by the Constitution when it provides that the 'Constitution is supreme and its provisions shall have binding force on

119. Cap A9 Revised LFN 2004.

all authorities and persons throughout the Federal Republic of Nigeria.'[120] Arguably, the executive falls within the category of all authorities. Similarly, the Nigerian Constitution provides that 'it shall be the duty and responsibility of all organs of government, and of all authorities and persons, exercising legislative, executive or judicial powers, to conform to, observe and apply the provisions of this chapter of this Constitution.'[121]

The fourth approach which may be adopted by Nigeria is for Nigeria to delegate its criminal jurisdiction to the state which has the custody of the fugitive and will not extradite to Nigeria unless the death penalty will not be imposed. While all the preceding approaches tend to face one obstacle or the other, this approach tends to balance Nigeria's preference to retain the death penalty with its obligation to investigate and prosecute crimes recognised under the Rome Statute in line with the principle of complementarity. With respect to states that are not parties to the Rome Statute, they can prosecute on behalf of Nigeria. With respect to states that are parties to the Rome Statute, Nigeria may successfully enter an admissibility challenge claiming that other states are acting as its agents. It is also possible that those states prosecuting on behalf of Nigeria may themselves successfully enter an admissibility challenge claiming that they are prosecuting on behalf of Nigeria. While the abolition of the death penalty as indirectly induced by states that will not extradite unless there is assurance that death penalty will not be imposed or, if imposed, will not be carried out leans towards the universalists agenda, the competence of Nigeria to delegate its criminal jurisdiction to the state that has custody of the fugitive accords with the pluralists stance with their deference for legal diversity as adopted in this book.

The competence of one state to delegate its criminal jurisdiction is not without foundation[122] as a number of treaties can attest to it.[123] In fact, the

120. Nigerian Constitution 1999, s 1.
121. Ibid s 13.
122. See Dapo Akande, 'The Jurisdiction of the International Criminal Court over Nationals of Non-Parties: Legal Basis and Limits' (2003) 1 *Journal of International Criminal Justice* 618, 622.
123. See The Tokyo Convention on Offences and Certain other Acts Committed on Board Aircraft (signed 14 December 1963, entered into force 4 December 1969) 704 UNTS 220; the Hague Convention for the Suppression of Unlawful Seizure of Aircraft (signed 16 December 1970, entered into force 14 October 1971) 860 UNTS 105; Montreal Convention for the Suppression of Unlawful Acts against the Safety of Civil Aviation (signed 23 September 1971, entered into force 26 January 1973) 974 UNTS 178; the Convention on the Prevention and Punishment of Crimes against Internationally Protected Persons including Diplomatic Agents (adopted 14 December 1973, entered into force 20 February 1977) 1035 UNTS 167; the New York Convention against the taking of Hostages (adopted 17 December 1979, entered into force 3 June 1983) 1316 UNTS 205; Convention against Torture and other Cruel, Inhuman and Degrading Treatment (adopted 10 December 1984, entered into force 26 June 1987) 1465 UNTS 85; the Rome Convention for the Suppression of Unlawful Acts against the Safety of Maritime Navigation (signed 10 March 1988, entered into force 1 March 1992) 1678 UNTS 222; UN Convention against Illicit Traffic

European Union (EU) Council Framework Decision is sufficiently clear with respect to delegation of criminal jurisdiction by one state to another when it allows an EU member to exercise jurisdiction over acts of terrorism committed on the territory of any other member.[124] Similarly, the European Convention on the Transfer of Proceedings in Criminal Matters 1972[125] allows a party to the treaty to transfer criminal proceedings commenced by that party to another party.[126] Article 6 of the convention allows transfer even when the state party to which it is transferred would not have had jurisdiction.

In the same vein, the Agreement between Member States of the European Communities on the Transfer of Proceedings in Criminal Matters 1990[127] permits transfer on similar terms. Its article 4 similarly allows transfer even when the party to which it is transferred would not have had jurisdiction. In addition, article 5(c) of the South Africa Development Community Extradition Protocol provides that a state party may refuse extradition if the state party which is requesting extradition would impose the death penalty but that the state that refuses to extradite may carry out the trial if the state requesting extradition so requests. This clearly indicates that a state may delegate another to exercise on its behalf its criminal jurisdiction.

The Treaty on Mutual Legal Assistance in Criminal Matters between the Government of the Federal Republic of Nigeria and the Government of the Republic of South Africa[128] arguably makes the transfer of the kind done by the EU members possible. The treaty provides that the two states agree to assist each other 'in connection with the investigation, prosecution and prevention of crimes and in proceedings related to criminal matters.'[129] Assistance within the meaning of the treaty include 'taking the testimony or statements of persons;'[130] 'providing documents, records and articles of evidence;'[131]

---

in Narcotic Drugs and Psychotropic Substances (adopted 20 December 1988, entered into force 11 November 1990) 1582 UNTS 95; the Convention on the Safety of United Nations and Associated Personnel (adopted 9 December 1994, entered into force 15 January 1999) 2051 UNTS 363; the International Convention for the Suppression of Terrorist Bombings (adopted 15 December 1997, entered into force 23 May 2001) 2149 UNTS 256; the International Convention for the Suppression of the Financing of Terrorism (adopted 9 December 1999, entered into force 10 April 2002) 2178 UNTS 197.

124. Council Framework Decision of 13 June 2002 on Combating Terrorism (2002/475/JHA), *Official Journal of the European Communities* L164/3–7, 22.6.2002, art 9(1).
125. European Convention on the Transfer of Proceedings in Criminal Matters (signed 15 May 1972, entered into force 30 March 1978) ETS No 73.
126. Ibid art 3.
127. Agreement between Member States of the European Communities on the Transfer of Proceedings in Criminal Matters 1990 (2009/C 219/03), *Official Journal of the European Communities* C219.7, 22.9.2009.
128. The Treaty on Mutual Legal Assistance in Criminal Matters between the Government of the Federal Republic of Nigeria and the Government of the Republic of South Africa (Ratification and Enforcement) Act Cap T24 Revised LFN 2004.
129. Ibid art 1(1).
130. Ibid art 1(2)(a).
131. Ibid art 1(2)(b).

'transferring persons in custody for testimony or other purposes;'[132] and any 'other form of assistance not prohibited by the laws of the Requested State.'[133]

The clause 'other form of assistance not prohibited by the laws of the Requested State' may accommodate transfer similar to that of the European Conventions earlier mentioned or that of SADC Extradition Protocol. This suggestion appears more persuasive in the light of article 4(3)(c) of the South African Implementation of the Rome Statute of the International Criminal Court Act 2002[134] which empowers the Republic of South Africa to prosecute any person who commits any of the crimes recognised under the statute once the person is found on the territory of the Republic of South Africa irrespective of where the crime has been committed.

As previously hinted, an agency relationship of a kind between Nigeria and the state of custody exists. Agency has been defined as a relationship 'in which one party (the agent) may act on behalf of another (the principal)' and that it is a device to 'enable [an entity] through the services of another, to broaden the scope of [its] activities.'[135] As rightly suggested, 'the duty to exercise criminal jurisdiction' within the context of complementarity should not be construed strictly, rather it should be considered an obligation 'to ensure that a genuine investigation be undertaken, be it by the State itself, be it by way of extradition to another State, or even by way of surrender to an international criminal jurisdiction.'[136]

132. Ibid art 1(2)(e).
133. Ibid art 1(2)(i).
134. Act No 27 2002.
135. Garner and others, *Black's Law Dictionary* (n 116), 70.
136. Claus Kress, '"Self-Referrals" and "Waivers of Complementarity": Some Considerations in Law and Policy' (2004) 2 *Journal of International Criminal Justice* 944, 946.

9 Conclusion and Recommendations

Conclusion

The coming into force of the Rome Statute has institutionalised putting an end to impunity gap. In achieving the goal of ending impunity, the Rome Statute has placed the primary duty of investigation and prosecution of crimes recognised under the Rome Statute in the hands of state parties. The primary duty of states to prosecute and investigate crimes recognised under the statute is what is known as the principle of complementarity and it is embedded in articles 1 and 17 of the Rome Statute. Since Nigeria is a party to the Rome Statute, it is also expected to investigate and prosecute crimes recognised under the statute.

In implementing the principle of complementarity in Nigeria, the question of whether the Nigerian legal system can successfully investigate and prosecute the crimes recognised under the Rome Statute becomes imperative, and it has been the preoccupation of this book. Meanwhile, the concepts of sovereignty, legal universalism and legal pluralism were found to be central to proffering answer to the question of whether the Nigerian legal system as it is can successfully investigate and prosecute crimes recognised under the Rome Statute. The exercise of criminal jurisdiction is an expression of a state's sovereignty. Thus, the primary duty placed on state parties by the Rome Statute reflects deference to the concept of sovereignty. By implementing complementarity, state parties, including Nigeria, would have given expression to the concept of sovereignty. The concept of legal universalism sets the International Criminal Court (ICC) as an ideal to which states must aspire in the investigation and prosecution of the crimes recognised under the Rome Statute. It tends to erode the concept of sovereignty. On the other hand, legal pluralism aims at the minimum required to ensure effective investigation and prosecution of crimes recognised under the Rome Statute. It tilts favourably towards the concept of sovereignty. As the Rome Statute implicitly admits of legal pluralism as distinct from legal universalism, this book adopted legal pluralism as its underlying theoretical framework. Thus, this book never set for itself the task of finding out whether Nigeria could investigate and prosecute crimes recognised under the Rome Statute the same way the ICC would do it; rather, it asked the question of whether the Nigerian legal system as it is could successfully implement the principle of complementarity.

The universalists, seeing the implementation of the principle of complementarity as a civilising agenda, have suggested that the general part of the Rome Statute, the principle of universal jurisdiction, the abolition of the death penalty, the compliance with fair trial guarantees and prison reforms are required for the implementation of the principle of complementarity. By necessary implication, for a successful investigation and implementation of the principle of complementarity, Nigeria must be prepared to carry out these reforms if it had not already carried them out. However, legal pluralism, which is the heart of the principle of complementarity, has obviated the need for all these reforms. To make the preceding reforms imperative for implementing the principle of complementarity was found to be a gross misconception of what complementarity requires. Thus, the general part of the Criminal Code in Nigeria was found to be sufficient to effectively implement the principle of complementarity. Should Nigeria adopt the principle of universal jurisdiction for any of its courts to assume adjudicative jurisdiction, it does so not because complementarity requires it but because it may choose to maintain a symmetry with Geneva Conventions Act, which has already adopted the principle of universal jurisdiction for the exercise of adjudicative power by the Nigerian courts with respect to grave breaches of the convention. Similarly, it was found that Nigeria can indeed maintain death penalty even though the ICC will not impose the death penalty with respect to the same crimes. Although Nigeria has fair trial guarantees, they were found not to be relevant except to the extent that failure to observe them have the consequence of unwillingness or inability. With respect to prison reforms, the so-called international standards which would have made a case for elaborate reforms were found to be quite unnecessary.

Thus, the scope was defined of what complementarity does not require of the Nigerian legal system through the concept of legal pluralism in contradistinction to that of legal universalism. But, this was half of the picture. To know what was required of the Nigerian legal system led to the examination of articles 1 and 17 of the Rome Statute within the context of the minimalist prescriptions of legal pluralism. In defining what is required of states to implement the principle of complementarity, articles 1 and 17 of the Rome Statute develop the concepts of unwillingness and inability. Thus, the ICC will take over the investigation and prosecution of crimes recognised under the Rome Statute from a state party only if that state is unwilling or unable to investigate and prosecute the crimes recognised under the Rome Statute. The concept of unwillingness has three criteria, namely shielding the person concerned from criminal responsibility, unjustified delay inconsistent with the intent to bring the person concerned to justice and a lack of independence and impartiality inconsistent with the intent to bring the person concerned to justice. With respect to the concept of inability, the criteria adopted are the collapse of the domestic legal system, inability of a domestic legal system to obtain evidence and inability of a domestic legal system to obtain the accused, all of which will justify the ICC intervention. While all these criteria will be applied in specific factual situations, nonetheless, they could be used to access the compliance of any domestic legal system with the principle of complementarity. Thus, in assessing whether the Nigerian legal system could successfully investigate and prosecute the crimes recognised under the Rome Statute, the preceding criteria were adopted.

Meanwhile, the idea of an ICC takeover does not arise when a state has not taken any step. Thus, mere inaction is sufficient for the ICC intervention without having had to examine the unwillingness and inability of a state party. Further, the criterion of unjustified delay inconsistent with intent to bring the person concerned to justice was not considered since it essentially depends on the circumstances of each case. Unlike other criteria, the criterion of unjustified delay with the intent not to do justice was found to be too fluid and amoeboid in nature, making it defy a cognisable boundary. This does not at all make a case for legal universalism. It is as un-cognisable for legal universalism as it is for legal pluralism. In the same vein, since this study is predicated on the existence of the Nigerian legal system, the collapse of the Nigerian legal system was not considered.

Having subjected the Nigeria legal system to those criteria stipulated in articles 1 and 17 of the Rome Statute, the Nigerian legal system was found to have abysmally failed. It was found that Nigeria does not have any law in place to prosecute international crimes recognised under the Rome Statute. This would justify ICC intervention without the need for assessing unwillingness and inability of Nigeria by the ICC since the situation arguably constitutes inaction on the part of Nigeria. With respect to the criterion of shielding from criminal responsibility as an expression of unwillingness, it was found that the existing legal regime in Nigeria which *inter alia* recognises immunities (executive, legislative and sovereign immunities), amnesties, pardon/the prerogative of mercy, plea bargain, the *ne bis in idem* principle, the principle of legality, the power of the legislative organ to enact statute of limitation with respect to any crime and the power of the prosecutor (attorney-general) to amend the law of evidence are latent, with the possibility of making the prosecution of crimes recognised under the Rome Statute in Nigeria difficult.

Similarly, with respect to the criterion of lack of independence and impartiality inconsistent with intent to bring the person concerned to justice as an expression of unwillingness, it was found that the prosecuting authority (the attorney-general) in Nigeria and the Nigerian judiciary lack the requisite independence and impartiality for the successful prosecution of the crimes recognised under the Rome Statute in Nigeria. The attorney-general could be appointed and removed at will by the executive and thus makes the person susceptible to being manipulated. With respect to the judiciary, judges are too dependent on the chief justice of Nigeria for their carrier prospect, and he or she, in turn, is subject to the executive in staying in the office. This makes the judiciary lacks the requisite independence and impartiality. With respect to the criterion of inability of a domestic legal system to obtain evidence as an expression of inability, it was found that there is no witness protection regime in Nigeria that would enhance the effective prosecution of the crimes recognised under the Rome Statute. Similarly, with respect to the criterion of inability of a domestic legal system to obtain the accused as an expression of inability, it was found that fugitives of the crimes recognised under the Rome Statute could readily escape prosecution due to a lack of a treaty arrangement between Nigeria and other state entities on extradition.

The preceding findings consequently inform recommendations made hereunder for effective prosecution of crimes recognised under the Rome Statute in Nigeria.

Recommendations

Inaction: Adoption of Implementing Legislation as an Aspect of Complementarity

In Nigeria, there is no legislation which punishes the crimes recognised under the Rome Statute. Thus, Nigeria will be perpetually inactive, which will consequently justify ICC intervention. To avoid inaction due to the absence of an implementing legislation, four legislative options were identified, each with its own advantage(s) and disadvantage(s). The first legislative option is incorporation of the crimes recognised in the Rome Statute by attachment. The second one is enacting the crimes in the Rome Statute as ordinary crimes. The third option is enacting the crimes recognised under the Rome Statute into law by criminalising gross violations of fundamental rights while the fourth option is making the crimes recognised under the Rome Statute part of the Nigerian Constitution.

With respect to the first option, the most important advantage it has is that the egregious nature of the crimes contained in the Rome Statute will be readily reflected. The most pertinent disadvantage is that the inelegantly worded section 12 of the Constitution of the Federal Republic of Nigeria (Nigerian Constitution) 1999 with its onerous requirements will apply. It would be recalled that section 12 requires the participation of the federal government and the state governments before the Rome Statute can be implemented although its inelegant wording is not clear whether 18 or all the 36 states of the Nigerian Federation are required for a successful passage. Similarly, it is not clear whether presidential assent is required without the possibility of being overridden or not required at all. Considering these disadvantages, it is not advisable for Nigeria to adopt this option.

With respect to the second legislative option, it would be recalled that the federal government can rely on the rule in *Attorney General Ondo State v Attorney General Federation*[1] and competently legislate on the crimes recognised under the Rome Statute once it is not claiming to implement a treaty. Similarly, states within the Nigerian Federation can also legislate on the crimes recognised under the Rome Statute under general legislative competence on crime once they are not claiming to implement a treaty. It would also be recalled that while the doctrine of covering the field may sometime nullify the effectiveness of state legislation, it does not appear to have this effect in this instance. The advantage of this approach is that failure of the federal government or any of the federating states in Nigeria to investigate and prosecute may not be an end to the doing of justice since others are available to do justice. Also, the problematic section 12 of the Nigerian Constitution 1999 can be technically bypassed. The only disadvantage is that since the Rome Statute will be prosecuted as ordinary crimes, the egregious nature of the crime may not be adequately reflected. However, this disadvantage could be avoided if the definitions of the crime are copied verbatim even without openly acknowledging that the Rome Statute is being implemented. This approach is at least preferable to the first.

Unlike the second option, the third option affords both the federal government and any of the federating states to openly implement the Rome Statute and still bypass section 12 of the Nigerian Constitution 1999. This is its greatest advantage. Unlike the second option where the crimes enacted as ordinary crimes may not reflect the egregious nature of the crimes recognised under the Rome Statute, this option permits both the National Assembly and any House of Assembly of any state to attach any relevant provision of the Rome Statute to an implementing legislation.

With respect to the fourth option, the advantage it has is that the Rome Statute and any of its provisions cannot be declared unconstitutional since it has acquired the status of being part of the Constitution. The disadvantage is that it leaves too much in the hand of the judiciary, and the option can, in every way, amount to the legislature's abdication of duty. Also, amending the Constitution is onerous.

In the light of the advantage(s) and disadvantage(s) of each approach, the third option, that is, enacting the Rome Statute into law by criminalising gross violations of fundamental rights is the most advantageous. It is therefore recommended for Nigeria. While amendment may be required in each case whenever the Rome Statute is amended to keep abreast with the definition in the statute, it is therefore recommended that any change in the definition should automatically take effect in Nigeria to avoid this situation. Thus, the Kenyan approach, where it is stated that crime against humanity 'includes an act defined as a crime against humanity in conventional international law or customary international law that is not otherwise dealt with in the Rome

1. [2002] FWLR (Pt 111) 1972.

Statute or in this Act,' is therefore recommended for Nigeria. Also, as the definition of war crimes in the Rome Statute is not identical in content with the definition of war crimes in the Geneva Conventions, it is recommended that an express stipulation like that of Uganda should be made that an implementing legislation would not affect the operation of the Geneva Conventions Act.

Meanwhile, apart from the definition of the crimes under the Rome Statute, other relevant issues in enacting an implementing legislation are the defences that are available to the defendants, the court that will assume jurisdiction, the principle for the assumption of jurisdiction and punishment to be meted. As previously established, defences under the Nigerian Criminal Code are sufficient. It is therefore recommended that Nigeria should rely on these defences, unlike Kenya and Uganda, which recognise international and domestic defences and make defences under international law superior to those under domestic laws in case of conflict. Recommending defences under the Nigerian Criminal Code for Nigeria accords with the minimalist prescriptions of legal pluralism as the Nigerian courts will be able to apply concepts with which they are familiar like their counterparts in the Netherlands.

With respect to the court to be conferred with jurisdiction, three approaches were identified, namely placing jurisdiction on an existing court as done by Kenya which confers jurisdiction on its High Court, creating a special division of an existing court as done by Uganda and creating a special court. While each of these approaches may be adopted by Nigeria, creating a special division like Uganda is preferable. This is because it encourages professionalism and better competences in the judiciary with respect to prosecuting international crimes. The nature of international crimes is highly technical, and professionalism of the highest order is required. While it is arguable that a special court may also offer identical professionalism, the danger inherent in special court is that it may not have an appearance of independence and impartiality. A special court may have an outlook identical with that of a court martial and it may be perceived as an instrument of witch-hunt by the masses whose 'heroes' may sometimes have to face this court. It is therefore recommended that the National Assembly in enacting an implementing legislation should create a special division of the federal high court. When any of the federating states chooses to enact an implementing legislation, it is recommended that a special division of the state high court should be created.

With respect to the principles for the assumption of jurisdiction, it is recommended that Nigeria should adopt the principle of universal jurisdiction based on the presence of the defendant in Nigeria. Combining this principle with other principles like active personality, passive personality and territoriality as done by Uganda and Kenya may be superfluous. Adopting the principle of universal jurisdiction based on the presence of the accused has a number of advantages for Nigeria. It will maintain symmetry with the Geneva Conventions Act, which adopts the same principle when read in conjunction with the

Nigerian Constitution, reflects its historical root,[2] accords with the present position of the development of the principle[3] and avoids bringing Nigeria in conflict with other states. As the experience of Belgium has shown, prosecuting foreigners for international crimes *in absentia* may bring a state in conflict with others.[4]

With respect to punishment to be meted, it is recommended that Nigeria should retain the death penalty like Kenya. This recommendation is in consonance with the doctrine of legal pluralism which requires the minimum to implement the principle of complementarity.

Unwillingness: Shielding From Criminal Responsibility

Executive Immunity

It would be recalled that the Office of the Prosecutor (OTP) of the ICC recognised immunities as one of the 'contextual issues' capable of yielding the notion of shielding from criminal responsibility. Similarly, article 27 of the Rome Statute prohibits immunity of any kind and any special treatment based on official capacity. Executive immunity is one of the expressions of these immunities. In Nigeria, the president, the vice-president, 36 state governors and their deputies all enjoy executive immunity in Nigeria. They all make a total of 74. They could not be made to testify in court or be prosecuted, although they could be investigated. Since they could not be prosecuted, they are shielded from criminal responsibility.

Four approaches were identified to solve this problem. The first approach is to remove the beneficiary from office before his or her prosecution. This approach may not be advisable for Nigeria because removing any of these officials may be difficult and the outcome largely unpredictable. The second approach is not to permit immunity with respect to crimes recognised under the Rome Statute because of their egregious nature. This is the approach adopted by Kenya. Kenya provides immunity generally for its president but limits it when it comes to international crimes.

The third approach is interpretative approach adopted by some states like Norway. The constitution is interpreted to avoid conflict with the Rome Statute. However, the provision on immunity in the Nigerian Constitution does not allow room for much judicial creativity. Therefore, this approach cannot be adopted by Nigeria. The fourth approach is 'probability ratio' adopted by some states, like Liechtenstein, which leaves immunity for leaders because it is considered unlikely that they will be able to commit international crimes.

2. Yana Shy Kraytman, 'Universal Jurisdiction-Historical Roots and Modern Implications' (2005) 2 *Brussels Journal of International Studies* 94.
3. See Princeton Principles on Universal Jurisdiction and Commentary thereon, principle 1(2).
4. *Case Concerning the Arrest Warrant of 11 April 2000 (Democratic Republic of the Congo v Belgium)* Judgment of 14 February 2002, ICJ Reports 2002.

This approach can only prove workable in a situation where the leader is a ceremonial figurehead. This approach cannot be available for Nigeria where the beneficiaries wield executive power. While the vice-president and deputy-governors may not really wield much power, it is inconceivable that they will be completely unaware of government policy geared towards committing international crimes recognised under the Rome Statute. In fact, the vice-president and deputy-governors can head ministries like ministers or commissioners, respectively. It is therefore recommended that immunity should not be made available to the president, the vice-president, governors and deputy-governors in Nigeria, just as Kenya limits the application of immunity with respect to crimes recognised under the Rome Statute.

Parliamentary/Legislative Immunity

Just as executive immunity is one of the expressions of immunities recognised by the OTP and prohibited by article 27 of the Rome Statute, legislative immunity is also another expression of immunities. Legislative immunity precludes a parliamentarian from being arrested or punished with respect to anything said on the floor of the house. In Nigeria, 109 Senators[5] and 360 members of the House of Representatives[6] enjoy legislative immunity. Members of each House of Assembly of a state also enjoy legislative immunity. While each state has its own number of members, there is no state with fewer than 34 members, and none has more than 40 members.[7] Since no member of the legislative house could be prosecuted for anything said on the floor of the house, parliamentarians in Nigeria who directly and publicly incite genocide cannot be prosecuted and are thus shielded from criminal responsibility. It is therefore recommended that parliamentarians should not be immune from prosecution for publicly inciting genocide.

Sovereign Immunity

Sovereign immunity like executive and legislative immunities is also an expression of immunities recognised by the OTP and prohibited under article 27 of the Rome Statute. There are two classes of sovereign immunity. The first one is personal immunity while the second one is functional immunity. Personal immunity is absolute as the beneficiary cannot be prosecuted for any acts whether sovereign or not. The time the alleged act took place is also irrelevant. Personal immunity is conferred to allow free flow of intercourse among states in their quest for peaceful cooperation and coexistence. Head of state and diplomats are entitled to personal immunity by virtue of customary international law. Special missions are, however, entitled to personal immunity by

5. Constitution of the Federal Republic of Nigeria (Nigerian Constitution) 1999, s 48.
6. Ibid s 49.
7. Ibid s 91.

virtue of treaty.[8] Head of states are conferred with personal immunity because they personify their respective states symbolically together with the indispensable function they perform. With respect to special missions, they enjoy personal immunity because of the functions they perform. But the number of officials entitled to personal immunity is not clear.

On the other hand, functional immunity attaches to state conduct and state officials. However, functional immunity does not prevent state officials from being prosecuted because the principle of individual criminal responsibility has supplanted functional immunity. However, functional immunity subsists for diplomats by virtue of the Vienna Convention on Diplomatic Relations (VCDR) 1961. This treaty applies to Nigeria by virtue of Diplomatic Immunities and Privileges Act No 42 of 1962.

For those who are entitled to immunity by virtue of customary international law, Nigeria can choose to limit the scope of the immunity and the number of officials entitled to it. Similarly, Nigeria also has exclusive jurisdiction on its territory by virtue of its sovereignty and any immunity accorded to other states is as a matter of courtesy. South Africa has chosen this path by virtue of Section 4(2) of the South African Implementation of the Rome Statute of the International Criminal Court Act 2002 which denies immunity to past and serving head of state under customary international law with respect to crimes recognised under the Rome Statute. However, South Africa later recognised the need for other states to be able to perform effectively on its territory.[9] It is therefore recommended that Nigeria should accord personal immunity for head of states and diplomats alone and deny all other officials who may be entitled to personal immunity under customary international law. This is to allow effective functioning of other states and limits the contours of customary international law. A head of state in this context means the leader of a state who performs a truly executive function.

Hersch Lauterpacht once developed an 'assimilative approach' to state immunity where he stated that a state enjoys immunity to the extent permitted other states.[10] The extent of immunity a state chooses to permit others is an attestation of the sovereignty a state maintains on its territory. Based on this approach, Ian Brownlie suggested that any legislation limiting the

8. Vienna Convention on Diplomatic Relations (adopted 18 April 1961, entered into force 24 April 1964) 500 UNTS 95, arts 29 and 31; Vienna Convention on Consular Relations (adopted 24 April 1963, entered into force 19 March 1967) 596 UNTS 261; UN Convention on Special Missions (adopted 8 December 1969, entered into force 21 June 1985) 1400 UNTS 231, arts 21, 31 and 39.
9. See *South African Litigation Centre v National Director of Public Prosecutions* High Court of South Africa (North Gauteng High Court) Case No: 77150/09 and the unsuccessful appeal of the decision by the South African Supreme Court of Appeal in *National Commissioner of the South African Police Service v South African Human Rights Litigation Centre* Case No: 485/2012.
10. Hersch Lauterpact, 'The Problem of Jurisdictional Immunities of Foreign States' (1951) *British Year Book of International Law* 220, 236–241.

sovereignty of other states should be communicated to those other states.[11] Therefore, it is recommended that Nigeria should communicate to other states once it has enacted a law limiting their sovereignty. It is further recommended that Nigeria should give ample time for other states to adjust before allowing the law to take effect. The law may be allowed to take effect after about five years.

Amnesties

Amnesties are also recognised by the OTP as capable of shielding a suspect of crimes recognised under the Rome Statute from criminal responsibility. Amnesties are intended to wipe out past offences to put an end to proceedings to be initiated, those already initiated or judgements that have been delivered. It may be by way of legislative enactment or executive order. Despite efforts to combat impunity, amnesties have continued to be a political reality. Broad amnesties foreclose prosecution and thus shield those concerned from criminal responsibility. Amnesties granted after conviction prevent punishment to be meted to the culprit and thus have him or her shielded from criminal responsibility. Conditional amnesties appear to be a bit tolerable if granted in good faith and do not completely foreclose some other forms of accountability. Although there is no amnesty law in Nigeria, the legislative organs can competently exercise their power to legislate on it. In addition, the president or the governor in granting pardon under the Constitution may bring about the grant of amnesty. It is therefore recommended that broad amnesties with respect to crimes recognised under the Rome Statute should be outlawed in Nigeria. Similarly, amnesties after conviction with respect to these crimes should also be outlawed in Nigeria.

Pardon/The Prerogative of Mercy

Like amnesties, pardon is also recognised by the OTP as being latent with the possibility of shielding a suspect of crimes recognised under the Rome Statute from criminal responsibility. Pardon, like amnesty, shields the person concerned from the consequences of his or her action which is punishment. In Nigeria, section 175 empowers the president to grant a pardon while section 212 empowers the governors to grant a pardon. The provisions do not indicate the manner of exercising the power. A pardon may be granted before conviction or after conviction. When granted, the person concerned is shielded from his or her criminal responsibility. When a pardon is granted on conditions, shielding from criminal responsibility will depend on the circumstances of each case. Self-pardon is permissible in Nigeria.

11. Ian Brownlie, *Principles of Public International Law* (3rd edn, 1979) 334 cited in Lee M. Caplan, 'State Immunity, Human Rights and Jus Cogens: A Critique of the Normative Hierarchy Theory' (2003) 97 *American Journal of International Law* 741, 763–764.

The constitutional provisions on pardon can be construed alone or placed within the constitutional scheme. Where the constitutional provisions are considered alone, the power to grant pardon is absolute and unfettered. This has the potential of giving rise to the notion of shielding from criminal responsibility. On the other hand, where the constitutional provisions are considered within the constitutional scheme, a pardon cannot be granted with respect to the crimes recognised under the Rome Statute since they are gross violations of human rights contrary to the fundamental rights provisions of the Nigerian Constitution 1999.

It is therefore recommended that the Nigerian judiciary adopts an interpretation that places the power to grant a pardon within constitutional scheme like its Indian counterpart. Meanwhile, while the judiciary maintains this attitude, it is safer to have a clear position outlawing the grant of pardon with respect to crimes recognised under the Rome Statute. Therefore, it is further recommended that the Nigerian Constitution 1999 be amended to deny granting pardon with respect to the crimes recognised under the Rome Statute.

Plea Bargain

It would be recalled that one of the 'contextual issues' capable of yielding the notion of unwillingness is 'powers attributed to institutions of the criminal justice system.' Plea bargaining is one of these powers. A plea bargain is of two kinds. The first one is when a more serious charge is dropped in exchange for a defendant's guilty plea to a less serious crime. The second one is when a prosecutor agrees to recommend a lighter sentence in exchange for a defendant's guilty plea. To the extent that Nigeria has the duty to investigate and punish crimes recognised under the Rome Statute, plea bargaining can be regarded as contrary to the principle of complementarity, where the factual bases of the crimes committed are distorted or ridiculous sentence discounting is occasioned. Plea bargaining has been found to have been occasioned by the complexity of criminal trials among several factors.

In Nigeria, the Administration of Criminal Justice Law of Lagos State 2011 and the Administration of Criminal Justice Act 2015 provide for plea bargaining. Since both the federal government and states within the Nigerian Federation can prosecute the egregious crimes recognised under the Rome Statute, the possibility of applying plea bargain to these crimes cannot be ruled out with the consequence that the implementation of the principle of complementarity embodied in the Rome Statute may suffer. However, when plea bargain is combined with truth and reconciliation process reminiscent of the South African truth and reconciliation process with its strict criteria on those entitled and those who are not entitled to some reprieve, the practice of plea bargain may not necessarily be contrary to the implementation of the complementarity principle embodied in the Rome Statute. This is because distortion of the factual bases of the crimes committed would have been addressed while those who are not entitled to reprieve would still have to serve their respective sentences in full without mitigation. The criteria to determine those entitled to reprieve can be laid down by the attorney-general of the federation or of any state within the Nigerian Federation.

It is therefore recommended as follows: (1) Plea bargaining should be the last option for Nigeria in the prosecution and punishment of crimes recognised under the Rome Statute. (2) Plea bargaining should only be practised when a lower-level participant may need to be made some compromises to apprehend the higher-level participants. This should be the only admissible criterion. (3) Since both the federal government and states within the Nigerian federation can prosecute egregious crimes recognised under the Rome Statute, excessive workload should not be a factor to be considered in plea bargaining. It is recommended that the federal government and states within the Nigerian Federation can complement one another when congestion and other factors want to occasion the failure of Nigeria to implement the principle of complementarity. This may be a form of complementarity within the Nigerian Federation. (4) The power of the attorney-general to lay down criteria for the practice of plea bargaining should be outlawed while only a statutory provision should lay down the criterion as identified earlier.

The **Ne Bis in Idem** *Principle*

The *ne bis in idem* principle prohibits prosecuting a person twice for the same crime. It is contained in article 20 of the Rome Statute although it is envisaged to be applied between the ICC and domestic prosecution and not within domestic jurisdiction. In Nigeria, the principle is embodied in the Nigerian Constitution 1999, the Criminal Procedure Act and the Administration of the Criminal Justice Act 2015. The principle can be a clog to the implementation of the principle of complementarity when there had earlier been sham proceedings, when new evidence came to light after the former trial and when amnesty or a pardon had been granted with respect to the former proceedings in certain instances.

With respect to foreign trial proceedings, Nigeria does not have to take cognisance of foreign proceedings in prosecuting any person with respect to the crimes recognised under the Rome Statute by virtue of section 36(9) of the Nigerian Constitution 1999. This favours the implementation of the principle of complementarity even though it may be detrimental to the person who had before undergone genuine trial in another state. While section 36(9) does not take cognisance of foreign proceedings, section 36(10) is not certain whether the Nigerian criminal justice system can take cognisance of pardon or amnesty granted by another state. An expansive approach to interpretation will take cognisance of a pardon granted by another state contrary to the spirit of complementarity while a restrictive approach will discountenance pardon granted by other states which is in line with the spirit of complementarity.

With respect to pardon granted in Nigeria, it is not certain whether once a state has granted a pardon with respect to the crimes recognised under the Rome Statute, no other state among the 36 states of the federation can subject the person to trial again thus shielding the person from criminal responsibility. A strict construction will bar prosecution by other states within the Nigerian federation while a broad construction will not. Similarly, it is not certain whether pardon granted by the president with respect to the crimes recognised under the Rome Statute can be considered binding on the states within the federation. Again, a strict construction will bar a state from prosecuting a beneficiary of presidential pardon, and it will also bar the federal government from prosecuting the beneficiary of a state pardon within the Nigerian Federation whereas a broad construction will not.

In Latin American states, a person can be prosecuted more than once when there had earlier been sham proceedings, when new evidence came to light after the former trial and when amnesty or a pardon had been granted with respect to the former proceedings. This is also the position in Europe under the amended European Convention on Human Rights and Fundamental Freedoms. It is therefore recommended that Nigeria should amend the Nigerian Constitution 1999, the Criminal Procedure Act and the Administration of the Criminal Justice Act 2015 to permit the prosecution of any person more than once where there had earlier been sham proceedings, where new evidence came to light after the former trial and where amnesty or pardon had been granted with respect to the former proceedings in certain instances.

Canada and New Zealand will consider the proceeding in another state, and where

> the proceedings in that court (a) were for the purpose of shielding the person from criminal responsibility; or (b) were not otherwise conducted independently or impartially in accordance with the norms of due process recognised by international law, and were conducted in a manner that, in the circumstances, was inconsistent with an intent to bring the person to justice,

then the person concerned will be tried again. It is therefore recommended that states within the Nigerian Federation should adopt this provision to allow for the prosecution of the person concerned again.

The Principle of Legality

The principle of legality prohibits prosecuting any person for an act or omission which at the time of commission or omission was not an offence. Article 22 of the Rome Statute provides for this principle although it is intended to be applied by the ICC. In Nigeria, this principle is stated in section 36(8) of the Nigerian Constitution 1999. The implication is that crimes being committed in Nigeria before the enactment of an implementing legislation cannot be prosecuted. The decision of the ECOWAS Court in *Hissène Habré c/ Republique du Senegal*[12] also reinforces the Nigerian position by prohibiting retroactive penal legislation. Having a retroactive penal legislation would have made it possible to have a domestic jurisdiction co-extensive with that of the ICC and reduce impunity for recent crimes. Meanwhile, article 50(2)(n) of the Constitution of Kenya (Kenyan Constitution) 2010 provides that every accused person has the right to a fair trial which includes the right 'not to be convicted for an act or omission that at the time it was committed or omitted was not—(i) an offence in Kenya; or (ii) a crime under international law.' With the Kenyan position, crimes recognised under the Rome Statute before an implementing legislation in Kenya are crimes under international law and could be punished. Implementing legislation in Kenya would have achieved a jurisdictional function as distinct from a substantive function since the substantive definition is already subsisting at the international plane. It is therefore recommended that the Nigerian Constitution 1999 should be amended along Kenyan line to make retroactive penal legislation possible to implement the principle of complementarity in Nigeria.

Statute of Limitation

Article 29 of the Rome Statute prohibits the application of the statute of limitation to the crimes recognised under the Rome Statute. Statutes of limitation are of two kinds. The first stipulates the time within which a criminal action can be instituted. The second stipulates the time within which a sentence can be enforced. The first one will make the prosecution of crimes recognised under the Rome Statute impossible once the limitation period has expired. The second one will prevent a convict of the crimes recognised under the Rome Statute from serving his or her sentence. A statute of limitation with respect to crimes does not generally apply in Nigeria, and this is in favour of the implementation of the principle of complementarity as embodied in the Rome Statute. However, the lawmaking organs reserve the right to enact a statute of limitation as it has been done with respect to certain crimes in Nigeria. This potentially poses a threat to a successful implementation of the Rome Statute complementarity principle.

Some states, such as Ecuador, Venezuela and Egypt, have found the need to specifically stipulate in their respective constitutions that statute of limitation of both kinds do not apply to egregious crimes. This is to curb the exercise of legislative power in enacting statute of limitation since the exercise

12. *Hissène Habré c/ Republique du Senegal* (ECW/CCJ/JUD/06/10) Judgment of 18 November 2010.

of that power is subject to the overriding supremacy of the constitution. It is therefore recommended that Nigeria should amend its constitution and specifically prohibits the enactment of a statute of limitation with respect to egregious crimes recognised under the Rome Statute. Meanwhile, in amending the Nigerian Constitution 1999 with respect to fundamental rights which are placed under chapter IV of the Constitution, the Nigerian Constitution 1999 stipulates that a four-fifths majority of the members of the National Assembly together with the majority of two-thirds of 36 states are required.[13] Since the prohibition of the statute of limitation with respect to these egregious crimes is also to secure the enjoyment of these fundamental rights as entrenched in the Nigerian Constitution apart from the fact that it is also meant to implement the principle of complementarity, it is therefore further recommended that the rule prohibiting statute of limitation should be placed under chapter IV of the Nigerian Constitution 1999 which would have made any effort to abrogate it subject to the preceding onerous requirement. This recommendation places fundamental rights and the rule advancing their enjoyment under the same pedestal.

The Power of the Attorney-General to Amend the Law of Evidence

As previously noted, powers attributed to institutions of the criminal justice system constitute one of the contextual issues recognised by the OTP which can yield the notion of unwillingness. The attorney-general of the federation and minister of justice is an institution in the Nigerian criminal justice system and by virtue of section 255 of the Evidence Act 2011, he or she is empowered to amend the law of evidence. It would be recalled that the attorney-general of the federation is the chief prosecutor at the federal level, and all other prosecutors at this level are subject to his or her control. It would also be recalled that the attorney-general could be appointed and dismissed at will by the president. Similarly, the attorney-general could choose to prosecute, take over any prosecution instituted by others or stop any prosecution.

As earlier found, this power is unfettered and can be abused since the attorney-general has always been appointed based on political consideration and could be appointed and dismissed at will. Thus, the possibility is that the bar of admissible evidence may be raised to make prosecution more difficult contrary to the spirit of the principle of complementarity where the interest of his or her appointer is at stake. Although it is possible to mitigate any abuse of the power of the attorney-general to amend the law of evidence in certain instances, nonetheless the possibility is latent. It is therefore recommended that section 255 of the Evidence Act should be repealed.

13. Nigerian Constitution 1999, s 9(3).

Unwillingness: Independence and Impartiality Inconsistent With Intent to Do Justice

Independence and Impartiality of the Prosecutor

Among the 'contextual issues' recognised by the OTP are the constitutional role, the separation of powers and powers attributed to institutions of the criminal justice system and the parameters of prosecuting powers and discretion. The relevant institution of the criminal justice system is again the attorney-general. The independence and impartiality of the attorney-general as the prosecutor are reflected in the manner of appointment and the exercise of prosecutorial discretion. Thus, since the appointment of the attorney-general is often motivated by political consideration and the attorney-general remains in office at the pleasure of the person who appointed him or her, the attorney-general is not likely to perform his or her duties without political interference. This is unlike the position in Kenya, where the director of public prosecution (DPP) holds office for a term of eight years and in Uganda where the DPP holds office till the age of 65 years.

With respect to the exercise of prosecutorial discretion, the attorney-general has the discretion to initiate criminal proceedings, take over criminal proceedings initiated by others or stop criminal proceedings initiated by others. The power to stop criminal proceedings initiated by others is called *nolle prosequi*. While all discretionary powers are now subject to judicial review in modern jurisprudence, the discretionary power of the attorney-general with respect to *nolle prosequi* is not amenable to judicial review in Nigeria. This is unlike other Commonwealth states where the power of *nolle prosequi* is reviewable in line with modern jurisprudence.

It is therefore recommended that (1) the attorney-general should be removable by way of judicial process which allows for the presence of foreign judges (preferably from the Commonwealth states) on the panel, (2) the prosecutorial discretion of the attorney-general in all forms should be made amenable to judicial review, (3) a member of the Commonwealth should be capable of being appointed as it obtains in Kenya and application should be welcomed from different parts of the commonwealth and (4) the process for appointment should be open and transparent.

The Right of Private Prosecution

The right of private prosecution subsists in Nigeria under the Criminal Procedure Act and the Administration of Criminal Justice Act. While the right could have fostered prosecution by aggrieved individuals under the Criminal Procedure Act, a number of impediments have reduced its potency. The first one is that a law officer must give his or her consent before a private person can initiate criminal proceedings. The second one is that the amount required to enter into a recognisance may be raised to discourage private prosecution. The third impediment is that the attorney-general may enter a *nolle prosequi* even after he or she has given his or her consent. The fourth impediment is that public interest private prosecution by foreign counsel may be difficult by the decision of the Supreme Court of Nigeria in *Awolowo v Usman Sarki, Minister of Internal Affairs.*[14] The last impediment is that the power of the attorney-general to amend the Evidence Act may be used to frustrate any private prosecution. It is possible for the attorney-general to raise the bar of admissible evidence to frustrate successful prosecution initiated by any private person.

While the first impediment has been obviated under the Administration of the Criminal Justice Act 2015, other impediments remain with the additional clog of limiting the right of private prosecution to crimes not punishable by death and life imprisonment with the consequence of having crimes recognised under the Rome Statute excluded since they are likely to be punishable by death or life imprisonment. It is therefore recommended that all the previously mentioned impediments should be removed. But the right of private prosecution can also be abused. Although costs may be awarded against the private prosecutor under the Administration of Criminal Justice Act 2015 if the defendant is acquitted; however, this is not a sufficient safeguard. It is therefore recommended that any abusive use of the right of private prosecution should be checked by the court by setting up a panel to review it before prosecution proceeds while a new judicial panel is composed to sit on the substantive trial should the review decision stated that a *prima facie* case is made.

Police Independence

As earlier stated, some of the 'contextual issues' recognised by the OTP include constitutional role, separation of powers and powers attributed to institutions of the criminal justice system and parameters of prosecuting powers and discretion. Just as the attorney-general is a relevant institution of the criminal justice system, the police are also a relevant institution, and the mode of appointing those who man this institution and the manner of exercise of their discretion is important for a successful prosecution of crimes recognised under the Rome Statute. The police are expected to perform their duties without fear or favour. This is known as police independence. The independence of the police as the investigator is as important as the independence of the attorney-general as the prosecutor. Under the common law, police independence manifests the widest expression. The common law position has, however, been modified in Nigeria to the extent that the President may issue directions to secure public safety and public order. This does not necessarily undermine the competence of the police to investigate the crimes recognised under the Rome Statute. This is because, while the president may issue

14. 1966 1 All NLR 178; 1966 NSCC 209.

directions to secure public safety and public order, police independence with respect to the investigation of crimes and laying of charges is not affected. This position coheres with that of Kenya except that the Kenyan position is clearly well articulated in the Constitution.[15] Also, any direction given must be in writing in Kenya.

While police independence with respect to the investigation of crimes subsists, the appointment of the inspector-general of police who has the command of the police in Nigeria has, however, undermined it since the president can appoint and remove the inspector-general of police at will. It would be recalled that the nature of governing body has been recognised by the OTP as relevant in determining independence. Although other officers in Nigeria apart from the inspector-general of police are appointed, promoted and disciplined by the Police Service Commission, nonetheless they are all subject to the overriding control of the inspector-general of police.[16]

Police independence is further undermined by the appointment of members of the Police Service Commission. It would be recalled that members of the Police Service Commission are appointed by the president subject to the confirmation of the Senate and that the members could be removed at will by the president. The commission's power to formulate and implement policies aimed at the efficiency of the Nigeria police force[17] may also undermine police independence where the police are ill equipped which is, in fact, the situation in Nigeria. Similarly, the orientation of the police in Nigeria, which is pro-executive and punitive in line with colonial heritage, also undermines police independence.

It is therefore recommended that (1) the appointment of the inspector-general of police should be based on merit determined on clearly stipulated criteria and that it should be done by the Police Service Commission; (2) application should be welcomed from among commissioners of police; (3) shortlisted applicants should be made known to the public and petition should be welcomed with respect to their character and professional competence; (4) interviews geared towards appointment should be publicly conducted and televised, and members of the public should be permitted to question them in respect of their character and professional competence; (5) the removal of the inspector-general of police should be by way of judicial process on clearly stipulated grounds; (6) police officers should be properly educated to change their pro-executive orientation; (7) the Police Service Commission should be made up of members appointed on clearly stipulated criteria like the knowledge of international criminal justice, criminal law, criminology and so on, and interviews should be publicly conducted and televised while the removal of any member should be by way of judicial

15. The Constitution of Kenya (Kenyan Constitution) 2010, art 245(2)(b).
16. Nigerian Constitution 1999, Third Schedule Part I para M ss 30(a) and (b).
17. Police Service Commission (Establishment) Act 2001, s 6(1)(e).

process; and (8) police should be well equipped and properly trained to foster the investigation of crimes recognised under the Rome Statute.

With respect to equipping and training the Police, the decision of the Pre-Trial Chamber I of the ICC in *Prosecutor v Saif Al-Islam Gaddafi & Abdullah Al-Senussi*[18] becomes relevant. In the instant case, the Pre-Trial Chamber I of the ICC took cognisance of the fact that Libya had allocated resources to its investigation of the crimes which are the subject of admissibility challenge.[19] This decision implies that Nigeria needs to equip and train its police.

Independence and Impartiality of the Judiciary

The independence of the Nigerian judiciary is a myth. This is largely accounted for by the composition of the National Judicial Council (NJC), where the chief justice of Nigeria (CJN) nominates 19 out of 22 members, and its procedure, where five members are sufficient to take decisions including disciplinary actions. It would be recalled that the nature of the governing authority has been identified by the OTP as relevant to determine independence. The governing authority in this instance is the NJC. It is therefore recommended that the CJN should no longer have the power of nomination; rather, the president of the Court of Appeal, the chief judge of the federal High Court, presidents of the Customary Courts of Appeal, grand kadis of the Shari'a Courts of Appeal and the chief judge of each state of the federation should be members as of right. The rationale behind this suggestion is that if judges of the federal courts are adequately represented, there is no reason why judges of state courts should not.[20] Just as chiefs of federal judges would have to justify their nomination of any judge, so, too, would the chief of judges of each state have to justify his or her nomination of any judge. It is incongruent that the NJC, which is meant for the appointment, discipline, removal and funding of the state High Courts and Abuja, should have had a fair representation of federal judges without having a fair representation of state judges.[21] Similarly, if 36 state and Abuja are adequately represented in the National Assembly and each state of the federation has a minister in the Federal Executive Council and other federal executive bodies, there is no reason why the judiciary should be different.[22] With respect to procedure, a

18. *Prosecutor v Saif Al-Islam Gaddafi & Abdullah Al-Senussi, Decision on the admissibility of the case against Saif Al-Islam Gaddafi*, ICC-01/11-01/11, dated 31 May 2013.
19. Ibid para 182.
20. Ademola O. Popoola, 'The Bench, the Bar and the Challenges of Democratic Consolidation in Nigeria: Issues and Prospects' Being the Text of a Commemorative Lecture Presented on the Occasion of the 20th Year Anniversary of Chief Wole Olanipekun SAN's call to the Inner Bar, 19 July 2011 at the Trenchard Hall, University of Ibadan, Nigeria, 72–73.
21. Ibid., 71–72.
22. Ibid., 72–73.

two-thirds majority of the number of suggested members should be required for taking decisions.

With respect to the appointment of the CJN and other chief judges, it is recommended that (1) the appointment should be based on merit determined on clearly stipulated criteria, (2) applications should be welcomed from any legal practitioner or judge with 15 years' post-call experience, (3) the names of all applicants should be published and petitions welcomed from the public in respect of their character and professional competence and (4) interviews geared towards appointment should be conducted openly and televised, and members of the public should be allowed to question them in respect of their character and professional competence. With respect to composition, it would be recalled that the requirements for appointing judges in Nigeria do not make it possible for foreign judges to sit in Nigerian courts. This is unlike Kenya[23] and Sierra Leone.[24] While the independence of judges is generally sustained by the security of tenure, this is not so with the prosecution of international crimes. In fact, the security of tenure may be an impediment. This is because tenured judges have their carrier prospects to worry about which may, in turn, affect their duty to do justice. Similarly, judges are also members of their society, and they may also pander to ethnic sentiment which may become relevant in the prosecution of such crimes like genocide as they may not want to be a betrayal of their ethnic groups. It is therefore recommended that foreign judges from other Commonwealth states should be allowed to sit with their Nigerian counterparts in prosecution of crimes recognised under the Rome Statute in Nigeria. The same number of foreign and domestic judges may be allowed to sit, and when there is a tie, it should be taken that the prosecution has failed in proving its case beyond reasonable doubt and in successfully rebutting the presumption of innocence of the defendant. It is worthy of emphasis that making a case for foreign judges is not recommended to do justice as the ICC would do it (a universalist stance); rather, it is necessitated to cure the defect in the domestic mechanism to achieve international justice.

The need for foreign judges in prosecuting international crimes recognised under the Rome Statute is best illustrated by the Kenyan experience. Following post-election violence in Kenya, a Commission of Inquiry known as the Commission of Inquiry into Post-Election Violence (CIPEV) was established.[25] It was mandated to investigate circumstances surrounding post-election violence in Kenya. The commission recommended that a Special Tribunal for Kenya (STK) should be established. The court was to have an international character and be made up of judges who are non-Kenyans

23. Kenyan Constitution 2010, s 166(2).
24. Constitution of Sierra Leone 1991 (Act No 6 of 1991), s 121(1).
25. The Commission is sometimes informally referred to as the Waki Commission, after its Chairman Justice Phillip Waki.

together with Kenyans.[26] In fact, CIPEV feared that the Kenyan judiciary might be subdued by political interference and suggested more roles for foreigners.[27] The STK was to put an end to impunity which was considered by CIPEV to be at the heart of the post-election violence in Kenya. CIPEV noted that the post-election violence in Kenya was 'more than a mere juxtaposition of citizen-to-citizen opportunistic assaults' and that they 'were systematic attacks on Kenyans based on their ethnicity and political leanings.'[28]

Apart from the utilitarian value of foreign judges, having foreign judges also have a symbolic value. It would be recalled that Hagenbach was tried on 4 May 1474 by an alliance of Austria, France and knights of the neignbouring regions at the marketplace in Breisach and that the bench which presided over his trial was made up of judges from Austria, the Allied cities and 16 knights representing the Order of Knighthood. Although it has been contested that the tribunal which tried Hagenbach was not of an international character because Europe at the time was under the hegemony of the Holy Roman Empire,[29] however, if the European Court is considered a court with an international character despite its being under the European Union, the tribunal which tried Hagenbach cannot be denied an international character. Just as each of the Allies which prosecuted Hagenbach retained its criminal jurisdiction under the Holy Roman Empire, so, too, does each member of the European Union retain its criminal jurisdiction under one political entity known as the European Union.[30]

In addition to the symbolic value of having foreign judges, having foreign judges must have succeeded in gathering international opinion of a judicial character against the perpetrators of the crimes recognised under the Rome Statute. Arguably, the approach adopted in prosecuting Hagenbach must have been to gather world opinion against his criminal actions. Although it was argued that Hagenbach was really tried for murder,[31] there would be no reason to gather world opinion to convict him of murder. The egregious nature of his crimes must have been the rationale behind the approach adopted by the Allies.[32] In any event, international crimes are no less serious because the same crime could be characterised as murder domestically.[33]

26. Christine Alai and Njonjo Mue, 'Complementarity and the Impact of the Rome Statute and the International Criminal Court in Kenya' in Carsten Stahn and Mohamed El Zeidy (eds), *The International Criminal Court and Complementarity: From Theory to Practice* vol II (Cambridge University Press 2011), 1224.
27. Ibid., 1225.
28. Ibid., 1224.
29. Robert K. Woetzel, *The Nuremberg Trials in International Law* (Stevens & Sons1960), 21.
30. Deji Adekunle, 'International Criminal Court: A Historical Account' in J.O. Fabunmi (ed), *Themes on Jurisprudence and International Law* (Total Communications Ventures 2009), 109, 111.
31. Ibid.
32. Ibid.
33. Ibid.

With respect to the court martial, it would be recalled that independence is lacking since the judicial decision handed down by the court is subject to confirmation by the executive arm. Since a special division of the high court has earlier been recommended, there is no reason why the court martial should still be used to prosecute international crimes in Nigeria. It is therefore recommended that the court martial should not be made to prosecute international crimes in Nigeria whether committed by people subject to service law or not.

Apart from the composition of the judiciary, the need to have the judiciary well resourced and equipped to enhance the effective prosecution of the crimes recognised under the Rome Statute is also worthy of consideration. It would be recalled that lack of necessary personnel, judges and judicial infrastructure are recognised by the OTP as capable of yielding the notion of inability. Similarly, in *Prosecutor v Jean-Pierre Bemba Gombo*[34] the Trial Chamber III while considering the question of the inability of Central African Republic (CAR) held that because of insufficient number of judges and human resources and inadequate budgetary allocation, the CAR lacked the requisite capability to try the alleged offences and thus its judicial system was unavailable. Therefore, the Nigerian judiciary must be well resourced and equipped. It would also be recalled that the primordial dependence of the judiciary on the executive had occasioned a dwindling fortune for the judiciary by way of inadequate budgetary allocation resulting in its inefficient administration of justice. Now that the judiciary does not have to depend on the executive with respect to its budget (at least on current expenditure), the judiciary should be alive to the need to have the judiciary well resourced and equipped.

Inability

Inability to Obtain Evidence

It would be recalled that lack of witness protection law in Libya was considered by the ICC to find a case admissible. This makes witness protection imperative in Nigeria. Some states have witness protection as a matter of policy while others have it as a matter of statute. Irrespective of the approach adopted, any witness programme must indicate protection measures that may be put in place, criteria for admission of witnesses and conditions for their application, a procedure to be followed; the authority responsible for the implementation of the programme, the reason for the termination of the programme, the rights and obligations of the parties and the confidentiality of the operations of the programme.

34. *Prosecutor v Jean-Pierre Bemba Gombo,* Decision on the Admissibility and Abuse of Process Challenges ICC-01/05-01/08-802 Pre-Trial Chamber III, 24 June 2010.

Witness protection is a relatively recent issue in Nigeria. The Nigerian Terrorism Act 2011, Terrorism (Prevention) (Amendment) Act 2013 and the Administration of Criminal Justice Act 2015 make provisions for witness protection. Similarly, the Nigerian Constitution 1999 also has some provisions which may accommodate the idea of witness protection. However, the provisions of the Nigerian Constitution are not sufficient to accommodate all the issues identified earlier for a successful witness protection programme. Also, the three statutes in Nigeria cannot serve as useful models since the above issues are not adequately addressed. However, witness protection programme of Kenya takes cognisance of these issues. It is therefore recommended that Nigeria should adopt the Kenyan Witness Protection Act 2006 and Witness Protection (Amendment) Act 2010 subject to such modifications as the Nigerian circumstances may occasion. Statute is preferable as distinct from policy because policy may be changed at will by the executive arm of government.

Inability to Obtain the Accused

The inability to obtain the accused implies that the custody of the accused cannot be obtained which makes the prosecution of such an accused by Nigeria impossible since trial *in absentia* does not obtain in Nigeria. This is sufficient to trigger ICC intervention even if the ICC cannot obtain the accused as well. To be able to obtain the custody of the accused, other states that have the custody of the accused would be prepared to extradite the accused to Nigeria. This can only be done by way of an extradition treaty between Nigeria and any of these states. However, some states, like the members of the European Union, would not extradite unless there is an assurance that the human rights of the fugitive would not be violated. The imposition of the death penalty and the poor conditions of prisons in Nigeria may make it impossible for some states to extradite to Nigeria. The death penalty may violate the right to life and the right not to be subjected to inhuman and degrading treatment. The poor conditions of prisons in Nigeria may violate right not to be subjected to inhuman and degrading treatment. With respect to prison conditions, two options were identified as being open to Nigeria. The first one is that Nigeria may choose to improve its prison conditions and makes extradition to it possible. The second option is that Nigeria may delegate the state which has the fugitive to imprison the fugitive. The second option is therefore recommended for Nigeria because it accords with the pluralist stance adopted in this book with its minimalist prescriptions.

With respect to the imposition of death penalty, four options were identified as being open to Nigeria. The first option is for Nigeria to abolish the death penalty by amending its Constitution. The problems with this option are that amending the provision on the death penalty is especially onerous, and heated debate will be generated. The second option is for Nigeria not to impose the death penalty for crimes recognised under the Rome Statute in its implementing legislation. The problems with this option are that the federal government could not prevent states from imposing the death penalty and failure to impose the death penalty for crimes recognised under the Rome Statute while it is being imposed for less egregious crimes may be contrary to the constitutional right of equal treatment. The third option is for Nigeria to retain the death penalty but grant moratorium as a matter of policy to crimes recognised under the Rome Statute. But this option may also violate the constitutional right to equal treatment since policies like statutes are amenable to the test of constitutionality. The fourth option is for Nigeria to delegate its criminal jurisdiction to the state which has the custody of the fugitive. This option does not have any problem attached to it and it balances Nigeria's preference to retain death penalty with its preference to investigate and prosecute crimes recognised under the Rome Statute. This option also accords with legal pluralism not only because it admits of legal diversity but because it requires the minimum to implement complementarity. It is therefore recommended that Nigeria should delegate its criminal jurisdiction to any state that has the custody of the accused and is not prepared to extradite to Nigeria for failure to obtain assurances that death penalty would not be imposed. This can be done by entering into treaties on mutual legal assistance on criminal matters with these states.

Bibliography

Books

Adekunle, D., 'International Criminal Court: A Historical Account' in Fabunmi, J.O (ed), *Themes on Jurisprudence and International Law* (Total Communications Ventures, Lagos 2009).

Akinseye-George, Y., *Improving Judicial Protection of Human Rights in Nigeria* (Centre for Socio-Legal Studies Abuja, Abuja Undated).

Alai, C. and Mue, N., 'Complementarity and the Impact of the Rome Statute and the International Criminal Court in Kenya' in Stahn, C. and El Zeidy, M. (eds), *The International Criminal Court and Complementarity: From Theory to Practice* vol II (Cambridge University Press, Cambridge 2011).

Asein, J.O., *Introduction to Nigerian Legal System* (2nd edn, Ababa Press Limited, Lagos 2005).

Bassiouni, M.C., 'International Criminal Investigations and Prosecutions: From Versailles to Rwanda' in Bassiouni, M.C. (ed), *International Criminal Law: Enforcement* vol II (2nd edn, Transnational Publishers Inc, Ardsley, New York 1999).

Bernaz, N. and Prouvèze, R., 'International and Domestic Prosecutions' in Bassiouni, M.C. (ed), *The Pursuit of International Criminal Justice: A World of Study on Conflicts, Victimization, and Post-Conflict Justice* vol I (Intersentia, Antwerpen 2010).

Bois-Pedain, A., *Transitional Amnesty in South Africa* (Cambridge University Press, Cambridge 2007).

Boister, N. and Cryer, R., *The Tokyo International Military Tribunal: A Reappraisal* (Oxford University Press, Oxford 2008).

Broomhall, B., *International Justice and the International Criminal Court: Between Sovereignty and the Rule of Law* (Oxford University Press, Oxford 2003).

Brownlie, I., *Principles of Public International Law* (3rd edn, Oxford University Press, Oxford 1979).

Combs, N.A., *Guilty Pleas in International Criminal Law: Constructing a Restorative Justice Approach* (Stanford University Press, Stanford, California 2007).

Denning, A.T., *The Family Story* (Butterworths, London 1981).

Dublin, M.D., *International Terrorism: Two League of Nations Conventions 1934–1937* (Kraus Microform, Millwood, New York 1991).

Due Process of Law Foundation, *Digest of Latin American Jurisprudence on International Crimes* (Due Process of Law Foundation, Washington DC 2010).

Dyani, N., 'Is the International Criminal Court Targeting Africa? Reflections on the Enforcement of International Criminal Law in Africa' in Nmehielle, V.O. (ed), *Africa and the Future of International Criminal Justice* (Eleven International Publishing, The Hague 2012).

El Zeidy, M.M., 'The Genesis of Complementarity' in Stahn, C. and El Zeidy, M. (eds), *The International Criminal Court and Complementarity: From Theory to Practice* vol I (Cambridge University Press, Cambridge 2011).

El Zeidy, M.M., *The Principle of Complementarity in International Criminal Law: Origin, Development and Practice* (Martinus Nijhoff Publishers, Leiden/Boston 2008).

Ferdinandusse, W.N., *Direct Application of International Criminal Law in National Courts* (TMC Asser Press, The Hague 2006).

Gallant, K.S., *The Principle of Legality in International and Comparative Criminal Law* (Cambridge University Press, Cambridge 2009).

Garner, B.A. and others, *Black's Law Dictionary* (9th edn, Thomson Reuters, St. Paul, MN 2009).

Gonzalez, P.V. and Ferstman, C., *Ending Threats and Reprisals Against Victims of Torture and Related International Crimes: A Call to Action* (Redress, London 2009).

Greppi, E., 'Inability to Investigate and Prosecute under Article 17' in Politi, M. and Gioia, F. (eds), *The International Criminal Court and National Jurisdictions* (Ashgate, Aldershot 2008).

Henckaerts, J. and Doswald-Beck, L., *Customary International Humanitarian Law* vol I, Rules (Cambridge University Press, Cambridge 2005).

Hollis, D.B., Blakeslee, M.R. and Ederington, L.B. (eds), *National Treaty Law and Practice* (Martinus Nijhoff Publishers, Boston/Leiden 2005).

Holmes, J.T., 'The Principle of Complementarity' in Lee, R.S. (ed), *The International Criminal Court: The Making of the Rome Statutes, Issues, Negotiations, Results* (Kluwer Law International, The Hague/London/Boston 1999).

International Centre for Criminal Law Reform, *International Criminal Court: Manual for the Ratification and the Implementation of the Rome Statute* (3rd edn, International Centre for Criminal Law Reform, Vancouver 2008).

Jayawickrama, N., *The Judicial Application of Human Rights Law: National, Regional and International Jurisprudence* (Cambridge University Press, Cambridge 2002).

Ladan, M.T., *Materials and Cases on Public International Law* (Ahmadu Bello University Press, Zaria 2007).

Lattanzi, F., 'The Complementarity Character of the Jurisdiction of the Court with Respect to National Jurisdictions' in Lattanzi, F. (ed), *The International Criminal Court: Comments on the Draft Statute* (Editoriale Scientifica, Naples 1998).

Mahony, C., *The Justice Sector Afterthought: Witness Protection in Africa* (Institute for Security Studies, Pretoria 2010).

Maluwa, T., *International Law in Post-Colonial Africa* (Kluwer Law International, The Hague/London/Boston 1999).

Martins, E.A. (ed), *Oxford Dictionary of Law* (5th edn, Oxford University Press, Oxford 2004).

Mbazira, C., 'Prosecuting International Crimes Committed by the Lord's Resistance Army in Uganda' in Murungu, C. and Biegon, J. (eds), *Prosecuting International Crimes in Africa* (Pretoria University Law Press, Pretoria 2011).

Mégret, F., 'Too Much of a Good Thing? Implementation and the Uses of Complementarity' in Stahn, C. and El Zeidy, M. (eds), *The International Criminal Court and Complementarity: From Theory to Practice* vol I (Cambridge University Press, Cambridge 2011).

Morris, J.H.C. and McClean, D., *The Conflict of Laws* (5th edn, Sweet & Maxwell, London 2000).

Nmehielle, V.O., 'Taking Credible Ownership of Justice for Atrocity Crimes in Africa' in Nmehielle, V.O. (ed), *Africa and the Future of International Criminal Justice* (Eleven International Publishing, The Hague 2012).

Nouwen, S., 'Complementarity in Uganda: Domestic Diversity or International Imposition?' in Stahn, C. and El Zeidy, M. (eds), *The International Criminal Court and Complementarity: From Theory to Practice* vol II (Cambridge University Press, Cambridge 2011).

Ntoubandi, F.Z., *Amnesty for Crimes Against Humanity Under International Law* (Martinus Nijhoff, Dordrecht, Netherlands 2007).

Nwauche, E., 'Is the End Near for the Political Question Doctrine in Nigeria?' in Fombad, C. and Murray, C. (eds), *Fostering Constitutionalism in Africa* (Pretoria University Law Press, Pretoria 2010).

O'Shea, A., *Amnesty for Crime in International Law and Practice* (Kluwer Law International, The Hague/London/New York 2002).

Okonkwo, C.O., *Criminal Law in Nigeria* (2nd edn, Spectrum Books Limited, Ibadan 1980).

Olusanya, O., *Double Jeopardy Without Parameters: Re-Characterisation in Inter-National Criminal Law* (Instersentia, Antwerp-Oxford 2004).

Oluyede, P.A.O., *Constitutional Law in Nigeria* (Evans Brothers (Nigeria Publishers) Limited, Ibadan 1992).

Pillai, K.N.C., *Double Jeopardy Protection: A Comparative Overview* (Mittal Publications, Delhi 1988).

Radstan, R., 'Situation and Case: Defining the Parameters' in Stahn, C. and El Zeidy, M. (eds), *The International Criminal Court and Complementarity: From Theory to Practice* vol I (Cambridge University Press, Cambridge 2011).

Robinson, D., 'The Inaction Controversy: Neglected Words and New Opportunities' in Stahn, C. and El Zeidy, M. (eds), *The International Criminal Court and Complementarity: From Theory to Practice* vol I (Cambridge University Press, Cambridge 2011).

Robinson, D., 'The Rome Statute and Its Impact on National Law' in Cassese, A., Gaeta, P. and Jones, J.R.W.D. (eds), *The Rome Statute of the International Criminal Court: A Commentary* (Oxford University Press, New York 2002).

Ryngaert, C., 'Horizontal Complementarity' in Stahn, C. and El Zeidy, M. (eds), *The International Criminal Court and Complementarity: From Theory to Practice* vol II (Cambridge University Press, Cambridge 2011).

Schabas, W.A., *The Abolition of the Death Penalty in International Law* (3rd edn, Cambridge University Press, Cambridge 2002).

Schabas, W.A., *An Introduction to the International Criminal Court* (3rd edn, Cambridge University Press, Cambridge 2007).

Schwarzenberger, G., *International Law as Applied by International Courts and Tribunals: The Law of Armed Conflict* vol II (Stevens & Sons Ltd, London 1968).

Seils, P., *Handbook on Complementarity: An Introduction to the Role of National Courts and the ICC in Prosecuting International Crimes* (International Center for Transitional Justice 2016).

Shaw, M.N., *International Law* (6th edn, Cambridge University Press, Cambridge 2008).

Stenning, P., 'The Idea of the Political "Independence" of the Police: International Interpretations and Experiences' in Beare, M.E. and Murray, T. (eds), *Police and Government Relations: Who's Calling the Shots?* (University of Toronto Press, Toronto 2007).

Stigen, J., *The Relationship Between the International Criminal Court and National Jurisdictions: The Principle of Complementarity* (Martinus Nijhoff Publishers, Leiden/Boston 2008).

Triffterer, O., 'Legal and Political Implications of Domestic Ratification and Implementation Processes' in Kress, C. and Lattanzi, F. (eds), *General Aspects and Constitutional Issues* (Baden–Baden/Fagnano Alto (L'Aquila), Nomos/II Sirente 2000).

The United Nations War Crimes Commission, *History of the United Nations War Crimes Commission and the Development of the Laws of War* (HMSO, London 1948).

Wierda, M. and Otim, M., 'Courts, Conflict and Complementarity in Uganda' in Stahn, C. and El Zeidy, M. (eds), *The International Criminal Court and Complementarity: From Theory to Practice* vol II (Cambridge University Press, Cambridge 2011).

Williams, S.A., 'Issues of Admissibility' in Triffterer, O. (ed), *Commentary on the Rome Statute: Observers' Notes, Article by Article* (Baden-Baden, Nomos 1999).

Willis, J.F., *Prologue to Nuremberg: The Politics and Diplomacy of Punishing War Criminals of the First World War* (Greenwood Press, Westport, Connecticut 1982).

Woetzel, R.K., *The Nuremberg Trials in International Law* (Stevens & Sons, London 1960).

Wyngaert, C.V. and Ongena, T., 'Ne Bis In Idem Principle, Including the Issue of Amnesty' in Cassese, A., Gaeta, P. and Jones, J.R.W.D. (eds), *The Rome Statute of the International Criminal Court: A Commentary* (Oxford University Press, New York 2002).

Articles

Ajulo, S.B., 'Sources of the Law of the Economic Community of West African States (ECOWAS)' (2001) 45 *Journal of African Law* 73.

Akanbi, O., 'The Myth of Judicial Independence in Nigeria' (20 April 2012). http://ssrn.com/abstract=2175933 accessed 7 August 2017.

Akande, D., 'The Jurisdiction of the International Criminal Court Over Nationals of Non-Parties: Legal Basis and Limits' (2003) 1 *Journal of International Criminal Justice* 618.

Akande, D. and Shah, S., 'Immunities of State Officials, International Crimes, and Foreign Domestic Courts' (2011) 21 *European Journal of International Law* 815.

Akintayo, J.O.A., 'Legislation in Democratic Governance in Nigeria' (1999) 11 *African Humanities Monograph* 14–26.

Allan, K., 'Prosecution and Peace: A Role for Amnesty before the ICC?' (2011) 39 *Denver Journal of International Law & Policy* 239–301.

Amar, A.R., 'Double Jeopardy Law Made Simple' (1997) 106 *Yale Law Journal* 1807.

Ambos, K., 'Establishing an International Criminal Court and an International Criminal Code: Observations from an International Criminal Law Viewpoint' (1996) 7 *European Journal of International Law* 519.

Bassiouni, M.C., 'Human Rights in Criminal Justice: Identifying International Protections in National Constitutions' (1993) 3 *Duke Journal of Comparative & International Law* 247.

Belsky, A.C., Merva, M. and Roht-Arriaza, N., 'Implied Waiver Under the FSIA: A Proposed Exception to Immunity for Violations of Peremptory Norms of International Law' (1989) 77 *California Law Review* 365.

Benzing, M., 'The Complementarity Regime of the International Criminal Court: International Criminal Justice Between State Sovereignty and the Fight Against Impunity' (2003) 7 *Max Planck Year Book of United Nations Law* 591.

Bianchi, A., 'Denying State Immunity to Violators of Human Rights' (1994) 46 *Austrian Journal of Public & International Law* 195.

Blakesley, C.L., 'The Practice of Extradition From Antiquity to Modern France and the United States: A Brief History (1981) 4 *Boston College International & Comparitive Law Review* 39.

Bottini, G., 'Universal Jurisdiction After the Creation of the International Criminal Court' (2004) 36 *New York University International Law and Politics* 503.

Caplan, L.M., 'State Immunity, Human Rights and Jus Cogens: A Critique of the Normative Hierarchy Theory' (2003) 97 *American Journal of International Law* 741.

Çinar, A. and Nierkerk, S., 'Implementation of the Rome Statute in the Netherlands'. http://ssrn.com/abstract=996521 accessed 7 August 2017.

Combs, N.A., 'Procuring Guilty Pleas for International Crimes: The Limited Influence of Sentence Discounts' (2006) 59 *Vanderbilt Law Review* 69.

Duffy, H., 'National Constitutional Compatibility and the International Criminal Court' (2001) 11 *Duke Journal of Comparative & International Law* 32.

Duru, O., 'The Doctrine of Separation of Powers Under the Nigerian Constitution: A Critical Overview'. 6 September 2009. http://papers.ssrn.com/sol3/papers.cfm?abstract_id=2142933 accessed 6 August 2017.

El Zeidy, M.M., 'From Primacy to Complementarity and Backwards: (Re)-Visiting Rule 11 *Bis* of the Ad hoc Tribunals' (2008) 57 *International & Comparative Law Quarterly* 403.

El Zeidy, M.M., 'The Principle of Complementarity: A New Machinery to Implement International Criminal Law' (2001–2002) 23 *Michigan Journal of International Law* 869.

Gevers, C., 'Immunity and the Implementation Legislation in South Africa, Kenya and Uganda'. http://ssrn.com/abstract=1975788 accessed 7 August 2017.

Goldmann, M., 'Implementing the Rome Statute in Europe: From Sovereign Distinction to Convergence in International Criminal Law?' (2005) 16 *Finnish Yearbook of International Law* 5.

Gurule, J., 'United States Opposition to the 1998 Rome Statute Establishing an International Criminal Court: Is the Court's Jurisdiction Truly Complementary to National Criminal Jurisdictions?' (November 2001–February 2002) 35 *Cornell International Law Journal* 1.

Halpenny, A., 'The Governance of Military Police in Canada' (2010) 48 *Osgoode Hall Law Journal* 1.

Heller, K.J., 'The Shadow Side of Complementarity: The Effect of Article 17 of the Rome Statute on National Due Process' (2006) 17 *Criminal Law Forum* 255.

Jennings, R.Y., 'The Caroline and McLeod Cases' (1938) 32 *American Journal of International Law* 82.

Kalt, B.C., 'Pardon Me?: The Constitutional Case Against Presidential Self-Pardons' 106 *The Yale Law Journal* 779.

Kraytman, Y.S., 'Universal Jurisdiction-Historical Roots and Modern Implications' (2005) 2 *Brussels Journal of International Studies* 94.

Kress, C., '"Self-Referrals" and 'Waivers of Complementarity': Some Considerations in Law and Policy' (2004) 2 *Journal of International Criminal Justice* 944.

Kumar, P., 'The Executive Power to Pardon: Dilemmas of the Constitutional Discourse' (2009) *2 NUJS Law Review* 9.

Lauterpact, H., 'The Problem of Jurisdictional Immunities of Foreign States' (1951) *British Year Book of International Law* 220.

Mallinder, L., 'Amnesties and International Criminal Law'. http://ssrn.com/abstract=1531701 accessed 8 February 2014.

Mba, O., 'Judicial Review of the Prosecutorial Powers of the Attorney-General in England and Wales and Nigeria: An Imperative of the Rule of Law' (1 March 2010) *Oxford University Comparative Law Forum* 2 (2010). http://ssrn.com/abstract=2056290 accessed 7 August 2017.

Møse, E., 'Main Achievements of the ICTR' (2005) 3 *Journal of International Criminal Justice* 920.

Moy, H.A., 'The International Criminal Court's Arrest Warrants and Uganda's Lord's Resistance Army: Renewing The Debate Over Amnesty and Complementarity' (2006) 19 *Harvard Human Rights Journal* 267.

Naidike, T., 'Doctrine of Covering-The-Field in Federal Constitutional Theory'. http://tnaidike.wordpress.com/doctrine-of-covering-the-field-in-federal-constitutional-theory/ accessed 7 August 2017.

Naqvi, Y., 'Amnesty for War Crimes: Defining the Limits of International Recognition' (2003) 85 *IRRC* 583.

Newman, D.G., 'The Rome Statute, Some Reservations Concerning Amnesties, and a Distributive Problem' (2005) 20 *American University International Law Review* 293.

Okagbue, I., 'Private Prosecution in Nigeria: Recent Developments and Some Proposals' (Spring 1990) 34(1) *Journal of African Law* 53.

Olowu, D., 'Nolle Prosequi and the Law in Nigeria: Concept, Issues and Analysis' (2002) *Law Monograph Series 1 Demyaxs Law Publications* 33.

Petrig, A., 'Negotiated Justice and the Goals of International Criminal Tribunals with a Focus on the Plea-Bargaining Practice of the ICTY and the Legal Framework of the ICC' (2008) 8 *Chicago-Kent Journal of International & Comparative Law* 1.

Pichon, J., 'The Principle of Complementarity in the Cases of the Sudanese Nationals Ahmed Harun and Ali Kushayb before the International Criminal Court' (2008) 8 *International Criminal Law Review* 185.

Rauxloh, R.E., 'Plea Bargaining in International Criminal Justice: Can the International Criminal Court Afford to Avoid Trial?' (2011) 1(2) *The Journal of Criminal Justice Research* 1.

Robinson, D., 'Serving the Interests of Justice: Amnesties, Truth Commissions and the International Criminal Court' (2003) 14 *European Journal of International Law* 481.

Sebba, L., 'The Pardoning Power-a World Survey' (1977) 68 *Journal of Criminal Law & Criminology* 83.

Solera, O., 'Complementarity Jurisdiction and International Criminal Justice' (2002) 84 *International Review of the Red Cross* 145.

Spiga, V., 'Non-retroactivity of Criminal Law: A New Chapter in the Hissène Habré Saga' (2011) 9(1) *Journal of International Criminal Justice* 1.

Swaine, E.T., 'Does Federalism Constrain the Treaty Power?' (2003) 103 *Columbia Law Review* 403.

Tallgren, I., 'Completing the "International Criminal Order": The Rhetoric of International Repression and the Notion of Complementarity in the Draft Statute for an International Criminal Court' (1998) 67 *Nordic Journal of International Law* 107.

Tobechukwu, O.H. and Chukwuma, S.C., 'Rethinking the Power of Nolle Prosequi in Nigeria: The Case of State v Ilori' (March 2014) 2(1) *Global Journal of Politics and Law Research* 1.

Tomonori, M., 'The Individual as Beneficiary of State Immunity: Problems of the Attribution of Ultra Vires Conduct' (2001) 29 *Denver Journal of International Law and Policy* 261.

Villa-Vicencio, C., 'Why Perpetrators Should Not Always Be Prosecuted: Where the International Criminal Court and Truth Commissions Meet' (2000) 49 *Emory Law Journal* 205.

Warbrick, C., 'Immunity and International Crimes in English Law' (2004) 53 *International & Comparative Law Quarterly* 769.

Watts, A., 'The Legal Position in International Law of Heads of State, Heads of Government and Foreign Ministers' (1994-III) 247 *Recueil des Cours* 13.

Wilt, H., 'Equal Standards? On the Dialectics Between National Jurisdictions and the International Criminal Court' (2008) 8 *International Criminal Law Review* 229.

Wyngaert, C.V. and Stessens, G., 'The International Non Bis In Idem Principle: Resolving Some of the Unanswered Questions' (1999) 48 *International and Comparative Law Quarterly* 779.

Thesis

Kok, R.A., 'Statutory Limitations in International Criminal Law' (PhD thesis, University of Amsterdam 2007).

Documents

1994 International Law Commission Draft Statute in 1994 International Law Commission Report 37.

1994 Yearbook of International Law Commission, vol I.

Amnesty International, 'The International Criminal Court: Checklist for Effective Implementation' AI Index IOR 40/011/00 (2000).

Amnesty International, 'Nigeria: Prisoners' Rights Systematically Flouted' AI Index: AFR 44/001/2008 (February 2008).

Basic Principles on the Independence of the Judiciary (the Basic Principles) adopted by the Seventh United Nations Congress on the Prevention of Crime and Treatment of Offenders held at Milan from 26 August to 6 September 1985 and endorsed by General Assembly Resolutions 40/32 of 29 November 1985 and 40/146 of 13 (December 1985).

Decisions Taken by the Preparatory Committee at its Session Held 4 to 15 August 1997, UN GAOR, 52 mtg, UN Doc A/AC.249/1997/L.8/Rev.1 (1997).

Draft Code of Offences against the Peace and Security of Mankind GA Res, 177 (II), 2nd Session, 123rd Plenary Meeting (21 November 1947).

Draft Proposal by Italy 44 UN Doc A/AC 249/1997/WG 3/IP 4 (5 August 1997).

The Eight United Nations Congress on the Prevention of Crime and the Treatment of Offenders in its Guidelines on the Role of Prosecutors A/CONF. 144/28/Rev.1.
Eighth United Nations Congress on the Prevention of Crime and Treatment of Offenders 1990 UN Doc A/CONF 14/28/Rev 1.
Explanatory Memorandum to the Code on International Crimes, Parliamentary Papers II, 2001/2002, 28 337. no. 3, 29.
GA Res 43/164 (1988), 76th Plenary Meeting.
GA Res 44/32 (1989), 72nd Plenary Meeting.
GA Res 44/39 (1989), 72nd Plenary Meeting.
GA Res 49/53, 9 December 1994.
Human Rights Committee (HRC), General Comment No 13: Equality Before the Courts and the Right to a Fair and Public Hearing by an Independent Court Established by Law (13 April 1984).
The International Association of Prosecutors' Standards of Professional Responsibility and Statement of the Essential Duties and Rights of Prosecutors.
International Bar Association (IBA), 'Judicial Independence Undermined: A Report on Uganda' (September 2007) paras 4.49–4.50.
International Bar Association (IBA), 'Witnesses Before the International Criminal Court: An International Bar Association International Criminal Court Programme Report on the ICC's Efforts and Challenges to Protect, Support and Ensure the Rights of Witnesses' (July 2013).
International Crimes Working Document 2009 (Uganda).
International Federation for Human Rights (IFHR), 'International Criminal Court: Implementation of the Rome Statute in Cambodian Law' no. 443/2 (2006).
The Judicial Integrity Group, 'Commentary on the Bangalore Principles of Judicial Conduct'. March 2007. www.coe.int/t/dghl/cooperation/ccje/textes/BangalorePrinciplesComment.PDF accessed 7 August 2017.
Max du Plessis and Jolyon Ford (eds), 'Unable or Unwilling? Case Studies on Domestic Implementation of the ICC Statute in Selected African Countries' (March 2008) Institute of Security Studies (ISS) Monograph Series No 141.
Office of the Prosecutor (OTP), Informal Expert Paper 2003.
Office of the Prosecutor (OTP), Informal Expert Paper: The Principle of Complementarity in Practice ICC-01/04–01/07–1008- Annexe 4.
Office of the Prosecutor (OTP), 'Paper on Some Policy Issues before the Office of the Prosecutor' (September 2003).
Office of the Prosecutor (OTP), Policy Paper on the Interests of Justice 2007.
Pal Wrange, 'The ICC Bill, Complementarity and "Retroactivity"' 30 September 2008 in Sarah Nouwen, 'The ICC's Intervention in Uganda: Which Rule of Law Does It Promote?' University of Cambridge Faculty of Law Legal Studies Research Paper Series, Paper No 22/2012 (August 2012).
Princeton Principles on Universal Jurisdiction and Commentary thereon.
Principles and Guidelines on the Right to a Fair Trial and Legal Assistance in Africa.
Procedures for the Effective Implementation of the Basic Principles on the Independence of the Judiciary 1989, Economic and Social Council Resolution 1989/60, 15th Plenary Meeting (24 May 1989).
Report of the Ad hoc Committee on the Establishment of an International Criminal Court UN GAOR, 50th Sess, Supp No 22, UN Doc A/50/22 (1995).
Report of the Commonwealth Expert Group on Implementing Legislation for the Rome Statute of the International Criminal Court Revised (April 2011).

Report of the Preparatory Committee on the Establishment of an International Criminal Court, UN GAOR, 51st Sess, vol 1, Supp No 22, UN Doc A/51/22 (1995).

Report of the Preparatory Committee on the Establishment of an International Criminal Court, Draft Statute and Draft Final Act, UN Doc A/Conf. 183/2/Add.1 (1998).

Report of the Preparatory Committee on the Establishment of an International Criminal Court, UN Doc A/Conf. 183/2 (14 April 1998); UN Doc A/Conf. 183/SR.2; UN Doc A/Conf. 183/SR.3; UN Doc A/Conf. 183/SR.4; UN Doc A/Conf. 183/SR.5; UN Doc A/Conf. 183/SR.6; UN Doc A/Conf. 183/SR.7; UN Doc A/Conf. 183/SR.8.

Report on Prosecutorial Strategy (RPS) 2009–2012 of 1 February 2010 (ICC).

Report on Prosecutorial Strategy (RPS) of 14 September 2006 (ICC).

A Review of the United Kingdom's Extradition Arrangements (Following Written Ministerial Statement by the Secretary of State for the Home Department of 8 September 2010) Presented to the Home Secretary on 30 September 2011.

Sarah Nouwen, 'The ICC's Intervention in Uganda: Which Rule of Law Does It Promote?' University of Cambridge Faculty of Law Legal Studies Research Paper Series, Paper No 22/2012 (August 2012).

Summary Record of the 11th Meeting, 22 June 1998, UN Doc A/CONF. 183/C 1/SR 11.

Summary Records of the Meetings of the Thirty-Fifth Session (3 May–22 July 1983), 1983 Yearbook of International Law Commission, vol 1.

Terry Coonan, 'Prosecuting and Defending Violations Of Genocide and Humanitarian Law: The International Tribunal for the Former Yugoslavia' 1994 American Society of International Law Proceedings 239.

The United Nations Commission on Human Rights Resolutions 1999/61 (adopted April 28 1999) and 2000/65 (adopted April 27 2000).

United Nations Convention against Transnational Organised Crime, General Assembly Resolution 55/25, Annex I.

United Nations International Law Commission Draft Code of Crimes against Peace and Security of Mankind with Commentaries, Yearbook of the International Law Commission, vol 2 Pt 2 (1996).

United Nations Office on Drugs and Crime, 'Good Practices for the Protection of Witnesses in Criminal Proceedings involving Organised Crime' (2008).

Universal Declaration of Human Rights (UDHR) (adopted 10 December 1948 UNGA Res 217 A(III).

Yearbook of the International Law Commission, Volume II (1967).

Internet Sources

American Non-Governmental Organisations Coalition for the International Criminal Court (AMICC), 'Kenyatta Case at the ICC: Three Options Available for the ICC Judges, the Issue, the Importance of the Status Conferences for the International Community and for the African Countries'. http://amicc.blogspot.com/2014/10/kenyatta-case-at-icc-three-options.html accessed 7 August 2017.

Federación Internacional de los Derechos Humanos (FIDH), 'Comments on the ICC's Prosecutorial Strategy'. 1 December 2009. www.fidh.org/IMG//pdf/FIDHCommentsProsecStrategy2009-12_FINAL_REV.pdf accessed 7 August 2017.

International Criminal Court, 'States Parties-Chronological List'. https://asp.icc-cpi.int/en_menus/asp/states%20parties/Pages/states%20parties%20_%20chronological%20list.aspx accessed 6 August 2017.

International Criminal Court, 'The States Parties to the Rome Statute'. https://asp.icc-cpi.int/en_menus/asp/states%20parties/Pages/the%20states%20parties%20to%20the%20rome%20statute.aspx accessed 6 August 2017.

International Military Tribunal for the Far East (Indictment). www.trumanlibrary.org/whistlestop/study_collections/nuremberg/documents/index.php?documentdate=0000-00-00&documentid=18-2&pagenumber=1 accessed 7 August 2017.

Index